POLICING

CANADIAN

society

POLICING

DENNIS FORCESE
Carleton University

CANADIAN

SECOND EDITION

society

Prentice Hall Allyn and Bacon Canada
Scarborough, Ontario

Canadian Cataloguing in Publication Data

Forcese, Dennis, 1941–
  Policing Canadian Society

2nd ed.
Includes bibliographical references and index.
ISBN 0-13-941386-3

1. Police—Canada. 2. Law enforcement—Canada. I. Title
HV8157.F67 1999   363.2'0971   C98-930667-4

Prentice-Hall, Inc., Upper Saddle River, New Jersey
Prentice-Hall International (UK) Limited, London
Prentice-Hall of Australia, Pty. Limited, Sydney
Prentice-Hall Hispanoamericana, S.A., Mexico City
Prentice-Hall of India Private Limited, New Delhi
Prentice-Hall of Japan, Inc., Tokyo
Simon & Schuster Southeast Asia Private Limited, Singapore
Editora Prentice-Hall do Brasil, Ltda., Rio de Janeiro

Vice President, Editorial Director: Laura Pearson
Acquisitions Editor: David Stover
Marketing Manager: Christine Cozens
Associate Editor: Lisa Phillips
Production Editor: Avivah Wargon
Copy Editor: Charis Cotter
Production Coordinator: Kathrine Pummell
Permissions/Photo Research: Susan Wallace-Cox
Cover Design: Julia Hall
Page Layout: Carol Magee

1 2 3 4 5   WEB   01 00 99

Printed and bound in Canada

Visit the Prentice Hall Canada web site! Send us your comments, browse our catalogues, and more at
www.phcanada.com. Or reach us through e-mail at **phabinfo_pubcanada@prenhall.com**.

Statistics Canada information is used with the permission of the Minister of Industry, as Minister responsible for Statistics Canada. Information on the availability of the wide range of data from Statistics Canada can be obtained from Statistics Canada's Regional Offices, its World Wide Web site at **http://www.statcan.ca**, and its toll-free access number 1-800-263-1136.

Contents

Preface

To the Revised 2nd edition

This book is about the Canadian public police. These are the men and women who are front-line public servants, sworn to uphold the public interest. There are many persons and agencies in our society engaged in regulation and control. But only the public police are supposed to serve us all, and be accountable to us all, insofar as we are prepared to conform to general social expectations and laws.

Working from this ideal conception, in the book I have attempted general description, illustration, and commentary to represent policing throughout Canada. It is of course the case that there are numerous local idiosyncrasies and variations that a reader might have to fold into the general information. Details differ. Police work-shifts vary, for example, as between 8-hour, 10-hour, and 12-hour shifts. Rank structure labels vary: there are lingering military designations such as Corporal in the RCMP, and sometimes Lieutenant in Quebec, in addition to more universal rank labels such as Constable, Sergeant, Inspector, and Superintendent; in some services the rank of Inspector is being phased out. The specifics of special units operating within police services, or the precise name and form of civilian overseeing bodies, vary. And of course, there is always organizational tinkering, with changes under way even as this book goes to press. I trust nonetheless that the basic descriptions and generalizations in the book are apt and reasonably corroborated, such that the policing represented in the book is recognizable wherever in Canada the reader may live.

I am not nor have I ever been a police officer. I am a long-time observer of policing. I have taught a university course on policing for more than 20 years, lectured intermittently on Canadian society at the Canadian Police College throughout that time, undertaken several research projects to do with policing, and generally have had the opportunity to know and talk with many officers over very many years. In particular I have learned a good deal from the officers attending my lectures. As a rather naive Canadian graduate student, the first course that I taught, in St. Louis in 1968, found me tutored by two of my students, African American police detectives who leavened my "book-learning." Having learned a valuable lesson, in this book I therefore use a good deal of informal information as well as that from the published literature.

This revised edition inevitably includes corrections, information updates, and altered organization. Some new narrative occurs throughout. There are three altogether new chapters on police work, community policing, and a concluding chapter considering developing issues. The most marked change is the greater attention to community policing, as that American-developed concept has rapidly become the flavour of choice in policing. Because of the attention to community policing, I have even recanted my first edition refusal to reproduce the so-called Peel principles of policing!

More literature has come available and has been consulted, although it remains the case that the research literature for Canada is scant, especially now that the *Canadian Police*

College Journal no longer publishes. The reader should be aware of the huge influence of American models in policing. It is not just the academic research literature, but the techniques, equipment, and interpersonal contacts that influence Canadian police agencies. We might wonder that we are enormously influenced by a society where policing has always been enormously flawed and that incarcerates and executes more persons, most of them from minority groups, than any other Western democratic industrial nation. I have used a good deal of American research, attempting to be judicious in seeking critically innovative work, of which there has been a good deal. There are some undoubted commonalities in the experiences of policing in North America's two great settler societies. The reader, though, should be wary, and realize that the two societies and their policing do also differ, and that many of the research generalizations derived from the literature have not been replicated in Canada.

In the absence of a large Canadian literature on policing, I employ numerous news reports. News reports permit one to flesh out and to illustrate with contemporary incidents the generalizations found in the formal research literature—much of it American. News reports are data. Media reports, of course, also introduce a bias. They favour the sensational and the critical. Many more news reports are available to illustrate police misconduct, for example, than to illustrate community policing. I am aware of this, as should be the reader.

I am a critic of policing, although, I believe, a critic with a tolerant and respectful edge. Some readers will be disappointed that the book is not an exercise in "cop bashing." Others will find altogether too much "bashing." I have great respect for the complexity of policing, and the commitment and the thoughtful restraint of so many police officers. I also consider that the people doing policing, as the people doing other jobs in our society, make mistakes, commit misdeeds, and need to be scrutinized and restrained. There is a necessary relationship of dependency with the public, a relationship flawed in its outcomes by virtue of inequalities in society that police officers did not make, but which they help maintain. Working on that relationship can make for better policing.

Ours is a highly differentiated public. The task of public policing is to somehow fairly represent that diversity in an evenhanded and caring way, even as police themselves are restrained by the social and legal structure of Canadian society. Police interaction with informed citizens is a means to attempt to achieve that impossible ideal objective.

Dennis P. Forcese
Ottawa
January, 1998

POLICING

CANADIAN

society

THE IDEA OF POLICE

This chapter introduces the concept of policing. It considers the elemental components of the policing role, as expected by police and public. Policing as a conceptual ideal is posed as a benchmark against which to evaluate the realities of policing in Canada.

Ask Canadians today what they expect police to do, and usually the response will focus upon crime. They expect that police will protect the "law-abiding" from "criminals" and apprehend those who commit criminal violations. Additionally, our Jane or Joe Public will expect the police to be willing to extend general assistance in times of need. There will also be some expectation of appropriately sensitive and restrained by-law enforcement, for example, attending to someone else's noisy party or bad driving. There will be an emphasis upon protection and social order, especially if Jane and Joe are upstanding middle-class Canadians; yet all Canadians, irrespective of social class, gender, or race, will expect their persons and property to be protected. What may vary is the perception and confidence that police meet these expectations.

Control of crime and deviance and social order have always been the business of police. And there has always been policing. In all human societies there have been persons, norms, and laws acting to achieve conformity, to control the behaviour of their members. In simpler and smaller societies, more homogeneous socialization and relatively slight role specialization and lifestyle options minimized deviance or non-conformity. Where deviant acts did occur or were threatened, the entire community, the kin, or group leaders might act in defence.

Such intervention was a form of policing, of enforcing conformity, and protecting the interest of others in the community. This simple "law enforcement," however, did not depend upon role specialists, persons designated as responsible for policing as a full-time occupation.

Today in Canada's First Nations communities some people are attempting to re-establish such community forms of social responsibility and control. These efforts to adapt our concepts of modern policing to aboriginal communities are imperfectly reminiscent of First Nations pre-European contact, where one might have found a shared or collective engagement in social control. In traditional Iroquois societies, for example, the clan, not specialists, dealt with social deviance and dispensed a justice that was negotiated to satisfy all parties: the offender, the offended, and their relations and neighbours.

As societies increased in population size and economic complexity, in Western societies (Robinson et al., 1994), other forms of collective response to social violations developed, such as the "hue and cry" of England or the fabled posse of the American frontier. Specialized occupational roles associated with control tasks began to appear. King's men, soldiers, and sheriffs, under the direct control of local nobility or a monarch, represented a clearer definition of policing roles. The role specialization eventually culminated in the numerous trained, uniformed, and specialized police personnel of today, whose role continues to evolve.

THE CONTRADICTION WITHIN POLICING

There is no good reason in historical fact or theory to suggest that policing or some form of police force was ever absent, or could be eliminated in complex societies. The more heterogeneous a society, the greater the need for specialized personnel to impose a modicum of control and conformity. Although for some people the police are equated, with reason, with oppression and curtailment of liberty, for others, again with reason, they are the security against personal violation and anarchic resort to force. Both the violence in the streets of nineteenth-century London, directed as much or more at working-class persons than at the privileged who had means of protection, and the rule of might on the American frontier, led to policing specialists enforcing some legal expression of social expectation that also infringed upon personal liberties. These infringements, or restraints, are inherent in social life, and become more overt as specialists authorized to use force or its threat enforce regulation and conformity, perhaps with infrequent reference to community definitions.

While the policing role in all societies has always been social control, the basis of such control has ultimately always been force. Where social pressure and persuasion fail, the threat of force or actual forceful intervention is invoked. That is no less true in modern societies, where police are uniquely authorized to employ appropriate force. And in the nature of socially stratified societies, the less fortunate and less powerful are more apt to be the objects of forceful intervention.

When Robert Peel's legislation created the benchmark for modern urban policing in 1829, the London Metropolitan Police, the nine principles of policing (see Figure 1-1) were high-sounding and idealistic. The principles suggested that persons should and could be treated equally in law and police contact, even though English class inequalities were very pronounced. At least, the principles provided some goals and some restraints.

Peace enforcement or social control has always been intrinsically contradictory. Personal freedoms are curtailed so that personal freedom may be expressed. Social constraints are enforced so that social democracy may be sustained. Social advantage and, conversely, social disadvantage are reinforced so that social opportunity and mobility may be realized.

FIGURE 1-1   **Principles of Policing, as attributed to Robert Peel and developed for the London Metropolitan Police in 1829 by Richard Mayne and Charles Rowan**

1. The basic mission for which the police exist is to prevent crime and disorder as an alternative to the repression of crime and disorder by military force and severity of legal punishment.

2. The ability of the police to perform their duties is dependent upon public approval of police existence, actions, behaviour, and the ability of the police to secure and maintain public respect.

3. The police must secure the willing cooperation of the public in voluntary observance of the law to be able to secure and maintain public respect.

4. The degree of cooperation of the public that can be secured diminishes, proportionately, the necessity for the use of physical force and compulsion in achieving police objectives.

5. The police seek and preserve public favour, not by catering to public opinion, but by constantly demonstrating absolutely impartial service to the law, in complete independence of policy, and without regard to the justice or injustice of the substance of individual laws; by ready offering of individual service and friendship to all members of the society without regard to their race or social standing; by ready exercise of courtesy and friendly good humour; and by ready offering of individual sacrifice in protecting and preserving life.

6. The police should use physical force to the extent necessary to secure observance of the law or to restore order only when the exercise of persuasion, advice, and warning is found to be insufficient to achieve police objectives; and police should use only the minimum degree of physical force which is necessary on any particular occasion for achieving a police objective.

7. The police at all times should maintain a relationship with the public that gives reality to the historic tradition that the police are the public and the public are the police; the police are the only members of the public who are paid to give full-time attention to duties which are incumbent on every citizen in the interest of the community welfare.

8. The police should always direct their actions toward their functions and never appear to usurp the powers of the judiciary by avenging individuals or the state, or authoritatively judging guilt or punishing the guilty.

9. The test of police efficiency is the absence of crime and disorder, not the visible evidence of police action in dealing with them.

Source: W.L. Melville Lee, *A History of Police in England*, London: Methuen, 1901.

There is no doubt that enforcement is to the advantage of the privileged in society, for their property and favoured lifestyle are protected. But in complex societies virtually everyone has some property they wish protected, and seeks physical protection for themselves, kin, and friends. Persons of all social classes desire civil protection. All do not, however, receive equal or adequate protection (Robinson et al., 1994).

Problems of police insensitivity, non-responsiveness to needs, or abuse of class disadvantaged and ethnic minority communities are more pronounced in societies where the inequalities are themselves more pronounced or extreme. Police abuse in Latin American nations, or apartheid South Africa, would be cases in point. Extreme inequality and community isolation generally tend to be reflected in policing attitude and style. Police become alien agents, unlike Peel's police, who were themselves members of the public and the community. Because these police belong to large paramilitary organizations, which emphasize political as well as crime control to the exclusion of social service functions, they will be less apt to respond to a diversity of publics and needs.

Police action to control behaviour essentially affects the maintenance of public order. Order, of course, is in the interests of the privileged, who require that their persons and their property be protected, and that established society and its distribution of benefits not be radically altered. Developing as they did in highly differentiated societies, the police were created to protect the "peace loving propertied classes" by controlling the "dangerous classes" (Silver, 1966; Parks, 1970; Harring, 1981). But while civil order undoubtedly sustains the privileges of the upper classes, it does also permit the less fortunate to live out their relatively disadvantaged lives on the basis of some rules or laws. The quality of the laws and their enforcement, as experienced by persons of different social status or class, will, however, be quite variable.

The diverse regulatory functions of police, although skewed to favour the privileged, as do the regulations themselves, are a general expectation of all publics. Some elements of the population are better able to care for themselves without frequent police intervention. Homogeneous communities, with social control vested in the extended family and community organizations, for example, require less assistance for protection and regulation. Heterogeneous communities, such as those consisting of migrants, or of elements who are vulnerable for physical and economic reasons, such as the elderly or women, are more in need of the formal intervention of police personnel. Single-parent women, for example, who are often below the poverty line and living in public housing, are a segment of the population in comparatively greater need of police service; yet they often reside in areas the police are reluctant to enter except for periodic punitive incursions. Those demonstrated to have the greatest fear of victimization by criminals, the aged and women, also show the lowest levels of satisfaction with policing (Canada, 1985).

Police do not deliver the same protection to persons of class and racial minorities as they do to privileged members of society. Lower-class persons are associated with attitudes and behaviours that the middle class deplore, and the police, despite working-class origins, become quintessential representatives of middle-class ideology. As in the school setting, where the cooperative, polite behaviour of middle-class children is positively valued while the relatively belligerent, aggressive, and non-skillful conduct (by school standards) of working-class or some immigrant children is negatively valued, so police officers' encounters with lower-class persons often involve punishment. Police, like the larger middle-class public, come to see lower-class communities and their residents as problems rather than victims.

Police failures are most pronounced in service to the less privileged. Most middle-class white Canadians are relatively satisfied with policing, because they and their property are relatively well protected. Where the advantaged do criticize, it is because police do not respond quickly enough, or fail to protect their homes. But police inattention and failure are, in fact, most frequent in subcommunities of welfare residents, new immigrants, and visible minorities. Inadequate protection of the less privileged, as well as over-attention to lower-class communities in regulatory zeal on behalf of the privileged, in some part account for the low regard in which police are held in lower-class communities. And, of course, the relationship is self-perpetuating.

In Canadian society, therefore, while it is undoubtedly the case that most citizens benefit from some police protection, all do not benefit equally. This difference in degree of protection is the result of a complex of reasons ranging from organizational flaws and police prejudice and self-interest to faults in the public structures governing and controlling police. Students of policing must consider all of these influences in their attempts to comprehend policing: the selection or recruitment of police of different social and personality types, the organizational or "mechanistic" characteristics associated with the structure of policing, and the subcultural and the environmental influences upon persons who engage in policing (Grimshaw and Jefferson, 1987:5–18). Group and cultural biases of police conduct must also be considered.

Modern police are recruited from, and operate within, societies with many different components. But they have never been representatively recruited, that is, coming in reasonably representative numbers from all social classes, racial or ethnic populations, and both genders. They are public servants, by definition responsible to public authorities and to the general public. But they work within well established organizations, with traditions, norms, restraints, and demands—paramilitary, bureaucratic, and at times political. Police act for governments and the state, and in democracies, governments are presumed to act for the general populace. As such, the police are not independent. Like any occupational group, however, they exercise significant discretion. Once set in motion, police operation has a good measure of autonomy. In some societies that autonomy has been relatively unchecked by authorities, and the police may come to enforce their own norms of conduct as much as those of the legal system. Or the police system may become synonymous with state factions, with the police enforcing policing and ideological control as much as or more than the control of crimi-nal deviance and civil protection. Therefore, as one observer remarks (Berkley, 1969:4–5), "the very antithesis of democracy is called the 'police state'."

POLICE AUTONOMY

There are many textbook definitions of policing. In one text widely used in law enforcement training, six major aspects of policing are listed: preservation of the public peace, protection of life and property, prevention of crime, enforcement of the law, the arrest of offenders, and the recovery of property (Clift, 1970). These elements are the traditional core of police definition of their job, and also encompass the main aspects of public expectation, though the emphasis has shifted from the historical one of maintaining public order to the current one of capturing thieves and recovering property (Wilson, 1969).

An interesting contrast in job definition was made by a sociologist. The seven components of the police role, says Weiner (1976), are: maintenance of order or, in other terminology, preservation of the peace; support of the dominant group, the sociological counterpart of protection of life and property, albeit suggesting a class bias in such protection; to be a buffer between the advantaged and the disadvantaged—suggesting again an order function in a class society; to provide a symbol of authority, an element implying social control with no counterpart in the law enforcement inventory; to act as a measurement of social tolerance, again absent in the law enforcement inventory; law enforcement—the element in closest agreement between the two inventories; and service, the element that research finds occupies the majority of police time, but which has no parallel in the traditional law enforcement concept, since it encompasses "helping" activities not related to criminal conduct. But, while service may be marked as the significant omission in the 1970 law enforcement inventory (it would not be overlooked today!), so in the sociological inventory of 1976, a notable omission was prevention of crime.

A merger of the two inventories would appear to be worthwhile. It may be understood that several of these role elements are often in contradiction, reflecting the contradictory expectations of the public and the police. Generally, the public expect efficient policing *and* flexible policing, with police not only rigidly enforcing the law but dispensing justice too. The police, on the other hand, are apt to think of themselves as enforcing the law as impartially as the system and the job allows. The discretion inherent in policing may be acknowledged, and even the differential enforcement between socio-economic groups in society; but, community policing (to be discussed) notwithstanding, their view is apt to be that there is little they can do about it.

Within the police organization people develop and acquire an occupational ethic and subculture with its own attitudes and definitions of appropriate behaviour. The physical dangers and emotional demands upon police tend to produce powerful networks or bonds, which until recently have been exclusively male. Police officers, by and large, interact with their own kind, and are isolated not only from the prosperous and from the very well educated, but from most of their working-class and middle-class neighbours.

The isolation and independence of police can produce, in extreme cases, quite violent police behaviour. If violence is lauded, romanticized, or simply tolerated and left unchecked, especially in a society with marked social differences and animosities, the practices of police officers can become exceedingly abusive of class or ethnic minorities, who become, as in apartheid South Africa, victims of systematic and quasi-legitimate violence. The police are not society's only agency of control and order, but they are its more direct and forceful one. The more conflicts there are within a society, especially those associated with inequality, the more apt there are to be numerous police and numerous police interventions. In such a context, with minimal social consensus and public compliance, the police interventions will be more forceful and violent as the police respond to controlling class interests or to their own subculture's interests (Jacobs, 1979).

Social differences may also incite exaggerated police responses in periods of international tension or conflict, responses that may be consistent with public biases and government policies. In association with government practice, in wartime and between the two twentieth century world wars, enemy "aliens" (or prospective enemy aliens in the case of interwar fear of communism) were subject to massive police surveillance. Immigrant and Canadian-born populations, such as Japanese, Italians, Ukrainians, and Germans, were deemed untrustworthy. In World War II the police assisted in detentions, and between the wars in surveillance and expulsions. The so-called Cold War against the Soviet Union was replete with such police activity (Whitaker and Marcuse, 1994).

There are also elements of police autonomy deriving from cross-national collaboration among police, with actions sometimes taken in contradiction of government policies. Hannah Arendt wrote of the cross-national solidarity of the police, often acting in the name of national security, that at times amounts to "an independent police initiative in matters of foreign policy" (quoted in Berkley, 1969:13). Leon Trotsky (quoted in Berkley, 1969:13), no fan of the state police, stated that "There is only one international: the police." Police, including Canadian police, may be trained abroad or influenced from abroad, by non-Canadian police technologies or by non-Canadian investigative data, usually American. They may also be influenced by other national ideologies, such as the "Cold War" extremism of the United States. Canadian police and security personnel depend upon the investigative reports of police agencies in other countries, especially when they are interested in person(s) who have lived abroad for any length of time. Information from the FBI, when a check is being done on a Canadian who has lived in the United States, will be coloured by American investigative and ideological biases, such as those that characterized the FBI during the extended direction of J. Edgar Hoover. The United States has invested massive amounts in equipping and training Third World police personnel, just as the RCMP have had a role in external police organization and training, as in Grenada and Haiti.

Overall, however, in the democracies police behaviours and the relatively autonomous elements of police organization are checked. Consensus regarding rules of conduct and the hierarchy of authority in democratic societies, with periodic regulatory interventions into police conduct, subordinate policing and its very definition to laws, to the elected government representatives who frame the legislation, and to the courts that interpret the legislation. By definition, the police are agents of the law, subordinate to the law, required to enforce the law objectively and impartially, and generally expected not to participate in the framing of the laws that they are called upon to enforce. In actual practice, of course, the distinction is imperfectly maintained, even in a democracy such as Canada, as we have already seen. Not only do police respond to variable social conditions in variable fashions, and periodically abuse their power and discretion, they also, unavoidably, participate in shaping social conventions or norms, and the operational meaning of the laws themselves. Some laws are more diligently enforced than others; some laws are deemed by the police to be more significant than others. Moreover, as they are called upon to enforce laws, they inevitably in some measure interpret laws. Thereby, too, they interpret and define crime, or even by selective interventions, "make crime" while also "reproducing social order" (Ericson, 1981b; 1982; Manning, 1977, 1980).

Most police officers are simply persons caught up in social circumstances that they may reinforce but they did not create. They are persons living out lives and careers, with little time, opportunity, or inclination to reflect upon the complex meanings and consequences of their own activities.

PUBLIC CONTEXT

Today the concept of policing, which began as an attempt to offer civil protection, that is, to respond to disorder and to crime, has become somewhat confused. Police themselves are criticized for failing to realize that they are now expected to be much more than merely law enforcement officers. Yet, at the same time, there is an undeniable public priority attached to law enforcement. People wish to be protected. Observers may remark upon the extensive service role of police, and call for organizational changes that more explicitly respond to service demands. The current emphasis on community policing to some extent reflects more service-oriented policing. But public satisfaction or dissatisfaction remain focussed, as do the police themselves, upon crime control and order. When, therefore, there is comment upon the failure of police, intrinsic to the indictment is a middle-class view that police have failed to protect the "respectable" and deserving elements of society. Of only secondary importance—although it is increasingly in the media—is criticism associated with allegations of the police having unfairly and inefficiently provided civil protection to less privileged class or ethnic minorities.

Police agencies have capitalized upon public needs, fear, and demands for protection. In stressing their basic law enforcement obligations the police have in some measure been effective in perpetrating a public fiction. The public need, and the romance of the police response, have enabled police agencies to win regard by celebrating successes. The well publicized successes, of course, are not the service successes or preventative work, but conspicuous responses to crime. The irony of this public relations tactic is that in building an imagery around crime and giving it such prominence the police create a public perception of danger and a level of fear that not only sustain public support for police actions and the associated expense, but also render police vulnerable to the criticism that they are unresponsive and inefficient in "stamping out crime." Unsolved break-and-enters, murders, and other dramatic acts of violence will generate public complaints that diminish the police reputation as much or more than will publicized instances of police misconduct. And where confidence is lost in the public police, self-help and private police are resorted to by those who have the financial wherewithal.

There is another significant consideration in outlining the context within which police work. Today, working within massive urbanized regional jurisdictions, with large police organizations and specialized personnel, the police have been relatively isolated from communities, including the middle class. In addition, therefore, to their relative autonomy as major, self-renewing organizations, they are increasingly subject only to the rather indirect public control that is vested in government, as contrasted to the direct restraints inherent in local community participation and visibility. For the most part, the controls are not local, but provincial and national. Large municipal police forces are therefore only intermittently steered by local concerns. The police have day-to-day discretion as to interventions, while legislators, appointed boards, and very infrequently local municipal representatives, set the broader policing policies. The more removed that policy formation is from local interests, the less it disrupts the autonomous day-to-day police powers, and the more it inhibits effective local police–community relations and integration.

In Canada, the provincial police forces (the Ontario Provincial Police and the Sûreté du Québec), are directly controlled by the provincial governments, and the Royal Canadian Mounted Police (RCMP) is controlled by the federal government and to some extent by the provinces by contract relationships. Historically, governments have often used the police for partisan purposes under the guise of legitimate and objective social control. The recurring example is police intervention in labour disputes. A related activity is police surveillance for political reasons, whether by the RCMP with respect to the Communist Party or the séparatistes in Quebec. In this sort of investigative role the police are pitted against specific elements of the society, consistent with our earlier premise of policing in a stratified society. As long as such a role, which will be perceived as partisan, persists as part of policing, the police will be estranged from large segments of society.

The contemporary demand upon policing is for more local responsiveness. But local communities are diverse and non-consensual. The Canadian police today, as they have been since their inception, are in a state of change. Canadian society remains a "settler" society made up of heterogeneous populations, whether their members were born within Canada or abroad. Most of these people reside in cities, especially in the large metropolitan centres of Ontario. The police, less than ever before in Canadian history, cannot take for granted a social consensus as to behavioural norms. They can neither assume nor depend upon voluntary conformity, compliance, or passivity to the extent that may once have been true in a more homogeneous Canada of rural and small town populations. In addition, traditional agencies of social control—the family or the churches, for instance—are conspicuously less effective today in controlling the behaviour of members of society. The individual today is more nearly that, an individual, less fettered by the constraints of primary groups. The anonymity of urban life, the less compelling value systems, and the plethora of cultures and lifestyles serve to produce more deviant behaviour, and increase the frequency of the appeals for more formal regulatory measures, and most of all, the interventions of the police.

POLICE EVOLUTION

Policing has become more complex and more problematic. And police organizations, like all large bureaucratic organizations, are difficult to change. The technology of policing, of course, continues to alter rapidly. Where the automobile revolutionized policing in mid-century, information technology has radically altered policing in the late twentieth century. But less dramatic, though more difficult to integrate into the police culture, are social changes. More heterogeneous recruitment, with better gender and ethnic representation, is a continuing demand upon police forces. Better educated persons, to deal with more sophisticated crimes and with complex public conduct, are also required.

Demands for changes in policing, such as those remarked above, are a reflection of major transformations in Canadian society. As Canada has become not merely urban but characterized by the megalopolis, as population heterogeneity has become more marked with changed immigration patterns, as more Canadians, especially women, have increased education and are more mobile, and as the media, especially the electronic media, have aggressively assumed a near hegemony over the attention and opinion forming of Canadians, no organization, let alone one so visible and crucial as policing, can avert scrutiny, critical and often sensational reporting, and demands for reform. The public demand for quality service from educators, physicians, government, and the police is insatiable and a perfectly proper and desirable feature of a healthy democratic society. The opinions of all citizens, or their more outspoken representatives, are not always well informed or fair, but they cannot be ignored. Where police, like many others, may utter the all-too-familiar theme that the press have got it wrong, or misrepresented, or misquoted, there is little doubt that the imperious "no comment" is ultimately damaging for any public body. The Canadian police, therefore, are ostensibly seeking to engage the public, and to change.

Of course, the police services have evolved from their very outset. They have continually adapted to altered circumstances and social expectations, though in doing so, have maintained a very cohesive and generally secretive organization. The closed character of policing is now itself being fundamentally changed. Policing is being obliged, at least for the time being, to be more responsive, more accountable, and more civil.

Where the police respond affirmatively to such expectations, they retain the high regard that has traditionally characterized the Canadian attitude. Conversely, where they cling to outmoded attitudes and practices, they are more apt to find their relationship to their public an adversarial one. An appreciation of the ongoing tension of change, and of police relations to diverse and complex communities, permeates the consideration of policing through the following chapters.

CONCLUSION

These preliminary orienting observations will inform this narrative. They are not intended, nor is the text that follows, to condemn the police, or for that matter, politicians. Police cannot change society. But if these opening remarks are accurate, they enable us to comprehend the nature, the limits, and the possible reforms of policing in Canada. Law enforcement personnel are the direct agencies of intervention in Canadian society, redefining and reinforcing dominant norms, behaviours, and interests. Conceivably, however, with the support of the organized publics, they can offer more socially sensitive representative policing. Only then will there be an adequate approximation to the ideal of policing in a democratic society.

Our consideration begins with an overview of the origins of Canadian policing vested in the colonial link to Britain. These origins, and the features of Canadian policing discussed thereafter, are offered in juxtaposition to a brief account of contemporary policing in the United States and in Britain.

ANNOTATED READINGS, CHAPTER ONE

Ericson, Richard. *Making Crime: A Study of Detective Work.* Toronto: Butterworths, 1981. Richard Ericson is the most dedicated and prolific academic observer of policing. In this work, based upon study of the Peel Regional Police Force, he analyzes police conduct as an expression of discretion that helps shape the definition and awareness of crime. Ericson's work is pertinent throughout this book.

Ericson, Richard. *Reproducing Order: A Study of Police Patrol Work.* Toronto: University of Toronto Press, 1982. In this work, also examining the Peel Regional Police Force, Ericson further applies his interactionist analysis of police work and the relationship of police discretionary behaviour to the definition of crime. Where in the companion volume he considers detective work, here he offers information and interpretation regarding police patrol conduct. The book includes a fascinating statement by the Peel Police, who objected strenuously to Ericson's published analyses.

Grimshaw, Roger and Tony Jefferson. *Interpreting Police Work: Policy and Practice in Forms of Beat Policing.* London: Allen and Unwin, 1987. In addition to offering a useful account of British patrol policing, replete with implied comparisons with Canadian policing, this book offers what is arguably the most coherent overview and application of sociological theory to the study of policing.

Klockars, Carl B. *The Idea of Police.* Newbury Park: Sage Publications, 1985. Written for an introductory course on police, Klockar's book questions stereotypes and misconceptions of policing. The content and style are designed to engage the reader and provoke thoughtful consideration of the police role.

Martin, Maurice. *Urban Policing: An Aging Craft.* Montreal and Kingston: McGill-Queen's University Press, 1995. This book affords a friendly but thoughtful account of the evolution of the police role in Canadian society. The emphasis is upon the need for police reform so that the craft or trade of policing can in fact become a profession.

ORIGINS AND COMPARISONS

This chapter discusses the origins of Canadian policing, stressing British and American influences. The military model and the importance of the frontier are noted. The policing that has evolved in Canada from colonial days is a hybrid; because of local Canadian circumstances, it is distinguishable from both the wilder, more violent American mode, and the older, more restrained British tradition. But there are also commonalities, especially when policing in these three societies is contrasted with other policing traditions, the most important being the concept of police serving and enforcing "neutral" laws rather than protecting or serving particular political masters or ideologies.

Canadian policing is obviously to be placed within the traditions of Western European society. As a former colony of Britain, and a neighbour of the United States, inevitably both these nations helped shape Canada's policing. In a general sense, we find in Canada a blend of the administrative control achieved over policing by the British, and the more forceful and technology-driven policing of the United States.

There are several interactive influences to consider in the origins and development of Canadian policing: the nightwatch, British urban policing, British policing of Ireland, the military, the frontier, and American policing style and technologies. Throughout the evolution of Canadian policing, the emphasis has visibly been upon maintaining order, especially in an immigrant-frontier society—and markedly so with respect to controlling labour job actions—in addition to the prevalent modern focus on criminal law enforcement.

ORIGINS: EUROPE

In medieval Europe a nobleman or monarch would have law-enforcement personnel, a sheriff and men, to collect taxes, enforce property laws, and protect the peace. But with urbanization large elements of the population were left unprotected by this system, except those wealthy enough to hire bodyguards. Towns resorted to watches: men hired not by the nobility but by local merchants or by entire neighbourhoods. The community watch might consist of volunteers, persons receiving no remuneration whatsoever, or persons on some sort of retainer (Paul, 1982:201). Remnants of this system can still be found in Continental Europe, with block watchmen on duty at night. From an historical perspective, all modern police forces in Western Europe and North America have their origins in the nightwatch.

High constables might be named to manage the watch, and be paid from public levy. The constable might also call upon the townspeople to mobilize to apprehend an offender in the Saxon tradition of "hue and cry," not unlike the American frontier use of a posse of local townspeople. Other law enforcement demands were met by thief-takers: bounty hunters who hunted offenders for a reward. The thief-taker also became a familiar part of frontier life in North America in the nineteenth century, coexisting with publicly appointed officers and private police, such as the Pinkertons.

As cities grew, the problem of protecting persons and commerce also grew, and outdistanced the capacity of the watch or local action. Only persons with the means to employ substantial staff enjoyed effective protection from robbery and assault, and as cities grew, even that measure of protection began to be insufficient. More organized policing responses were therefore implemented. On the continent, France formed the Sûreté in 1810. It included many former criminals, and was devoted to detection and criminal work, as distinguished from the political police enforcement associated with post-revolutionary France (Paul, 1982:198).

In England, authorities were increasingly concerned about street crime and rowdiness, much of it related to the widespread availability of gin, reminiscent of today's drug-related crimes. The British citizenry, with its democratic experience, was wary, however, of an organized force for internal policing, and especially sensitive to the example of political policing in revolutionary France. The prospect of a powerful organized force, like the army but for internal deployment, was a matter of concern. But by 1829 Sir Robert Peel established his London Police Force, the beginnings of the now-famous "bobbies," to deal with street crime (Paul 1982:199). Despite some opposition, they were uniformed, but in relatively dull colours in contrast to the flamboyant military uniforms of the day. Peel's police were the first modern police force, unlike the French Sûreté consisting not of thieves and criminals, but of relatively upstanding persons. Ironically, and with persisting implications, although the English feared an internal military force, bringing to mind images of Cromwellian dictatorship or presumed French excesses, the only organizational model they found apt was the military. Rank designations, training, discipline, command style, and the first several commanding officers were from the military. But unlike the military, they did not bear arms.

The model of urban policing established in Britain influenced the United States and Canada. Britain did export at least one other policing tradition for colonial administrations, to locations as diverse as Canada, South Africa, and Australia, based upon a much more military force after the style of the Royal Irish Constabulary. This was a force intended to act like an occupying or colonizing army. But as local civic government grew, local municipal policing emerged, influenced by the model of the London Metropolitan.

ORIGINS: NORTH AMERICA

As towns and cities grew in Canada and the United States, a gradual transition from watch and local constables to police departments was taking place. The municipal departments then employed suitable young men to keep order.

In the older settled communities away from the more fluid frontier, towns and cities in British North America had depended upon citizen watches, or special constables, with chief constables sometimes in place. Local magistrates or justices of the peace were responsible for these amateur law enforcement personnel, who had no identifiable uniform or symbol of authority and were unarmed. In serious circumstances, the militia was called out. At least as early as 1651 there was a constable in Quebec City and in Montreal (Talbot et al., 1984:260). By 1793 there were high constables in each of the four districts of Upper Canada (Higley, 1984:28). Such constabulary, in that they were not full-time paid persons, did not constitute police officers in the modern sense, but were obvious antecedents of policing as we find it today (Stenning, 1981a:8–13). They were expected to enforce by-laws and to keep order.

Across the border in the new United States, in New York City, for example, by 1802 at the latest organized watch was in operation. The day personnel were known as "rounds-men," and at night as "watchmen." By 1827 the New York City watchmen began to be identifiable by their leather helmets and came to be popularly known as "leatherheads." As was typical, they were not otherwise uniformed, nor were they trained.

By 1835 in Toronto there was a force of three full-time paid constables and at least fourteen specials under the control of a high constable. Not until 1837, however, were they uniformed (Cooper, 1981:39; Higley, 1984:29). By 1840 Hamilton had a chief constable, and in Bytown (to become the city of Ottawa in 1855 and the nation's capital in 1867), a chief constable was appointed in 1847 (Cooper, 1981:39; Higley, 1984:29; Horne, 1984:5). Earlier, in Quebec, Lord Durham legislated a police force for Quebec City in 1838, where there had been a chief of police as early as 1833 (Kelly and Kelly, 1976:3; Talbot et al., 1984:262). In 1843 Montreal had a police force with a chief, 3 officers, and 48 men (Kelly and Kelly, 1976:3, Talbot et al., 1984:262).

By 1859 the governments of the provinces of Canada required that each city and incorporated town have a chief constable and at least one and possibly more constables, paid by the municipality (Higley, 1984:29). In 1859, too, the Parliament of Upper Canada required boards of police commissioners for the public's control of the police (Cooper, 1981:40). In 1866 the city of Ottawa, about to become the capital of a new nation, established a paid constabulary of 11 uniformed men, who were also armed with revolvers after 1867 (Horne, 1984:11).

One year after Confederation, in 1868, a Dominion Police Force was created, charged with the duties of guarding the Parliament Buildings, and given general responsibilities relating to federal laws. The Police of Canada Act, federal government legislation, authorized the new force to enforce criminal and other federal laws. Significantly, the force was not a matter of local responsibility but was created to operate nationally, and was subject to government appointments and control, most directly through police commissioners (Stenning, 1981a:40–41). The Dominion Police operated in the Atlantic provinces as well as in Ontario, engaged in policing as glamorous as protecting against counterfeiting and "white slavery," and the mundane enforcing of liquor laws (Higley, 1984:70). By this point a gradual transition had been achieved: from the older tradition of the watch and the constable with authority under common law and local mandate, to the concept of police officer and peace officer, the paid professional, mandated by legislation and subject to political control (Grant, 1980:19–20). In 1870 two other pieces of legislation followed the example of the Police of Canada Act, in Manitoba, and in Quebec, where the Quebec Provincial Police Force was created. Although it was not part of the federation, in Newfoundland the Newfoundland Constabulary, modelled after the Royal Irish Constabulary, was founded in 1871 (Kelly and Kelly, 1973:7).

The potential now existed for the new police employees to be used by governments for tasks other than those related directly to crime control and relatively minor matters of public order. The potential now also existed of divorcing the police from their communities. In part the state control of policing was prompted by the demands of the frontier. The new Canadian government was seeking to extend sovereignty over vast underpopulated territories. Trade and settlement had to be regulated, and the aboriginal populations needed to be controlled.

In the West, by 1871 the Manitoba Provincial Police were formed, created by a Constables Act (1870) modelled after the national statute that created the Dominion Police (Stenning, 1981a:41–44). This new police force had province-wide responsibilities and, of course, was dealing with a frontier rather than the older and better established communities of central Canada and the east. What would later become Winnipeg was then just a sparsely populated settlement scattered around Fort Garry. However, by 1874 it too had its own police force of a chief and two constables (Higley, 1984:70; Kelly and Kelly, 1973:10).

The frontier played a significant role in the development of modern Canadian policing. Where the Americans resorted to the Army and assorted adventurers and gunmen for major frontier ventures, the new Canadian government merged the policing concept with the military influence already apparent in European antecedents. Eventually, as provincial forces were founded, in Quebec (1870) and Ontario (1909), the military organizational and command model was dominant. But in the West, the military model was also the major influence on the NorthWest Mounted Police (1873).

In 1906 the new province of Saskatchewan passed legislation similar to Manitoba's, with a Constables Act creating the basis for a provincial force, and in 1908 Alberta enacted a Constables Act that was amended a year later to more nearly resemble the Manitoba model. Not until 1917, however, did Alberta pass its Alberta Provincial Police Act, and not until 1920 did Saskatchewan pass its Police Act, enabling constables in these provinces to act as provincial police. Hitherto province-wide policing had remained with the NorthWest Mounted Police (Stenning, 1981a:46).

As policing continued to evolve, a divergence in American and Canadian experience emerged. The more rapidly expanding American cities, true melting pots, found themselves with police as part of the local political machine. Politicians and industrialists used police for local interests to an extent not true in Canada. In the Canadian cities, the norm of British police neutrality and objectivity was more seriously attempted. Where the British sought for their internal policing a politically neutral, publicly accountable (that is, government-accountable), and administratively controlled police, and in no small part achieved this, the Americans developed fractious policing as part of immigrant politics and urban political "machines." Police early on, as in Boston and New York, became a political force in their own right, a style that lives on, as demonstrated in some New York City police referring to themselves as the "biggest gang of them all." Referring to corruption, inefficiency and ineffectiveness, one American observer remarked that one could only find consolation in the fact that police were not an instrument of any particular local politicians, because they were such an independent force in their own right (Klockars, 1985:49).

In the United States the police moved from crisis to crisis, in cycles of exposed corruption and violence. Reform preoccupation, and some public distrust, has historically always been part of public attention to policing in the United States. In Britain, the United States, and Canada working-class men were recruited, and not necessarily models of moral rectitude. Rowdiness and drunkenness were problems, but in Britain, and in Canada, but less evidently in the United States, the police were early on controlled by the police administrators and once-removed political masters. They were disciplined, and dismissed. And in what was to become the RCMP, military discipline as well as military structure and trappings were soon in place. All three societies experienced drinking problems, brawling, late reporting for work, discourteous behaviour, disorderly uniforms, and like offences, and these were frequently sanctioned in Britain and in Canada. But in the United States police were refusing to wear uniforms, "assaulting superior officers, refusing to go on patrol, extorting money from prisoners, and releasing prisoners from the custody of other officers" (Klockars, 1985: 43).

Canadian municipal and state police were long dominated by a British link. Persons of British military experience were common and deliberately sought. So too were Irish Protestants and officers with experience in the Royal Irish Constabulary. This recruitment tradition is documented for the city of Toronto, for example, where for decades English, Scots, and Irish, often with "old country" policing experience, were sought. In 1930 almost one-half of former British police recruited to Toronto had served with the Royal Irish Constabulary or Irish municipal forces (Marquis, 1987:165).

The deliberate British recruitment bias and somewhat more apolitical policing culture in Canada continue to mark a difference between the two North American nations. Yet, as the twentieth century unfolded, media images, technological innovations, and organizational features of American urban policing undoubtedly were imported to Canada. Motor patrol, radio communications, weapons, and special units such as SWAT teams influenced Canadian police enough to render them at least superficially more like American rather than British police services.

POLICE QUALITY

As organized police services developed, there was inevitably some uncertainty as to police capacity and quality. This continued well into the twentieth century in Canada when, for example, governments considered municipal police politically suspect, especially as they might be too sympathetic to labour interests. Generally, too, police organizations recruited large, vigorous, ill-educated young men, often deliberately for toughness. An advertisement in Windsor specified "three suitably big men" (Gervais, 1992:11). The ability to brawl was often a requisite skill, as a good deal of policing had to do with regulating working-class men in the bars and taverns of Canadian cities. Coming from working-class backgrounds where fighting was a survival skill, and called upon to enforce rough and ready public order, the police were themselves subject to misbehaviour. In Windsor, for example, police offences were largely those of accepting bribes and drunkenness.

Only gradually were the police rendered more respectable and deserving of the confidence of the middle and upper classes to which they were outsiders. Even outfitting the police was an aspect of distinguishing not just the role but also the quality and propriety of police. Uniform and equipment standards were progressively specified and enforced, entrusted to the policemen who were responsible for this public property. In 1876 Windsor Town Council passed a bylaw by way of a code of conduct for police. The code specified dress, to the effect that each constable would be supplied with "one blue coat, one light, two pairs of trousers, one instruction booklet, one baton, one whistle and in addition one great coat and one cap to be supplied every second year" (Gervais, 1992:21).

Urban policing developed. But confidence in them grew much more slowly; as Canada experienced massive immigration and industrial development, the evolving municipal police workers found themselves viewed with some suspicion by government. They were suspect as ineffective and politically unreliable. They were themselves often immigrants. They were working class. And they were too local.

It is useful to distinguish within Canadian policing between local and central or state-controlled activities. The authority of municipal police forces was historically vested in local communities and reflected the biases of, as well as a generalized responsiveness to, local needs. To the extent that local settlements were relatively homogeneous culturally, policing was adequate. As Canadian society grew more heterogeneous in terms of cultural, ethnic, and class composition, local policing became suspect in contrast to state-controlled provincial or national police forces. Labour conflicts, for example, prompted the use of state-controlled forces, since local, municipally controlled constabularies would have been unable to handle large-scale altercations, and may, in any case, have sympathized with local grievances. Ultimately, both local and state-controlled police came to be removed from direct community contacts, evolving into centralized bureaucratic organizations that segregated the "citizens in uniform" from the communities and populations they were intended to serve and to protect.

STATE POLICE

By mid-twentieth century, Canada was overwhelmingly an urban nation, with most residents living in towns and cities. Municipal police forces therefore came to be of paramount importance as the rural population decreased. The municipal police force, although subject to provincial legislation, tended to be more community sensitive. They were local. But in Canada's history, right down to the present, there has been a marked senior government attempt to oversee local town or urban interests, to weaken local influences, and make police forces more subject to direct government command. Police forces were wanted to be more directly the instruments of the state or the provincial or national governments.

State police featured early in the history of Canadian policing. For the provincial state, a Quebec Provincial Police was in place in 1870, the Newfoundland Constabulary in 1872, and the Ontario Provincial Police in 1909. At the federal level, the new Canadian government established the Dominion Police in 1868, and with an eye to the frontier, the NorthWest Mounted Police in 1873. The latter had the designation "Royal" appended in 1904, and merged in 1920 with the much smaller Dominion Police and was renamed the Royal Canadian Mounted Police.

Earlier in Canada's history there were several provincial police forces, including Manitoba (1870), Saskatchewan (1906), Alberta (1908), British Columbia (1871), Nova Scotia (1910), New Brunswick (1927), and Prince Edward Island (1930) (Stenning, 1981a:40–49). For the most part these forces were displaced by the 1930s, prompted by the economic depression, with their duties assumed by the RCMP. The RCMP assumed provincial policing in Saskatchewan in 1928, in Manitoba, Alberta, Nova Scotia, New Brunswick, and Prince

Edward Island in 1932, and in British Columbia in 1950, and also in Newfoundland a year after it entered into Canada's 82-year-old Confederation (Grant, 1980:34; Stenning, 1981a:48).

Where municipal police in Canada have been expected to maintain local order, especially with respect to crime and by-law enforcement, the provincial police forces, the Ontario Provincial Police (OPP) and the Quebec Police Force (later to be named Sûreté du Québec), as well as the national police force, the NorthWest Mounted Police, were expected to act for order in the larger sense of representing the government in the face of political threat. Each of these forces performed regular policing duties, from alcohol law enforcement to criminal investigation. But especially in the disruptive days when unions were fighting for recognition and labour–management confrontations were often violent, these forces were expected to intervene when local police were viewed as unreliable (Juliani et al., 1984:538–540). It is noteworthy that the OPP and the Sûreté are today granted the right of employee association and collective bargaining, but are explicitly prevented in the law from affiliation with organized labour, and denied the right to strike in favour of compulsory binding arbitration (Fisher and Starek, 1978:135). The RCMP remain the only Canadian police force without an employee association. Although for some years now they have had the right in law to associate, efforts thus far by a group of pro-association members, most of them in Montreal and British Columbia, have been futile. Many RCMP members have been hostile, and politicians not encouraging.

NWMP/RCMP

Today's RCMP have evolved from what was first the NorthWest Mounted Police (NWMP) and later the Royal NorthWest Mounted Police (RNWMP) (1904), founded in 1873 by Act of Parliament in order to secure and police the western territories. The NWMP were modelled after forces such as the Royal Irish Constabulary, which had been formed to police Northern Ireland—an expression of central colonial state control. The first commissioner, George Arthur French, and some of the first recruits, had served in the Royal Irish Constabulary (Kelly and Kelly, 1973:14, 21, 24). The NWMP were formed with an initial authorized strength of 300 men. Their deployment in the western territories was quite rapid, spurred by a massacre of 36 Assiniboine Indians by American whisky traders in the Cypress Hills (now southeastern Alberta and southwestern Saskatchewan). In the very year of formation, 150 men were in Lower Fort Garry, and by 1875 Fort Walsh was built near the site of the massacre (Kelly and Kelly, 1973; *The Canadian Encyclopedia*, 1985).

The United States and Canada shared a frontier. Or, better put, they contested a frontier. The new Canadian federation was intent upon claiming the west in advance of expansionist and hegemonic Americans who deemed it their manifest destiny to own the continent. Where the Americans swarmed west in a freebooting fashion, with law and law enforcement belatedly following population, the Canadian government used the NWMP to impose civil order on the prairies almost before the settlers arrived. They were especially effective with the native people, and in controlling traders. When the Métis rebelled in 1885, the military had to be called in. But by and large, the NWMP established and demonstrated Canadian sovereignty. In contrast, the American frontier expansion was more anarchic and violent. Adventurers and settlers poured into the West without an organized legal force to protect them. Self-protection, vigilantes, and hired guns, the stuff of American Western films and still an important part of American mythology, were the norm. And the law, when it came, was every bit as violent. The American army frequently resorted to force in dealing with native peoples, in a punishment mode, in contrast to the NWMP who sought to prevent problems and, as in the example of the legendary Superintendent James Walsh, routed the alcohol merchants and adopted a protective, albeit patronizing, attitude to the aboriginal populations (Jennings, 1977:50–65).

The NWMP continued to evolve to meet changing state requirements. In 1920 the Royal NorthWest Mounted Police Amendment Act created the Royal Canadian Mounted Police, by amalgamating the RNWMP, who had operated in the West, and the Dominion Police, who had operated in the East (Stenning, 1981a:49). Later, the RCMP headquarters were moved from Regina to Ottawa, signifying the national status of the Force, which had previously operated mainly in the West. They had gained distinction as the oldest national police force in the western hemisphere (Sallot, 1979:8).

The newly reconstituted Mounted Police began actively to develop a model of police service that merged national police responsibilities and local municipal and provincial policing. The RCMP contracted with other levels of government for police services. The first policing contracts between the NWMP and the provinces of Alberta and Saskatchewan, which had been fixed in 1905, were discontinued in 1917, but were reinstituted with the formation of the RCMP. The first municipal contract with the RCMP was signed in 1935, with Flin Flon, Manitoba (*Contact* 1, Fall–Winter 1982:16).

The costs of the contract policing are shared, with the federal government until the 1980s assuming somewhat more than 50% of the costs. In 1981 agreements with the federal government called for a sliding scale of cost-sharing up to 1990. By 1987 the cost of provincial contracts were borne by provinces at 64%, municipalities with under 15 000 population also paid 64%, and municipalities over 15 000 paid 87% of the costs. By 1990 the costs declined further for the federal government, with the provinces and large municipalities bearing 90% of the costs, and municipalities with under 15 000 population paying 70% of the costs.

Today the RCMP have jurisdiction in all provinces and territories, and in over 100 municipalities. In all cases they are ultimately managed by a commissioner, who reports to the solicitor general of Canada. The nature and extent of their operations vary with local or provincial policies. In Ontario and in Quebec they have no provincial or municipal policing responsibilities, as these are assigned to the provincial police forces and municipal forces operating under provincial acts. Only in these two provinces do the RCMP not enforce provincial statutes. In all of the Atlantic provinces they are responsible for rural policing, and some of the towns and cities. In the West they are the provincial police, under contract to the provincial governments, and also under contract to most smaller communities. In addition, in Alberta and in British Columbia they police many of the urban and suburban municipalities. In the northern territories they are the only police. Finally, in all regions of the nation where federal statutes must be enforced, including customs and excise, or where federal property is to be policed, such as some parks and buildings in Ottawa, the RCMP have authority.

Canada is today an urbanized society, and consequently most of our discussion in this book deals with urban policing. But there remains, of course, a significant rural police presence. While some small-town police forces persist in Ontario, in Canada generally, rural and small-town policing services are provided either by the RCMP, or, in Ontario and Quebec, by Canada's two major provincial police forces, or, and in a very limited fashion, by the Royal Newfoundland Constabulary in Newfoundland. All are responsible to provincial legislative authority. In Ontario and in Quebec, small detachments of police from their respective forces serve small towns and the adjacent hinterland. In these two provinces, the two most populous regions of Canada, the so-called national police force have least responsibility.

The Ontario Provincial Police

Colonial Ontario, as elsewhere in North America and in Europe, depended upon local residents performing constabulary functions and on some system of the watch. A more specialized system began to emerge in the last half of the 19th century. In 1864, by Order in Council, a constabulary force was created in Essex County in Upper Canada: a "frontier" police, with constables named by a magistrate. In 1865 a force of constables called the Niagara River Frontier Police, were in service around Fort Erie, and by 1874 they were being paid by the province. By 1877 a provincial statute allowed the appointment of provincial constables who were authorized and intended to work outside of the organized counties, tending the frontiers of northern and northwestern Ontario. In the northwest, by 1883 there was a constabulary force for the Thunder Bay District. The Ontario Provincial Police (OPP) force was founded in 1909 to deal with problems in northwestern mining towns. It was responsible to the provincial attorney general, headed by a superintendent, and divided into a southern and a northern division, each under a divisional inspector. It was in active service as of January 1, 1910. In that year two officers were suspended for refusing to wear a uniform, as the concept of uniformed police was opposed by many members of the new force. By the end of 1910 a western division was hived off from the northern division, and another, the middle division, was formed in 1913. By 1921 there were six divisions, and then the system was amended to nine districts under district inspectors, operating out of Windsor, Niagara Falls, Kitchener, Toronto, Belleville, Ottawa, Cobalt, Sudbury, and Port Arthur. The Criminal Investigations Department operated out of Toronto from Queen's Park offices (Higley, 1984:30–133).

Just as military origins can be identified for the RCMP, as the government required a forceful arm for frontier expansion, so too in the case of Ontario policing the military influence is apparent. The early commissioners had military backgrounds, with two successors to the inaugural commissioner coming from British and Canadian military service. The third commissioner, assuming office in 1922 and serving until 1937 until 70 years of age, especially stressed the military mode for the force. The fourth commissioner came from a policing and not a military background, with years of service in the Toronto Police Service and the Ontario Police Force. He assumed office in 1937, commanding a force of 379 uniformed and civilian personnel. His successor in 1953 had municipal policing service in Kitchener, and service in the Ontario Provincial Police, preceded by military service during World War I (Higley, 1984:361). He was to be the last appointee with military experience.

The founding of the OPP in 1909 was a response to the development of the Ontario northwestern frontier and resource communities. Historically, too, the OPP have been ordered to control and curtail labour demonstrations, strikes, and conflicts, a practice continued aggressively into the 1990s.

In 1944 the Municipal Act was passed in Ontario, allowing contract police service by the OPP for communities. The first such communities to contract with them in 1945 were the

Village of Rockcliffe Park, the upper-class neighbourhood of Ottawa; the village of Port Stanley; and the township of McKim. The strength of the force by war's end was 510; by 1949 strength was at 1083, including 999 uniformed personnel. The new recruits largely came from military service, and the expansion was associated with additional communities contracting for police service. Municipal policing became more clearly defined in 1946 and 1949 with Police Acts. By 1984 the OPP was for a time the third largest police force in North America, after the RCMP and the California Highway Patrol. They are responsible for their own training, for which they operate the Provincial Police Academy, located initially in Toronto and in Brampton since 1981 (*Ottawa Citizen*, May 15, 1984; Higley, 1984:570). The OPP have recently been displaced in many communities by expanded regional police. They continue to police a huge province, however, working rural and wilderness areas, small towns and villages, and suburbs of larger cities. Even though they have lost contracts for policing, they do, in a somewhat more competitive environment for policing services, also bid successfully to contract for policing in Ontario communities.

The Quebec Police Force

The Sûreté du Québec or Quebec Provincial Police Force, founded by legislation in 1870 as the Quebec Provincial Police, was Canada's first provincial police force, although its duties were initially confined to tasks such as prisoner escort. Today, with sworn employees in excess of 4000, and a major training academy at Nicolet, it is one of the most powerful police organizations in Canada after the RCMP. The force's full range of tasks includes an intelligence operation, with a labour/political surveillance role similar to that which the RCMP has played historically on a national basis.

Some of its labour interventions have been notorious among labour historians, especially its role in breaking the 1949 Asbestos Strike in the northern Quebec mining towns of Asbestos and nearby Thetford Mines. The strike, which has been identified as a watershed event in the social history of Quebec leading to the liberalization of the "Quiet Revolution," lasted for five months. In May a pitched battle was fought with the Sûreté, and some officers were taken hostage and later released. The Riot Act was read, police reinforcement brought in, and 200 men arrested. According to the accounts of some participants, statements were forcefully extracted by police (Beausoleil, 1974:167–173). The event was a clear instance of the provincial police as the arm of government assisting a major corporation (*Ottawa Citizen*, May 6, 1989).

Since then, the Sûreté has itself become a significant force as an organized labour group in the province. Unlike the Ontario force, it has been quite militant in its relations with its state employer. In 1977, for example, although police strikes are not legal in Quebec, the members withdrew services for seven days in a dispute where the police union was insisting upon 24-hour two-officer patrols, following the killing of an officer in a rural area. Eventually they settled for two-officer patrols for overnight shifts from 3:00 p.m. to 8 a.m. (*Ottawa Citizen*, April 13, 1977; April 20, 1977).

Responsible to the justice minister of the province, the Sûreté acts throughout the province, not only policing rural areas and small towns, but as provided in the Police Act of 1968, at the will of the Quebec government having jurisdiction "in the entire territory of Quebec" and intervening in any Quebec municipality (Barot and Berand, 1981; Stenning, 1981a:79). Unlike its Ontario counterpart or the RCMP, it does not operate in Quebec towns on a contract basis (Kelly and Kelly, 1976:35, 50), but as an agency of the Quebec government. The director general of the force is appointed by the government, as are senior officers, on the recommendation of the director general (Stenning, 1981a:79). A 1968 Act created a provincial police commission that has some control and investigative functions, but the Quebec force remains a direct arm of the provincial government.

The Newfoundland Constabulary

The Royal Newfoundland Constabulary, formerly the Newfoundland Rangers, was established by legislation in 1872. It had in fact become operational a year earlier, in 1871 (Talbot et al., 1984:256–257). Like the Royal Canadian Mounted Police, the constabulary was modelled after the Irish Constabulary as a means of colonial control by England. It operates today mainly in the capital, St. John's, although it does maintain some posts in the hinterland, working in Corner Brook and the Wabush area of Labrador (Montreal *Gazette*, January 29, 1989), and contingents have intervened elsewhere in instances of civil disturbances (Talbot et al., 1984:258). The Constabulary, used as an expression of provincial power and autonomy, expanded in 1984, assuming policing responsibilities in some communities in Labrador that the RCMP had carried (*Globe and Mail*, December 30, 1983; *Ottawa Citizen*, July 3, 1984). But the RCMP role has remained well established, and elsewhere in the province policing is largely an RCMP responsibility. The Constabulary was unique in North America as an unarmed police service, until April 3, 1998, when following extensive lobbying by the police union, the government announced that henceforth sidearms would routinely be worn (*CBC Radio News*, April 3, 1998).

THE STATE, POLICE, AND LABOUR

Through the first part of the twentieth century, especially after World War I, a pronounced role for the police in Canada, as in the United States, was the control of labour actions, which were often viewed by governments, sometimes correctly, as political movements intent upon revolutionary change. Anti-strike police action would consist of protection for strike-bound property and for replacement labour, measures probably expected by the wider public. Additionally, however, they harassed and arrested strikers and prior to the post-World War II period, frequently intervened in communities to deter meetings and to intimidate and detain labour leaders (Harring, 1981:304). Labour still complains of police protection of strikebreakers as often "provocative and intimidating." They have also complained that the numerous former police officers working for private security agencies creates sympathy and collusion between police and guards (Zwelling, 1972:93, 100–101).

Especially the RCMP and the two provincial forces, the OPP and the Sûreté, were used in such a role since they were viewed by governments as more reliable than local municipal police. They intervened with unionists, immigrants, and the unemployed, as the arm of government. The labour radicalism of the West especially influenced government with respect to a role for the RCMP, following the RNWMP's violent intervention in the Winnipeg General Strike of 1919. Labour historians (Jamieson, 1973; Abella, 1974; Penner, 1979) have been unforgiving of the RCMP intervention, considering the use of force unnecessary and excessive, where in contrast William Kelly, a former commissioner, described the intervention as one provoked by violent and abusive strikers, and the situation as saved only by the "discipline" of the police (Kelly and Kelly, 1973:149–150). For Kelly, the RNWMP action "prevented the revolutionary movement from developing further." The Winnipeg General Strike is noteworthy in the history of policing for another reason. The Winnipeg Police Force had previously joined the strike, and eventually all its officers were dismissed and never regained their jobs. A later example of the massive use of RCMP intervention was the Dominion Day police charge in Regina that broke the "on to Ottawa" trek of 1935.

Writing for the Task Force on Labour Relations, Jamieson asserts (1973:12) that the intervention of the RCMP has throughout Canadian history "been felt with enough force to tip the scales of battle in hundreds of strikes and labour demonstrations." A similar view of the manner in which the NWMP and the RCMP earned their keep has been expressed by Brown and Brown (1978). The NWMP's role in defending the interests of the Canadian Pacific Railroad against native peoples and labour (24–32), founding unionists and the fledgling labour movement (33–50), unemployed Canadians during the Great Depression (58–78), and against protest and dissident political groups (50–57; 79–126) are inventoried in their book, which is well known but not well loved by members of the Force.

Similar accounts are offered of the OPP and the Sûreté. Of these provincial police Jamieson writes (1973:12): "When up to 400 Ontario Provincial Police marched into Kirkland Lake during a 1942 miners' strike, when 100 Quebec Provincial Police invaded the town of Asbestos to protect hundreds of strikebreakers in the 1949 Asbestos workers' strike, and when 300 OPP constables arrived in Sudbury during the 1966 strike at International Nickel Company of Canada, Canadian authorities were repeating a history of official sanction of the use of force in labour disputes in North America." As for the Quebec police, Dumas (1975:19–69) identifies the police as the arm of government in breaking strikes and arresting workers who were eventually tried, imprisoned, or deported, in major strike actions in northern mining towns such as Rouyn-Noranda.

The state police have frequently functioned covertly. Until 1981 the RCMP operated a national Security Service responsible for security checks and counter-espionage. Like the provincial police forces, who also have operated intelligence units whose work was defined as preventive, the RCMP Service devoted considerable attention to labour and political groups. The Security Service, which was sometimes a source of resentment among regular officers, operated as an organization within an organization. Although subject to RCMP chain of command and ultimately the commissioner, its duties were in their very nature more political. They often contradicted the law enforcement functions for which members had originally been recruited and trained; agents were obliged to work covertly and to tolerate illegalities in the national interest (Sawatsky, 1980:18–20). Monitoring dissidents, and by some accounts, even opposition politicians, particularly in the New Democratic Party, was historically an important area of activity for the provincial and especially the federal police force. Policing labour, anti-communism, and the Cold War were mixed up, as state police variously monitored and intervened in the conduct of Canadians (Whitaker and Marcuse, 1994).

In the pages to follow, as we focus on general policing, the state role of provincial police and the RCMP will periodically intrude. The emphasis in our discussion, however, will be municipal policing and the regulation of daily civil life. While the responsibilities of state conducted forces for special social-control duties are an underlying element of the totality of policing in Canada, they are not its dominant characteristics as experienced by most Canadians on a day-to-day basis.

Modern Canadian policing bears inevitable similarities to other industrialized urban police organizations, today especially to the American rather more than to the British, from which Canadian policing derived. Relative to many other societies, the Anglo-American policing tradition, of which Canada is a part, has represented a publicly responsible tradition of policing that has only in limited manifestations been overtly associated with the direct interests of a particular political ideology or regime.

ANGLO-AMERICAN POLICING

The forms, behaviours, and reputations of police forces vary widely around the world. In the Anglo-democracies the police have in common their origins in the watch system and a citizen constabulary. With police forces instituted for public protection and order, albeit a rather privileged public, and not for the imposition of government regimes, municipal police retained some affiliation with their communities. Police have tended to be more localized, although there has obviously been a centralized role for government, and even national state police, as with the Federal Bureau of Investigation in the United States and the RCMP in Canada.

The Anglo-democratic police forces from their origins have had a basis in criminal law enforcement and civil protection, and not in political control. This is very much unlike police in most continental Western Europe democracies such as France and Germany, in post-colonial developing societies, and in nondemocratic states, where the police have a more explicit role in political or state control. They are thereby more subject to political direction in their very nature and definition, and to control through a state bureaucratic apparatus rather than local community direction. As Bayley has observed, "Where police forces, as well as tasks, have grown out of the needs of governance, the police system tends to be centralized and supervised by a civilian bureaucracy. Where police forces and tasks have grown out of private needs, police systems tend to be decentralized and to have little civilian bureaucratic supervision" (Bayley, 1971–72:96).

In Canada, the United States, and Great Britain the number of police employees, including sworn police officers, increased significantly in the 1960s and 1970s as did public expenditure upon policing. In 1962, in Canada there were 1.5 sworn police officers per 1000 population, contrasted to 1.7 in the United States and 1.7 in the United Kingdom. By 1977 there were 2.3 sworn police per 1000 population in Canada, 2.1 in the United States, and 2.3 in the United Kingdom (Canada, 1980:165).

Canadian policing is similar to, and yet distinctive, when compared to Britain and the United States. The evolution from the watch in our early cities to citizens in uniform responsible to local elected authorities has been akin to the British development of policing. Historically, this early policing has been much less characterized by corruption and loyalty to political bosses than has been true of policing in the United States. At the same time, since Canada then consisted largely of frontier, we adapted a British paramilitary model in the NWMP (as is obviously symbolized by their dress uniforms) and a somewhat more explicit state police component in order to ensure orderly settlement and labour control.

American influences, however, have been unavoidable, and these have been most evident in our adoption of their technology and organizational structures, from the dependence upon motorized patrol to special tactical units. Nonetheless, Canadian police have remained distinct in their character from the American forces, not least in the lower levels of violence and corruption.

Great Britain

It is undoubtedly the case that the police most admired by the Canadian public, and still serving as an idealized model for Canadian police, are the British. Where Canadian public and police alike are prone to speak disparagingly of American policing because of their violence, corruption, and low recruitment and training standards, the British police on the other hand have, at least until recently, been regarded as approximately the ideal. For the non-British public, the British police are perceived as polite, incorruptible, politically neutral, and reluctant to resort to force. The reality, of course, is somewhat at odds with the ideal.

The more than 100 000 police officers in England and Wales work in a system balancing centralized and local elements. Police are responsible to the Home Office of the national government, but policing in Britain is also effectively decentralized into more than 40 local forces in England and Wales, each commanded by a chief constable (Mark, 1977:13–15). The Home Office responsibility consists of setting nation-wide standards of recruitment, training, and compensation, with training delivered in seven centres around the United Kingdom. Training is to a standard curriculum (Mark, 1977:16–19; Manwaring-White, 1983:226), quite unlike either the United States or Canada.

A prominent feature of British policing has been its ostensible apolitical character. The model of the detached public servant has remained a prevalent one in Britain. A noteworthy exception to the norm of avoiding political statement and public sentence was Sir Robert Mark who, when retiring from his role as head of Scotland Yard, became a very effective and outspoken representative of police interests, strongly advocating an active role for police in policy information and application. He disparaged the "curious, old-fashioned belief that there is something vaguely improper in a policeman talking about the law, the courts and lawyers" (Mark, 1977:72).

Rank-and-file British police have had relatively slight political influence. Unlike police in North America and Europe, they have not been very effectively organized in employee groups that would permit them internal and external influence. The Police Federation, in contrast to North American police associations and unions, has been very ineffectual, without even the right to engage in contract bargaining, and the police generally have been loath to participate in political debate. There have been exceptions. The Police Federation was very aggressive in the mid-1970s, and sought the right to strike in 1977. In this period, too, they actively mounted a law-and-order campaign (Reiner, 1978b:179). In Britain, as in Canada, the death penalty has been a provocative issue, eliciting police comment. In 1983 when Parliament declined to restore hanging, Police Federation representatives reacted bitterly. Noting that 30 British police officers had been killed since hanging was abolished in 1964, a spokesperson remarked that "Parliament is not concerned about the problems officers face in the front line." The federation urged a vigorous application of existing sanctions following the reconfirmation of abolition (*Toronto Star*, July 15, 1983).

In addition to legal restraints, the absence of police union militancy had been attributable, in part, to public support of the police. But in the 1970s the police were besieged. Major race-related conflicts occurred, such as the Notting Hill clashes in 1976 surrounding the West Indian Carnival. Several hundred people, including more than 300 police officers, were injured (*Economist*, August 18, 1979:23). Accordingly, by the late 1970s and early 1980s both the public and the police were increasingly dissatisfied, with the police uncharacteristically under critical attack by the public, and the police unhappy with their pay levels and duties. Prime Minister Thatcher's law-and-order emphasis, however, helped restore some police satisfaction. In 1977 police had been sufficiently angry to demand the right to strike, despite such utterings in themselves being illegal (*Globe and Mail*, May 25, 1977). But the Thatcher government's rhetoric and its actions restored police confidence. One of the first acts of the Thatcher government upon taking office was awarding a 20% pay increase to police in 1979, keeping a campaign promise. The Home Secretary, in announcing that the increases would be effective immediately, went on to state that "By this action, the government has demonstrated very clearly its support for the police and their role in society" (Montreal *Gazette*, May 10, 1979). Since the Thatcher period, however, the image of British policing has been subject to serious renewed doubts, with revelations of major instances of evidence-tampering and subsequent unwarranted convictions, especially associated with police anti-terrorist investigations.

The support of Mrs. Thatcher's Conservative government may also have had the consequence of reinforcing the inherent conservatism of police personnel. Where the British police have had some excellent public spokespeople who have conveyed a sense of responsible, albeit conservative, interests, recently prominent senior police have been associated with extremist views. The chief of Manchester, for example, labelled by the press as "God's Own Policeman" because of his fundamentalist religious views, provided *Woman's Own Magazine* with an interview in 1987, uttering remarks such as "I'd thrash some criminals myself ..." and "They should be punished until they repent their sins." In other interviews he had offered the view that rapists should be castrated, homosexuality banned, and that victims of AIDS are "swirling in a human cesspool of their own making." The chief has claimed that his views derive from prayer and divine inspiration (Montreal *Gazette*, December 15, 1987).

British police apparently not only have a rather negative view of pubic morality; they also, like their American and Canadian counterparts, consider the public to be hostile and non-supportive (Reiner, 1978b:175–176). Yet research indicates generally very favourable public views of policing, as illustrated by a measure of London public opinion in an extensive survey in the late 1960s (Belson, 1975). But some deterioration in public sentiment developed in the 1970s, essentially deriving from major corruption scandals and racial problems.

In the 1970s the mass media exposed major, indeed systematic, police corruption in Scotland Yard, especially among drug and morality investigators. The corrupt activities and inept or indifferent internal investigations into complaints over a period of years led to major investigations, and eventually the government appointment in 1972 of Robert Mark, a police officer from outside London—as commissioner of Scotland Yard. Mark, in turn, had to depend upon outside detectives as he pursued a clean-up of Scotland Yard that eventually included a massive turnover in personnel, with many persons returned to uniformed service, as he worked to establish the ascendancy of the uniformed branch over the detective branch (Cox et al., 1977; Mark, 1978:116, 126–130). In Mark's words, he responded to the recognized "need to bring the CID under proper control for the first time in nearly a hundred years."

In 1989 revelations regarding use of excessive force and perjury further called into question the reputation of British police. In the city of Birmingham the Serious Crime Squad was disbanded, and detectives were suspended or reassigned following evidence of faked or extorted evidence. The most famous incident involved six Irishmen who in 1980 were convicted of terrorism. According to the 1989 revelations the convictions followed police beatings and perjured police testimony (*Chicago Tribune*, October 22, 1989). Similarly, in 1990 the press reported forged confessions by the West Midlands Serious Crime Squad, which had led to the conviction of an Arabic man on charges of armed robbery (*Sunday Times Magazine*, July 15, 1990).

Public polls have clearly suggested some diminishment in public regard for police. A London Times poll in 1980 found that 71% of respondents rated police as "good" (*Ottawa Citizen*, September 11, 1980). A national newspaper poll in 1981 reported that 25% of respondents had decreasing confidence in the police (Manwaring-White, 1983:213). By 1989, although 89% of respondents found it simple to agree with a leading and ethnocentric statement that "Despite their faults I would rather have our police than those I have seen in other countries," as put in a *Daily Express* poll, another research group found that of those polled only 11% trusted their police "just about always" (*Economist*, April 1,1989:53). Forty-seven percent had the opinion that corruption is not uncommon, although only four percent believed that it was widespread. More telling perhaps, the poll data showed a decline in public satisfaction with policing in the community, from a rate in the high 70s in 1981 to below 60% in 1987. On the other hand, examination of police opinion indicated alarming attitudes. An independent research study commissioned by the Metropolitan London Police reported racial prejudice, sexism, alcoholism, and corruption. They particularly stressed racist sentiments, noting racist graffiti in police stations, racist language, and special police attention to young black males (*Globe and Mail*, October 17, 1983).

Violent rioting in Tottenham (London) in 1985 resulted in injuries to hundreds of police officers, and one police death. Pitched battles were fought, with black rioters and police both armed. The rioting broke out after a woman died, apparently of a heart attack, during a police search of her home in search of stolen goods following the arrest of her son (*Globe and Mail*, October 7, 1985). Rioting also occurred in Leicester when police arrested black youths in connection with the police officer's death (*Ottawa Citizen*, October 11, 1985).

An analysis of police development in several western traditions concludes that the British police, the most "benign" of police forces, has, in its response to the crisis politics of the current decades, become more interventionist and more explicitly the arm of the central state (Bowden, 1978:264–273). Since the 1960s the police in Britain have had to contend with a multiracial society for which they were unprepared. Bowden sympathetically characterizes the breakdown in acceptable British policing as a consequence of their having been required to police social circumstances beyond their control.

Other observers noted the loss in public confidence and consequent deterioration in citizen cooperation, especially among less privileged communities, leading to the failure of police to cope with crime. A vicious circle was established of differential enforcement, ineffectual solutions, loss of confidence, and mutual police–public distrust and low regard, leading to further partiality and imperfect enforcement (Kinsey et al., 1986). Another very friendly analysis argued that declining government support and loss of public regard has harmed the police ability to deal with crime and generally has jeopardized British policing (Evans, 1974).

In addition to contending with a racially heterogeneous society, British police have had to contend with a very clearly demarcated class society. In industrial conflicts, British police have been interposed between workers and management, and have themselves become the object of violence. During major coal miners' strikes in 1984 police and strikers fought bitterly (*Ottawa Citizen*, September 24, 1984; *Toronto Star*, October 18, 1984). Firebombs and homemade spears were used by strikers attempting to stop a police convoy of strike-breakers. Throughout the strike police were blamed for provoking picket-line fights, and were featured in an anti-police resolution at a Labour Party convention. In contrast to the historically favourable public view of the police, after the clashes with the striking miners signs were seen in shop windows in Yorkshire that read "Policemen will not be served" (*Ottawa Citizen*, November 13, 1984, October 2, 1984; *Toronto Star*, October 5, 1984).

Police violence and race riots such as those in Brixton in 1981 and Tottenham in 1985 led British police authorities to modify their recruitment and training. British police have sought to upgrade and diversify recruitment, especially with regard to women and visible minorities. They have also been more willing than North American forces to allow flexibility in uniform dress to accommodate minorities. Sikh police officers, for example, are allowed to wear turbans and, below the uniform jacket, the ceremonial dagger (*Toronto Sunday Star*, February 23, 1986). And as previously remarked, they have developed basic training curricula and standards for all British police officers, in contrast to the widely varying standards characteristic of North America.

But recruitment and training efforts have not been markedly successful. In 1990 it was estimated that only 520 of the 28 000 London Metropolitan police officers were non-white. Only in 1990 did the London force abandon minimum-height requirements of 173 cm (5'8") for males and 162 cm (5'4") for females as a measure to enhance minority recruit selection (*Ottawa Citizen*, January 23, 1990). Inevitably, too, police efforts to diversify their composition cannot solve the racial inequality and tension of British society, and British police still find themselves in repeated clashes with minority populations.

In this charged environment British police have resisted, but not avoided, the use of weapons. The Brixton riot was set off by a police shooting. Searching for a young black man, police mistakenly shot and wounded his mother. Also in 1985, police in Birmingham shot and killed a five-year-old boy during a police raid. A member of the tactical firearms unit placed his handgun on a pile of clothing on a bed in order to search for weapons, and the gun discharged, killing the child hidden beneath the bedclothes (*Toronto Sunday Star*, August 25, 1985; *Ottawa Citizen*, October 3, 1985). In recent decades British police have more frequently been issued arms for special operations, though the number of officers regularly carrying guns decreased in the mid-eighties: of Scotland Yard's 27 165 members in 1984, 2970 were authorized to carry guns, a reduction in that year from 3780 (*Toronto Sunday Star*, May 4, 1986). In the five years from 1980 through 1985 there were only two accidental deaths arising from police use of weapons, including an unborn child when a woman being held hostage was hit by police bullets in 1980. The contrasting estimate from the United States is 200 people per year. In 1984 British police fired only a total of 17 shots in the course of 6 incidents (*Ottawa Citizen*, October 3, 1985).

Violence by and towards police is less pronounced in Britain than in North America. But as in Canada and the United States, perceptions of the frequency and severity of violent encounters have prompted more elaborate offensive and defensive equipment and techniques. The famous "flying squad" and armed encounters are normal. Increasingly there have been attempts to afford protection for officers; body armour is standard issue. In fact, in 1997, having removed body armour prior to a search for a man in violation of bail, a British female police officer was stabbed to death—the first female British police officer to be killed in the line of duty. Immediately the London Metropolitan Police Commissioner stated that the death was not an incident warranting the issue of firearms to police (*Ottawa Sun*, October 26, 1997).

It remains true that in the normal routine of police duty, the "bobby" is unarmed except for a truncheon or nightstick. Moreover, rank-and-file police officers in Britain have favoured not being armed, with the policy being endorsed by the Police Federation (*Toronto Star*, December 20, 1981). Despite the rising use of weapons in offences, British police have persisted in their commitment to their theory of "opposite force," the notion that if police do not carry arms, by and large offenders will not either, while if police are armed, the use of weapons in crime will escalate (*Ottawa Citizen*, December 16, 1981).

Yet there has been some increased demand for arms in Britain, associated with the increase in violent crime. In London, offences in which guns were used rose to 2356 in 1985 from 1401 in 1976 (*Toronto Star*, May 5, 1986). The police have, in turn, responded by arming special personnel. In 1983, for example, an unarmed policeman was shot during a robbery in London. An incident three days earlier involved robbers armed with a shotgun. Following the robbery some police officers on patrol were issued guns, albeit not without protest in the British press and in Parliament. Elsewhere in Britain, in Manchester, "small mobile units of armed and highly trained officers" were assigned to patrol the city in response to a marked increase in armed offences. In 1983, therefore, in Britain for the first time, regular patrols of British police were armed (Montreal *Gazette*, April 7, 1983). The decision to arm some Manchester City Police was well publicized by the press, and widely criticized, even by other police services (*Toronto Sunday Star*, April 10, 1983).

In 1987 it was estimated that 93% of British police still did not carry guns. But also in that year police in London lay in wait and shot to death two armed men attempting a payroll robbery (*Ottawa Citizen*, July 11, 1987). In 1988 more than 200 policemen, many armed with rifles, were deployed in Trafalgar Square to deal with an armed hostage-taker. A police marksman shot and wounded the man (*Ottawa Citizen*, December 3, 1988).

There have also been incidents involving armed special units in Britain. In 1985, the Technical Support Unit of Scotland Yard, known as the "Watchers," were involved in a well-publicized blunder. Two officers, in civilian clothes and masked, invaded the grounds of a man under surveillance, without a warrant. When discovered, one officer was stabbed to death. The defendant when tried claimed that he was defending himself from unknown men who confronted him and did not identify themselves as police officers. The man was acquitted of a charge of murder (*Ottawa Citizen*, December 16, 1985). Two years previously, armed undercover Scotland Yard officers shot a man sitting in a car. Mistaking the man for a wanted and dangerous criminal, a warning shot was fired by one of the officers. *That* shot was mistaken by another policeman for shooting from the car, and further shots were fired, seriously wounding the man. The victim had been shot five times by police, and was battered in the head with his gun butt as he lay wounded in the street, and then handcuffed (*Toronto Sunday Star*, January 23, 1983; *Toronto Star*, October 10, 1983). He later recovered. The two police officers were tried for attempted murder and acquitted by a jury on the grounds that the police had feared for their lives and had shot in self-defence, even though they were mistaken. There was no apparent public dissatisfaction with the verdict (Montreal *Gazette*, October 26, 1983).

For all the violence and corruption that have recently come to be associated with British policing, overall the apparent character of British policing has remained somewhat less suspect than American counterparts. The British police, more often on foot and still relatively rarely armed, have also been less technology-driven and less remote from the public than in either the United States or Canada. One work does strongly indict the British police for their new technological dependence and increased remoteness from their communities, itemizing complaints familiar to any North American observer of policing about labour interventions, violence, poor training, and the like (Manwaring-White, 1983). But still, the foot patrol or beat police officer, for example, remains intrinsic to British policing (Grimshaw and Jefferson, 1987:4), unlike the shift to automobiles and elaborate specialization in North America that only now is being addressed by the relatively recent rediscovery of community-based policing. In Britain "normal" policing has remained predominantly foot patrol/beat policing with consequent "reassuring contacts with the public" (Grimshaw and Jefferson, 1987:4).

The United States

The quality of American policing varies enormously in both recruitment and training. American policing has been at one and the same time conservative and anachronistic, progressive and innovative. The contradiction may exist even within one organization, and certainly is evident when contrasting the several hundred police forces in the United States. It was estimated in a Rand report that in 1969 there were about three-quarters of a million police in the United States, consisting of approximately 324 000 local or municipal sworn officers, 71 000 state and federal sworn personnel, and 290 000 private police (Johnson, 1976:91). Extrapolation from this estimate would suggest a figure well in excess of one million law enforcement personnel (U.S. Bureau of Justice *Statistics Bulletin*, 1992; 1993). At the municipal level, in cities such as New York, they are less well paid than in Canada, with entry-level salaries for officers averaging $18 910 in 1990 (U.S. Bureau of Justice *Statistics Bulletin*, 1992). There is federal policing in the form of the Federal Bureau of Investigation, state police forces such as the New York State Police, and a plethora of local municipal police forces and law enforcement agencies, in a wildly diversified system utterly lacking in uniform standards of selection, training, or conduct. There are approximately 40 000 distinct policing agencies in the United States, often with overlapping jurisdictions. In Chicago, within a radius of 50 miles, there are 350 different forces.

In 1970, as America emerged from the rowdy 1960s, a British police superintendent observed at a conference of British chiefs that their American counterparts fluctuated between community relations attempts and outright oppression (Germann, 1971:62). "Their role can be likened to Jekyll and Hyde—on the one hand they are furiously promoting community relations programs to woo over their public—and on the other they are shooting, beating, and bombing their public to keep them in order."

Some American police forces have outstanding levels of qualification and training. Others, such as Detroit and New York City, have difficulties in attracting recruits, and often bring in personnel with only a low level of high school, arm them, and place them on the streets with little preparation. The cost of training police personnel has influenced communities to seek poorly paid private police to supplement regular service, and to take other measures such as hiring additional civilian employees. There has also been experimentation with combined functions, as in Kalamazoo, Michigan, where the fire and police departments were integrated. All personnel are trained as firemen and as policemen, and then enter service as "public safety officers" (*Toronto Sunday Star*, March 6, 1983).

Historically, the development of police forces in the United States was congruent with similar development in Britain and in Canada. In the United States, however, in contrast to Britain and in some degree to Canada, urban police forces, especially in the North, depended very heavily for their recruits upon immigrant populations. The immigrant waves of Irish and Italians in particular contributed to police composition, and to the police integration into local politics and the Catholic Church (Johnson, 1976:93–94). From the start, then, the police have been involved in the politics of American urban immigrant communities, and as Wilson put it, "have repeatedly been in conflict with new urban migrants of whatever color" (Wilson, 1969:130). Police intervention has, therefore, generally had a conservative nature, as police forces have acted to restrict and harass new immigrants while protecting their interests in the urban politics of the day.

In part, the early growth of private policing, such as the Pinkerton Detective Agency, was an effort by the middle class to have reliable policing responsive to their interests (Johnson, 1976:94). The municipal police with their political connections were perceived as riddled with corruption, part of the illegal activities of the underclass of urban immigrants. Corruption in the cities such as New York was evident as a public problem from the early days of the force (Richardson, 1970:175–189).

While in Canada, business interests and the government turned to a national police force to secure frontier development, or to provincial forces responsible to the state, such as the OPP, in the United States, faced with corrupt and working-class-dominated municipal policing, business interests resorted to private police. On the frontier, where massive force was required, the army was called in; and otherwise, pople were expected to fend for themselves. The notion of the armed citizenry, with a right and a responsibility to defend themselves, persists today as a limitation upon social and police reform in the United States (Bayley, 1977). It is generally correct to note that in the United States, in contrast to Britain and Canada, the middle-class public, and especially the business elite, have never had confidence in the public police, and periodic attempts to reform police or to curtail their activities have their basis in this context of non-confidence (Johnson, 1976:101–103).

Private police forces have been created by such diverse groups as corporate interests, such as the railroads who fostered the original Pinkertons, to entire communities who seek to rid themselves of dependency upon police whom they perceive to be ineffective and brutal. Communities will contract with security firms who recruit unskilled young men with little or no background checks, arm them, and assign them to patrol duties. One such situation in a California community produced a sensational rape/murder, committed by one of the security personnel (*Sixty Minutes*, December 11, 1988). But in the United States there is an additional element that seems unique. There has been widespread use of modern bounty hunters. Taking advantage of an upsurge of outstanding felony warrants and associated rewards, as many as one thousand bounty hunters, usually working for bail bondsmen, are operating in the United States (Montreal *Gazette*, September 10, 1987). There is no doubt that the bounty hunters have operated illegally in Canada, and in one incident were apprehended, tried, and convicted.

It appears incorrect to argue, as Johnson (1976) does, that the public police in the United States are an arm of the working class. They were intended, as were most other forces, to regulate the lower classes (Miller, 1977:16–18; McDougall, 1988b:14). Their political character did, however, render them open to immigrant politics and upward mobility. A somewhat similar dynamic, moderated by the prestige of British recruitment links, characterized early Toronto policing (Marquis, 1987).

The police have, therefore, at times acted to protect working-class immigrant interests, and police careers themselves have been an important avenue of social mobility and political influence. By the same token, they have, as Johnson remarks (1976:104–108), thereby been a means of expressing white, working-class racial antipathy, and have generated deep mistrust of police by blacks. Noting almost two hundred years of commissions on law enforcement and crime with scant reform, one observer remarked upon "a strong feeling that the police target is not criminality, but social, political, and cultural deviance" (Germann, 1971:416). The expectation in the United States, more explicitly than in Britain or in Canada, is that the police are associated with right-wing politics. This includes an expectation of racism. As Lipset wrote (1969): "Although there is a general understanding that the police should be politically neutral, their role as public employees has inevitably involved them in local politics. ... In many communities, the police were part of the machine organization."

Police unions, resurgent in the late 1950s and especially in the 1960s, also appear to have reinforced a conservative political attitude among police officers. Skolnick (1969:268–292) cites as a major example police association opposition to civilian review boards, a police attitude that Canadians were to witness in the 1980s in Toronto. For example, the Fraternal Order of Police fought the civilian appeals board formed in Philadelphia in 1958 (the first of its kind in the United States) for more than eight years. Finally, the board was discontinued in 1967, in the context of a mayoralty campaign explicitly involving police as the issue and as major political players (Halpern, 1974:63–75). But by the 1970s, for police managers, government, and the public, the power of police unions was conspicuous, and with a flurry of strike action in the 1970s labour stoppages came to be viewed by some as "a problem of national scope" (Gentel and Handman, 1979:v). Police as a powerful interest group, therefore, loosely controlled by local, state or national civil authorities, have been a reality in major American cities such as Chicago, Philadelphia, and New York City since the 1960s (Ruchelman, 1974). This development has led one observer to remark that "the major problem with the police today is political" (Bent, 1974:168).

The politics of American policing were noted by an observer of the Canadian and American elections in 1988. George Bush was supported by three hundred uniformed and cheering police officers in a rally in New York City as he was formally endorsed by them and presented with the badge of an officer killed in a drug-related encounter (*Globe and Mail*, October 24, 1988). Such explicit police allegiance to a political candidate remains virtually unknown in Canada, although there have been interventions in municipal politics.

An additional illustration is to be had from a full-page colour advertisement in *Life* Magazine (May 1989:25). The National Rifle Association, a notoriously conservative and powerful lobby, featured the 1988 police officer of the year, who was a member. The award is an annual presentation by *Parade* Magazine and the International Association of Chiefs of Police. The officer, from Cloverdale, California, was cited as having "shot a paroled murderer" in a hostage-taking incident. The shooting was remarked upon first in the citation itself, and as having saved a fellow officer's life. The officer is quoted as crediting his NRA training, arguing that armed American citizens deter criminals, and that "we need to get tough with criminals." The officer is quoted further: "The NRA's training and support helps police preserve law and order. Together we make a good team."

The conservative political allegiance of police in the United States is also reflected in vociferous criticism of the judicial system. This negative view of the judicial process has at times created a police response of "street justice," in the view that otherwise offenders will escape adequate sanction. Beatings by police are not uncommon and in extreme instances such "street justice" has involved deadly force. When several instances of brutality were exposed by the media in Philadelphia in the 1970s, resulting eventually in U.S. Justice Department intervention, police justified their actions as arising from frustration and "outrage" at the frequency of court acquittals of criminal offenders (*Sunday Post* of Canada, August 26, 1979). In Houston in 1977, six police officers were implicated in the beating and murder of a Mexican-American man, as they laboured to "talk some sense into him" (Katz, 1977:53).

Another rather dramatic illustration of extrajudicial police action was exposed in Los Angeles in 1988. A newspaper enquiry found that a Special Investigations Section of the Los Angeles Police Department had routinely allowed suspects under surveillance to commit offences (*Ottawa Citizen*, October 1, 1988). Rather than intervene prior to the offence, police allowed the events to unfold in order to be in a position to bring more serious charges. Thereby the public was put at risk, rather than protected, in order to maximize the sanctions available through the judicial process. In San Antonio, Texas, a patrolman became notorious as the "vigilante cop." He was eventually shot and killed by his police partner, who claimed that he was threatened with death for knowing too much. In the dead patrolman's home police recovered 5 shotguns, 6 rifles, 18 handguns, and 100 000 rounds of ammunition. At the time of his death he was alleged to be plotting the death of the district attorney and two deputy chiefs following his having been indicted for brutality (*Toronto Star*, September 28, 1986).

New York City Police also developed an undesirable reputation for brutality. Complaints are regular and numerous, with 25 officers in a force of 27 000 charged with crimes in the period January–April, 1985. They assumed somewhat greater significance in 1985 when the public were informed of the arrest of five officers for eliciting confessions from suspects by using electric stunguns. The practice seemed to have become standard in one precinct, and one of the five officers charged was the so-called precinct "integrity officer" responsible for preventing misconduct. The police officers charged were all white, and the victims all were black (*Toronto Star*, May 5, 1985). In 1988 a report concluded that New York City Police behaviour in controlling a demonstration, or riot, at a park in Manhattan involved excessive force. The confrontation grew as police sought to enforce a curfew. Officers were videotaped having covered over their identification plates and badges, chasing and beating demonstrators with their billy clubs (*Boston Globe*, August 25, 1988).

Other major police forces in the United States, such as Philadelphia and Houston, also have unenviable reputations for police brutality. The Philadelphia Police have a lengthy history of notoriety (Pennsylvania, 1974). In Philadelphia the former police commissioner was elected mayor and set about producing what he called the "toughest cops in the world." In seven years of his administration more than 150 people were killed by police, over half of them unarmed, with no police suspensions or discipline as a consequence. Police attributed their conduct to anger with the justice system's leniency, and suggested that they were "encouraged" to be violent by their superiors. In 1979 the U.S. Justice Department filed a lawsuit against the city, the mayor, and 18 city and police officials for allowing "systematic police brutality" (*Sunday Post* of Canada, August 26, 1979). The suit was eventually dismissed by the U.S. federal court, ruling that the government did not have the authority to bring such a general charge (*Ottawa Citizen*, October 31, 1979).

The Philadelphia police were responsible for one of the most outrageous police operations in American history when, in 1985, they literally bombed a neighbourhood of their city.

In an attempt to take a house occupied by a radical cult, the police evacuated an entire block in the black neighbourhood of West Philadelphia. After 80 minutes of gunfire and three hours of fire department water cannon, without success, the police dropped explosives on the roof of the besieged building. The bomb burned more than 50 houses and killed at least 11 people, including 4 children. The action was so extreme that it was criticized by police in other American cities. The Executive Director of the American Federation of Police declared that "They broke every rule in the book" (*Toronto Star*, May 16, 1985; Montreal *Gazette*, May 21, 1985; *Maclean's* Magazine, May 27, 1985:28–29).

In the United States, use of deadly force by police officers is frequent, in contrast to Canada. With American police by and large failing to support gun control, unlike their Canadian and British counterparts, weapons encounters are numerous. One of the significant risks of American police officers is to be shot by another police officer, especially in encounters with non-uniformed personnel. To cite just one example, in Houston in 1982 an undercover female police officer was shot to death by a uniformed policeman in the course of a drug raid (*Ottawa Citizen*, August 19, 1982).

The biases in American policing, especially the racism, were brought to the fore during the 1960s when the insulation of the middle class from the conduct of police temporarily broke down. For a brief period the sons and daughters of middle-class Americans were subjected to the harassment and the force that police usually inflicted upon the racial and economic lower class of the United States. Police violence, including killings, as frequent and "routine" behaviour, came to be widely analyzed and publicized (Stark, 1972:55–84). For the first time they had an impact upon an influential segment of the nation. The inefficiency of police, and the resort to crude actions with a political bias as well as a race prejudice became the focus of public enquiry.

Corruption, too, has come to be associated with the reputation of American policing. One of the most conspicuous examples has been the huge New York City Police Force (Grosso and Rosenberg, 1978). Through the 1970s and 1980s several scandals surfaced, most involving drug-related payoffs and gambling. In the 1970s corruption was found to be widespread and institutionalized, that is, the normal practice among New York City Police. Despite the exposés and prosecution, violations continued. In 1986, for example, all police officers in a Brooklyn precinct were ordered off patrol to the station house, where they witnessed 17 officers being suspended without pay for extorting drugs and money from dealers (Montreal *Gazette*, September 25, 1986).

In the face of apparently unprofessional, politically and morally corrupt, violent, and racist police, there have been incessant attempts to repair and reform American policing. The make-up of American policing has changed in some significant ways in the previous few decades. The composition, with respect to minorities, women, homosexuals, and most recently with respect to age, have altered. The emphasis upon recruiting minority persons and women preceded Canadian programs by about a decade, working to the now familiar assumption that police forces must be representative of population heterogeneity in order to be effective and just (Cox and Fitzgerald, 1983:177). Unlike Canadian forces, homosexuals have been recruited to major police forces for several years, naturally with a lot of publicity. Major recruitment efforts were under way in San Francisco by 1980, with a view to having enough homosexual police officers that they would cease to be an oddity in policing, where hitherto they had been barred (Montreal *Gazette*, April 24, 1979). In Washington, D.C., a homosexual officer and a transsexual were teamed on patrol. He had acknowledged homosexuality at time of application, and she had previously served on the force as a male (*Toronto Star*, March 6, 1983).

In 1985, a court ruling preventing age discrimination allowed the successful graduation from the Los Angeles Police Academy of a 53-year-old black man, the first such recruit (*Ottawa Citizen*, May 29, 1985). American police were many years ahead of their Canadian counterparts in recruiting women as regular police officers. To date in Canada there are no all-female police teams. But in Washington, D.C., early in 1980 the police department assigned the first all-female police patrol team in the world. This is not to suggest, however, that the role of women in policing is widely accepted in the United States. In El Paso, Texas, a police union newsletter referred to "police broads," in what was reported to be an attempt at satire. Twenty-one female police officers on the El Paso police force filed suit for unspecified damages (Montreal *Gazette*, March 10, 1990).

The most significant change in American policing over the previous three to four decades has been with respect to the role of blacks. As blacks were first recruited to police forces, they were effectively segregated. Within major police forces parallel employee associations existed, one for whites and another for blacks, the latter often to protect black police officers against harassment from within the force. By the early 1980s, blacks still represented only 10% of the more than half-million sworn municipal American police officers. They have, however, achieved prominent roles. In 1985 it was reported that in four of the six largest cities in the United States—New York, Chicago, Houston, and Detroit—the police chiefs are black. By the mid 1980s, in the 50 largest American cities, there were 12 black chiefs (*Ottawa Citizen*, July 23, 1985).

Black recruitment and promotion have made black associations less relevant in some forces, but have by no means eliminated police racism, and in many urban police forces black police officers have persisted with their own employee groups in the face of continuing racism. In California, a police sergeant in Hawthorne, a suburb of Los Angeles, on leave for stress related to on-the-job racial harassment, worked with a group called the Police Misconduct Lawyer's Service of Los Angeles. Together with a local television station he operated a "sting" against the Long Beach Police force, about whom the group had received many complaints. He and an off-duty corrections officer were pulled over in a high-crime area, allegedly for straddling lanes. Out of the car, the off-duty police sergeant was ultimately shoved through a plate glass window, and then charged with interfering and challenging police, as well as a traffic citation. The victim's analysis is that he was stopped for no reason. Though he denied the alleged moving violation, he was nonetheless cooperating, but the Long Beach police officer used force as a "first resort" (*Ottawa Citizen*, January 17, 1989).

Innovations are constantly being attempted in the United States, intended to bring the public police back into community contact. A minor example, now also to be found in Canada in most major police services, has been bicycle patrol, a variation upon the limited return to foot patrol. In Madison, Wisconsin, for example, male and female police officers, in uniform, ride bicycles on city streets while on patrol (*Ottawa Journal*, August 13, 1979). In Los Angeles police on bicycle patrol wear quite atypical dress, patrolling in t-shirts marked LAPD, shorts, white socks, and sneakers (*Globe and Mail*, October 29, 1983).

Another, more remarkable innovation was the Menlo Park uniform experiment. In 1969 the entire police force of Menlo Park, California, with the exception of a single motorcycle patrol officer, changed to civilian uniforms consisting of an identifiable green blazer with the city crest on the breast pocket. Above the crest was a tag identifying the officer. The gun was concealed beneath the blazer. No hat was worn, and no indication of rank (Tenzel et al., 1976:22). Initially there was embarrassment and resentment on the part of the police. Morale dropped, and there was high turnover. But as new recruits were selected, in part, for amenability to the dress and that which it symbolized, turnover dropped, and in the fourth year of the experiment, had diminished from 25.5% in the first year to 2%. As the uniform experiment progressed morale increased, with the force increasingly defining itself as engaged in a "professional public service."

> As the stereotypic police identity began to change, the concept of the police role began to broaden to include tasks and ideologies that had previously been considered antithetical to police work. Many of the public service duties which occupy approximately 80% of police time (animal complaints, first aid, finding lost children, family counselling, traffic control) and are considered an irritation by most police officers, became incorporated into the new role concept" (Tenzel et al., 1976:27).

As the paramilitary concept shifted to a civilian definition, contacts with the community also altered. Assaults on police officers declined by 30% in the first 18 months, and injuries to citizens declined by 50% (Tenzel et al., 1976:27). The removal of the threatening symbolism of the uniform and gun would appear to partially account for the changes, as would the altered role definition and behaviour of the police themselves in encounters with the public.

In the attempts to reform American policing, so vigorously renewed during the 1960s, major emphasis was placed upon better education (Weiner, 1976, 1977; U.S. Government, 1967). The untested—and unrealistic assumption—was that higher education would in and of itself produce better policing. Especially as the higher education consisted of specialized police programmes, it did not, in fact, demonstrably alter the police subculture. In one notorious instance, it was found that programmes were produced to recruit police students in order to generate revenue. In New Hampshire College, near Boston, a programme in criminal justice was offered that included no courses in criminal justice, a four-year degree with the possibility of two years advanced credit for five years of police experience, and that required 16 weekends of work over 16 months. The quick degree satisfied pay incentive programmes within area police forces, and generated revenue for the college (*Boston Globe*, March 26, 1985).

Another model, college-credit courses offered within police stations, also operates in the United States. As described in a Cambridge, Massachusetts instance, the courses are closed to any but police officers, maintaining the occupational isolation that police higher education should be intended to moderate (*Boston Globe*, March 26, 1985). Researchers observed that police education tended to narrow outlooks rather than broaden them, and focus upon the superficial paraphernalia of professionalism rather than training persons capable of exercising professional competence (Harris, 1973). A study of nation-wide police education commissioned by the Police Foundation noted the failure of such systems and recommended broadly based curricula rather than technical and specialized police-oriented content (Sherman, 1978).

Following the great emphasis in police reform for a fix through education, great stress has been placed upon community relations. The concept has, however, tended to mean anything but basic restructuring of traditional police organization, because of both management resistance and union opposition. Team policing, a form of local community service, for example, was attempted in many American cities, including Syracuse and Cincinnati in the early 1960s, but later abandoned (Cox and Fitzgerald, 1983:147). One of the better known attempts, probably that which first gained the attention of Canadian police personnel, was that of Venice, California in 1972, policed as a division of the Los Angeles Police Department, and a pioneer in community-based teams of police officers (Center for Research on Criminal Justice, 1977).

Many elements of American policing have made their way into Canadian policing. American literature, American suppliers, and American training (as at the FBI Academy where many Canadian police officers have taken courses) have been open to Canadian police. Equipment, from open holsters to helicopters, has origins in the United States. More recently, as standard field equipment, and as a safety issue (for reasons of skin cancer), wide-rimmed Stetson hats, similar to those of many state police (and the dress uniform of the RCMP) have been adopted by Ontario police. Much more significantly, organizational fashions have spilled into Canada. A notable example has been the resort to tactical units, probably having origins in Los Angeles. And presently looming so large, as we shall discuss, the related concepts of problem-oriented and community policing now pervade Canadian policing.

Other Societies

While the American and British policing experiences may be seen to have played a role in shaping Canadian policing styles, the character of policing in other societies has also had implications for Canadian society and the relations of police and the public. Other societies have been much less fortunate than Canada in the quality and the political neutrality of their police. As long as Canada drew the great majority of its immigrants from the United States, the United Kingdom, and to a somewhat lesser degree, Western Europe, there was a similar experience of policing, and therefore immigrants brought to Canada similar attitudes and expectations as those held by Canadians. But except for the democracies of Western Europe, policing in other societies is often used for the control of civil populations by despotic governments. The police are frequently an arm of the military, and are often extremely corrupt. Immigrants to Canada from such environments have no reason to expect different conduct from Canadian police, and these attitudes prejudice encounters.

In Mexico, for example, the public fear the violence and the corruption of their police. Poor salaries encourage corruption, with the normal expectation that income will be supplemented with "tips." One traffic officer, earning the equivalent of $9.00 Canadian a week, remarked that "You have to know the traffic regulations to make a lot of money. Someone will always break the traffic law. Then you can advise him that he doesn't have to take the ticket to a higher authority if he gives you money" (*Toronto Star*, January 4, 1987). Interagency rivalries for benefits have produced massive graft, and even murder of police officers. A notorious former chief of police of Mexico City made millions of dollars this way

(*Ottawa Citizen*, October 23, 1988). Mexican governments, recognizing the corruption of their police, promised to intervene, to "moralize" the police, as it was put in 1983 in a presidential inaugural address. Responding to the high rate of crime committed by police officers, especially graft due to low rates of pay, the President stated that the police must "guarantee public safety and order rather than cause their breakdown" (*Toronto Sunday Star,* February 6, 1983). Effective reform, however, appears slight. In the 1990s poorly paid Mexican police and their senior officers are still engaged in serious corruption, and the government has even resorted to using the military against police personnel.

In many Latin American societies police corruption is endemic, as in Mexico. Extremes of wealth and poverty, low paid public police, police misconduct, and public distrust abound. Just as the relatively low wages paid to police in the expensive American city of New York relate to police abuse, the low police salaries in many developing societies affect police behaviour, in more extreme manifestations. Civil and military police contend with one another, as in Brazil, and are seen to be engaged in crime and brutality. In Brazil it is reported that many persons will entrust their protection to "a paid bandit working privately for you more than a police [officer] in a uniform" (Schemo, 1994:10).

A notorious example of police as an agency of oppression is to be had from South Africa. Enforcement of the racial system of inequality produced in this "democratic" state a police agency that was an arm of political policy, and engaged in brutal repression. Evidence reminiscent of some Latin American experience reveals that police death squads operated in South Africa (*Globe and Mail*, April 21, 1990). A former police officer testified before an enquiry commission (the Harms Commission) in 1990 of orders received from senior officers, which he obeyed, to kill people. He described it as "part of the game" (*Ottawa Citizen*, April 26, 1990).

In other democratic societies police conduct may also differ from the North American expectation. In Israel, for example, policing is centralized, very military in structure, and confounded by security problems. Police have a reputation for low standards, ill manners, and brutality, especially against Palestinians. In an annual report in 1985 the State Comptroller indicated considerable police harassment and abuse of power. He cited detention of suspects for up to 48 hours without warrant or charges, or even "reasonable suspicion." The report indicated 4120 people detained in the first half of 1984, with only 600 criminal charges eventually filed. The comptroller wrote that "the figures show ... that in not a few cases the police are inclined to arrest first and ask questions later" (*Ottawa Citizen*, May 14, 1985).

Another example from among the democracies is that of Japan. Japanese police have the contrasting reputation of being very tough and ruthless on the one hand, and community-oriented and helpful on the other. In fact policing in Japan is quite dichotomized between a rather prestigious national force with responsibility for major investigations and actions and local patrol officers (Bayley, 1976; Miyazawa, 1992). The latter are in effect a form of community policing. This community character is expressed in local decentralized units organized into "kobans" or police boxes. These small posts (around 1240 in Tokyo), each with 10 foot-patrol officers, are conspicuously and continuously operated. Every neighbourhood will have a koban, some more elaborate than others, often located by a transportation stop (*New York Times* Magazine, February 6, 1994). The officers are expected to assist people, even loaning money, finding addresses, and lending telephones. The locally assigned officers make house-to-house calls twice a year, to achieve mutual familiarity with the patrol zone and its occupants (*Toronto Star*, November 28, 1982). They will post bulletins, collect information about residents and their possessions (such as cars), offer general assistance, and organize community crime prevention.

In Japan, though, rather like the Israeli situation, the police are authorized to detain persons without charge in the course of an investigation. The system of pre-trial detention has allowed Japanese police to detain and question an estimated 100 000 people per year. Critics allege that a consequence is that police produce confessions, sometimes through abuse, rather than investigative clearance of cases. Suspects may be detained up to 23 days and are not ensured of the benefit of legal advice during questioning (*Ottawa Citizen*, September 22, 1988).

Similar preventive detention practices were in force in France until the government repealed the law in the early 1980s, and also curtailed police powers of search and identity checks. Shortly thereafter, when two police officers were killed, hundreds of officers marched through the streets of Paris to protest in front of the offices of the justice minister, calling for a reinstitution of their previous powers (*Ottawa Citizen*, June 4, 1983).

In other democracies policing may be regarded as comparable to that of North America in its responsibility to an informed public. But the balance between localism and central political control has generally leaned far more in the direction of the state in other nations than in Canada and the United States. And often police in other societies will lack credibility and public support—a circumstance of relevance to Canada as immigrants bring with them local perceptions of police roles and conduct.

CONCLUSION

Canada's policing reflects the experience and influences of urban/industrial society. Policing is delivered today by large and complex organizations, and contends with numerous and complex public demands. Yet police personnel in Canada, as in the United States, the United Kingdom, and elsewhere have been increasingly divorced from most if not all of their publics. The occupational subculture develops its own dynamic, and the isolated police-specific culture is reinforced by technology, bureaucracy, and political direction. These influences generate police abuse, and public criticism in return. In response, police in Canada, like those abroad, are now seeking means to regenerate public support. The local character of Canadian police, distinguishable through much of its history until the post-World War II drive to centralization, is now desperately being reinvented. The attempt to establish effective citizen contacts, which are crucial to effective policing, is coming to be a prevalent ambition of modern police in Canada.

ANNOTATED READINGS, CHAPTER TWO

Brown, Lorne, and Caroline Brown. *An Unauthorized History of the RCMP*. Toronto: James Lorimer and Company, Publishers, 1978. This counter-establishment polemical history of the RCMP infuriates police officers. The account stresses the role of the RCMP as an agent of the state in controlling or suppressing labour, native persons, and dissidents.

Kelly, William, and Nora Kelly. *Policing in Canada.* Toronto: The Macmillan Company, 1976. The literature capturing the history and nature of policing in Canada is sparse and uneven. This volume remains the only work that attempts some account of all levels of policing in Canada from historical conception to the 1970s. It is a rather uncritical, non-issues-oriented work.

Miller, Wilbur R. *Cops and Bobbies: Police Authority in New York and London, 1830–1870.* Chicago: The University of Chicago Press, 1977. This is an interesting historical analysis of the origins of the policing reputations and styles of New York and London.

Robinson, Cyril, Richard Seaglion, and Michael Olivero. *Police in Contradiction: The Evolution of the Police Function in Society.* Westport, CT: Greenwood Press, 1994. This is a comparative look at policing, with ethnographic and historical material. A theme throughout is the relationship between inequality and policing.

3

POLICE AND
THE PUBLIC

*This chapter considers the relationship of Canada's police to its pub-
lic. We begin with an account of images and stereotypes. We also review
police relations with the courts and the media representatives who mediate and help shape the general public images of policing in Canada.*

In seeking to regulate the communities and the society in which we live, Canadians, like all
other societies, have vested certain persons with the right and the power to intervene in our
conduct. The principles of policing elaborated in Robert Peel's original conception of the
British public police stressed that the police required public respect and approval. Ultimately,
police power was to derive not from threatened or real resort to force, but from public regard
and willing collaboration. So empowered, and subject to effective restraint and informed responsibility, the police may enhance the quality of democratic social life. If improperly restrained, however, and imperfectly held accountable by the public whom they are intended
to serve, the police become an impediment and a threat to their communities, or mere agents
of special interests.

IMAGES AND STEREOTYPES

There are extreme and diverse views of the police in Canadian society. Depending upon
social class, gender, age, race, and simply the happenstance of personal experience of police

officers, individuals will have differing views of police attitudes and conduct. The academic literature itself can be shown to have divergent models of policing. The mainstream literature views policing as a necessary role that must be monitored, constrained, and reformed. Most American and Canadian scholars subscribe approximately to this view, even those who are viewed as exceedingly critical (Skolnick, 1975; Reiner, 1992). Others tend to be unremitting in finding dire consequences of policing, whatever police intend or do, perhaps attributing greater influence and deliberateness to policing than most observers would credit (Ericson and Haggerty, 1997).

It is interesting to find that police themselves tend not to view themselves as very powerful. They are apt to complain of non-support and interference, and being obliged to enforce bad laws. They resent media criticisms and public complaints. And they tend to feel helpless to change society, or even to influence the laws and judicial interpretations that matter to them.

They do, however, attempt to influence public and media images of policing, often by playing to the public's fear of crime. They may be seen to "thrive on useful myths" and ceremony, and are not averse to "distorting aspects of crime" (Ericson, 1989:222). Police collaborate in television drama that celebrates police action and they even stage their own events, such as elaborate police funerals (Skolnick, 1975; Crank, 1998) or national Police Days in Canada and the United States. The police memorial in Washington, D.C., was dedicated by the president of the United States, and annually attracts millions of visitors. Police even market paraphernalia, just like sports teams; the RCMP have a licensing and marketing agreement with the U.S. firm of Walt Disney Corporation.

In so doing they contribute to public stereotypes of policing. As policing has become more arcane and hidden from the outsider, much of the public has been left naively trusting police to be virtually infallible, or on the other hand, sullenly suspicious and hostile, seeing police as unfair and incompetent. In the context of isolation and poor information, persistent stereotypes of the police have developed, each containing a fragment of truth. Little effort is made to acquaint the public with "real life" policing, and conversely, too little effort is made to diminish the isolation from the public that tends to romanticize and distort the police experience.

One extreme stereotype is that of police officer as oppressor and bully. This image, less prevalent among second- or third-generation Canadians than among recent immigrants from non-Western nations and aboriginals, results in an unwillingness to collaborate with police. Images of totalitarian European or Latin American states come to mind, where the police are agents of government suppression.

The more prevalent Canadian stereotype, shared with the United States, is much more romantic, the stuff of television and movies, the heir to the good guy–bad guy imagery of western movies. In Canada this idealization has been best expressed with regard to the RCMP, honoured on stamps, coins, currency, and many symbolic occasions. The police are brave heroes, often battling against fearsome odds, unremitting in their integrity, dedication, and skill. A "realistic" account, such as Stroud's work (1983), very selectively describes vignettes in the lives of patrol officers in the inner-city zones of major urban centres, capturing some of the reality of policing, especially the alienation from the public. Yet for all the skill in representing real people at work, it still adds to the exaggerated conception of police officers almost exclusively engaged in law enforcement.

Whereas the negative stereotype exaggerates the iron fist of policing, and deters the consensual and collaborative citizen response upon which effective policing depends, the positive stereotype also has undesirable consequences. It deters public participation and awareness of the limitations and the flaws of police operations and personnel. The affirmative stereotype, like the negative extreme, encourages opting out, in the view that there is no need for public discussion.

Conversely, because police have failed to meet the exaggerated public expectations—sometimes generated by police propaganda itself—some segments of the public have lost confidence in their police. This is especially so in major cities such as Montreal and Toronto. In the context of perceived police incompetence, social response comes full circle, turning to private retainers (security personnel), vigilantism (neighbourhood defence groups, such as the Guardian Angels), and frontier-style personal application of force.

Like the police in their responses to the public, members of the public also respond on the basis of images, stereotypes, and cues. Preconceptions as to police behaviour, or even the paraphernalia of policing—the uniforms, the weapons, the automobiles—will be perceived and evaluated differently by different segments of a highly differentiated public. For the majority of Canadians, for example, the uniform elicits respect and even pride, to the extent that a great many people resisted adapting the RCMP and other police uniforms to accommodate Sikh police officers.

For many Canadians, though, especially new Canadians, the uniform may elicit fear, suspicion, and hostility. Just as police attitudes, work schedules, and organizations may serve to isolate police personnel from meaningful interaction with members of the public, so too the isolation may be reinforced by accoutrements that come to have a negative symbolic loading. And the unintended symbol or cue may be a provocation.

Even the buildings housing the police may emit cues. Some of the older buildings once also served as city jails, and still look like fortresses. Even many of the new buildings, with their high-tech security measures, look unpleasant and foreboding. Their very architecture serves to isolate their inhabitants from the public they are intended to serve. The uniform, the car, the centralized building—all serve to distance the police officer from the community.

Of course, whatever the public stereotype, that of extreme suspicion and vilification, or that of romance and adulation, the reality is much more prosaic. Policing is a job. The policeman is a public employee. He or she is neither especially virtuous (although recruitment and institutional checks should tend that way) nor especially corrupt (although there are many temptations). He or she is an ordinary person called upon to perform a complex job, with much less training than is demanded of other complex jobs. The job is relatively well paid and secure, yet subject to hazards and periodic intense public attention. It is a stressful job, but also a job allowing extraordinary discretion and power. Many occupational groups tend to isolate their members from the rest of society, so it is only natural that this should happen to police officers too. But in their case, it is particularly unfortunate that people who must sometimes make life-saving or life-threatening decisions are so insulated from the reality check that all members of a well-functioning society require, most of all those charged with its protection.

THE JUDICIAL SYSTEM

In 1962 the Ontario Royal Commission on Police declared that "The police should be powerful but not oppressive; they should be efficient but not officious; they should form an impartial force in the body politic, and yet be subject to a degree of control by persons who are not required to be impartial and who are themselves liable to police supervision" (Ontario, 1962).

This declaration re-expressed the historic Canadian commitment to a police themselves not part of politics, but subject to public control by duly elected political partisans. The power of the police, therefore, is to be found in the responsibilities assigned them to regulate the social order in a manner determined by others.

The police officer does not make the formal rules or laws, although he or she can choose among them for purposes of intervention and enforcement. Because of delegated authorization, and because of discretion, the police officer is a significantly powerful person. He or she has the delegated right to arrest persons, even to use force against persons. An officer's interventions are usually discretionary, in that he or she must decide whether the conduct warrants police action. So too the actions in the course of intervention are to a considerable extent governed by the officer's judgement. The actions may subsequently be subject to review and criticism, especially if the police encounter results in charges and a court appearance, but generally persons subject to police interventions are very vulnerable. The citizen carries the burden of reacting to police, who carry the full weight of social authority, and who have the benefit of a high degree of public and court confidence.

A police intervention sets in train an often costly justice process, even as it is due process—costly in time, money and reputation. As Daley said of a police encounter,

> His mere presence stripped subjects of their rights. Most saw this immediately and became afraid. Whatever the Constitution might say, their rights were in abeyance, had become illusory. Subjects could not exercise them without causing trouble or themselves ... (Daley, 1985:157).

The legislatures and the courts in Canada and the United States have, of course, attempted to limit police power and to protect the rights of citizens against improper police exercise of power. As fabled in television drama, for example, American Supreme Court rulings have long since obliged police officers to advise persons of their rights, including the right to an attorney at time of arrest, while similar practices have become normal in Canada as a consequence of the Charter of Rights and Freedoms and subsequent court rulings. Canadian police officers, like their American counterparts, now impart precise information to a person when arrested or detained. Gradually in Canada, as long established in the United States, correct police procedures, as measured against overriding principles of civil and human rights, have come to supercede simpler conceptions of offence or guilt. Police must not only apprehend offenders, they must do so properly, respectful of legislative and court-defined procedural proprieties and protections (see Beaudoin and Ratushny, 1989:458–477). The cautions imparted to persons being detained by police in Canada are simulated in Figure 3-1.

Police, of course, continue to have opportunities and means to circumvent rights. An intervention by a police officer is often private, with no witnesses other than the officer and perhaps other police. As illustrated later, police do sometimes lie about incidents, and do sometimes resort to "cover" charges, such as disturbing the peace or resisting arrest, to protect themselves at a citizen's expense where misconduct has occurred. Police, even where not overtly violating rights, are quite simply intimidating to most people because of their power and potential to damage.

The police are the front line of the criminal justice system. Many of the public believe that the police do an in-the-trenches job that others in the criminal justice system then undo. For the police, and many of the public, justice means something different than for the judiciary, something to do with security and retribution and the victim, as against procedural and collective

---

FIGURE 3-1   Example of Caution by Police

1. NOTICE UPON ARREST
    I am arresting you for   . . . .
    　　　　　　　　　　　　　　 (briefly describe reasons for arrest)

2. RIGHT TO COUNSEL
    It is my duty to inform you that you have the right to retain and instruct counsel without delay.

    Do you understand?

    _____

    _____

    _____

    You (are charged, will be charged) with . . . .
    Do you wish to say anything in answer to this Charge?
    You are not obliged to say anything unless you wish to do so, but whatever you say may be given in evidence.

    If you have spoken to any police officer or to anyone with authority or if any such person has spoken to you in connection with this case, I want it clearly understood that I do not want it to influence you in making any statement.

Source: A composite created from information given in the *Toronto Sunday Sun*, May 11, 1986.

---

safeguards. Perhaps because the police and the public are nearer in their conceptions, the police are generally accorded high regard, higher than that given to lawyers and judges.

It is difficult to accurately estimate the prevailing public view of the different elements of the justice system, and especially the extent to which they cooperate with each other and are effective. Public opinion polls that invite an estimate of public respect generally allocate police officers a favoured status in contrast to other criminal justice personnel, despite their lower occupational standing, as measured by indicators such as education. Guards and parole officers seem to have relatively scant social standing in the view of the public, and while lawyers are recognized as important, they are not well liked. Judges are respected, but perhaps suffer the stigma of the legal profession, and from the prevalent criticism, encouraged by police, that they are too lenient on crime. Often, too, the public perceive judges to be unqualified political appointees, rather than skills-related appointees. Occasional demand occurs for an elected judiciary, as in the United States, to better reflect public attitudes. By and large, therefore, and despite public complaint, police occupy a favoured role, one which allows them, much as Ericson (1983:32–39) has argued, to shape the justice process. Police make the decision on whether to intervene or not, define the intervention, lay charges or not, and help shape the prosecution. In the process, however, there seems to be resentment, even animosity, between the elements of the system—the police, the courts, and corrections personnel (Kelly and Kelly, 1973:610).

In the face of increasingly complex legal prohibitions upon their authority, the demands of complicated white collar/financial crimes, and internal labour relations problems, a rational police response is to have their members trained in law. Some forces, especially the RCMP, have been doing so. But the legal profession is reluctant to allow acting police officers to practise as lawyers. In Quebec in 1988, for example, a Quebec Provincial Police officer, working in internal affairs, was refused admission to the bar despite full qualifications, including the mandatory apprenticeship. The bar's code of ethics defines some occupations, including police officer, as "incompatible" with that of a lawyer. The refusal was upheld by a professional tribunal made up of three provincial court judges (Montreal *Gazette*, January 16, 1988).

It is not difficult to find examples of antagonism between police, lawyers, and the judiciary. An interesting case is that of a Toronto lawyer who had been convicted of contempt of court following a newspaper interview in which he stated that the "courts and the RCMP are sticking so close together you'd think they were put together with Krazy Glue." An Appeal Court overturned the conviction on the grounds that it violated guarantees of freedom of speech in the Charter of Rights (*Ottawa Citizen*, November 28, 1987).

Judges are often viewed by the police as out of touch, isolated from public opinion and concerns, and therefore flawed in their sentencing decisions. Recently the chief of the Ottawa-Carleton Regional Police, generally regarded as a progressive, complained that judges were "too aloof and out of touch" with the community, unlike the new-style proactive police. In turn, the chief was chastised by the president of the Defence Counsel Association of Ottawa for vague and unfair criticism (*Ottawa Citizen*, January 11, 1998; January 17, 1998).

Police appear to perceive lawyers as unprincipled, willing to be hired to serve any interest but justice. Reciprocal police–lawyer criticism is frequent. Lawyers will tend to perceive police as persons committed to conviction above all else, including justice and fair play. The antagonism was illustrated in 1982 in Ottawa when the president of the Defence Counsel Association of Ottawa addressed a meeting of the Canadian Bar Association and stated that "conviction-oriented" police seek to be a law unto themselves, finding ways around Charter protection, and would even perjure themselves to gain convictions. Police reaction was prompt and angry, demanding evidence, while other defence lawyers chimed into the fray, stating that they also believed that police would and do commit perjury (*Ottawa Citizen*, September 4, 1982).

Just as police may often not think highly of lawyers and judges, members of the legal profession often have low regard for police. The poor educational standards of police, placing them relatively low in the status hierarchy compared to lawyers and other university-educated professionals, may account in part for the negative views. In general, the legal profession's views are the converse of police views. Where police see lawyers as too lenient, lawyers see police as too intolerant. One lawyer has written of a "general fear that too often police constables will become partisan and in their desire to convict, they will tailor their evidence ... " (Teed, 1981:119). Lewis accounts for these reversed images of one another by reference to the quite different roles and norms of behaviour, where "the police are interested in actual guilt and the lawyers and the courts can be concerned with legal guilt" (Lewis, 1981:103). In other words, lawyers and police have two quite different concepts of justice.

A decision handed down in Quebec in 1989 dealt with a celebrated incident of what lawyers thought of as unprincipled police conduct, and conversely what police thought of as unprincipled legalism. A man charged with arson in a PCB warehouse fire was acquitted when the presiding judge ruled that a confession was obtained illegally. Having viewed a videotape of the interrogation, the judge harshly criticized police because the suspect had not been allowed to have a lawyer present during questioning and had been intimidated (Montreal *Gazette*, February 2, 1989). Editorial criticism of the police was unqualified in the Montreal *Gazette*. In a news report of the acquittal, the views of constitutional lawyers were cited, suggesting that police need training in legally correct procedures of interrogation, given the willingness of courts to exclude improperly acquired evidence (Montreal *Gazette*, February 9, 1989). Responding to statements by the president of the Quebec Police Association, who defended the police methods in the case and called their work "excellent," editorialists and lawyers described the methods as obviously unacceptable and "out of step" (Montreal *Gazette*, February 4, 1989; February 5, 1989). The Quebec justice minister subsequently ordered two enquiries. The Sûreté was ordered to investigate police misconduct in the investigation, while the Police Commission was ordered to evaluate investigation and interrogation techniques in the province (Montreal *Gazette*, February 4, 1989).

Yet there is some evidence that the judiciary are often very supportive of police actions. An indicator is the issuance of warrants, and of wiretap authorizations. Available data suggest that Canadian police are rarely disappointed in their request. For example, in 1984 the annual report to the federal solicitor general revealed that only 1 of 699 applications by federal prosecutors or the RCMP were turned down by judges (*Ottawa Citizen*, May 11, 1984). The response of the judiciary to police applications for wiretaps has frequently been criticized by observers. A University of Montreal criminologist referred to Canada's courts as having "totally failed" to control police wiretaps. He noted that in the period 1974 to 1982 there were 5200 applications to judges for wiretaps and only ten were turned down (*Globe and Mail*, October 24, 1983).

Despite evidence of collaboration, police have a view of themselves as in antagonism to the courts, and court time is a distinct cause of police stress. A prevailing attitude among police officers in Canada, as in the United States, is that the courts and other bodies, such as parole boards, are not supportive and undermine their efforts by leniency. Police complain of the "revolving door" character of the judicial system, with offenders prematurely released likely to offend yet again (Vincent, 1979:95–97). The chief of the Ottawa police issued a public statement in the fall of 1988 criticizing court leniency with drug offenders, for example, and incurred the ire of lawyers in Ottawa (*Ottawa Citizen*, November 7, 8, 1988). The chief complained that the criminal system was not working, and that the courts "are not working in concert with the police" to deal with drug offenders.

Similar criticism had occurred in 1984, when Ottawa experienced a wave of bank robberies. A contrast was drawn with Montreal, where the Montreal Urban Community Police (MUC) had collaborated with the Crown to win heavy sentences for offenders, working with two especially assigned Crown prosecutors. In contrast, Ottawa police argued that sentencing in their region was too light. One spokesperson attributed the killing of a Nepean police constable to leniency, as the offender had a lengthy record of armed robberies (*Sunday Herald*, September 9, 1984). Also in 1984, several police killings prompted police officers to express frustration with the criminal justice system, seeking restitution of capital punishment, and generally less lenient sentencing. The chief of the York Regional Police (Ontario) complained that "We get the feeling that most judges seem to look for a reason for coming down on the policeman instead of the accused" (*Toronto Star*, October 10, 1984).

In Toronto, following a seven-day sentence for a man convicted of selling "crack" to an undercover police officer, the Metro police stated that they would begin to systematically monitor sentences, and wished to have judges accompany them on drug investigations "to show them what is going on in the streets." Police referred to the sentence as a "joke" (*Toronto Sunday Star*, February 12, 1989).

A widespread, though not always articulated police sentiment, is that lawyers and judges who make the rules are often uninformed. In Great Britain, Sir Robert Mark, former head of Scotland Yard, argued persuasively that of all the actors in the criminal justice system, only the police have been excluded from drafting and interpreting legislation. The police perception is that they are denied influence and their opinions are ignored, despite their being on the front line and well informed. A report of the Canadian Association of Chiefs of Police in 1985 was illustrative of this kind of resentment. It harshly criticized the Law Reform Commission of Canada, which had worked to reform and streamline Canadian legislation. A spokesperson for the chiefs stated that the report was "the culmination of years of pent-up frustration with the commission. ..." The brief developed the theme that the commission had not attended to the protection of society, and in its reform proposal had ignored victims and law enforcement in favour of offenders, all the while seeking to inhibit the power of police to act. Where the commission defended its recommendations as seeking to reconcile law with the Charter of Rights, the chiefs resented measures to limit police power of search and seizure, questioning of suspects and witnesses, and investigative measures such as surveillance and fingerprint procedures. The chiefs declared that "the commission does not understand the role of criminal law or the psyche of Canadian society. Its fundamental philosophy is not to simplify the law, but rather to control police powers in an attempt to combat a perceived erosion of individual liberties" (*Ottawa Citizen*, May 31, 1985).

Part of the police argument is attributable to frustration with a judicial system that is perceived to be offender-biased rather than victim-oriented. In this the police, the media, and the general public appear to be of like attitude, and therefore general public regard for policing may be reinforced. Some of the police attitude, too, has to do with what the police perceive as unfair demands and costs attached to policing, in properly executed arrests, processing charges, preparing for trial, and not least, in contending with offenders whom the police believe have been improperly released by the court system. The police have not had, however, a very effective representative of this point of view, although from time to time members of the policing community have been outspoken. In 1981, Robin Bourne, formerly head of the much-criticized and now defunct RCMP Intelligence Service, was appointed Assistant Deputy Minister of Police Services in British Columbia, responsible for coordinating all police services in the province. Following his appointment, in an address to newly inducted police officers at the Justice Institute of British Columbia, he criticized the court and spoke of a "justice breakdown," urging the police to try to set matters right. He complained of overloaded courts, police budgets used to pay witnesses who are never called in court, and unnecessarily prolonged trials with associated costs for witnesses and police personnel (*Vancouver Sun*, August 9, 1981).

Police, like the general public, have generally been critical also of post-sentence processes. Well-publicized incidents in which offenders have been issued day passes or paroled without prior consultation with or notification of relevant police services have generated police antagonism. In an ineffective attempt to address the problem, as early as 1973 a nation-wide joint committee of the Canadian Association of Chiefs of Police and the National

Parole Board was established, arising from a recommendation of the Canadian Association of Chiefs of Police conference in that year (*Liaison*, July–August, 1988:10–15; *Contact* 1, Fall–Winter 1982:1). Local "zone" committees were to meet regularly and bring in correction personnel, Crown counsels, and police personnel to discuss common problems. In 1985, for example, police reports were discussed, noting that on a national basis, in approximately 15% of cases before parole boards, a police report was absent; in a survey of one region, 50% of the time a police report was not on file (*Contact* 4, Fall 1985:3). Wherever the fault rested, indications such as this that police evaluation was not even relevant in release decisions did not impress already cynical police officers.

THE INFLUENCE OF THE CHARTER OF RIGHTS

Police have also held the view that while the judicial process is lenient on offenders, and protective of their rights through procedural rulings, at the same time police actions are unfairly restricted. In Canada, all evidence, even that illegally obtained, had been admissible in court, following a Supreme Court decision in 1970, until the Charter of Rights was implemented in 1982. Also, unlike in the United States, cases had not been dismissed merely because of police violations of rights. In fact, many rights presumed by Canadians to apply, as a result of watching American television shows, were not in existence here.

That changed with the Charter of Rights and subsequent court rulings, such as the right to counsel or a police caution. For example, in 1984 the Ontario Supreme Court upheld a lower court decision dismissing a case against a person in possession of drugs on the grounds that police had not informed him of his right to call a lawyer. The Supreme Court of Canada refused to hear an appeal, effectively accepting the Ontario interpretation (*Ottawa Citizen*, October 12, 1984). With such rulings police sentiment has been that, as they had predicted in their opposition to the Charter, Canadian practices are being "Americanized."

Before the Charter of Rights, police interventions were decidedly less restrained than in other democracies. Cases would not fail on the basis of illegally obtained evidence, for example, nor was there any clear requirement to inform suspects of their legal options and rights. The Charter, however, allows the courts a significant basis for intervention and interpretation. In particular, three clauses bear upon police conduct:

1. (Section 8) Everyone has the right to be secure against unreasonable search or seizure.

2. (Section 9) Everyone has the right not to be arbitrarily detained or imprisoned.

3. (Section 10) Everyone has the right on arrest or detention
      (a) to be informed promptly of the reasons therefor;
      (b) to retain and instruct counsel without delay and to be informed of that right; and
      (c) to have the validity of the detention determined by way of *habeus corpus* and to be released if the detention is not lawful. (*Liaison*, November 1982:26–27; Beaudoin and Ratushny, 1989)

Canadian police officers have fretted over judicial interpretations of the Charter of Rights. When the Charter was first proposed police vigorously opposed it in public statements on grounds that it would "Americanize" Canadian law enforcement and unfairly restrain them. Many judgments are in, and the nuanced thrust of argument has varied with the changing composition of the Court. The police have had reason to be encouraged and discouraged. A prevalent view is that court decisions leave the police in a situation of uncertainty for extended periods until decisions can be appealed or legislation amended. In 1986, for example, the Supreme Court ruled on a Charter appeal that the police had the right to enter a residence without warrant to arrest a suspected offender, a judgment that gives Canadian police more power than their British or American counterparts (*Ottawa Citizen*, March 1, 1986). Yet in 1997 police were found by the Supreme Court to be at fault in entering a residence without a warrant in an instance where they had reason to expect to find and apprehend an offender alleged to have bludgeoned an elderly neighbour to death. Ruling that at least a judge's approval was needed before forcibly entering a home, important evidence in the case was lost to the court. More consoling to the police, in 1998 the Supreme Court confirmed broad police powers of search without warrant, ruling that police may search a person or vehicle if the search is "truly incidental" to an arrest. That is, the Court found that there must be some reason genuinely related to the arrest to undertake the search, including the safety of the police or public, to protect evidence from being destroyed, or to discover evidence (*Ottawa Citizen*, January 23, 1998).

Court rulings allowing illegally obtained evidence to be presented in court also suggest a persisting difference between Canada and the United States. Although the Charter invalidates such information (Section 24.2) if its use would "bring the administration of justice into disrepute," courts have taken the view that illegalities must be blatant to be disreputable. The British Columbia Supreme Court, in 1987, turned down three appeals in drug cases on grounds that although the constitutional rights of offenders may have been violated, precedence is attached to the justice system and enforcement. The court concluded that although police erred, they "acted in good faith" (*Ottawa Citizen*, April 10, 1987).

On the other hand, a Supreme Court ruling in 1989 was consistent with police expectations. The Court, in a 7-0 ruling, concluded that evidence in a case against a Quebec motorcycle gang member was not admissible because it has been acquired with a defective warrant and because unjustified force was used in a police raid. The police drug warrant was vague and described by the chief justice as permitting a "fishing expedition." The judgment also concluded that "the extremely large number of police involved in the search, the failure to give any warning beforehand, and the amount of force used to break into the house, all suggested that the search was unreasonable." In its defence the Crown had conceded the unreasonable search, but argued that to disallow the evidence would "bring the administration of justice into disrepute" (Montreal *Gazette*, January 27, 1989).

Generally, and often involving young offenders, criticism has become more frequent, led by police, that an unelected, unrepresentative judiciary is thwarting police and the public will, and in the words of the Manitoba Justice Minister making life "administratively difficult" for the police (*Ottawa Citizen*, January 9, 1998). The courts are perceived, because of their "liberal" Charter rulings, to favour the rights of offenders as the key to justice rather than the individual and collective rights of victims or potential victims. The police for their part have overtly associated themselves with opinion and statements of supportive policy on behalf of victims.

In 1989 the Supreme Court brought down another decision relating to police conduct. Upholding two lower court decisions, the Supreme Court ruled that confessions of breaking and entering and theft obtained from two men by police in Windsor were obtained illegally and were inadmissible as evidence, as were stolen items found at their residence. The conclusion was based on the view that the police did not have reasonable grounds to suspect the men and hold them in their car and that it was, in effect, an unjust arrest (Montreal *Gazette*, January 27, 1989).

In these cases, then, police predictions regarding Charter rights as having precedence over demonstrable guilt in criminal cases were borne out. Overall, along with some persisting tolerance of police actions that may infringe rights, as has been the Canadian custom, modern judicial interpretations have tended to limit police actions.

Court-imposed restraints upon police actions—the cautionary procedures, or due process to protect individual rights—are the contemporary expressions of the ongoing tension between police powers on the one hand, and civil or public democratic rights on the other. The tension can never be utterly relieved. Rather, it is in a constant state of flux, or rebalancing, as norms of tolerable conduct on both sides are revised and tested. The individual seeks to resist unfair social restraint or imposition, and society, the collectivity of individuals, through its delegated enforcement agents, seeks the correct accommodation that allows complex group life wherein one individual's liberties do not jeopardize those of others.

Police are one of the most direct means whereby this accommodation is defined and maintained, for the police put to the test evolving social expectations as expressed in often imprecise laws. By reacting when they do, as they do, and testing their reactions in public courts, police help make norms, or conversely, as Ericson (1981a) put it, help make crime. Police operate backstage and onstage, not only effecting control and maintaining order, but defining the limits of control and order.

POLICE POWER IN DEMOCRATIC SOCIETY

From the very inception of public police forces in the democracies, a fine balance has been sought between police agencies that are sufficiently strong to maintain order and to protect the citizenry without, however, being so powerful and interventionist as to threaten or to violate those citizens' liberties. The Task Force on Policing in Ontario again gave expression to these "two competing social principles ... which will never be perfectly harmonized, but must be properly balanced" (Ontario, 1973:145). Such an assertion, of course, is an idealization. Society is not homogeneous, and the justice system does not represent everyone equally. Nevertheless, it is a goal that an egalitarian society should approach.

In their interventions, even if perfectly legal, the police inevitably enforce social biases and inequalities. Especially in a multi-ethnic immigrant society there will be interventions that will be intolerant of some minority values and practices. For example, consider reactions to standards of physical discipline among Muslim immigrants, or to the sale of live animals in ethnic markets. Laws are themselves a reflection of social cleavages and inequalities, written, interpreted, and enforced by people in relatively privileged social strata (Chambliss and Seidman, 1971). All elements of the justice system are therefore reacting in a differential enforcement mode, not just the police who are called upon to be the front-end of the system, enforcing legislation which they, often to their frustration, had no hand in framing but which they interpret in practice. The courts later test, accept, or reject those front-line interpretations.

Police themselves complain of the great difference in the way that working-class crime and middle-class crime are punished. Violations such as theft and robbery are, in monetary value, cumulatively less significant than white collar crimes such as embezzlement, fraud, and price-fixing, yet they are severely punished while many of the latter are rarely punished at all. But street-level crimes are more conspicuous, more personally threatening to members of the public, and easier to detect, so they become the focus of considerable legislative and penal practice and demand the bulk of police attention. By being "forced" to respond to conspicuously deviant or antisocial behaviour, the police are used to control and order society, a society that is inherently class-bound. Police interventions may, therefore, be understood as response to conduct defined by the more privileged elements of society to be significant criminal deviance. The police serve the Canadian public, but are subject to the directives of privileged elements of the general public.

In Canada the police have, by and large, conformed to the expectation in the British tradition that they be politically neutral in the sense of not initiating autonomous political action. Police neutrality means, in addition—though this has been less convincingly achieved—that police are not used for the partisan interests of a given political party or government. Also, police personnel are not to be explicitly affiliated with a political party, a normative expectation enforced in Police Acts. It must be realized, however, that police political neutrality in Canada has not meant indifference or inactivity, but only the avoidance of explicit affiliation or independent political support.

The requirement of political neutrality has inevitably been breached as police have acted to enforce the established political order. Police interventions in labour disputes and labour surveillance, as remarked in Chapter Two, and even surveillance of opposition party personnel, such as the CCF/NDP, have been common in Canada. The provincial and federal police forces especially were intended to have a capacity for political intervention where the municipal forces were deemed unreliable. An analysis prompted by the Quebec separatist crisis of the 1970s suggested that police actions can be aptly summarized in the single sentence: "Political policing is a major aspect of Ottawa's 'national unity' offensive" (Fidler, 1978:12). In other words, police, as agents of the state, have covertly and with relatively little violence, been employed in actions intended to deter political dissent.

The RCMP became a national police for precisely such a role, especially as the government viewed local police as unreliable after the police role in Winnipeg in 1919. The perceived threat of Bolshevism and labour union challenges to the established Canadian order were to be controlled by a national police agency, untainted by local sentiments and loyalties.

Police action in explicit response to government policy was used, for example, to break Canada's most famous labour action, the Winnipeg General Strike of 1919. Thereafter, through the Depression especially, police were frequently involved in labour disputes. In 1931, for example, a wildcat strike in the Souris coal field, typical of western Canadian labour radicalism, was broken in familiar fashion, with violent police action. The local Estevan police and the RCMP went into action when the strike was a month old, intervening in a street demonstration on September 19, 1931—"Black Tuesday." Three miners from the town of Bienfait were killed in the battle with the police, and eight others badly injured with bullet wounds; nine police officers were injured (Abella, 1974). Afterwards, a monument was placed in the local cemetery. Sponsored by the Ukrainian Labour Temple, a stone listed the names of the three miners killed, and, as recalled by Tommy Douglas, the words, "murdered in Estevan, September 29, 1931, by the RCMP." Reference to the RCMP was subsequently removed by order of the village council (Shackleton, 1975:54).

Historical examples abound. Another famous intervention occurred in 1935, when the "On-to-Ottawa" trek, a demonstration by unemployed workers intent upon taking their demands for employment to the authorities in Ottawa, was broken by an RCMP mounted charge in Regina on Dominion Day (Liversedge, 1973). At Asbestos, Quebec, in 1949, one of Canada's most famous strikes ended after five months of battle between strikers and local police when the Quebec Provincial Police were used to force the miners back to work (Isbester, 1974). A well-publicized police action involved a strike by female workers in Exeter, Ontario. The Fleck manufacturing plant, owned by an Ontario cabinet minister, experienced a strike for five and a half months by 75 workers, and met by a massive police presence, estimated at 7000 police days, from the Ontario Provincial Police (White, 1980:95–102). There are many other examples, from OPP intervention in Kirkland Lake in 1942 and in Sudbury in 1966 (Jamieson, 1973:12), to the meat-packers strike in Edmonton in 1984. In all such cases, as state employees, the police were called upon to intervene, involving the threat of force, or its actual application. As recently as 1997, the Ontario Provincial Police were explicitly engaged in government-ordered actions to curtail public sector protests by teachers and others at Queen's Park, Toronto. Following a forceful OPP intervention, the state police actions were criticized by a representative of the Metropolitan Toronto Police Association.

As armed servants of the state, police may too easily be called upon—or think it's their duty—to intervene illegally on behalf of governments facing intransigent opposition. This occurred most explicitly during the 1970s; the RCMP's "dirty tricks" and illegal investigation in Quebec associated with the so-called FLQ crisis are illustrative of a police force making its own rules, using its own definition of the public interest. But in doing so, Force members from the rank and file to high-ranking senior officers, perhaps including the commissioner, were also responding to government cues, although probably not explicit orders, and reinforced the political strategy and the popularity of the Liberal government of Pierre Trudeau.

Information indicates police subjection to political influence in Newfoundland in the 1970s. The Royal Newfoundland Constabulary, investigating sexual abuse allegations in regard to the Mount Cashel orphanage, sought the advice of officials in the justice department with respect to laying charges. Ultimately, charges were not laid. Reports also indicate that an investigating officer of the Royal Newfoundland Constabulary was ordered by his chief to terminate his 1975 investigation and to rewrite his report, deleting all reference to sexual offences. The chief attributed the demand to the orders of the minister of justice (*Ottawa Citizen*, September 13, November 22, 1989).

In another controversial case, the RCMP were obliged by the federal government to mount a major investigation of the budget leak in 1989. A television journalist had been given a copy of the budget summary and had broadcast it, forcing the finance minister into a premature budget announcement. The investigation, at government insistence, resulted in charges against five persons, including the television reporter. The cost of the investigation was estimated at $60 000 or 2220 person hours, with personnel drawn from other duties that Force managers would likely have preferred to attend to (*Ottawa Citizen*, January 27, 1990). Trial testimony indicated that investigating RCMP officers did not wish to lay a charge against the journalist. The senior investigating officer was removed and charges eventually were put following orders from the deputy commissioner (Montreal *Gazette*, November 8, 1989; *Ottawa Citizen*, February 13, 1990). One investigating officer was later quoted as having "formed the opinion that they [the charges] were intended to please elected officials." A former deputy commissioner remarked that if proven, the interference would be "devastating" on morale (*Ottawa Citizen*, November 7, 11, 1989).

In another case, the commissioner of the RCMP admitted delaying an investigation that eventually led to the conviction of a government member of parliament on charges of fraud, breach of trust, and bribery. Search warrants were delayed until after the federal election of 1988 (*Ottawa Citizen*, November 21, 1989). Whether this was a partisan act, or a case in which the police sought *not* to appear to be influencing a political decision, in effect the politically sensitive response of the police intruded upon police actions.

In 1989 the RCMP commissioner was the object of criticism when he disclosed that as many as 11 members of Parliament were under investigation. The information was conveyed to a justice committee without persons being named and without charges pending, inciting charges of police smear tactics (*Ottawa Citizen*, December 14, 1989).

Arguably, another major example of police involvement in politics, and perhaps government use of the state police, was that of the RCMP investigation of former Prime Minister Brian Mulroney. While the government has been obliged to pay the former Prime Minister compensation, it remains unclear as to the extent of RCMP initiative in the investigation, the quality of evidence prompting the investigation, and latterly, the RCMP role in case damage by way of information "leaks" to the media.

The case of the RCMP versus Richard Hatfield is illustrative of another sort of police politics, where police take initiatives against political figures. For some years the RCMP and Premier Hatfield of New Brunswick were at odds. Perhaps the strain was first evident when the premier determined to create the New Brunswick Highway Patrol, displacing the RCMP, in 1980. The Patrol was responsible for enforcement of traffic regulations, while the RCMP retained broader policing responsibilities. The Liberal Party, in opposition, feared that eventually the patrol would become a full-fledged provincial police force, and saw it from the outset as a slap at the RCMP. As soon as they came to power, they abolished the Patrol, which they had always seen as inefficient and formed only for political reasons (Montreal *Gazette*, January 31, 1989). In 1984 the press carried stories about marijuana having been found by the RCMP in Premier Hatfield's luggage during a royal visit. It was reported that the premier was not advised of the discovery for three days, but that the find was leaked to the press within two hours (*Ottawa Citizen*, October 24, 1984). An RCMP staff-relations officer in the province wrote to the justice minister in 1986 (with a copy to the press), stating that the Force had little confidence in the justice department. The letter brought a reprimand from his superior (Montreal *Gazette*, September 20, 1986). The premier may have voiced a common perception when he stated that the police were attempting to embarrass him, while the opposition claimed there was a "plot" to replace the RCMP in the province.

In the previous few decades another element has emerged in police organizations that has influenced the police's political role. Police unions, which became powerful in Canada in the 1960s, have altered the police officers' image of neutrality, as is evident in their public comments, and in their having supported court challenges to Police Act restrictions on political participation. An interesting decision was handed down in 1981, with implications. In the 1980 federal election an Ontario Provincial Police constable ran unsuccessfully for Parliament as a Conservative candidate. His candidacy was in violation of the Police Act. An arbitration board, however, to whom the case had gone with the support of the police association, ruled that he could not be disciplined for the violation (*Globe and Mail*, January 20, 1981).

Police unions have been bold enough to react publicly in a way that police managers have been unable or unwilling to do. Police union opposition to the abolition of capital punishment is a case in point. Similarly, their willingness to criticize politicians has not been matched by senior police officers. Where senior officers have dared to venture opinions on public policy, they have been subjected to criticism, in the view that they had no such right. When in 1983, for example, the deputy chief of the Ottawa Police criticized the attempt to restrict police rights of search and seizure, and also reproved women's groups for impeding police action on prostitution, he was rebuked by the city mayor, who sought police commission backing for his censure of the deputy chief (*Ottawa Citizen*, September 15, 1983).

There is thus an inherent tension within the very nature of policing in democratic societies, between the need to control police, on the one hand, so that they do not act outside the law, and on the other hand, the requirement of police autonomy, so that they are not used by political officials for partisan ends or, as in the budget leak incident, for government and political priorities. The police must at one and the same time be relatively independent, that is, not be controlled by political factions, but must also be subject to legitimate public control, so that the personal freedoms and human rights of law-abiding citizens are protected. Moreover, police must have the ability to adapt to changing pubic perceptions of what is right and wrong, and must be accountable to the ultimate body politic, the citizens whom they protect.

In a democratic society such as Canada, it is necessary to find and maintain an acceptable role for police, one affording them sufficient power to protect the public and to enforce laws of conduct, but not so much power that the police become a law unto themselves. There is an obvious compromise involved, an expression of the compromise inherent in all group living, wherein individual liberty must be reconciled with social conformity. In a complex society, social agencies are charged with enforcing the balance, agencies such as schools and police forces, and these agencies must themselves be subject to ongoing review and control.

Today, "the cops" don't just chase thieves; there is a greater stress upon general public service. Though not everyone would readily call the police in an emergency (for some classes and ethnic groups still lack confidence in the police), by and large police have established a legitimate and respected role in modern Canadian society, and offer a desirable substitute for reliance upon personal strength, private retainers, and vigilantism. The counterbalancing consequence, of reliance upon outside experts, of course, is a deterioration in self-help and personal or civic responsibility.

The police not only protect, they serve in a multitude of ways. They are a catch-all service agency. Police are called upon to handle untended urban social difficulties from care for the indigent to family discipline, from traffic control to "crime-fighting." Probably we have come to expect too much of the police, not in the sense of standards of conduct, but in the sense of a plethora of tasks or duties. The policing role has become cluttered; they have been left with the residue of all the tasks no one else wants to do. Rather like social garbagemen, they deal not only with the tawdry social phenomena of crime, but with traffic problems arising from bad urban planning, with juvenile offences deriving from the changing family and educational failures, and with welfare problems from drunkenness to child and elderly abuse. They contend with, but cannot prevent or resolve, the inequities and associated behaviour of racial and class distinctions. They do so in the absence of clear performance guidelines, clear definition of public expectations, or consistent public participation, and with low standards of recruitment and relatively little training. As a result, the police officer often feels abused, isolated, and unsupported—walking the clichéd "thin blue line," holding on, coping.

In the face of demands expanding beyond traditional law enforcement, police services have not developed skilled personnel as rapidly as they have needed to, for reasons of budget and also for reasons of organizational or subcultural conservatism. In order to cope with the extraordinary, complex, and sometimes dangerous demands upon them, police, like persons in all occupational roles, develop a modus operandi. They acquire behaviours and group support to help them cope, in accordance with their perceptions of citizen attitudes and conduct—perceptions skewed by their encounters and by the media.

PUBLIC OPINION

Over the previous three decades there appears to have been a slow but steady increase in public attention to policing. Police forces in Canada, as elsewhere, have grown enormously in the twentieth century, in personnel numbers, costs, and scope of operations. They bear faint resemblance today to their predecessors in the nineteenth century. As they have grown, there has been increased media and public attention upon them. Police have for decades counted upon public support, in the context of public fear of crime, to lobby politicians for resources. The public have characteristically favoured taxation for police services. A poll in Ottawa, for example, found that the highest public importance of all services was policing, and more than half of the respondents suggested a tax increase rather than cuts in policing (*Ottawa Citizen*, June 29, 1995).

The police have evolved in the context of a consensual society that operates democratically. They are clearly subordinate to civil authorities, from whom they derive their legitimacy, and are also aided by the willing support of most members of society, who depend upon them for protection and order. They are, indeed, one of the most important symbols of social order (Reiss, 1971; Manning, 1977; Dowling and MacDonald, 1983). In contrast to attitudes in totalitarian societies, and even other democracies, police forces in Canada had, prior to the 1970s, rarely met with public distrust or serious criticism. During the 1960s, when policing in the United States was subject to considerable criticism and abuse, the police in Canada were largely immune. In fact, the contrast with America police excesses enhanced a sense of pride and confidence in Canada's apparently more disciplined and professional police forces.

Public perceptions of police in Canada have changed, however, especially with the advent of a more heterogeneous urban population. Where previously Canadian police had been highly regarded, honoured, and even venerated and idealized, increasingly Canadian police have been subject to greater scrutiny from minority groups, the media, social scientists, community groups, and perhaps belatedly, government. Having operated with a relatively free hand, police officers have had to adjust to this scrutiny, and to what many of them believe has been unfair criticism.

While a broadly based public consensus persists among Canadians that attaches value and regard to police, that consensus has been eroded in the last 20 to 30 years. Among the factors responsible, we suggest, are police unionism, the relatively new multiracial character of Canadian society, and more aggressive media reporting.

Unionism

The establishment of effective employee groups in the 1960s, to be discussed in Chapter Five, while quite evidently improving police salaries and working conditions, also eroded some of the mystique of policing in the public viewpoint. All Canadian police services except the RCMP now have effective employee representation in the form of police associations or unions. Where the police had previously been perceived as nobly pursuing a vocation to public service, they now came to be seen as merely another occupational interest group. Especially in jurisdictions where police withdrew services to reinforce their demands, as has frequently been true in Nova Scotia, or engaged in other job actions, the public regard diminished.

Unionism affected public opinion in at least four ways. As police threatened or resorted to job action to back demands, the public-service pedestal on which the public had placed the police crumbled. Police were revealed as humans, and not superheroes.

Additionally, the adversarial relations that unionism introduced often brought the police employee organizations into open conflict with municipal authorities and police managers. An example is found in Montreal, where the Montreal Urban Community (MUC) Police Brotherhood has been continuously and publicly in conflict with management. In such circumstances, the issue of who is running the police comes to the fore. Similarly, in Toronto, where the police association assumed a public relations role in defending police against racism charges, and contested many issues in the 1980s with Mayor John Sewell, the objectivity of police was called into question in a way that isolated incidents of misconduct could not do.

A fourth sort of union activity that can affect public perceptions, albeit in an unintended manner, may be seen when the police unions deliberately engage in a public advertising campaign. Years ago police association campaigns in favour of capital punishment probably hardened Canadian abolitionist opinion. Extremist rhetoric misplayed again during the Oka crisis in 1990, when the Mohawks in Quebec were under military and Sûreté du Quebec siege. The Sûreté was vigorously criticized by the media and the rights groups for its actions. The Canadian Police Association, the national umbrella body for police employee groups, prepared an advertisement for publication that was headlined "We oppose terrorism," and went on to claim that the police did not fire a shot (contrary to news reports) and that the police officer killed on July 11, when the prolonged incident began, was "murdered." Many newspapers across Canada printed the advertisement. Two major newspapers, however—the *Globe and Mail* and the *Ottawa Citizen*, refused (*Ottawa Citizen*, September 18, 1990).

In Ottawa in 1997 the police association was publicly conspicuous in an enquiry involving alleged misbehaviour by a deputy chief. When the chief of police initiated an enquiry, the association claimed that the investigation was threatening its own members. Beyond the adverse publicity surrounding the alleged misbehaviour, therefore, was the media reported impression of a police service in turmoil, with the association and the chief at loggerheads. The further implication was that the association had reacted publicly because of their resistance and resentment of management-initiated reforms in policing. The deputy chief was subsequently fully exonerated, and senior major crime officers were reassigned, amidst contending charges conspicuously reported in the print media. The chief of police suggested that investigating officers had failed to bring the matter to his attention in a timely fashion, and the police association appeared to persist in the view that the chief had not properly investigated, even though investigators external to the Ottawa Carleton Regional Police had been called in (*Ottawa Citizen*, February 14, 1998, February 18, 1998; *Ottawa Sun*, February 14, 1998, February 15, 1998, March 15, 1998).

Minority Groups

Many police union actions have been in response to charges that the police are racist. There have been criticisms of police across the country in regard to encounters with minorities, whether native persons or other visible minorities. In part the problems may be associated with segments of the Canadian public who, unlike previous generations, distrusted and feared the police because of previous experiences quite unlike those of the white middle-class Canadians. Thus black young people in Montreal refer to police as "beasts" and "beast boys." Police, for their part, have distrusted the minorities, and have had little basis in experience to understand them. In this context of cultural separation, incidents involving police and minority group members invariably came to be viewed as racist, whether the police response was warranted or not. Police shootings of minority group members dramatized relations that were otherwise not publicly visible, and prompted calls for altered police composition and more public control of police.

While the police have struggled to adapt to a new multicultural Canada, the signals from their heterogeneous public have not always been clear. Criticism from minority groups has been strident, but polls show continued overall support of the police. Minorities and intellectuals have demanded more liberal recruitment and other practices, but other segments of the public have opposed measures that might alter their traditional conceptions of policing. For example, in 1986 the Peel Regional Police Force was petitioned not to allow Sikh police officers to wear turbans and ceremonial daggers. A petition organizer stated that "the police uniform should be left [as it is] simply because it is Canadian and it's known as Canadian" (*Globe and Mail*, March 4, 1986).

Because police work is in the limelight of public scrutiny and prone to dramatic and sometimes tragic outcomes, it has become the focus of minority group attention, frustration, and criticism. It has also become the focus of the energy of reformers intent upon changing police composition, training, and conduct, but who have, however, given no precise direction to police for the changes. The police have, perhaps, become a whipping post for a society working out its multiracial tensions. The coincidence of two newspaper headlines illustrates the point. The articles appeared on the same page. The first read: "Four out of ten Canadians want fewer immigrants: poll." The second declared: "Police urged to hire ethnic recruits" (*Ottawa Citizen*, November 2, 1985). One reported the results of a study sponsored by the Canadian Association of Chiefs of Police urging the recruitment to police forces of more minority group members. Above it were the results of a Gallup poll, revealing that only 14% of Canadians would increase immigration, while 42% favoured a decrease.

It is obvious that policing as a job experience alters with heterogeneity. While Canada has always been a settler society, the immigration of the 1980s from Third World countries has introduced a cultural diversity encompassing race, religion, and a range of customs that Canada has not previously experienced. Effective policing depends upon a measure of behavioural consensus in a society, associated most strongly with homogeneity. Thus, as Banton (1964) remarked in contrasting policing in Scotland to policing in the United States, informal control and compliance diminish in the relative lack of integration associated with the highly diverse multicultural urban society. The circumstance is one that is not of the police officer's making, but one to which he or she must adapt.

Public pressure for changes in policing has tended to centre around changing population composition and public complaints. Heavy media reporting, lobbying, and possibly police intransigence, accounted for the move in Toronto to independent civilian review of police conduct, another level of public control in addition to management, a police commission, and government. For approximately a decade, public bodies had been calling for reform in complaints procedures before finally being met by government legislation in 1981 (McMahon and Ericson, 1984), which was further strengthened in 1990. In 1981 in Toronto, a group labelled the Citizens' Independent Review of Police Activities (CIRPA) was formed to pressure for police reform. The group at first was confrontational and even extremist, but was eventually moderated to cooperation, or co-optation, with a public Complaints Commissioner's Office and Police Commission.

An analysis of CIRPA's history illustrates the entrenched character of policing, and the accommodations required of reform groups in order to realize any change in the highly legitimated institution of policing. Authorities control the public commentary or rhetoric, and in limiting or "policing the boundaries of the discourse," they inhibit the actions of reformist groups (McMahon and Ericson, 1984:139). Ultimately the process is one of ongoing reciprocal lobbying and adjustment. Change, especially independent review, did come to exist in Toronto, despite fundamental police opposition. Later the practice of civilian review boards was extended province-wide, only to be eliminated in 1997 by another government.

By the early 1980s the topic of police–multicultural relations had become a common one in police assemblies, especially for the chiefs of police. In 1984 a national meeting of chiefs of police and minority community representatives held in Vancouver was described as a "landmark event" (Canada, 1984c). Recommendations from the symposium included research into: the means to increase minority recruit applications, altered testing and selection procedures, intercultural in-service training, and local committee liaison. A National Police Multicultural Liaison Standing Committee was also established, with the support of the federal Minister of State for Multiculturalism, intended to deal with problems of community contact, recruitment, and training of police. Federal funding was provided for research into these topics, under the direction of the former chief of police in Vancouver. The report of the symposium was released in the context of the Association of Chiefs of Police commitment to increased visible-minority recruitment.

In March 1989 the RCMP sponsored a major national conference on "Policing for a Pluralistic Society," with minority group and police participation. While stressing measures such as representative recruitment and cross-cultural training, the underlying theme of the conference was to establish or re-establish a broad-based social consensus with regard to policing and public support, cooperation, and respect.

Police treatment of native persons is a particular problem. The most famous, or infamous case, of course, is that of Donald Marshall, who was unjustly convicted of murder in Nova Scotia following a biased and bungled police investigation. In Western Canada especially, there is concern that the aboriginal population is overpoliced, and perhaps mispoliced. Native persons are vastly overrepresented in penal institutions, and have frequently been subject to violent police actions. In April 1990 the *Globe and Mail* ran a three-part analysis of policing in the provinces of Manitoba, Saskatchewan, and Alberta, looking at the municipal police and the RCMP, and reported that native persons have come to expect police bias. Moreover, there is good evidence that alleged police misconduct rarely results in satisfactory enquiry or sanction. In the five years of its operation, the Law Enforcement Review Agency in Manitoba, for example, upheld only two of a hundred complaints, one of which was later overturned. Similarly, in Alberta there are few successful complaints to the Law Enforcement Appeal Board; nor are complaints apt to bring consequences from the Board of Commissioners in Saskatchewan (*Globe and Mail*, April 21, 23, 25, 1990).

Yet it may also be remarked that minority criticism of police is itself often discriminating and biased. Police may face hostility and non-support, because they are persons in a uniform representing a system in which they occupy a disadvantaged position. Specific complaints cases may therefore be brought forward in an atmosphere of cynicism and scant credibility for both sides, and with the consequence of greater police defensiveness and solidarity.

Policing is a two-way interaction, and sometimes the interaction is distorted by citizen perception of the uniform. During an enquiry in 1989 in Manitoba into aboriginal justice, sensational testimony accumulated regarding police abuse of native persons. But where reformers stressed minority recruitment as a solution, one native, a former officer with the RCMP, testified that he left his job because he was abused by the native people, for whom he had become a traitor (*Ottawa Citizen*, March 29, 1989).

Early in 1989 an Ottawa-area native woman was left by Hull Police with her friends at the side of a bridge on New Year's Eve. The woman, blind, had been struck by an automobile, but it is not evident that police were told of her being injured. Eventually she made her way to the market area of Ottawa, where she was found by Ottawa Police and taken to hospital, where she died. Native rights groups called for an enquiry, alleging racism. In the following days the supervising officer of the Hull policemen who appeared to have acted incorrectly, expressed his frustration, referring to a "witch hunt" (*Ottawa Sun*, January 16, 1989). Later, in February, when the provincial task force conducting hearings into police–minority group relations met in Ottawa, ethnic advisory committees criticized Ottawa police for poor minority relations, citing the Hull incident and another involving provincial police, which the Ottawa force had finally investigated only after misconduct was alleged. The chief of the Ottawa police expressed amazement at the criticism (*Ottawa Citizen*, February 14, 15, 1989). Yet even the head of the federal Human Rights Commission chipped in, in the absence of specific complaints about the Ottawa force, and testified of failures in hiring and internal policing (Montreal *Gazette*, February 16, 1989), while the *Ottawa Citizen* editorialized about the need for review boards given public "mistrust," and cited the same two incidents.

In Toronto over the last decade the police have been subject to criticism for their treatment of minority group members, especially blacks. Police already skeptical have frequently wearied of being criticized and "lectured." In 1989 the antagonism boiled over in connection with several police shootings. Public statements by black spokespeople and by police suggested relations of such distrust and antagonism that no "quick fix" was conceivable, and brings to mind the observations of an American researcher. William Westley (1970:xiii) remarked that "civil strife ... has the effect both of increasing the conflict between the police and the public, and of increasing the physical and social dangers to which the police are subject. It is then reasonable that the police should protect themselves by drawing closer together and becoming more hostile to the public." Thereby the opposite of reformist intentions is achieved.

Following heavily publicized incidents involving Toronto police and blacks, a task force was established. The well-reported hearings were, in the words of one newspaper headline, "testy." In one instance, the chief of the Metro Toronto Police was told by a panel member that his presentation on minority groups and employment standards, prepared by two staff members, was poorly prepared and unprofessional. The panelists declared that in a corporation "you guys would be fired." The chief, in turn, complained of unfair criticism, and warned, "The effect of the recent media hype has been devastating on force morale. I know of no time when morale has been lower" (Montreal *Gazette*, February 8, 1989).

Later in Toronto, while the task force was holding meetings elsewhere in the province, a Metro Toronto staff inspector, in the course of a meeting with New York's community committee on race and ethnic relations, released figures stating that while blacks made up only 6% of the population of the Jane-Finch area (a high-density, lower-class housing development), they accounted for 82% of robberies and muggings, 55% of purse-snatchings, and 51%

of drug offences. The press publicized the statements, the head of the task force reacted with anger, and the police officer publicly apologized a few days later for an "inappropriate" statement (*Ottawa Citizen*, February 18, 1989; Montreal *Gazette*, February 20, 1989). As the task force concluded its hearings, it was expected to recommend renewing calls for accelerated minority recruitment, including recruitment abroad and at ranks above the level of constable. This would have run contrary to stubborn police tradition in Canada where every new recruit, irrespective of previous work experience, is expected to work up from the bottom. Media opinion, as expressed in the *Ottawa Citizen* (February 27, 1989), was supportive of such measures, in order to check the alienation of the public.

The Ontario task force reported in April 1989. It made 57 recommendations, with the suggested sanction of withholding provincial funding for non-complying police forces. The recommendations stressed urgent minority recruiting, including lateral entry. A province-wide recruiting agency was recommended, without subsequent implementation. Also—perhaps the most insightful recommendation—the report noted the utter inadequacy of present in-service ethnic relations training, suggesting that the substandard courses actually may reinforce biases. The recommendation was that courses be developed and offered by appropriately trained university-educated experts. A police response, as expressed by the Ottawa chief of police, was that imposed minority recruitment would damage the high standards of selection. Similarly, lateral entry would jeopardize the rigorous competition within police forces (*Ottawa Citizen*, April 11, 12, 1989).

Days after the closing of the task force hearings, a letter to newspapers from the president of the Canadian Police Association complained of the unfair criticisms levelled at police, which was damaging morale and driving police officers to seek early retirement and other employment. Describing the hearings as a "public media circus," the president noted that calls for accelerated recruitment were unrealistic, given the illegality of "press gangs." More seriously, the letter argued that the persistent public attention damaged the reputation of policing as an occupation, and thus further deterred minority applications (*Ottawa Citizen*, March 5, 1989).

Later, another police shooting of a black woman by Toronto police was investigated by the Ontario Provincial Police and a charge was brought against the officer for careless use of a firearm. The Police Association publicly supported the officer, but a new chief of police, reputed to be less comfortable with the Association than his predecessor, personally visited the wounded woman's family as a "matter of courtesy" (*Ottawa Citizen*, December 5, 1989; *Globe and Mail*, November 3, 1989).

In the police view, minority group criticisms and expectations are often unrealistic and unfair. A minor but illustrative incident in Montreal marks the point. Attempting to coordinate with minority residents, representatives of the crime prevention programme of the MUC Police met with Chinese Canadian businesspeople in what they had expected to be an informal contact and exchange of views. When, instead, the police were presented with an elaborate brief, they walked out of the meeting, thus exacerbating rather than ameliorating the tension between the two groups (Montreal *Gazette*, July 8, 1986).

Amended recruitment has been a conspicuous demand of organized groups and the media, and has been endorsed by the chiefs of police. Yet it is fair to acknowledge that while a public expectation of representative composition may be desirable, its consequences for the quality of policing are by no means clear. Minority-member policing of minority-group persons does not of itself mean better policing, although the general expectation that a representative force will have more knowledge of minority persons has some validity. Expertise on the multicultural character of society is the key goal to be attained, by all means, including training of existing personnel. Some services, such as Calgary, have responded by sending personnel abroad, for example to Hong Kong, to acquire new skills. Toronto employs a police officer formerly with the Royal Hong Kong Police, who has a Master's degree in international relations, speaks several languages, and is used as an expert in Chinese organized crime (he has had a novel on that theme published, *The Glorious East Wind*, by K.G.E. Konkel).

Most police in service have been recruited from working-class and lower middle-class backgrounds, and there is little reason to expect them to have attitudes other than those associated with such backgrounds. These attitudes include distrust of immigrants and minorities, and outright racism. In 1989, in the context of renewed antagonism between blacks and Toronto police, the media reported the results of research by Joseph Fletch, whose national survey found that police were less tolerant than better educated Canadians. Fully 73% of police agreed that immigrants frequently bring discrimination upon themselves (*Toronto Star*, January 15, 1989). In the police point of view, they do genuinely seek to treat everyone alike, and avoid special or privileged treatment. But, like many working-class Canadians, they believe that the onus should be upon immigrants to "Canadianize," and not upon Canadian institutions to change to suit immigrants.

A survey of Canadians at large, and of "elite" subcomponents such as lawyers, legislators, and police, found that police were more apt to agree with the proposition that immigrants "should try harder to be like other Canadians." Where 65.5% of police respondents agreed in some manner with the statement, only 42.5% of legislators agreed, and 35.8% of others agreed (Fletcher, 1989:4–12). Similarly, police were more apt to agree that "immigrants bring discrimination upon themselves" (73.1% versus 50.6% for legislators and 41.3% other), and were more apt to agree that "races are certainly not equal," with 30.4% of police agreeing, 16.5% of legislators, and 11.3 others.

In Toronto, a city where minority groups now make up approximately 40% of the population, and where the majority of immigrants to Canada find themselves at one time or another, it may be estimated from data in the late 1980s (see Table 6-1) that approximately 5% of Toronto police are from visible minority groups. This statistic, at least of symbolic if not also operational import, is resistant to change. Efforts by Toronto police to adapt to immigrants, such as the formation of an ethnic squad, seem trivial in the face of this basic statistic, the attitudes underlying it, and several major antagonistic incidents. An early attempt to reach out, the Danforth Avenue "mini-station" shared with social service agencies (*Globe and Mail*, October 11, 1983), was but a drop in the large puddle of crisis and suspicion that permeate Toronto. Unlike some communities, where such initiatives can be proactive, in Toronto, as in Montreal, the police are running from behind.

The problem for police is not simply their own behaviour. They must also contend with the ingrained expectations and perceptions of immigrant segments of the public. Many immigrants believe, on the basis of their previous experience, that racist conduct will occur, and where any questionable action takes place they may quickly hypothesize racism as the cause. The suspicion of police, in fact, goes beyond misbehaviour that can be documented. Clare Lewis, who was an Ontario public complaints commissioner, remarked that he had heard very few complaints about police behaviour. Rather than view this, however, as to the credit of the police, he stated that many people were simply too afraid to complain, thereby implying that there was much misbehaviour that never came to light (Montreal *Gazette*, January 31, 1989). Whether damned by evidence, therefore, or damned by *lack* of evidence of misconduct, the police are ultimately in a demoralizing position that they are not able to rectify.

Variation in evaluations of police by membership in ethnic groups is regularly identified in research. In the city of Toronto, high rates of affirmative evaluation were associated with people of European, Anglo-Celtic, and remarkably, Caribbean backgrounds, while low evaluations were associated with Italian and East Indian respondents. In the high-problem Jane-Finch neighbourhood, however, Caribbean respondents tended to rate police more poorly, along with East Indians (Murphy and Lithopoulis, 1988:22–32).

Other factors have been identified as consistently relating to public attitudes towards police. Age is an important variable, with satisfaction associated with greater age, and low approval with younger respondents (Koenig, 1980; Brillon, 1984; Murphy and Lithopoulis, 1988). In their work in Toronto, Murphy and Lithopoulis found that respondents under age 25, irrespective of their neighbourhood and its economic character, were apt to have more negative perceptions of police in general, and also with respect to specific policing performance characteristics such as enforcing the law, promptness, and approachability. Findings of the Canadian Urban Victimization Survey were consistent with other research noting an age relationship (Canada, 1985c:6).

A 1981 survey of Quebec, Ontario, and Manitoba found that 86% of respondents reported satisfaction with police services. The dissatisfaction was higher in Quebec (26% versus 8% in Manitoba and 7% in Ontario), and among younger people, consistent with other research findings. Satisfaction declined where there was also less knowledge among respondents concerning police service or helping programs (Brillon, 1984:137–38).

Majority and minority Canadian publics have come to concede that police are not paragons of fairness. Still, the majority have not been prepared to abandon the traditional regard for policing, but merely to qualify it with a touch of skepticism. A survey proximate to well-publicized criticism of RCMP conduct in Quebec in the 1970s produced very favourable public evaluations of the police. A press poll of 32 Canadian cities found that far more Canadians—by a factor of 2—reported increased respect for police than decreased respect. Sixty-four percent rated their municipal police as good or excellent and 27% rated them as adequate. This was slightly better than the RCMP, who had been the object of high-intensity press coverage. Sixty-one percent rated the federal force as excellent or good and 19% as adequate. Eight percent believed that police were honest and 87% considered them courteous. Only 67%, however, considered them to be impartial in their treatment of the public, with 27% believing them capable of bias or prejudice (*Weekend Magazine*, August 26, 1978).

In 1979, after several tragic shootings and public criticism, the *Toronto Star* surveyed residents, and found that 87% considered that the police were doing a good or an excellent job. A comparable survey in 1978 had elicited an approval percentage of only 78%. The 1979 survey was conducted in an environment not only of criticism, however, but of a public relations counter-offensive by police (*Toronto Star*, November 25, 1979). The Metro Police Association, for example, had paid for advertisements that requested the support of the public. "We believe that most Torontonians are proud of their police officers and we believe that we've earned that respect," declaimed the advertisement. Continuing with a description of Toronto as safe, the advertisement went on to observe, "That's because of you. It's because you won't stand for anything less than real security for yourself and your children. It's because you've always given your police men and women the vote of confidence they need to deal with crime on a professional level." The advertisement continued, evoking emotional-laden sentiments, and concluded by asking for expressions of support, and with the sentence: "We need to know because more than a few of us have died for you" (*Toronto Star*, September 13, 1979). Little wonder that a public survey found support had grown from already traditionally high levels. Nonetheless, the survey also found that 20% of respondents considered police to be prejudiced against blacks, Pakistanis, and homosexuals.

Almost 20 years later, in Canada's most ethnically diverse city, another survey produced disconcerting results. In an attempt to estimate perceptions of fairness in the police treatment of ethnic populations, researchers asked respondents to make comparative estimates. They found that blacks (79%) perceived overwhelmingly that police treated blacks worse than they did whites, while in contrast, just under half (46%) of Chinese perceived that police treated Chinese worse than whites. Even 60% of Chinese respondents and 50% of whites perceived that the police treated blacks worse than they did whites. Generally, then, a majority of respondents in this research sample did not believe that equal treatment of all citizens was to be had from Toronto police. Additionally the researcher found that 72% of blacks, 46% of Chinese, and 40% of whites believed that poor people were treated worse than the wealthy, younger people worse than older people (78%, 60%, 71% respectively of black, Chinese, and white respondents), and non-English speakers worse than English speakers (57%, 64%, and 47% respectively of blacks, Chinese, and whites) (Northrup, 1996:4).

Research such as that done in Hamilton-Wentworth suggests that even where general expressions of satisfaction may be high, when respondents are queried about specifics such as response times, relations with minorities, or use of force, the rate of satisfaction declines. The public seems to hold a positive image of policing in the abstract, but generally direct contact or knowledge of specific programs is modest, and evaluations are vague and neutral rather than hostile (Dowling and MacDonald, 1983:41–47).

Research has suggested that direct personal contact with police, as well as generalized awareness of policing, determines the attitudes of members of the public. The police officer's conduct in an encounter shapes the views, supportive or negative, of the citizen. Attitudes are especially negative, therefore, where people experience or witness police misconduct. Anecdotal information also shapes attitudes where the information is understood to refer to the direct contact of persons familiar to the individual whose attitudes are being shaped (Klein et al., 1978:448–451). Even where the police encounter with a citizen involves enforcement or sanction, the citizen response is not necessarily negative; the quality of the encounter, such as promptness and politeness, determines the citizen evaluation (Munn and Renner, 1978; Groves et al., 1980). Klein and his colleagues (1978:452) found that even arrest situations can generate favourable impressions. In Canada, with a history of relatively benign police–citizen relations, there has been a culture of support for policing. But that support is reinforced or diminished by direct contacts, depending upon the quality of encounters. One might infer, too, that vigorous and sustained media reporting of police treatment of "ordinary" citizens will generalize the sentiments generated in such encounters. It has been found that people who have been victims of crime generally give a less favourable opinion of police, though not by a large margin (see Table 3-1).

Similarly, the degree of isolation of police from the public can have a self-fulfilling consequence of increased isolation and reduced public understanding and support of the

TABLE 3-1	Proportion of Victims and Non-Victims Who Rated Police Favourably, by Age							
Aspects of	**16–24**		**25–39**		**40–64**		**65+**	
police behaviour	**V**	**N-V**	**V**	**N-V**	**V**	**N-V**	**V**	**N-V**
Enforcing laws	47	54	50	58	61	66	65	70
Responding promptly	40	42	48	47	58	56	66	58
Approachable	51	54	61	61	72	69	75	67
Supplying crime prevention information	36	37	38	42	43	46	45	46

Source: Canada, 1985c:6.

police, or vice versa. In a British Columbia survey of RCMP attitudes, for example, Koenig found that police had an accurate impression of community support, attributable to their being less socially isolated than their counterparts in the United States or Britain where comparable research found less accurate police perceptions (Koenig, 1975a:315; Thomas and Hyman, 1977). Research suggests that social ties with stable residents favourably affect evaluations of police, while geographically mobile or transient persons are less easily influenced by community-based policing (Murphy and Lithopoulis, 1988:45–52).

Another interesting factor is public perception of crime. Interestingly, Murphy and Lithopoulis (1988:34–57) found in Toronto that public perception of crime clearly was related to more negative perceptions of police. Rather than create a loyalty and regard for policing, the perception of widespread crime seems to translate into a sense of failed police services and a need for improvement. Similarly, having been a crime victim tends to relate to lower regard for police.

Public perceptions of police and policing needs are related, in an imperfectly understood manner, to public perceptions of personal safety. The Canadian Urban Victimization survey of the 1980s, co-conducted by Statistics Canada and the solicitor general, documented that as much as 57% of the incidents in which persons were victims of crimes were unreported to police. The survey canvassed seven cities—Metro Vancouver, Edmonton, Winnipeg, Toronto, Halifax-Dartmouth, and St. John's—and found that theft of personal property was the least reported offence (reportedly only 29% of the time) and theft or attempted theft of a motor vehicle the most reported (70%) (Canada, 1983:4, 5). When questioned as to reasons for non-reporting, 61% of the time people suggested that "police could do nothing about it anyway." This was also the most common reason (52%) for not reporting sexual assault, but in addition, 43% "cited concern about the attitude of police or courts." Especially for domestic assault, as contrasted to non-domestic assault, which usually involved males, the perception of police or courts unable or unwilling to respond was prominent in the survey findings (Canada, 1988b:7). Table 3-2 displays the data in detail.

There is evidence to suggest that when police are subject to criticism they see as interfering and unsympathetic, they react as any group does by becoming defensive, secretive, and even more prone to the use of force. Police have always distrusted the media (Mery, 1971). Westley found that police secrecy and solidarity in the face of public criticism was a paramount norm. In his research sample he found 77% of police respondents preferring to perjure themselves rather than testify against another police officer (Westley, 1970:151). To protect self-esteem and image, and the integrity of the group, police may therefore become more insular, and in fact, more prone to the misbehaviours that initially prompted the criticism. Westley remarks that "The police are, after all, only ordinary men, working collectively to protect their interests and self-esteem. They are, however, placed under extraordinary strain, and to compensate for these strains and threats, they can become exceptionally brutal and withdrawn" (Westley, 1970:xvii). Hostile reactions to critical press attention have been visible in several Canadian jurisdictions including Kitchener-Waterloo, Winnipeg, Toronto, and Montreal.

Media Relations

There can be little doubt that the mass media have been powerfully influential in shaping public impressions of policing, and in so doing, have also helped form police self-conceptions, especially that of crime-busting action heroes (Manning, 1996). The media, especially the electronic media and the tabloid press, are action-oriented in their reporting, and the police are inevitably prone to news coverage. Elements of risk and force, and the potential error and misconduct, are grist to media production.

The police and the media in Canada have generally not enjoyed a cooperative relationship. Police usually have a negative view of the media, both news reporting and entertainment. In news reporting, say the police, the sensational content is too often unfairly critical of police conduct. Viewing the press as a "nuisance," rank-and-file and senior officers often impede the media (Kelly and Kelly, 1973:621).

The media, for their part, are fascinated with policing. The drama of police action, even police misconduct, is the epitome of sensational news, and their persistence in ferreting out uncomplimentary stories arouses police officers' ire.

The Winnipeg Police Force dramatically illustrated the animosity between Winnipeg police and the press in the 1980s when it engaged in deliberate efforts to trick and embarrass press representatives, and publicly stated its lack of regard for the quality of reporting in the city. At one point the chief of police banned a reporter from police press conferences, only to have his ban overruled by city lawyers (*Globe and Mail*, April 20, 1985).

Another dimension of police–media disagreement relates to police use of media files and tapes. The press have resisted angrily when the police have seized evidence from print or electronic media offices in the course of a criminal investigation. It is of concern to the press that police searches often have to do with internal police matters rather than criminal investigations. Two such incidents were cited in a letter to the federal solicitor general from the Ontario Press Council. These raids involved RCMP visits, the first to Canadian Press offices in Montreal, and the other to offices of Radio-Canada in Ottawa, both visits in search of possible information concerning a security service employee who may have divulged information to the press (*Ottawa Citizen*, November 2, 1988).

The media create further problems for police when they become an intrinsic component of a situation that police are trying to control. As Scanlon (1981) has argued, for example, in terrorist or hostage-taking incidents, the media, especially television and radio, can become the vehicle for the offenders to convey messages. Police therefore are required to establish control over media influence, and to prevent the media from becoming intermediaries, or inducements, to the offenders. Police action in Springhill, Nova Scotia in 1979 is illustrative of the dilemma. The police were controlling access to a bomb disposal site where a World

TABLE 3-2 **Reasons Given for Failure to Report Incidents to the Police, by Crime, in Percentages**

	Sexual Assault	Robbery	Assault	B & E	Motor Vehicle Theft
Nothing taken	33	47	28	42	51
Police couldn't do anything	52	54	51	58	57
Fear revenge	33	10	11	3	—*
Protect offender	16	9	16	5	—
Too minor	26	56	63	65	56
Inconvenience	—	33	24	20	19
Personal matter	27	22	29	8	—
Reported to another official	—	—	7	7	—
Negative attitude of police	43	14	12	7	—
Overall unreported	62	55	66	36	30
Number unreported	11 000	27 000	185 000	81 000	12 000

Columns do not add to 100% since respondents could indicate more than one reason for failure to report any one incident.

*count too low to be significant

Source: Canada, 1983:7.

War II bomb was to be detonated by an armed forces disposal crew. In the police view, representatives of the newspaper who were seeking to report on the road closure and the reasons for it were willfully interfering. The managing editor and a reporter of the Amherst *Daily News* were arrested and charged with obstructing a police officer (*Ottawa Journal*, October 1, 1979).

Very few police forces have assigned professional public relations staff to represent them to the media. The Calgary Police Force has done so, and generally has received very sympathetic media attention. In other jurisdictions, however, tension or outright animosity prevails. The police tend to view press reporting as unfair, and their presence and attitudes as obstructionist.

In 1971 the Association of Chiefs of Police attempted an agreement with the Canadian Association of Broadcasters, calling for joint committees and greater cooperation. The print media refused to participate, and eventually the electronic media withdrew when criticized following a hearing by the Canadian Radio and Television Commission (Kelly and Kelly, 1976:624).

Media reports of misconduct, and especially of alleged racism, have been frequent since the 1980s. In the Ottawa region in 1986, a flurry of well-publicized cases of misconduct rocked that area's police forces. Incidents ranging from sexual misconduct to theft and favouritism prompted suggestions from the police themselves—also, of course reported in the press, that public confidence in the police had diminished, which was adversely affecting police–citizen encounters in the normal performance of duties (*Ottawa Citizen*, November 8, 1986).

Household Theft	Personal Theft	Vandalism	Total Number	Percentage of Total
8	6	28	179 000	19
64	64	69	564 000	61
1	2	2	40 000	4
3	5	3	60 000	6
71	62	73	606 000	66
26	24	25	224 000	24
7	13	6	123 000	13
7	27	4	109 000	12
7	5	6	75 000	8
56	71	65		
227 000	243 000	136 000	921 000	58

The press in several major Canadian cities seem to have a special predilection for stories of police errors. In Montreal, the *Gazette*, and in Toronto, the *Toronto Star* pointedly feature stories on police misconduct and errors, and frequently editorialize about them. The *Gazette* ran a front-page story speculating about the police director's possible retirement, claiming that he was seeking his pension plus salary, then editorialized in criticism of the director as having "discredited himself with demands for a large and unseemly increase in pay" (Montreal *Gazette*, January 15, 1989). On the same day, the *Toronto Star* followed up on its reporting of tense relations between blacks and city police and the charging of three police officers, with an editorial damning the president of the Police Association for his blatant call for public support, and also blasting the chief for misstatements denying problems in his force. In the editorialist's view, he was acting more like an association member than a chief (*Toronto Sunday Star*, January 15, 1989). That most damaging of editorial comments, the cartoon, has also been employed against the police.

The Montreal *Gazette* regularly featured reports that alleged police racism, as in 1987 when a black businessman charged harassment and beating by off-duty police officers who had accosted him in a street because he was with a white woman. He was confronted and manhandled, then arrested. While in custody in the police car he was beaten, and ordered to repeat "I am a nigger" three times. Two police were charged with aggravated assault (Montreal *Gazette*, December 4, 1987; December 8, 1987).

The media reporting of police errors and misconduct in Montreal appears to have had an effect. A Gallup poll conducted early in 1989 found a very low level of public approval of police, at 60%, in contrast to a 76% approval rate in Toronto. The overall approval rate in

Quebec was 70%, contrasted to 76% in the Atlantic, and 79% in Ontario and British Columbia. Forty percent of Montreal respondents indicated that they believed their police to be prejudiced, while in other areas of the province only 27% expressed this belief. This contrasts with 38% in Toronto, and only 13% in the Maritimes (Montreal *Gazette*, February 23, 1989).

Although most police believe that they are rule-bound, harassed by the media, and lacking public support, as one police stress counsellor stated (Montreal *Gazette*, December 17, 1987), they do in fact have considerable discretion. Street encounters are still not scrutinized. What perhaps has changed is the willingness of the public to complain, and the willingness of the media to publicize complaints in an unsympathetic way. Therefore, when an officer errs, or apparently uses discretion in an unreasonable or silly way, the publicity may be considerable. Such was the case, for example, when MUC police arrested and handcuffed a woman for posting signs offering a reward for her stolen cat. The Montreal *Gazette* reported the incident extensively and prominently. The incident was observed by a friend of the woman, who attempted to dissuade the police from their action, and according to the news report was threatened by police, with a constable allegedly saying, "Do you want trouble too, you little bastard?" The friend, born in Columbia, was also asked by police, "What kind of Canadian are you?" Covering the court proceedings, the *Gazette* described the constable present as having "sneered and laughed at defence witnesses" (Montreal *Gazette*, January 8, 1988).

In 1984 the *Toronto Star* published a major article entitled "Why police are never convicted in shooting" (*Toronto Sunday Star*, October 28, 1984). The article was prompted by the acquittal of a Sherbrooke police detective in the mistaken shooting of a carpet layer during a motel raid, and also cited acquittals in two Toronto police shootings of black men. Following a complaint by a lawyer who had acted for the Toronto Police Department, to the Ontario Press Council that the article was "unfair, unbalanced, and biased," the Council ruled that there was no bias but that "there was a degree of unfairness and imbalance because the article focused mainly on criticism of the way the justice system treats police officers, particularly in two Toronto cases, and did not contain comment from people holding contrary views" (*Ottawa Citizen*, March 22, 1985).

Where police actions are conspicuous, the media can be aggressively attentive. In the summer of 1990 the Mohawk dispute in Quebec generated very negative media coverage of police actions. The Sûreté was accused of brutality against the Mohawks and reporters. But in this major event, there was also a sense that the media were becoming players of a different sort, not only reporting actions but overtly influencing perceptions and behaviours.

It is probably fair to say that the public, generally remote from police actions, have an image of the nature of policing deriving from media content. It is probably also fair to state that mis-impressions have their origin in the media. Television programming and movies offer a violent and glamorous image of policing, stressing crime-busting rather than service, and law-bending and violation as much as law enforcement.

The print media, supposedly presenting news rather than fiction, inevitably reports crime-related incidents and police error and misconduct rather than the non-newsworthy minutiae of everyday policing. Even non-news items seem to pick up on the stereotypes, as in a column by a Halifax reporter who spent two days in a Halifax Police Department training program. The program itself extended over 26 weeks, but the reporter wrote a column, which was picked up elsewhere in Canada, stressing the use of force in subduing and handcuffing offenders and learning "how to shoot to kill" *(Toronto Sunday Star*, December 11, 1988). Similarly, an adulatory essay in *Quebec Magazine* recalled the careers of two "legendary" Winnipeg police detectives. Crime-busting was the theme of the article, celebrating two old-fashioned "real tough cops" who got things done by bending the rules. "We were the aggressors," they said (MacDonald, 1983:52).

There are, of course, more accurate journalistic accounts. Some journalists have written of the changing character of policing, with an emphasis on service, and also on the subject of more police precision and skill in a society bound by the Charter of Rights (Monteiro, 1982). But such analyses are relatively infrequent, and obscured in the waves of media sensationalism.

Media stories that are neutral, as when offering a feature article on the experiences of women in policing (Montreal *Gazette*, March 11, 1989), do occasionally have a favourable effect. Very uncommon are "good news" stories stressing affirmative actions by police. One such exception was the quite extensive coverage of police response to the murder of a Quebec boy by his hockey coach. The stories followed the actions of two Sûreté detectives who had worked on the case but who also spent considerable time with the victim's family. The detectives and their superior were later presented by the parents with plaques that read: "To an extraordinary police officer, whose incomparable support allowed us to come through the horror, in spite of the atrocious pain, for your entire collaboration and your profound compassion, be forever thanked, for your extreme generosity, sealed by the sincerity of a wonderful friendship" (Montreal *Gazette*, March 2, 1987).

Canada's entertainment media have generally not celebrated police officers in drama. The RCMP has to some extent been romanticized, but the Force, like its municipal counterparts, has shunned visibly strong personalities who might be celebrated. The RCMP had colourful figures from its early history on the frontier, such as James Walsh who contended with Sitting Bull (Turner, 1973). But however prominent the Force is in history, it has operated with a firm commitment to what has been described as a "cult of impersonality" (Sallott, 1979:9). Yet, while avoiding the sensational individual, especially among serving members, the RCMP has been anxious to promote the romance of the Force collectively, and literally to profit from its image. Its marketing agreement presently in place with the Disney Corporation, which has prompted criticism by observers for selling out to the Americans and jokes about the Mickey Mouse Force, is an attempt to market RCMP paraphernalia globally.

Much of the imagery of policing for Canadian is imported from the United States. For that matter, it must be admitted, much of the social science research literature is also imported from the United States. Television programs, fiction, non-fiction narrative descriptions, and research results permeate American culture, reflecting a pervasive and persisting fascination with policing. These items, in turn, influence Canadian views. By and large the American work stresses violence, corruption, and sordid aspects of policing, somehow managing nonetheless to make it all glamourous.

Novels such as the several works of Joseph Wambaugh or Robert Daley (e.g., Daley, 1985; Wambaugh, 1975) operate from a basis in experience, but like all fiction, seize upon usable themes such as danger and sex that command the publishers' and the readers' attention. So too, the authentic narrative accounts of real life on the streets (e.g., Baker, 1985; Stroud, 1987), offer a pseudo-ethnographic format, with the police players allowed to speak for themselves, and their activities, graphically depicted, conveyed to the avid reader. But unlike the less titillating social science descriptions (e.g., Rubinstein, 1973; Vincent, 1979), not only are such accounts unburdened by elaborate interpretation, they tend also to be un-burdened by routine police duties and encounters with non-deviant citizens. Their "real-ism" ultimately is sensationalism, as in one work, described on the cover by crime/thriller writer Elmore Leonard as being "as authentic as you can get." United Press International is also quoted, remarking "sirens screaming and blue lights flashing." And the *New York Times* is cited, invoking the words "bizarre" and "terrifying" (see Baker, 1985). Such exposés are not out-and-out falsehoods; they are exaggerations and caricatures, which seize upon gen-uine elements, even genuine persons and situations, and imply that they can be generalized as normal police experience.

In a rather unrealistic effort of its own, the British Columbia Association of Chiefs of Police sought to have the television industry delete sensational images of policing from their television broadcasts. Their president issued a statement protesting against the "continued and widespread false presentation of policemen." The public receive an incorrect impression of what police officers are like, and recruits with unsatisfactory qualities, such as interest in weapons use, seek policing careers, suggested the chief. "In a typical movie or TV presen-tation, the policeman is regularly portrayed as arrogant, abusive of public rights, brutal, and gun-happy. In almost any television show, he may be seen behaving in a manner which, in British Columbia, would result in his being either sternly disciplined under terms of the British Columbia Police Act or charged in the criminal courts" (*Globe and Mail*, June 17, 1981).

Media entertainment content resurfaced in police opinion again in 1984 following a spate of police murders. The Metro Toronto and Peel Regional police chiefs stated to the press that they deplored the violence depicted in films and on television. The statement followed the shooting death of a Toronto police officer by a man dressed in combat fatigues, appar-ently imitating behaviour in the violent film "First Blood." The chiefs also objected that "These programs are portraying policemen as idiots" (*Ottawa Citizen*, September 24, 1984). The executive director of the Canadian Police Association echoed the sentiments in a state-ment to the press, blaming the psychotic "Dirty Harry" stereotype of policing for distorting the public impression of Canadian police, and also for misguiding some recruits. Suggesting that the distorted image creates morale problems for Canadian police, he suggested that as a consequence "We're not judged on our best [men], we're judged on our worst."

Police public relations efforts rarely have succeeded with the media and the public to whom they report. Police participation in community programs has traditionally been a low-prestige task, delegated to very small units of one or a few personnel. And because they are often not thought out or taken sufficiently seriously, they have unanticipated neg-ative consequences from time to time, as the police mistakenly convey to a public their own flaws and biases. Such was the case in Toronto in 1979, for example, when the Metro Toronto Police offered an enrichment course at an area school to 11- and 12-year-olds en-titled "Cop Shop." The course showed a film, and required pupils to respond to a checklist describing suspects. The headings and choices of suspects revealed far more than intended of police biases and stereotyping. They included: "Deviate—homosexual and lesbian; Amputations and deformities—plate in head, appears feeble, simple-minded and thick lips; Colour—white, black, yellow, red-Indian, brown-Malay, East Indian, Egyptian; Apparent Nationality—Italian, French-Canadian, Jewish, Gypsy, Oriental and Canadian" (*Ottawa Citizen*, June 7, 1979).

Another public relations blunder transpired in Toronto in 1980. The pastor of a church in North York had asked the Metro police to provide a speaker. The chief of police assigned a staff sergeant who delivered a 45-minute lecture to churchgoers, replete with grisly photographic slides of murder victims, including children. The presentation, and the pastor's sermon that followed, were intended to support capital punishment (Montreal *Gazette*, December 30, 1980).

The intriguing matter of "group sex" elicited another manifestation of police public expression of opinion. The House of Commons considered in 1982 an amendment to the Criminal Code that would legalize group sex among consenting adults. The Association of Chiefs of Police, appearing before a justice committee, protested the proposed amendment on grounds that it "would permit any number of persons to engage in all manner of indecent acts ... and would seriously inhibit law-enforcement officials from controlling such behaviour" (Montreal *Gazette*, March 11, 1990).

Yet Canadian police forces have had some striking public relations successes. No other nation, not even the British and their "bobby," have had such an affirmative image of police as have Canadians. This is, of course, most clearly expressed in the Canadian respect for and willingness to publicize the RCMP. The "Mountie" is probably Canada's most widely recognized symbol. The RCMP are sent abroad with their horses to represent us at major events, from the Rose Bowl Parade to the Olympics. They appear on our currency, and are quite literally trotted out for national events, such as the Grey Cup Parade, where they receive the appreciative if perfunctory applause of the crowd. The RCMP quite naturally encourages this. The Musical Ride is a deliberate and costly enterprise with full-time personnel because it powerfully conveys the Mountie myth. Other municipal or provincial forces have not had the panache of the RCMP.

CONCLUSION

The benefits of media attention are public support, both financially and in terms of public collaboration. There is a relationship of mutual dependency between the police and media representatives, neither of which feels quite comfortable with, or free of manipulation by, the other.

In their relations with Canada's diverse and widely distributed population of more than 30 million people, Canadian police personnel have been in the forefront of social change. By and large they have been reactive, obliged to adapt to altered circumstances. But the pressure to adapt has been enormous, and unrelenting. The traditions of policing in Canada have been imbued with public regard and police restraint. Increasingly, however, there has been some sense of police and public as antagonists. The changed social circumstances and altered public attitudes have created difficulties for the vast, bureaucratically ponderous, and conservative police organizations. Initial police responses were superficial, with an intent to downplay the need for change. Lately, though, there appears to be serious intent to modify the basic character of Canadian police organizations, and to render them more responsive to their diverse publics.

ANNOTATED READINGS, CHAPTER THREE

Banton, Michael. *The Policeman in the Community.* New York: Basic Books, 1964. This book is a classic, and not only stands the test of time, but appears even more relevant with the contemporary commitment to community-based policing. Looking at the United States and Great Britain, Banton analyzes the actual and proper role of police officers in relation to their publics in democratic societies.

Grossman, Brian. *Police Command: Decisions and Discretion*. Toronto: The Macmillan Company, 1975. When there was no Canadian police literature, there was this book. It offers a straightforward and non-romantic view of police duties and responsibilities, from the command-level to the street, with a consistent reference to the requisite role of police in a Canadian democratic society.

Sewell, John. *Police: Urban Policing in Canada*. Toronto: James Lorimer and Company, 1985. This survey is offered by a former Toronto mayor who throughout his career was concerned with the quality and the public responsibility of police officers. The book reflects his interest in issues of police–public interaction and improvement.

THE ORGANIZATION OF POLICE SERVICES

This chapter provides an overview of the many police service organizations in Canada. The size, composition, and cost of Canada's police are presented, and the organization and management of police work are outlined. We explore the paramilitary origins of police services, and study the nature of the current large, centralized organizations.

The work of policing has its basis in legislation, the police acts passed by provincial and federal governments. The authority of police, the general rights and responsibilities, and the basic structure and configuration of police organization and hierarchy are to be found in these acts. Additionally, the work of policing is delimited by collective agreements, which contain negotiated terms and conditions of employment agreed upon between public authorities and police management with the representatives of organized police officers, the employees (see Chapter Five).

It must be recalled that among the plethora of police and police-like agencies in Canada, our concern is with the public police, persons with general peace officer status and responsibility to extend service and protection in our communities. Private policing, security intelligence services (e.g., Canadian Security Intelligence Service, or CSIS), and regulatory bodies (e.g., Canada Customs, or Parks Police) are a massive component of Canada's regulatory and social control net, and are themselves deserving of a volume; it is not this volume. Policing for our purposes, therefore, consists of municipal and state police services mandated by police acts.

The complexity of urban policing in modern Canada is dazzling, beginning with the maze of laws and statutes that created police forces and defined crimes. As Stenning (1981a:40,

130) observed, to generalize about police and their legal status in this country is perilous. From the outset, the national structure divided federal and provincial responsibilities in an imprecise manner, with the federal government having the authority to enact criminal law but the provinces understood to have authority for "administration of justice." Yet municipal police have similar authority across the country, depending upon provincial Police Acts.

Canada itself has changed substantially from the way it was at the inception of our police services. No longer a frontier society, or a rural society, Canada is a congress of large and small cities, each with a distinct history and a different experience of population mobility and immigration. Although no longer a frontier society, Canada remains a settler society, experiencing an annual influx of approximately 250 000 immigrants. And the immigrants no longer come predominantly from Anglo-American nations, but increasingly are from Asia and the Caribbean—the new "visible minorities." These immigrants, unlike previous generations, are not land-grant settlers, entering a new society of only six or seven million, taking on sparsely populated territories as middle European immigrants did in western Canada. They are entering an established society of more than 30 million inhabitants, and turning to the cities for their livelihoods—especially to Toronto, Montreal, and Vancouver. There they encounter Canadian customs and institutions, including Canada's police.

POLICE AUTHORITY

All of Canada's police are authorized to serve by acts of provincial legislature or Parliament. The RCMP, for example, function under the provisions of the 1959 Police Act of the Parliament of Canada. Thereby they undertake their national responsibilities, subject to the authority of the federal solicitor general. As a federal force they are responsible for enforcing federal statutes, and additionally they offer skilled services (e.g., crime records forensics) to other police. They also work in provinces and municipalities as local police, in contract relationships, and therefore also enforce provincial statutes and are nominally subject to the authority of provincial government, and ministers of justice, attorneys general, solicitors general, and even ministers of correctional services. Similarly, provincial police, such as the Ontario Provincial Police (OPP), and municipal police are subject to police services Acts, and the administrative authority and control of provincial governments by way of one or more of the above offices. In addition, in most provinces, provincial and municipal police are responsible to government-appointed police service boards, provided for in police Acts. Lastly, to some varying degree, local municipal governments will have some oversight of police services, more evidently so in jurisdictions without police service boards.

Police acts tend at one and the same time to be detailed and general. There is imprecise specification of the actual work of police officers, but general reference to responsibilities and duties, recruit requisites, rank structure, standards of conduct, and discipline. The details of actual police work are left to the organizational directives, informal police subculture, and to police collective agreements.

Consider three examples: Newfoundland, Ontario, and Canada. The Constables Act of Newfoundland, 1970, is "respecting the organization, operation, functions, powers, duties, rights, and privileges" of the Newfoundland provincial police. In its 20 pages, the duties of the chief and others are noted as subject to directives from government. Officer behaviour considered offences under the Act is indicated, and there is an explicit prohibition on trade union membership (not to be confused with non-certified and/or affiliated employee association; see Chapter Five). Six pages of the Act are devoted to spelling out appropriate contract bargaining.

The Ontario Police Services Act (1990) is even more elaborate. Having recently been reviewed and amended, it is a document of over 150 pages in English and French. Included in the Act is specification of the line of political and civil authority (attorney general, solicitor general, minister of corrections, police service commissions), the powers and duties of police, criteria for hiring, discipline, and complaint procedures, labour relations, general regulations and codes of conduct, rank structure, and even appropriate rank insignia. Where sheer bulk would suggest in Newfoundland a concern with collective bargaining, in Ontario one finds 25 pages devoted to oversight and complaints procedures, some of which have recently again been amended.

The RCMP Act is also voluminous, almost 60 pages in either official language. Among the details, it specifies senior management and administrative control in the person of a commissioner, rank structure, qualifications, general conditions of contract policing, authority for member compensation (the Treasury Board), discipline procedure, and even an "oath of secrecy" prohibiting disclosure of information acquired as a member. Including the specification of an External Review Committee and a public complaints commissioner, over 40 pages of the Act are devoted to matters of discipline.

CONTRACT POLICING

A distinct feature of Canadian policing that has developed is contract policing. Historically, as we have seen, the state police have been responsible for frontier and rural regions. The NorthWest Mounted Police initiated a practice of also entering into contracts with local provincial and/or municipal authorities to police towns, cities, and entire rural areas. The RCMP developed the practice further, the OPP followed suit, and today even major municipal services have offered to contract for services in adjacent areas.

Presently the RCMP commits about 57% of its budget and 47% of its members to contract policing. Costs are shared between the senior government, that is, the federal government in the instance of the RCMP, and the contracting government. Provinces and smaller municipalities meet 70% of the costs, and municipalities of over 15 000 population meet 90% of the costs. Current agreements provide for a review of costs every five years (RCMP Web site, 1998).

A contracted police service provided by a larger organization becomes a local police agency. For a community, there appear to be disadvantages and advantages. There have been complaints that the contracting community receives insufficient attention, and that they don't have enough influence and control. The commissioner of the RCMP, for example, is responsible to the federal government, and even though local contracts are supposed to engage responsibility to the local authorities, it has been suggested that the overall command hierarchy is not sensitive to the local authorities. But on the other hand, they receive the services of a large service with major facilities. Moreover, contracts expire, and the community then has alternatives. More care is being taken to write in police performance specifications in the contracts. In considering the number and size of Canadian police services, therefore, it is necessary to be aware that local policing does include the state police services.

THE SIZE OF POLICE SERVICES

In Canada there are several hundred police services, from the large national RCMP Police, with more than 15 000 sworn members, and huge municipal forces such as the Montreal Urban Community Police or Metro Toronto Police, to small-town forces consisting of just

TABLE 4-1 Major Municipal Forces, 1993	Number of officers	Population per officer
Metropolitan Toronto	5 507	407
Montreal Urban Community	4 020	397
Calgary	1 177	622
Edmonton	1 126	559
Winnipeg	1 074	574
Vancouver	1 108	448
Peel Regional	1 104	677

Source: Statistics Canada, *Juristat*, Catalogue No. 85-002, Volume 16, Number 1, 1996:7.

a few personnel (see Table 4-1). In Canada, every town with a population of 10 000 or more must have a police force, whether operated by the town or under contract to the RCMP or a provincial police force. A close estimate puts the number of Canadian police services at between 500 and 600. The numbers continue to fluctuate as regional mergers occur, and as small towns give up policing to provincial services or the RCMP under contract. In 1994 the estimate was 578 municipal police services, plus the four state police services (Newfoundland Constabulary, Sûreté du Québec, OPP, RCMP). Of the 578 municipal services, 364 were independent, 201 were RCMP contract services, and another 13 OPP contract services (*Juristat* 16, 1996:13). In 1994 these police organizations employed 74 902 persons, of whom approximately three-quarters, or 53 865, were sworn police officers. There was 1 police officer for every 523 Canadians in 1994 (*Juristat* 16, 1996:17). This number excludes other government enforcement agencies and private security operations. Table 4-2 shows the change in numbers over 32 years and is rather revealing. Over the 32-year period from 1962 to 1994 the number of sworn police officers more than doubled. The ratio of population to police officers indicates that police strength relative to population improved significantly in that period. Moreover, civilian employees of police agencies more than tripled, suggesting that the relative capacity of police agencies vastly exceeded population growth. All Canadian regions in 1994 demonstrated population to police ratios superior to the national average in 1962 (see Table 4-3).

The RCMP, with over 15 000 officers, is overwhelmingly Canada's largest police service, almost three times as large as Metropolitan Toronto Police, the largest municipal service and the second largest police organization in Canada. Both the OPP and the Quebec Provincial Police (Sûreté) are smaller than Metro Toronto; the OPP, Sûreté, and the Montreal Urban Community (MUC) Police all fluctuate near 4000 members. In the 1990s, the RCMP represents approximately 28% of total police numbers in Canada, Metro Toronto almost 10%, and Sûreté, MUC, and OPP fluctuate under 8%, leaving all others making up slightly over 39% of total police numbers (*Juristat* 16, 1996:7).

The RCMP operates nationally as a federal police agency and, under contract, as a provincial police force in the West and all the Atlantic provinces. The RCMP also serves as a municipal police force in many western and Atlantic jurisdictions. Canada's two largest provinces have major police forces, the OPP and the Sûreté, operating in rural areas and policing under contract in small towns. In Newfoundland, while the unique Newfoundland Constabulary, paid for by the province, polices in St. John's, Corner Brook and Labrador City, other areas in Newfoundland are RCMP policed.

TABLE 4-2	Police Personnel in Canada, 1962–1994		
	Officers	**Civilians**	**Population per Officer**
1962	26 129	5 699	711.2
1963	27 333	5 935	692.6
1964	28 823	6 665	669.3
1965	30 146	7 133	651.6
1966	32 086	7 583	623.8
1967	33 792	8 018	603.0
1968	34 887	8 351	593.4
1969	36 342	8 963	577.9
1970	37 949	9 936	561.2
1971	40 148	10 597	548.6
1972	41 214	11 762	540.7
1973	43 142	12 297	522.9
1974	45 276	12 085	505.2
1975	47 713	13 794	486.4
1976	48 213	14 377	487.8
1977	48 764	15 231	488.0
1978	48 705	15 749	493.5
1979	48 990	15 001	495.6
1980	49 841	16 410	493.4
1981	50 563	16 999	492.5
1982	50 539	17 738	498.7
1983	50 081	17 342	508.3
1984	50 010	17 503	513.9
1985	50 351	17 702	515.2
1986	51 425	17 855	509.6
1987	52 510	19 140	505.6
1988	53 312	18 985	504.5
1989	54,233	19 099	504.8
1990	56 034	19 330	496.0
1991	56 774	18 997	495.3
1992	56 991	19 614	500.8
1993	56 901	19 495	508.6
1994	55 865	19 037	523.5

Source: Statistics Canada, *Juristat*, Catalogue No. 85-002, Volume 16, Number 1, 1996:17.

The RCMP are organized nationally in 14 alphabetically designated divisions. Headquarters in Ottawa is a Division, as is Training or Depot in Regina. The other operational

TABLE 4-3	Police Officers by Province, 1994–1997			
	1994		**1997**	
	Officers	**Officers per Population**	**Officers**	**Officers per Population**
Newfoundland	880	662	794	710
Prince Edward Island	193	697	204	673
Nova Scotia	1 611	581	1 624	584
New Brunswick	1 297	585	1 304	584
Quebec	14 712	495	13 743	540
Ontario	20 742	527	21 335	535
Manitoba	2 130	531	2 230	514
Saskatchewan	1 896	536	1 872	547
Alberta	4 472	607	4 478	636
British Columbia	6 383	575	6 747	583
Yukon	113	266	122	259
Northwest Territories	234	275	246	275
RCMP Training & HQ	1 202			
CANADA	55 865	524	54 669	554

Source: Statistics Canada, *Juristat,* Catalogue No. 85-002, Volume 16, Number 1, 1996:18 and *CANSIM,* 1998.

divisions correspond to the provinces and territories, and are located in the capitals, except for British Columbia (Vancouver) and Quebec (Montreal).

The very large RCMP alone operates at every jurisdictional level, from the municipal to the national. The concern has been expressed, consequently, that the Force is too powerful and insufficiently subject to public control, especially by the provinces (Grant, 1980:35). Kelly and Kelly (1976:10) dismiss this concern, arguing that in fact, at the municipal level the Force is marginally responsible to local and provincial authorities, and that while under provincial contract, the provincial solicitor general is in control. Yet it is fair to note that career loyalty for a Force member must be to the national organization, and former provincial authorities in Alberta and New Brunswick have questioned the control which they have had over the RCMP (Sallot, 1979).

The large number of separate police organizations in Canada poses some difficulties. In the metropolitan area of Ottawa–Hull, for example, with approximately one million residents, even with recent regional organization there are several police forces with a perplexing overlap of jurisdictions (Ottawa–Carleton Regional Police, RCMP, OPP, QPF, Hull Police, Outouais Regional Police). Problems are thereby posed to members of the public—who sometimes hardly know who to call!—and to police forces' efficiency. The Ottawa–Carleton Regional Police have assumed responsibility for many roads and areas previously policed by the RCMP and the OPP. Yet, in the capital region, as in other areas of Canada with provincial (and international) borders, all inter-agency problems cannot be met by merger. Inter-service collaboration, as basic as information provision, is often wanting.

Collaborative protocols have been worked out since an especially embarrassing incident. In 1986 a hostage incident took place at the High Commission of the Bahamas. The

Ottawa police were dealing with an armed man when the RCMP attempted to assume command and were rebuffed. According to one press report, the hostage-taker threatened to shoot if the arguing police officers were not quiet (*Ottawa Citizen*, June 19, 1986). Three weeks later the local RCMP chief superintendent, who had been on the scene at the High Commission, issued orders that the RCMP and not the Ottawa Police Force were responsible for traffic accidents and criminal offences on federal roads, of which there are approximately 40 kilometres in Ottawa. For more than 30 years it had been understood that the local city police had jurisdiction over them. The Ontario solicitor general and his federal counterpart received complaints, and eventually the RCMP withdrew their assertion of jurisdiction (*Ottawa Citizen*, June 12, 18, 19, 1986).

Police handling of a hostage-taking incident three years later indicated improved cooperation between the Ottawa Police and the RCMP, but serious breakdowns in communications and coordination within the RCMP and among the RCMP and Quebec police agencies. On April 7, 1989, a bus bound for New York City from Montreal was commandeered by a gunman. Harbour Police learned of the situation from a passenger released on the Champlain Bridge near Montreal.

Inexplicably they failed to inform MUC Police or the Sûreté, and even refused the Sûreté access for questioning when the provincial force had been advised by Greyhound Bus authorities. Assuming that the bus was continuing to New York, American state police were alerted. Once the Quebec police were informed, an alert was supposed to have been sent on to the Canadian Police Information Computer (CPIC), which links all forces. An Ontario police constable on patrol on the busy highway from Montreal to Ottawa reported that she had received no advisory, and similarly it was not noted by RCMP in Ottawa. Later reports suggested that more than two hours before the bus arrived on Parliament Hill, an alert appeared on the CPIC computer screen at RCMP headquarters in Ottawa, but the screen is not regularly monitored and the information was not noted or passed on. Therefore nearby OPP detachments, who depend upon CPIC referral from the RCMP centre, received no warning. Ottawa Police and Ottawa-area RCMP did not learn of the hostage taking until the bus was on Parliament Hill; and in fact, no police agency had been aware of the location of the bus's location in the interim. Moreover, hostages later stated that the police negotiator on Parliament Hill could not speak fluently in French, and had to be assisted by the bus driver! Also, at least one hostage remarked that as the hostages exited the bus, they were searched under arms by police, and then detained for several hours without refreshment. The "police were scarier than the gunman" (*Ottawa Citizen*, April 7–9, 11, 12, 1989; Montreal *Gazette*, April 9, 1989; *Toronto Sunday Star*, April 9, 1989).

Until a court decision in 1983 it was not even clear that a police officer could operate across a provincial boundary. The Supreme Court, while hearing the case of a Sûreté constable who had been previously convicted of illegal use of a firearm following his pursuit of a car into New Brunswick, ruled that, given the nature of Canada, it is unreasonable to curtail police powers at a provincial border. The constable was acquitted of the charge, in the view that he had the same powers in New Brunswick as in Quebec, and had the right to use his weapon at his discretion, subject to the procedures of his force. The only limitation noted by the judge was that the police officer acting across a provincial border must notify the appropriate police as soon as possible (*Ottawa Citizen*, March 25, 1983). Another interesting jurisdictional problem, in this instance transnational, was reported in 1988, when two Vancouver city police officers pursued a speeding car 20 kilometres into Washington state. In defending the action, the Vancouver Chief of Police underscored the need for regional coordination among the area's police forces, including American ones (*Ottawa Citizen*, November 30, 1988).

In fact, there is some measure of coordination. An elemental measure that has been used from time to time between police services is temporary exchange or secondment of personnel. The RCMP and the Ottawa Police have exchanged personnel for training officers in recognition of contiguous policing jurisdictions and occasions for joint operations (*Ottawa Citizen*, May 5, 1990). The RCMP has entered similar exchanges with other forces, such as the Laval police. In Quebec the Sûreté and the MUC Police traded inspectors for purposes of improved familiarity and liaison (Montreal *Gazette*, January 23, 1996).

Most Canadian police services are dependent upon the RCMP for some technical services, such as skilled forensics testing. And Canadian police cooperate with the RCMP in providing input data for the central information system managed by the RCMP. The Canadian Police Information Centre (CPIC), a computer link providing information on known criminals and suspects, is available nationally. The database, operated by the RCMP, is a computer-based information system that links 1180 RCMP detachments and specialized units and 1285 police departments and government agencies. It also accesses the U.S. National Crime Information Center and state databases. Data files relate to vehicles and other property, information on persons, such as wanted or missing persons, and criminal records. Even individual dental records are on file (RCMP Web site, 1997).

THE COST OF POLICE SERVICES

The sheer number of police officers in Canada, and the associated costs, are enormous (see Table 4-2). The number of police officers in Canada grew steadily from 1962, when statistics were first systematically kept, slightly decreasing only in 1982 for the first time. By 1985 some fluctuating growth resumed, with minor decline again by 1994, and slight national increase again in 1997. The pattern of fluctuation suggests a relative stability in police numbers, ignoring civilian personnel. But the overall growth has been considerable, and over this time, so too the seniority and related compensation of police service members. The costs of policing have been driven by increased employee demands, in no small part associated with police unionism. In 1985, for example, the cost per capita per year for policing in the city of Montreal was $145.04; in Toronto it was $136.98; and in Calgary it was $129.81. These costs contrast unfavourably to major American cities such as Los Angeles at $112.92 and New York City at $119.25. By 1985 the total cost of policing in Canada was $3.52 billion, and by 1994, $5.78 billion, a slight decrease over the year of –0.1%, the first decrease since Statistics Canada began collecting data (*Juristat* 16, 1996:11). Total expenses slightly increased to $5.86 billion in 1996 (*CANSIM*, 1998). Ontario and Quebec have the highest per capita costs for policing (see Table 4-4).

The major cost component, of course, is salaries. Salaries have consistently accounted for over 80% of the total costs of policing. All major services monitor salaries nationally, and bargain to retain comparable salary position.

The salaries for a first-class constable in major Canadian cities by the mid-1980s were $35 151 in Montreal, $33 489 in Toronto, and $36 752 in Calgary (*Toronto Star*, March 7, 1985). In 1988 the average salary for a first-class constable in Canada was $36 854, with average salaries of $38 925 in Quebec, $37 933 in Ontario, and $40 034 in the Atlantic provinces (*Juristat* 9, October 1989:1).

TABLE 4-4	Per Capita Spending on Municipal and Provincial Policing by Province, 1995

	Dollars per Capita
Newfoundland	103
Prince Edward Island	97
Nova Scotia	112
New Brunswick	122
Quebec	179
Ontario	169
Manitoba	142
Saskatchewan	141
Alberta	132
British Columbia	128
National average	157

Source: Statistics Canada, *Juristat*, Catalogue No. 85-002, Volume 16, Number 1, 1996:13.

These salaries, and those in other Canadian cities, seem to be rising continuously. With the exception of Atlantic Canada, major urban forces in Canada bargain for salaries on the basis of what is being earned in other cities, striving to be first, and continually adjusting upwards. The Atlantic police tend to be 10 to 15% behind central and western Canadian police salaries, while the RCMP maintains an approximate parity with the rolling average of major municipal police forces.

In the 1990s police salaries are quite attractive. A constable might expect to begin with a salary in the $25 000 to $29 000 range, and increase regularly with seniority. By 1994 salaries in major urban cities exceeded $55 000 for a first-class constable with eleven years of service, with a high of $55 586 in Vancouver. With compensation packages total remuneration often exceeded $60 000, as in Vancouver at $65 192. Total remuneration in Montreal was $60 792 and in Toronto $60 847, and for the RCMP $62 752 (Source: RCMP: 1995).The salary and benefit mix varies, and from year to year the relative salary position of one police service to another will alter. But the pattern is one of a well-compensated public sector occupational group.

Police associations and unions have successfully bargained for wages and at times costly working-condition provisions such as two-man patrols. The cost of policing now threatens the quality of public service, as governments monitor spending, while at the same time the public demands for service grow. Cost-cutting measures such as centralization and increased employment of civilian personnel have been implemented across the country, but an unintended consequence has been to create a perception of reduced services, which in turn has generated an increased reliance on alternative agencies such as private security personnel.

Through the seventies measures to moderate the costs of policing were sought, usually under the guise of police effectiveness, efficiency, or productivity (Engsted and Lioy, 1978). Yet, other than the use of civilian employees, no dramatic changes or benefits were realized. The traditional indicators of police efficiency—crime statistics, clearance rates (the percentage of offences police claim to have solved), response times—were increasingly being viewed as inadequate representations of police actions, as insensitive to the service and prevention elements of good policing. Indeed, productivity research revealed, if anything, not better measures of efficiency so much as the irrelevance of variations in some cherished police practices, such as patrol frequencies, response times, or detective work (Farmer, 1978:120–133). Police forces had, it appears, adapted technology to their operations, but had not fundamentally modified operational conceptions of the policing tasks.

PARAMILITARY ASPECTS

The structure of authority or command in all police forces has its origin in the military model. This is not only true of Canada, but of virtually all police forces in the world. "Although they may operate in a democratic, post-colonial, or totalitarian system, there is no police force which is not based on [a] military model" (Das, 1986:267). The military character will vary. In some societies the police and the military are all but indistinguishable. In highly industrialized North America, despite the long tradition of civil service, a paramilitary character can still be found in policing (Skolnick and Fyfe, 1992).

In Canada, with policing origins deriving from Peel's founding legislation in Britain, there has also historically been concern that despite the military antecedents and remnants, the police officer, as a civilian in uniform, must be distinguished from the soldier, and there should be a commitment to "unobtrusive" policing (Das, 1986:276). Some Canadian forces are more traditional in their adherence to prerogatives of rank and command, and are more evidently military in character than are others, from their training and manpower disposition to dress and designation. Even symbolically, those who maintain the label of police "force" underline the power, discipline, and application of force associated with military organizations, as contrasted to the client-orientation of those choosing to be called police "service." In 1989 the Ontario government determined that Ontario police in future would be known as "service," rather than the prevalent designation of "force."

The military model is one of unquestioning obedience to the orders of superior officers. An implied aspect of this structure is also unquestioning loyalty. By and large, Canadian police forces have been slow to deviate from this model, although public pressure and the pressure of police unionism have forced a move in the direction of managerial rather than command-style authority. Police themselves often like to characterize their services as "professions." Yet the bureaucratic and quasi-military structure, with continuing demands for conformity and discipline, the level of recruit qualification and training, the characteristic internal command-officer selection, the absence of lateral entry, and like factors contradict a professional label. As Perrier (1978:212) has written, "personnel are closely regimented in most departments," deterring personal initiatives and independent judgment of a professional nature. Within a rigidly controlled hierarchy, employees perform rather as tradespersons than as professionals, and are subject to elaborate disciplinary codes and processes.

Like a trade, and in this instance quite unlike the military, police work their way up through the ranks. There is no pre-educated and pre-commissioned officer corps. While there are many perquisites and paraphernalia of rank in the police, as in the military, in the police everyone must work up from the ranks. Chiefs were once constables. Usually they will have been constables in the police organization that they now head.

An overwhelming tendency to recruit commissioned personnel, up to and including the chief, from the ranks of the particular police force, has been characteristic of police forces, especially in large municipal forces. There is lateral entry from other police forces, especially in smaller organizations, and from the RCMP. But even such traditional lateral movement seems to be declining (Grant, 1980: 28–29) and there is virtually no lateral entry from non-police occupations or from non-Canadian police forces. As Alan Grant observed, "The 'mandarins' in the civil service do not commence work in the clerical grades, officers in the armed service do not work their way up from privates and the president of General Motors does not start out on the production line, but every chief of police starts as a constable" (*Globe and Mail*, March 28, 1981).

The chief of police will invariably have served many years in policing. Western Canadian municipal forces have frequently appointed chiefs from outside, whereas the major municipal forces in Ontario and Quebec have tended not to do so. There are, of course, notable exceptions, as in 1990 when Hull, Quebec appointed as its chief a youthful, high-ranking officer from the MUC Police. More usually the appointee is nearing the end of a career in policing, and as Grosman (1975:13) noted many years ago, is therefore not interested in change or controversy.

The rank structure of all Canadian police forces is broadly similar and defined in the pertinent police acts. In Ontario, for example, since 1973 there have been nine ranks: chief, deputy chief, staff superintendent, superintendent, staff inspector, inspector, staff sergeant, sergeant, constable. Promotion, in most cases, means moving through each of these ranks (see Figure 4-1). The lower rank of constable will itself be gradated from First through Fourth Class, usually subject to a year of satisfactory service in each, and some services will also have a probationary status of Cadet. In addition, with some form of detective branch in urban police services, one will find distinctions, as in the Ontario Police Services Act, that locate detectives, non-uniformed personnel, in the rank hierarchy. The Ontario Act specifies that "Where a force has a detective branch, detective sergeant is equivalent to the rank of staff sergeant and detective is equivalent to sergeant." With the rank, of course, is corresponding compensation.

Like military organizations, police services have been male-dominated. The proportion of women has gradually been increasing, but overwhelmingly, because of relatively recent recruitment, they are to be found in the lower ranks of constable (see Table 4-5). At this time there have been only two female chiefs of police in Canada, in Guelph and in Calgary. The chief in Guelph, appointed in 1994, was the first female chief of police in Canada (*Juristat* 16, 1996:5).

TABLE 4-5	Male and Female Police Officers by Rank, Canada 1986–1994					
	Officers		**Under Officers**		**Constables**	
	Males	**Females**	**Males**	**Females**	**Males**	**Females**
			%			
1986	5.14	0.01	25.32	0.12	65.66	3.74
1988	4.80	0.01	25.46	0.21	64.66	4.87
1990	4.65	0.02	24.75	0.32	64.23	6.04
1992	4.68	0.04	25.29	0.41	62.52	7.07
1994	4.43	0.06	24.79	0.56	61.73	8.43

Source: Statistics Canada, *Juristat*, Catalogue No. 85-002, Volume 16, Number 1, 1996:5.

FIGURE 4-1   Police Rank Structure in a Typical Police Department

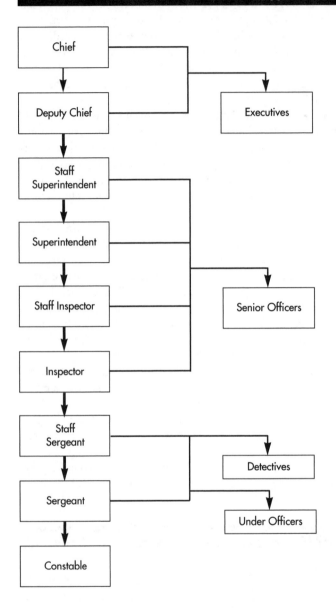

Also deriving from the military model in the Anglo-democracies has been the traditional requirement of police in Canada—much more so than in the United States—to be politically neutral. Police are to be the quintessential public servants, and although increasingly it is the case that police chiefs and police unions have offered comment on public policies, it remains unusual to have police representatives comment upon political candidates or parties.

Even more rare is to have a police officer engage in politics as a campaign worker, or as a candidate. Some few instances have, in fact, resulted in sanctions provided for in the pertinent Police Acts. In 1988, for example, an RCMP constable was determined to run for a school board seat in Nanaimo. At first he was told by his superiors to withdraw and then, when they acknowledged that they were uncertain about the correct interpretation of the RCMP Act, he ran and was elected. He was, however, transferred from the Island to Vancouver, with the Force claiming that it was a promotion and not a sanction, and in fact not at all related to his election. The constable, for his part, was determined to commute (*Ottawa Citizen*, November 23, 1988).

In another RCMP incident, a sergeant was ordered to resign his elected position as mayor of Saint-Blaise-sur-Richelieu, a small municipality south of Montreal. The sergeant had been warned that running for the office would be a violation, and he was suspended two days after winning the election. The suspension was fought in court, referred to internal grievance by mutual agreement (at which point he was reinstated with back pay, but not interest), and failing in a demand for interest on back pay, the sergeant has taken the RCMP to court, seeking interest, legal fees, and damages. Perhaps of relevance, the sergeant is founder and president of an association of Quebec RCMP members attempting to unionize (*Ottawa Citizen*, December 26, 1997).

ACCOUNTABILITY

Although the police are politically neutral, they must, of course, be accountable to the public through its duly elected or appointed representatives. The most common form of political accountability for municipal police forces is through the office of the chief, reporting directly to municipal councils (Hann et al., 1985:2). More recently the Atlantic jurisdictions and Quebec have resorted to police commissions. The second most frequent form of public accountability was represented by municipal contract police services, as provided by the RCMP and the OPP. These police units have the local police command authority moderated by divisional and ultimately central superior officers, with political control diffused through local councils, sometimes, as in Alberta, through boards of commissioners, and provincial political bodies. The third, and growing category of police–political relations is represented by boards of police commissions, government appointed bodies long established in Ontario and British Columbia. In British Columbia all municipalities with their own police services must have boards; in Alberta, all communities, even those with contract policing, with populations of 1500; in Saskatchewan, those with populations of 5000 or more; in Ontario, communities with populations of 15 000; in Prince Edward Island, populations of 1000; and in Nova Scotia, boards are called for where there are community populations of 1500. Elsewhere in Canada the existence of boards is not specified by provincial legislation and is left to local option (Hann et al., 1985:17–18). Boards include some local political representation, usually the mayor, and vary in the requirement of provincial appointees. For example, there are not provincial appointees in Saskatchewan or Prince Edward Island, but such appointees are the numerical majority in Ontario. Generally, these boards consist entirely of government appointees.

The public bodies, whatever form they take, rarely intervene in operational decisions of policing. Financial parameters do of course occupy their attention and do affect operations. Some personnel decisions also involve the public bodies, including bargaining and other relations with police employee groups, and the appointment of the chief executive officer, the police chief. RCMP detachments under contract are less affected by these public controls. Research suggests that Quebec police forces, operating without boards, tend to enjoy greater discretion, although they probably also offer more opportunities for direct intervention from political leaders (Hann et al., 1985:66–67, 77–78).

Public bodies such as police service boards act in a very broad administrative role. They are not particularly visible to or representative of public interests, nor are they apt to intervene in police management and internal operations, including allegations of police misconduct. Their general purview is the organization, not individuals within the organization. As will be discussed in Chapter Nine, over approximately the past decade a number of other civilian review bodies have developed that are intended to bring individual police officers to account for their actions.

WILSON'S TYPOLOGY

Within the common organizational model there have nonetheless evolved police forces of different character. Each police organization reflects the particular social environment in which it is located and the idiosyncrasies of its personnel. The interaction of these influences, along with its own history and general trends in policing produce a police organizational style. The range of possible styles is quite finite, and one author has offered a simple typology that appears to have some validity in comprehending differences in Canadian police organizations.

James Q. Wilson (1969, 1978), an observer of American policing, writes of three types of police force. He distinguishes the watchman, the legalistic, and the service styles of police organization. These three types reflect the internal police subculture, as well as factors having to do with interaction with the public, such as the quality and training of recruits and the nature of the community within which the police operate.

The watchman form of police service is dedicated to maintaining order rather more than enforcing the law. It is characterized by slovenly recruit selection, preparation, and service. Persons of low education are recruited, training is perfunctory, and the policing philosophy is to "keep the lid on." Such a style is characteristically associated with police misconduct, such as the unnecessary use of force, and corruption. The misconduct is not isolated, but is prevalent, what we refer to as elsewhere as institutionalized (Wilson 1978:140–171).

The legalist form of policing is dedicated to law as "the standard of community conduct." Contrasted to the watchman style, it is excessively "professional" insofar as emphasizing impartiality, though in another sense, it is only superficially professional in that it tends to substitute conformity to rules for initiative and independent thought (in both training and organizational structure). Such services may have members with relatively high education and offer quite elaborate, police-specific training. But they are bound by a rigid set of rules governing all aspects of their conduct and genuinely independent professional judgment is inhibited. Excellence is equated with consistency. Professionalism becomes a form of bureaucratization. A rule is a rule, an offence is an offence, and subsequently, the context of an event and the possible exercise of discretion are obviated (Wilson, 1978:172–199).

A hybrid of the above two styles is the service-oriented police organization. In this form, which is easily delivered in a homogeneous community, there is a sense of professionalism, but in keeping with the original meaning of the concept, not only are there high quality personnel selection and training procedures, but also an emphasis upon personal competence and discretion. Such police services tend to stress informal resolutions, and are less oriented than the legalistic services to arrest and formal punishment. Like the watchman mode, there is a sense of keeping the lid on, of keeping order. But the police actions are proactive and not merely reactive; the intervention is contextual and not strictly by the book; and the judgments are in the public interest and not that of individual police officers, the policing peer group, or special community interests (Wilson, 1978:200–226).

Wilson's typology is disarmingly simple. It does, however, approximately capture the empirical alternatives in policing. A police force that is not guided by some universal criteria of performance is subject to abuse—the watchman style. It is idiosyncratic, erratic, and corrupt. A police service, on the other hand, that seeks to define and to meet standards of performance, but does so by resorting to conformity to rules and regulations, becomes inflexible, rigid, and ultimately fails to reflect the complexity and the changes of the society in which it operates. Service standards become an end in themselves, displacing the original objectives or guidelines. The amalgam is, of course, an idealization. It allows for universalistic criteria, but also allows for moderation of criteria to reflect local community standards and realities, allowing and in fact depending upon police initiative. In true service-oriented policing, police seek to be sensitive to community members, and to mediate among them. This generally is the intent of community policing, to be discussed in Chapter Ten.

Another simple categorization of police forces that has been applied to Canada is simply to distinguish them in terms of administration and service style as regards their orientation to change. Some are "conservative," resistant to innovation and change, and others are "progressive," willing to adapt and change (Tomovich and Loree, 1989:29). As in so many established organizations in society, police officers are a mix of traditionalists and innovators, and in some individuals, and some organizations, one outlook or the other predominates.

PERSONNEL ORGANIZATION

Canada's large police forces have become very complex organizations, encompassing many specialized and often costly operations. Within the typical police structure there is an elaboration of administrative units. The maze of departments and subdepartments, with both sworn (persons "sworn" as regular peace officers, as contrasted to civilian employees) and civilian personnel, extends far beyond what one associates with the familiar, general duty street patrol officer. As Sewell (1985:77–82) concisely outlines, one may think of police services as characteristically tripartite. There is, as in all large organizations, an administrative sector, with senior sworn personnel and civilian support employees, engaged in policy and the gamut of fiscal and personnel management tasks. In the large forces, civilian specialists tend to concentrate in administrative posts, those positions having to do with technical skills such as accounting or forensics.

Secondly, there is a sector of staff operations. These consist of relatively senior and expert sworn personnel, with tasks relating to specialized investigative responsibilities (e.g., homicide, narcotics, morality), and to supporting roles such as vehicles and communications.

Thirdly, the core of the policing operation is the field operations. Here one finds the bulk of police personnel, and the least number of civilian employees. Within operations, the core is patrol, which in police forces in Canada and the United States comprises about two-thirds of the policing complement (Lundman, 1980a:vii). Operations also include specialized services such as general detective investigation and community ethnic liaison. It is in this sector, with the general patrol officer, that most contacts between police and the public occur. Investigatory specialists tend to be sworn employees, that is, police officers (MacDonald and Martin, 1986:201–202). Figure 4-2 gives an example of how a police force might be organized.

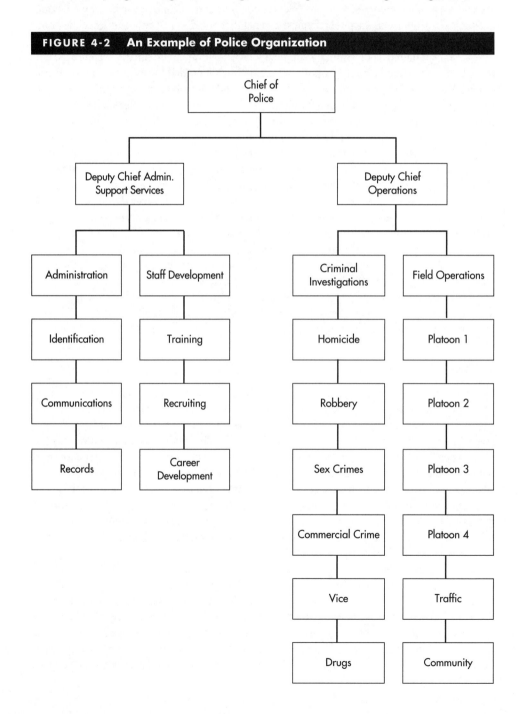

FIGURE 4-2   An Example of Police Organization

The RCMP is the best example of elaborate specialization, with national responsibilities ranging from regular policing under contract, to testing and backup, as in information systems, for smaller police organizations. The distinguishable operations of the very large municipal police organizations and the RCMP include specialization in major crime, morality, auto theft, drugs, fraud, major accidents, explosives, youth, crime prevention, tactical squads, marine/underwater units, and financial crime.

Within these complex and traditional bureaucratic organizations a major problem is internal communications. Ostensibly communication is effective and simple—that is, command-down. But command personnel are inevitably removed from the operational level, and with the specialization mentioned above, the police organization tends to stifle line initiative and to smother in paper. Policy statements, rules of conduct, and daily written orders and bulletins are the stuff of police management communications. Any flow of communication or information upwards in the hierarchy is formalized, and paper-oriented in the form of formal requests and reports (Adamson, 1987:243).

OPERATIONS

In the complicated police organization, much time is devoted to administering the elaborate system, including dealing with the paperwork and court time. Responding to calls for service, most of which are not crime related, is also very time consuming. Random patrol allows for rather more preventive work and police-initiated actions. The bulk of police time is engaged in patrol and other non-purposeful activity. The third main type of police work, besides administration and "random patrol," is detective work. The patrol officers, the anonymous persons in automobiles—are the first line of contact with the public and with offenders. They are usually the first on the scene at accidents, crimes, or calls for help. Yet their tasks are viewed as the least prestigious, the bottom of the pecking order, the assignment for rookies and for dead-end older constables.

Patrol personnel are organized into watches that operate for eight-hour, ten-hour, or twelve-hour shifts in four- or five-day weeks. Longer shifts result in briefer weeks. The patrols work zones or areas, but tend not to have stable assignments; location and shift time will vary. With some ad hoc adjustments, the personnel size of the watches is the same, despite variations in demand with the time of day or week, and there is no identification of personnel with a district, even though there may be some stability of assignment. In effect, one can think of cars rather than personnel that are assigned, and the assignment consists not of working as part of the district or community, but as being in a position to respond.

With the current emphasis upon community policing (see Chapter Ten), there is some attempt to "empower" the patrol officer, and to reduce the numbers of junior officers as found in traditional police organization. Officer rank positions, traditionally associated with the powerful tradition of top-down supervision, are reduced, and hands-on non-commissioned supervisors (sergeants) are increased. In Edmonton there has been some "flattening" of the police hierarchy with community policing, with the gradual phase-out of persons of Inspector rank. By 1995 in Edmonton, the personnel distribution included the chief, 2 deputy chiefs, 11 superintendents, 2 inspectors remaining to be phased out, 42 staff sergeants, 104 sergeants, 138 detectives, and 815 constables.

Detective work, on the other hand, is desired by most police officers, at least within the traditional centralized paramilitary force. It allows personal discretion, in the sense of relative freedom from supervision, and also the romance of crime busting. It is, however, second-stage policing, the most reactive of front-line police work. Detective work can itself be subdivided, with general investigation detectives, and others specializing in major crime, narcotics, morality, etc., yet research has repeatedly suggested that detective work is not especially effective. American research such as that of Niederhoffer (1967) and Reiss (1971), and especially the still controversial RAND Corporation investigation of 1975, has been tentatively corroborated in Canada by Ericson's work (1981b). It has also been suggested that detectives in collaboration with immediate superiors can control their selection of work, favouring those cases that are more likely to be cleared, and thereby can in a sense regulate and define crime—what Ericson calls "making crime" (Ericson 1981b:vii–viii).

Also featured in the operations of modern police organizations are special task groups, selected from other duties for temporary or extended work. Most prominent and prestigious among these have been tactical units, highly skilled in weapons use and negotiations, to be employed in crisis circumstances. Similarly, crowd control units may train for deployment. Their origins are probably in the experience of urban unrest in 1960s United States, especially Detroit and Los Angeles. Regular police appeared ineffectual, and combat-like units were subsequently invented. Members of these units, when not on response, will serve on regular patrol. "Tac units" are obviously reminiscent of the paramilitary character of policing, and it is a curious irony that they are thriving at the very moment that police services profess a commitment to community policing. The skills that they value, and their equipment, are exceedingly aggressive. Research in the United States suggests that since they have been put in place, they are used whether genuinely needed or not, supplanting regular police officers in routine activities, from preventive patrol to serving warrants—and conveying quite the opposite impression intended by community police officers (Kraska and Cubellis, 1997).

Another form of investigative unit, sometimes a permanent unit with fixed assignments or with persons temporarily assigned, are internal investigation or professional standards units. Their task is to investigate allegations of police misconduct. Unlike prestigious tactical units, professional standards is not often a welcome task.

At the margins of the police structure one sometimes finds police forces employing auxiliaries, or "specials." These semi-trained persons are civilian volunteers, unpaid and unarmed persons engaged in law enforcement under the supervision of the professional police. They are, therefore, in a weak sense, the modern heirs to the original concept of constables selected by the community (Willet and Chitty, 1982:188–189), although in fact the community today has little to say in their selection or training. In 1982, only 27 Canadian police forces operated auxiliary units. These included small as well as large forces, such as the OPP. That there were not more is probably attributable, at least in part, to opposition from police unions.

An auxiliary is an unpaid force, as in Toronto. The Toronto auxiliary force was formed in 1956 and was intended to be mobilized in disaster situations (*Toronto Star*, May 4, 1986). A special is an employee with a career line that does not extend into regular policing, as in the RCMP. They are persons with limited duties and lower qualifications and are often selected for their special characteristics, such as native status. They are called upon to perform a limited range of tasks associated with policing, such as patrol, crowd control, and searches. One also finds trainees or cadets serving as probationary police, a longstanding practice in Metro Toronto.

CENTRALIZATION

The specialized roles within police forces have been associated with the increased size and centralization of modern police operations. Students of the history of policing have remarked on the shift from the early conception of the local constable, a person acting for the community or some subset of the community, to the full-time paid employee responsible to central political authority rather than directly to the community members. Stenning's (1981a) survey of policy statutes in Canada outlines the shift to political bureaucratic control in Canada, right from the inception of the nation.

More than two decades ago, in one of the most influential books on Canadian policing, Brian Grosman wrote that "the more highly centralized the police becomes, the more it precludes consultation with minority groups prior to initiating policies." He went on to remark on associated impediments to good community relations, such as policy inflexibility, and a general non-responsiveness to a democratic public (Grosman, 1975:53). Yet, up until approximately the last decade, police and public bodies alike chose to ignore these basic considerations.

Since approximately the end of World War II, policing in Canada has become very centralized in its delivery of service to the public. From their inception, as we have seen, the police have been characterized by a paramilitary structure, with rigid hierarchy of command and rank that restrict the autonomy of the police officer in operation at the street level (Martin, 1982:101). In the nature of policing, however, with the basic service delivered by individual officers and not by large military-like units, the centralization inherent in the military model was moderated. The individual police officer exercised discretion, and often there was little or no opportunity to refer a decision to a superior.

Improved radio communications and the automobile, however, were seized upon by police commanders as a means of reimposing control. Now police in the streets were in continuous contact through a dispatcher with the chain of command. In fact, the command is still not as rigidly top-down as is intended. But the great size of the urban territories to be patrolled relegated the street police officer to the car, his connection to the command structure.

The move to the car appeared to eliminate the need for numerous local stations, which were, literally, within walking distance of the policeman on the beat. This went along with a movement towards greater efficiency and increased administrative control, and perhaps, as in the United States, a desire to segregate police from local communities where they were presumed to be susceptible to corruption (Kelling, 1986:12). In the postwar period virtually every major police force in Canada centralized, the most visible expression of this trend being a large central, physical location, and the merger region-wide of smaller services.

In Ontario, the Ontario Police Commission, guided by cost-efficiency criteria, concluded that in all cities of 500 000 or less, a single headquarters was desirable (*Ottawa Citizen*, August 11, 1982). Consequently, where officers had previously been known personally to the area's residents or businesses, they now became anonymous, and would be dispatched anywhere in the large urban area, rarely disembarking from their automobile to establish benign human contacts.

With urbanization, the number of offences, especially violent crime, increased, driving the need for larger police services and higher spending (Victor, 1977:199–206). More crime, and rising costs, suggested that policing must go "big," and realize economies of scale. Unification of several urban and suburban forces characterized Canada's two largest urban centres, Toronto and Montreal. Even smaller cities, however, judged such amalgamation and physical and administrative centralization as cost effective and operationally efficient. In the city of Ottawa, for example, as recently as the mid-1970s, the city considered the relative advantages of centralization, and elected to build a new police headquarters for the entire city rather than local offices. In an internal paper, a staff superintendent described American attempts at decentralization as failures, and argued in favour of the economies and the increased administrative control offered by centralization (Clarkin, 1979:10, 16). Foot patrol was viewed as "a thing of the past," and personal contacts between police and citizens, as opposed to telephone contacts, were viewed as of slight importance. Between the lines was the message that decentralization diminished the internal bureaucracy, and left the organization more open to the influences of the local publics.

In 1976 an Ottawa–Carleton commission of enquiry headed by a Carleton University political scientist captured the mood of the period by promoting centralization, which was being expressed in Ontario not only in Metro Toronto (prior to 1957 each of the municipalities had its own police force [Cooper, 1981:43; Beare, 1985]) but in the creation of regional police forces across the province. Considering the one area of the province managing to successfully resist regionalization, the Ottawa area, the Mayo Commission report urged amalgamation, for cost reasons, of the Ottawa, Vanier, Gloucester, Nepean, and Rockcliffe Park policing operations (Ontario, 1976:3–4). Eventually, in the late 1980s, the Vanier police were incorporated into the Ottawa City Police Force, but Rockcliffe Park retained OPP services, and Nepean and Gloucester, soon chartered as cities, retained independent and in many ways innovative police service. Rather than succumb to regional centralization, the surrounding jurisdictions maintained their own distinctive police forces, generally operated at lower cost levels than Ottawa. Coordination was nonetheless achieved among the forces for operational needs, as for example, with an Ottawa–Carleton regional drug squad consisting of members from the police forces of Ottawa, Nepean, Gloucester, the RCMP, and the OPP. But by the mid-1990s, regionalization of police services was finally imposed in the Ottawa metropolitan region.

Generally throughout the country, in urban/suburban areas, the dissolution of smaller police forces and the merger of services has been a persisting trend. Even rural areas are part of the tendency; through an area of Western Quebec, proximate to Ottawa, Canada's first regional rural police force began operating in 1997. Sometimes the loss of a local police service has been replaced by a contract with the RCMP or the OPP. For example, in 1997, a troubled independent police service in Hawkesbury, Ontario was replaced by the OPP. Or, sometimes even local contract services have been folded into larger regional conglomerates.

There is generally perceived to be economy of scale in the merging of smaller forces into large conglomerates. As the "metro" concept prevailed in urban government, so local police forces were merged into larger entities. In Montreal opposition petitions were presented opposing the closing of an old downtown station (formerly Station 10, made famous in a National Film Board documentary); similarly, opposition in the suburbs was expressed to the proposed closing of another station. A local mayor estimated that closing a substation saved approximately $50 000 in the first year alone, while the opponents stressed the need for local "physical presence" of police (Montreal *Gazette*, June 7, 1983).

With increased size and centralization came more specialized functions and units. The police generalist gave way to a more elaborate and bureaucratized command hierarchy and to specialized task-oriented units. These units attracted the senior—and presumably best—personnel, while street-level activity was left to less senior officers or those not on the fast track. At the bureaucratic level, planning units, research units, record units, etc., were inaugurated; at the service level, youth divisions, morality, homicide, underwater, traffic, accident, and a plethora of other sections came to be normal (Juliani et al., 1984:363).

An associated feature of centralization and automobile dependency has been the pseudo-professionalism of police, that is, a distancing supposedly related to professional expertise. In contrast to amiable, routine contacts with people, contacts are formalized, and usually occur in situations of difficulty or crisis for a citizen. A striking example is a regulation that was reported to apply to Toronto police. "Members shall not unnecessarily engage in conversation with any person while on duty which may result in neglect of duty" (*Toronto Star*, May 13, 1985). This imposed reserve is in large part what some police forces are now seeking to alter when they engage in forms of community-based policing.

As the number of police in Canada grew, therefore, they become, ironically, more remote and less visible to the public. The police officer became a distant crime fighter, not an agent of social service and social order. There was no effective interpersonal contact between the police officer and the citizen as the police officer disappeared into the automobile; reciprocal stereotyping was thereby allowed to flourish.

Members of the public notice foot patrol, with a consequent perception of security and confidence. Motor patrol is not noticed. "(I)f you increase or decrease the number of foot patrol officers, citizens recognize it immediately. If you increase or decrease the level of motor patrol, citizens generally don't have much sense of that police presence" (Kelling, 1986:15–16). Citizen fear versus confidence, and satisfaction versus dissatisfaction with police, varies with the visible police presence, and visibility is not effectively found in motor patrol. Further, as Kelling notes, the greater satisfaction occurs irrespective of the gender or race of the police officer. Motor patrol may shorten response time, but it does not satisfy the public.

Ironically, not only the public, but the police often prefer the foot service, for many of the same reasons, such as the opportunity for familiar contacts. Four police officers in the MUC Police, working out of affluent Westmount, were placed on the beat and declared that "it beats driving along in a prowl car." One constable went on to observe that "When you're in a car, you can't stop to take the time to get out and meet the store owners and citizens. You become isolated and out of touch" (Montreal *Gazette*, October 29, 1980).

Small towns as well as cities have been victims of the rise in costs and the response of centralized police service. As costs rose, with local police seeking comparable salaries to their big-city counterparts, towns across Canada began to give up their local police and contracted out to the provincial forces or the RCMP. The RCMP provided a prestigious and highly trained contingent of personnel, but also one immune to local politics and police unions, and susceptible to some cost-inefficiencies typical of the huge federal government bureaucracy. They also offered the backup of specialized services lodged in the larger national force.

This was, however, a mixed blessing. Sometimes the local force was utterly incompetent, and too often incorrect and abusive, with ill-trained personnel and too much power. On the other hand, sometimes the local police, perhaps working part time, were dedicated and competent, thoroughly familiar with the community, and capable of settling problems in a low-key manner.

Once towns gave up their local police, they did certainly notice a decline in visible police presence. Rightly or wrongly, the public have associated this centralization with a decline in the quality of police services. People have probably always complained about poor police service, but there seems little doubt that as police became more remote from residents, with urbanization, centralization, and vehicle dependency, the public's sense of collaborative relations with the police diminished. As centralization was achieved, people objected and resisted. In Ottawa, for example, when the last remaining substation was slated for closure in 1982, local businesses and residents complained strenuously, albeit to no avail (*Ottawa Citizen*, April 11, 1982). A short while after Vanier (a small city in the greater Ottawa area) implemented a cost-saving decision to have Ottawa police service the city, which had hitherto operated its own small force, residents complained of the non-visibility of police service. Although the mayor conceded no increase in problems or crime (in fact there was a decline), she remarked that personal contacts and confidence in police had diminished, and she sought increased patrols, preferably on foot, and a local satellite or storefront police station (*Ottawa Citizen*, February 2, 1989).

Consolidation and centralization, therefore, along with dependence on technology, have removed police officers from their communities. In an analysis of British policing Cain contrasted rural, small town, and urban policing. She had identified clear differences in policing style and attitudes associated with community intimacy. Rural police officers depended upon the residents, were knowledgeable of them, and friendly with them. The town police officers, especially when they were inexperienced outsiders and had brief postings, were isolated from residents and distrustful of them and their supervisors. They were "no longer imbedded in the local community" (Cain, 1973:227). The urban police officer, finally, was characterized by a strong group solidarity, an us–them relationship to the public. Specialization and separation from the community created scant understanding and empathy with the public. This summarizes, in effect, the distancing of police from their public in Canada as policing became another "big" bureaucracy and was associated with non-local government.

The two most frequent public responses to remote modern policing and declining public confidence and security are the employment of private police, or the formation of citizen groups of vigilantes. In Calgary, for example, proposals arose from meetings between police and dissatisfied citizens to form citizens' groups to patrol public areas (*Globe and Mail*, September 3, 1979).

Victim surveys in Canada have identified a perception of threat or fear of crime that seems clearly to be out of proportion to events, or even to the quality of police service. In particular, women and seniors express vulnerability and fear. In the United States, a survey found that 79% of 1101 women aged 18 to 35 approved of vigilante groups. They expressed the view that such groups did a better job in responding to crimes such as drug abuse and street violence. A large proportion, 45%, approved of illegal acts to curtail criminals (*Ottawa Sun*, November 17, 1988). Leaving aside, therefore, the question of actual police service and its quality, there is reason to believe that there is a perception problem that leads the public to dissatisfaction and attempts to correct the situation by resorting to measures other than police assistance. For example, in Goulbourn, a semi-rural bedroom suburb of Ottawa, municipal spokesmen expressed frustration with the quality of OPP service. In response to a vandalism problem, and failing in their demand for a more visible OPP presence in their community, the municipality pondered forming a citizens' group to patrol and protect the community (*Ottawa Citizen*, May 4, 1985).

In the Montreal area, increased violations, such as break-ins, have been attributed to the loss of local police and local police stations. The 1972 integration of 29 local police departments was largely justified on fiscal grounds, as a way to ensure that the suburbs shared equally in the costs of policing the metropolitan area. In Montreal, therefore, not only were area police forces merged organizationally, but local stations steadily closed. The local perception has been loss of control over police, loss of police visibility, and loss of service, especially in local by-law enforcement. One suburban mayor remarked in 1981 that in 1972 his city of Côte St. Luc paid $500 000 for policing, with five patrol cars. He estimated his city's costs in 1981 as $4.5 million, and went on to complain that "if we're lucky, we have one car on patrol." The suburban mayors therefore argued in 1981, with editorial support from the Montreal *Gazette*, that "limited local police forces" should be established since the MUC Force had not been able to protect the suburban communities (Montreal *Gazette*, June 14, 1981). Local Montreal communities have in fact reinvented their own local police by hiring private security firms to protect their communities in circumstances where they perceive that protection not to be properly delivered (Montreal *Gazette*, June 16, 1979). By 1985 as many as 13 of the municipalities had hired private security firms (Montreal *Sunday Herald*, January 13, 1985). These security personnel have very limited power, and are not authorized to enforce traffic regulations or to arrest people. But by 1987 at least nine area municipalities had passed motions asking the Quebec government for the right to have these personnel enforce traffic laws related to moving, as opposed to simple parking violations, with many also favouring powers of arrest (Montreal *Gazette*, March 28, 1987). Finally, in 1990 the MUC Police began experimenting with the introduction of local police stations.

Data published in the annual report of the MUC Police showed that the major crimes in the Montreal area in 1980 increased by 13.6%, but the police clearance rate sank to its lowest level since integration, one in every eight cases. Clearance dropped from 21% in 1971 to 14% in 1980 (Montreal *Gazette*, July 21, 1981). The statistics prompted comment by a criminologist, André Normandeau, who blamed bureaucratization and centralization for the decline in police performance, and advocated the establishment of "mini-stations" in every neighbourhood, and getting the police back out on the street. He also remarked upon a morale problem in the force, and the vigorous contention between the MUC Police Brotherhood and police management.

In order to amend performance, and perhaps also to increase middle-managerial control, the MUC chief attempted in 1979 to decentralize certain operations, with specialized personnel for homicide and robbery, for example, dispersed among stations rather than concentrated at headquarters. In doing so he encountered vigorous opposition from the Public Security Council (Montreal *Gazette*, May 19, 1982). The MUC Police Brotherhood had from the outset criticized the measures, and in 1980 released a special report that argued that attempts to decentralize within the overall structure of the MUC Police hindered police work because of poor coordination, and resulted in more crime (Ottawa *Sunday Express*, October 12, 1980).

In 1988, still contending with the problem, suburban mayors in the Montreal Urban Community indicated that they would welcome the creation of a cadet corps. These unarmed cadets would be trained by and attached to the MUC Police (Montreal *Gazette*, September 8, 1988). In addition to the cadet corps, the mayor contemplated an unarmed auxiliary corps, responsible for by-law and traffic enforcement. The police structure would become three-tiered, operating under the administrative responsibility of the MUC Police: the regular police, police cadets or apprentices, and police auxiliaries or parapolice. The proposal was made in the context of an agreement that MUC policing needed improvement, but the costs of additional regular police manpower would be too great (Montreal *Gazette*, September 12, 1988).

The proposal is reminiscent of the concept that emerged in the United States in the 1960s, when there was a generally perceived crisis within American policing. The President's Commission (1967), seeking a model that would render the structure of police organizations more congruent to, and therefore more responsive to, the structure of urban society, proposed a three-tier hierarchy, with the strata varying in qualifications, skills, and responsibilities. The idea was never implemented. Although many forces in the United States and in Canada use cadets and/or auxiliaries, the more elaborate stratification in the model suggested formidable career and organizational difficulties. In effect, a caste system would be created, with the parapolice relegated to limited career opportunities, much as troubled the RCMP special constables.

COMMUNITY-BASED POLICING

As centralization proceeded, police began to fear they were losing the fight against crime, and the public was less satisfied than ever. Police forces began to rediscover the notion of prevention and local community liaison. Community-based policing is the attempt by police forces to be less reactive, that is, to prevent offences and to stress service rather than to emphasize reaction to events after they have happened. This proactive or preventive policing is intended to reestablish police–community links. Since the 1960s there have been efforts to amend in some part the nature of policing, allowing police to prevent offences. The intention is not the old, simple objective of deterrence *per se*, but rather to take actions that remove the *occasions* of crime. Generally such measures involve some degree of community participation. To date, they have been attempted only in a marginal manner by police forces. Units devoted to community relations and prevention will have initiated "canned" programs such as Neighbourhood Watch, but have generally avoided strong collaborative organizational links with the public.

Since the 1970s, crime prevention, the original mandate of the public police, has again gradually become the fashionable ideology. The costly inadequacy of reactive policing in the face of crime, the expansion of the policing role to encompass a range of service functions that are not crime related, and public dissatisfaction with policing have generated a drive to return to the community. Several Canadian police forces, responding to academic and public criticism, and as always, influenced by American trends, began to respond to the real and the perceived problems of massive centralization. In effect, they sought to reintroduce local or community-based services within the overall organizational administrative structure of centralized policing. In 1976 the federal government inaugurated a "peace and security program" intended to encourage preventive policing in collaboration with police forces. A police officer was appointed as a consultant, working within the Ministry of the Solicitor General, to promote preventive measures nationally (*Liaison*, March 1977:15). Crime prevention was initially attempted in a manner that did not challenge traditional police organization and definitions of their work. Standardized prevention programs such as Neighbourhood Watch, Block Parents, and Operation Identification were initiated. Eventually, at a more sophisticated level, communities attempted to search the deeper problems and consult about them. Police awareness of environmental factors, the physical environment that communities created, was encouraged as police were advised of "defensible space" and the crime prevention aspects of neighbourhood design (Stanley, 1976; Moffat, 1981).

The entrenched bureaucracy did not allow genuine reorganization, but special programs were packaged and adopted across North America, intended both to reach into communities and elicit assistance, and to convey a proactive rather than reactive police attitude. Programs such as Block Parents, Neighbourhood Watch, property identification, target hardening (i.e., focussing upon a specific offence problem such as local drug abuse), sexual assault prevention, and environmental design, were in a sense the first generation of police community-oriented changes to ameliorate the effects of massive centralization.

Real amendment of centralized policing has been slow, for the changes had to occur within the context of the well-established and isolated organizational structure of traditional policing. The prevailing approach was to consider community relations as "public relations," often a low-prestige assignment and not integrated with other police service (Norris, 1973). Change-oriented organizations have been in the minority; perhaps the most successful have been in western cities such as Victoria and Calgary. Elsewhere, the changes were intentionally limited, and the pace generally controlled by the police. As Loree (1988:209) put it, "By virtue of their quasi-military, hierarchically structured and bureaucratic nature, police organizations have been reluctant to open the management and decision-making processes to those not of appropriate status." The complicated adaptation from a centralized, reactive, crime-oriented police organization to a localized, prevention-oriented police force probably must begin with management attitudes, and the leadership of the police chief in the still hierarchical police structure. But though change must originate at the top, it will not be successful unless the attitudes of street-level supervisors, the non-commissioned officers, also change to realign reward structures, community ties, service priorities, and overall policing ideologies (Loree, 1988; Deszca, 1988).

In the city of Toronto, community service officers were first appointed in 1967 and a Community Service Bureau in 1971 (Gandy, 1979:1–2). The police also participated in community committees on a trial basis. But the basic structure of reactive policing in the mammoth Metropolitan Toronto Police Force remained fundamentally unchanged, while society was changing rapidly about it,

In 1979 the RCMP established a Crime Prevention Centre to assist in community-based programs (RCMP, 1981:1). They also initiated a "police services community project" in the "typical" towns of Selkirk and The Pas, Manitoba, to develop techniques of preventive policing. The research program was generally intended to analyze local perceptions and needs related to policing, using police incident data, community surveys, and interviews. The objective was to identify problems that might then be addressed in police services. The findings did focus on some major community problems such as alcoholism, but also suggested a community "apathy" that would impede preventive programs. Significantly, the report of the Manitoba project illustrated the twofold obstacle to community-based police: on the one hand, police may resist, but the public may also be indifferent or resistant. For both, community-based policing requires information and activities to which they are simply not accustomed.

Through the 1980s the Canadian Police College in Ottawa has offered courses for municipal police in community-based policing and crime prevention. It employed a simulation, involving the fictional city of "Shebodan," where the course participants, working with offence report data and community data on problems, were required to devise a crime prevention program. In Montreal, the MUC Police have begun to attempt local neighbourhood contacts, despite a traditional and somewhat recalcitrant tradition, as a response to well-publicized public discontent. In Ottawa, the Ottawa Police Force, traditionally rather conservative and centralized, began in 1989 under a new chief to adopt community-policing measures, as rudimentary as four mini-stations in four distant geographical districts, under the command of inspectors, or as minor as introducing name tags to enhance the quality of police–public contact (*Ottawa Citizen*, January 6, March 12, 1990).

Another innovation attempted in several forces, such as in London, Ontario, and Vancouver, was to train teams in domestic crisis intervention. Reluctant police participation and low police regard for social workers impeded the programs. Working ties were difficult to maintain (Levens, 1978c). Training programs did, however, appear to moderate the negative attitudes and increase the rate of referral by police to other agencies (Dutton and Levens, 1976).

In Calgary, in the mid-1970s, the police implemented a program of counsellors in the schools. Each policing zone had at least one police officer assigned to high schools in that area. The police were in uniform, and they were available to participate in regular events, meet for private conversations, and generally be seen and contacted (*Liaison*, February, 1978:15–17).

Getting police officers out of their cars and into routine contact with citizens has also been a small part of the counter-centralization effort. It is not a popular practice, as it is viewed as costly and inefficient, despite longstanding research evidence of increased public satisfaction and greater probability of crimes being reported (Schnelle et al., 1975). Police managers, seeing foot patrol versus motor patrol as an all or nothing choice, resist foot patrol as time-consuming and impossible within the limits of their resources. Yet, of course, foot patrol and motor patrol are compatible, not only in the sense of mixing personnel, but in mixing the behaviour of the same personnel. A car can be parked, a walk completed, and motor patrol resumed. Such mixed patrols in Flint, Michigan have met with very favourable public response (Trojanowicz, 1986).

In 1986 the Ottawa Police Force announced that some constables would be walking daytime beats. The decision was taken, according to a police spokesperson, because of a "perceived need of the public to have a closer relationship with the police." He further stated that "We're encouraging these officers to get to know the merchants and the people who live in the vicinity" (*Ottawa Citizen*, April 14, 1986). Volunteers applied for the five new patrols in the downtown areas of the city. One constable remarked that "There's more contact with people in one morning on the beat than in a month in a car. It's like visiting friends all day long. You get the feeling you're accomplishing something" (*Ottawa Citizen*, May 16, 1987). Across the Ottawa River in Hull, Quebec, Hull Police reintroduced evening foot patrols on the downtown bar strip in 1986, with a consequence of immediate increase in arrests and reports of increased public confidence (*Ottawa Citizen*, March 17, 1986).

Foot patrol affords frequent opportunities for benign citizen–police encounters. There is, unfortunately, also reason to believe that foot patrol creates the illusion of more crime. Research literature suggests that a significant proportion of crime is not reported by victims or by observers. But foot patrol appears to increase the incidence of reported crime (Schnelle et al., 1975), presumably because of ease of contact and greater confidence in the police operations, and then higher rates of *reporting* are misconstrued as higher rates of *occurrence*.

A patchwork of changes has been associated with concepts such as proactive or preventive policing, team or zone policing, and community-based policing. They all involve some effort to amend the customary reactive, crime-response mode of police conduct.

There is an important distinction to be grasped. In genuine community-based team policing, the emphasis is upon the generalist, in the expectation that such police personnel can attend to most policing tasks and in doing so, within the context of community engagement, can maintain effective community relations. The alternative, one that attempts only marginal modifications, defines remote policing as the norm, and community relations personnel as just another form of specialist. As one widely used American text, purportedly a progressive text, suggests, community relations must not interfere with regular policing (Mayhall, 1984:1). Team policing, to the contrary, defines community relations, as contrasted to public relations, as the responsibility of all police personnel, and intrinsic to the police service.

Team or zone policing, a method used for community-based policing services, depends upon decentralization and de-specialization. Zones or sub-communities are identified, and police personnel are assigned responsibility for that area on a continuing and stable basis. Working with members of the community, and establishing better contact, the emphasis is upon identifying problem areas and preventing crime rather than reacting after the fact. As one guide put it, "Team policing is not a police–community relations program, yet police–community relations is one of the prime foci of team policing" (Basham, 1977:7). Coordination with other zone teams is maintained, as with a central command, although local zone commanders, often non-commissioned officers, are given considerable discretion. Specialist services from the larger organizations, like forensics, for example, are still available, but by and large the zone police officer has an almost total responsibility for events and cases, in contrast to the traditional model where the patrol officer would turn over a major crime to detectives (Wasson, 1975; Basham, 1977).

Wherever implemented, the process is gradual, with zones becoming operational over a few years' time. In Halifax, for example, a decision was taken in 1985 to move to a more decentralized zone model. Volunteers were selected, trained for several weeks at Dalhousie University, and the first zone came on stream in 1986, and two additional ones in 1987 (Clairmont, 1987:8). In the city of Toronto, which has Canada's largest metropolitan force, in 1982 the police began slowly and apparently with reluctance to develop and introduce elements of zone policing. Two areas of the city identified as having persisting policing problems, Parkdale and Jane–Finch, were targeted (Murphy and Lithopoulis, 1988:6, 8). A major six-volume report by Hickling-Johnson, a firm of management consultants, in 1983 recommended zone policing for Toronto.

Police in the city of Victoria altered their delivery of services with leadership from a chief who had for years been committed to team policing. Prior to his Victoria appointment, the chief had served in Ottawa under the aegis of the solicitor general, seconded while a sergeant on the Vancouver Police Force to act as a resource person on team policing. Committed to a thorough implementation of the concept, the Victoria Police delegated a constable to the city of Detroit to study the mini-station program that had been established there in 1974 (Walker and Walker, 1989:3–25). Starting with a succession of community meetings in Victoria and prompted by a Mayor's Task Force of businesspeople, the police moved to establish community mini-stations, with three in 1987 and an additional one in each of 1988 and 1989, plus a downtown office in the retail business district (*Liaison*, January 1989:7–9). They operate under the supervisory control of a sergeant in charge of the Community Services Section.

The Victoria program was begun with the aid of grants from the local business community and government. Through the period of implementation from 1980 on, police strength varied, but the system was developed with a force of approximately 150 sworn personnel, in a city of 5 distinguishable core neighbourhoods ranging from about 4000 people to 18 000 people each, and a total population of 64 700. City council approved the hiring of five new constables to meet the staffing demands of the new stations. Each station offers a crime prevention-oriented police service, with staff of 1 uniformed officer and 15 to 20 civilian volunteers who must complete a training course. All stations operate five days a week, although some also operate on Saturdays. Operations include routine telephone calls to seniors, and drug and alcohol abuse courses, with programs varying with local community needs.

Community-based policing places much more responsibility upon the individual police officer; there is less supervision than in traditional policing. For many police officers the job becomes more satisfying with this room for greater initiative. For some, though, the many demands in time and effort become unpalatable. Both reactions were observed by Clairmont (1987:18–20) in the Halifax program.

But increasingly through the 1980s, as community-based policing gradually came to be the progressive ideology of police personnel, closer police–public relationships were endorsed by police managers. As an Edmonton police inspector put it, "More than anything else, we have to start meeting normal people under normal circumstances on a regular basis. ... We must become students of the communities we live in" (Braiden, 1986:34–35). In effect, when people discuss the new localism and pluralism that should inform "modern" or "new" policing, as done quite explicitly in McDougall (1988a:1988b), what is being sought is some merger of current police organization and services with an earlier form of local constabulary.

When, in the 1970s, the Calgary Police Service (deliberately avoiding "Force" or "Department") implemented city-wide team policing, their chief, Brian Sawyer, spoke of a return to the original principles of policing. In a note in the annual report for 1977 he wrote of "going back to Robert Peel" and becoming a "people-oriented profession." The Service itemized several objectives or principles, such as "the basic mission ... to prevent crime and disorder." The cooperation of the public in the policing tasks, "impartial service," avoidance of force, and achievement measured by order and not by police actions, were included as the mandate and operational creed of the Calgary Police Service.

Productivity or effectiveness/efficiency measures in the traditional police force stressed police actions or "outputs," such as response times, man-hours on investigations, and clearance rates (Engsted and Lioy, 1978; Spring, 1984). An interesting illustration was the report of the auditor general of Canada on the RCMP (Canada, 1981:281–317), with its accounting/evaluation emphasis upon police responses relative to costs. In contrast, the model elaborated in Calgary and in other community-based systems sought to shift the emphasis: the police were to become truly part of the community, engaging in proactive measures that would be best measured in the *absence* of offences requiring charges. In a sense, police began to counter the cost-effectiveness pressure upon them, since the climbing costs of policing in the context of apparently high crime rates had, in any case, begun to deter rather than encourage increased public spending. With community-based policing, even in the absence of clear-cut efficiency measures of prevention, community satisfaction tends to increase, and with it, public willingness to accept policing costs.

It would be naive, however, to suggest that community-based policing and measures to increase police–citizen contact will correct all problems in policing. In fact, more frequent contacts, if mishandled, may exacerbate prejudices and problems. The research evidence is convincing that citizen attitudes towards police are greatly influenced by the quality of contacts (Klein et al., 1978). The polite and effective police officer, in frequent contact with citizens, will improve police–citizen relations. The impolite and ineffective police officer in more frequent contact will diminish the quality of citizen–police relations. The interaction effect also works with respect to police attitudes. Research findings demonstrate that more frequent contact with some minority groups, especially in the black ghettoes of the United States, adversely affect the police officer's views, whether the officer is white or black (Wilson, 1969:43; Black and Reiss, 1970:137–138).

Community policing, to be discussed further in Chapter Ten, can probably improve the quality of police–public relations. It is not rational to expect, however, that it can thoroughly transform policing. Large bureaucratic police organizations, responsible for massive geographic and population areas, are unlikely to decentralize sufficiently. Nor can all the occasions of police–public conflict be eliminated.

CONCLUSION

Policing in Canada comprises hundreds of distinct organizations, all delivering similar services within their bureaucratized structures. Police services are costly, and growing more so, as salaries and the numbers of police personnel increase. The post-World War II tradition of policing in Canada has been one of central organizational control, with police personnel detached from local community links. The police role, emphasizing law enforcement, has been remote from the general public, reinforced by a personnel composition that has been overwhelmingly white and male.

The prevailing military command style of operation, traditional conceptions of policing as primarily crime fighting, and the usual career paths are now seen to be ill-suited to modern demands. At present, there is a mounting pressure to diversify police composition, by gender and by ethnicity. And policing is being asked to be more community sensitive, with local contacts and some measure of local community control.

ANNOTATED READINGS, CHAPTER FOUR

Roberg, Roy and Jack Kuykendall. *Police Management* (2nd ed.). Los Angeles: Roxbury Publishing Co., 1997. This text has been used in courses at the Canadian Police College. It does convey a sense of police organizational complexity.

POLICE
UNIONS

*Police employee groups have had an important impact upon police
management, police–public relations, and of course, the nature and
the quality of the working environment of police officers. They are of
enormous importance and, arguably, growing more important. In this
chapter the activities and the influence of police associations are considered.*

The formal organization of police services and the occupation's peer subculture are parts of
the structure of policing. A third important element of police structure, affecting the formal organization, the police workplace, the media, and the general public is organized police employee groups. Police associations and unions exist everywhere in Canada, representing
rank-and-file officers, under-officers, and officers. In particular, associations of junior officers
have influenced the nature of police services and their public relations, and there is every indication that they will continue to do so in the future.

ORIGINS

Police unions are not new; they have existed through most of this century. The Vancouver
City Police Union, for example, has had a continuous history from the turn of the century.

The Toronto police were unionized in 1909 and went on strike in 1918 when several officers refused to give up union membership (Goldsmith, 1985). Police militancy, in fact, was to be found throughout the English-speaking democracies. Famous strikes occurred in Winnipeg, Boston, Liverpool, and Melbourne, all at about the same period, shortly after the conclusion of World War I. Police in the city of Winnipeg refused to work during the Winnipeg General Strike, forcing the government to use special police and the Northwest Mounted. In Melbourne, Australia, in 1923, local authorities, contending with striking police seeking better wages, were convinced of a "Bolshevist" element (Massingham, 1977:291), just as Canadian authorities had been convinced in 1919. In Britain in 1918, some police walked out in London and elsewhere, especially in Liverpool, striking for wages. As a consequence, a Police Bill was passed forming the still-existing Police Federation, a government-controlled employee body, and explicitly banning police unions (Manwaring-White, 1983:11). Similar reactions occurred in North America. The Boston Police Strike in 1919 was the American counterpart of the Winnipeg General Strike, with widespread fear of revolutionary change prompting government reaction (Russell, 1975). The Governor of Massachusetts, Calvin Coolidge, is viewed as having promoted himself to the American presidency on the basis of his reaction to the strike, having declared, "There is no right to strike against the public safety by anyone, anywhere, any time" (Maddox, 1975:10).

Although many police unions thereafter were subdued or suppressed, others persisted. The Americans effectively banned police unions and strike action after the Boston strike, for although employee organizations persisted, they were not affiliated with organized labour and not effectively reorganized until the 1940s (Gammage and Sachs, 1972:44–49), and more vigorously in the 1960s (Burpo, 1971:6; Halpern, 1974:6–14; Levi, 1977:7–8). Similarly, after the early experiences, in many Canadian jurisdictions the Police Acts did not allow unions, while provincial and federal police were bolstered as reliable backup to municipal police forces. Eventually, though, even the provincial police in Canada were granted effective association and collective bargaining rights. In fact, as especially evident in the case of the Ontario Provincial Police (OPP), this was seen as an aspect of modernization and building employee effectiveness and morale.

A major reorganization of the OPP took place in 1963, guided by a 1961 report prepared by Americans from the Traffic Institute of Northwestern University, "A Report to the Attorney General of Ontario on the development of a Police Traffic Supervision Program for the Ontario Provincial Police Force." The force was in some disarray, with morale problems and criticism following a lengthy enquiry of its "aiding and abetting" illegal gambling. The new commissioner, a lawyer with no police experience, set about implementing changes guided by the 90 recommendations of the Northwestern report. Most notably, recruit selection and training were improved, with some psychological testing and an increase in educational requirements. There was an expanded number of policing districts (17), with more decentralized command and 3 deputy commissioners. Merit displaced simple seniority for promotions, and more than 200 promotions were made in 1963 alone. Also in 1963, the government granted the Ontario Provincial Police Association collective bargaining rights. The association's first "memorandum of understanding" was achieved in 1968 (Higley, 1984).

The phenomenon of police employee groups, therefore, is not new and it is not peculiar to North America. In Western Europe most nations have unionized police, with the notable exception of Great Britain. Police strikes, too, are part of the European experience. In 1988, for example, the Belgian national police union called for a nation-wide strike. The strike began in Brussels and spread, with demands for improved salary, working conditions, and staffing (*Ottawa Citizen*, November 8, 1988). Other, more original forms of job action than the strike have also been employed by organized police in Europe. In Rotterdam, Holland, two police officers, a man and a woman, undressed in centre field during half-time of a soccer match to protest pay levels for police officers (*Ottawa Citizen*, November 14, 1988).

EMPLOYEE GROUPS

Today in Canada, virtually all police services follow industrial-style labour relations. The situation is different than in the United States. In the United States, although the police are the second most highly organized public sector employee group, some major city forces are still non-unionized (International Association of Chiefs of Police, 1977:42).

All significant police forces in Canada have employee organizations. Even provincial police forces in Ontario and Quebec are organized in employee groups, despite their historical role in opposition to organized labour. Rights to association even extend beyond the rank-and-file. Thus the Ontario Supreme Court ruled in 1987 that limits upon bargaining for the OPP were unconstitutional, thereby freeing junior officers to bargain (*Ottawa Citizen*, November 18, 1987).

Formally police employee groups are either unions or, more prevalently, associations. Whether unions or associations, both represent their members in negotiating elaborate collective agreements, thereby bargaining for wages and benefits, working conditions, and equipment. They also act to represent members in disputes. Grievance procedures specified in the agreements will proceed with employee association advice and representation, and they will also offer representational and financial support in misconduct enquiries. Additionally, police employee groups have financially supported members in civil and criminal court proceedings. Both unions and associations are acknowledged in provincial police acts, and if a union, in labour legislation. If a certified union, the group may choose to affiliate with a larger union body. Some American unionized police have been represented, for example, by the AFofL-CIO and by the Teamsters, but modern Canadian police unions have not done so, operating autonomously or in association with other police employee groups. Unions, unlike associations, may legally withdraw labour, that is, strike.

In Quebec the Association des policiers provinciaux du Québec argued unsuccessfully that they should be included under the labour code of Quebec on the grounds of the right of free association guaranteed in the Charter. The claim elicited a prompt editorial response from the Montreal *Gazette* (January 14, 1990), arguing that the police "are not ordinary workers" and that the right to strike would be "detrimental to the public interest." In part, probably, the brotherhood action was prompted by the government's determination to bring a code of ethics to govern police relations with the public under the authority of civilian review boards. The association had opposed the code as an infringement on their rights (Montreal *Gazette*, June 13, 14, 1989).

Municipal police associations are also affiliated in provincial umbrella associations that have been very effective in extending representation to smaller forces. This has been especially manifest, for example, in the activities of the Police Association of Nova Scotia (PANS), where numerous small associations have had the benefit of experienced bargaining advice. The provincial associations may also mobilize information sessions and media releases. The Police Association of Ontario holds an annual conference, dealing in issues such as management style and practices, women in policing, stress, bargaining, boards of enquiry, and virtually everything of current relevance to a police membership. With participants from not only provincial police associations but also government departments, law firms, universities, and usually a very healthy representation of interested senior police managers, the Association thereby seeks not only to inform, but to influence policies and administrative procedures.

There is also a national association, incorporated in 1953, loosely affiliated, but at least permitting exchange of contract information. The national association has, at times, been viewed as dominated by central Canada. In 1987 the Alberta Federation of Police Associations voted to withdraw from the Canadian Police Association, calling it a "social club" and charging that its lobbying with the federal government has not served western interests (*Ottawa Citizen*, December 15, 1987).

The single and significant exception to Canadian police unionism is the RCMP. Organizing efforts have been under way for at least three decades. A *Maclean's* Magazine article by a former mountie, Jack Ramsay, described low morale and stress-related problems such as alcoholism. He worked with the Public Service Alliance of Canada to win the right to unionize the RCMP. In 1974 RCMP members, including several disgruntled officers from the security service, met in Burnaby to attempt to gain support for an association. One night later the majority of Toronto-area RCMP officers attended a rally, and were addressed by the president of the Metro Toronto Police Association, Syd Brown. Interest in forming a union was expressed by 605 out of 620 voters, a vote that was itself illegal by virtue of a 1918 Order-in-Council prohibiting such association (Sawatsky, 1980:229–232). Eight days later, on May 10, RCMP members from Montreal, Toronto, and Ottawa met at the Ottawa Civic Centre, and were addressed by the person who had led the Montreal police out on illegal strike. The prohibition against association was discussed and condemned, and another vote taken, this urging repeal of the order by a vote of 1102 to 34. Since then, Quebec RCMP members have gone to court, unsuccessfully, to attempt to win the right to associate on a regional basis.

The force did react to discontent by creating in 1972 a system of division representatives, who gradually have attained some influence. At first the representatives were curtailed, sometimes even nominated by commanding officers. But by 1974, in the context of mass organizing meetings, meeting as a group in Ottawa for the third time the representatives found themselves with additional bargaining power. At that time a large pay increase, and the right to overtime pay was won. Just as pertinent, the representatives gained the right to represent members in discipline cases and grievances, and were placed on promotions and pay review boards. From this date the government has taken care to tag RCMP compensation to the levels of major municipal forces, thereby giving the RCMP the benefits of municipal bargaining (Sawatsky, 1980:234–237; Forcese, 1980). Moreover, within the division representatives system, members now have the right of formal grievance, a process that many managers in the Force deplore as no-cost opportunities by members to appeal everything.

The division representatives and the excellent compensation packages, as well as the national dispersion of the Force, have inhibited the persistent attempts at unionism, even as it became legally possible with the rescinding of the 1918 Order-in-Council in mid-1974. Union interest has, however, persisted. Since 1979 a loose national alliance known as the Association of 17 Divisions has sought support, with success in the large urban areas where the Force is employed, especially Montreal and Vancouver. In these locations, RCMP personnel were able to compare salaries, benefits, and working conditions with those of municipal police, and judged that they were in the unfavourable position. But these two sites have never brought the association near the requisite 50% of members needed for certification.

Several officers involved in the organizing efforts complained in 1985 that management had resorted to unfair labour practice, having been engaged in surveillance of their efforts since 1979 (*Ottawa Citizen*, October 10, 1985). In 1986 about 90% of the officers in the Quebec Division ("C" Division) of the RCMP, about 800 police, were signed up for accreditation. Ultimately the Canada Labour Relations Board, reconfirming the concept of an essential national service, turned down their application (Montreal *Gazette*, June 9, September 5, 1986). Members resorted to court challenge, and in 1989 were again unsuccessful in a bid to organize only Quebec when the Quebec Superior Court ruled that they had no guaranteed right, as they had argued, under the Charter to unionize (Montreal *Gazette*, December 1, 1989). The dispersed policing of the RCMP makes effective organizing and unionism all but impossible.

The issue of an RCMP union persists, as does the Association of 17 Divisions, and management resistance. The president of the Association of 17 Divisions, following his election as mayor of a small municipality in Quebec, has been in court over a suspension and damage claims, while implying that he has been treated severely because he is actively promoting an RCMP union (*Ottawa Citizen*, December 26, 1997). In 1996 a Parti Québécois Member of Parliament raised the issue in the House. He remarked that RCMP members are protected neither by the Labour Code nor by the Public Service of Canada Act. He went on to query their inability to form an association or union, and to bargain collectively. A government spokesman replied by way of claiming that the Divisional Staff Relations system in the RCMP was sufficiently effective. The exchange elicited, somewhat curiously, the favourable comment of the *Ottawa Sun* newspaper, expressing the view that police unions have been shown to be desirable. That is, said the *Sun*, they have been an effective lobby in favour of tougher laws dealing with crime (*Ottawa Sun*, October 9, 1996).

In general the dispute over RCMP unionism has divided members. Many RCMP officers explicitly prefer the absence of a union, considering it more "professional." They also may acknowledge the benefit of a divisional representative system that does not cost them dues, as the costs of the system are met by the Force. Moreover, in some sense, as the divisional representatives, management, and Treasury Board maintain the RCMP salary and benefits at the same level as those of other major police services, RCMP members bargain off the coattails of other associations. This last consideration may be pleasing to some, but displeasing and demeaning to some RCMP members, and a matter of irritation to other police associations.

Some RCMP members, and other associations, also find the large absence of the RCMP in the police union movement to inhibit lobbying and political action. RCMP members do not have in the divisional representative system the same degree of member representation and defence in matters of working conditions, internal regulatory procedure, and discipline. In 1997, for example, when a member was accused of leaking information in the airbus enquiry associated with former Prime Minister Mulroney (the member eventually negotiated a resignation) and was subject to internal hearings (intended to be confidential, but successfully challenged in court by the *Ottawa Citizen*), there was no union to offer assistance. Rank-and-file members were left to organize fundraising for the member's defence.

UNION–MANAGEMENT RELATIONS

While the RCMP has thus far resisted unionism, management attempts to prevent employee associations in other Canadian police forces failed. Not only did police organize, they appeared to catch police managers and police commissions ill prepared. The initial period of modern police unions in Canada was marked by complaints of lost command prerogatives.

During the late 1960s and 1970s, police unions appeared to have a bargaining advantage; they were better prepared and more aggressive than employers. Many police chiefs found it difficult to adjust to an industrial-relations style where they had been accustomed to a military tradition of command and deference (Jackson, 1980; Forcese, 1980).

Consequently, there persists a prevalent opinion among police managers and their civilian authorities that there has been a loss of management control. Police associations are perceived to have seized initiatives and diluted effective control of police organizations. For example, Metro Toronto named a chief whom the commissioners believed would be tough with the police association, and in so doing passed over an experienced and renowned candidate (*Toronto Star*, July 21, 1989).

In the traditional police force, whatever the resentments, the chief was a final court of no appeal. Police unions have obliged the chief to work in a world of management like other modern organizations, still powerful but not unchallenged. An aspect of that challenge is police union use of the media and public opinion. In Ottawa, the Police Association was thought to dislike a change-oriented chief of police, and has periodically cued the press and the public. In 1997, for example, the association objected to the chief's investigatory procedure in alleged misconduct involving a deputy chief. The association made the internal proceedings a public issue. Similarly, in Western Canada, disputes between the police associations and senior management—apparently over reform policies—have been conspicuous in Edmonton and in Winnipeg. In Winnipeg, for example, a chief of police committed to community policing, like the Ottawa chief, has met with public opposition and hostility from the association.

A major consequence of police unionism has been a deterioration in the command-like administrative authority of police managers. The unions have ensured that they have the means to influence department policy. Most basically, they effect department budget by wage-bargaining. But they also have influenced the disposition of personnel, and the sanctions imposed upon police officers. In addition, the unions have politicized policing by offering public comment on issues and political personalities. They have therefore assumed some of the role traditionally the prerogative of the chief, to represent the force publicly. There are instances, too, when police unions have intervened to improve the quality of police service. The police union in James Bay, Quebec, appealed to the Minister of Justice to investigate police misconduct on the force, from theft to the maltreatment of native peoples. The union claimed that the James Bay Power Company and higher officers in the 11-person force had interfered in the conduct of policing but had not properly supervised policing (Montreal *Gazette*, May 31, 1986).

Unions have rather often publicly criticized their superiors. The Montreal Urban Community (MUC) Police Brotherhood in particular has been consistently in conflict with its management, even when not bargaining on a contract. They have frequently defied or subverted management policy commands, and have been publicly outspoken in their disdain of superior officers. In the later seventies the brotherhood sought an amended shift schedule, and unilaterally implemented their preference. They also vigorously opposed a reassignment of detectives to area stations to work alongside uniformed personnel, a management response to a poor crime-solution rate. Rank-and-file resentments were very evident during the 1970s, associated with the appointment of police directors whom many believed were not the most appropriate within the organizations. In 1979 the police director claimed that the brotherhood had been "sabotaging" his efforts to change and to improve the force (Montreal

Gazette, September 8, 1979). In 1981, following the excessive use of force in the referendum night demonstrations, the director of the brotherhood testified before a police commission enquiry that there was a "defective distribution of orders" to the riot squad (Montreal *Gazette*, July 23, 1981). The union spokesman went on to suggest that if a recommendation to disband the squad was implemented, the brotherhood would "react" (*Ottawa Citizen*, July 23, 1981). When management determined to eliminate the MUC Police ambulance service in 1982, the brotherhood was aggressively opposed. It attempted a billboard advertising campaign dramatically advocating the service, but was denied billboard rentals by the Toronto-based billboard monopoly, which was accused by the brotherhood of fearing reprisals from the city (Montreal *Gazette*, February 9, 1982). Following a damaging delay in sending in riot control police following a Stanley Cup victory celebration in 1986, the president of the brotherhood publicly criticized management (Montreal *Gazette*, May 29, 1986). In 1988, 75% of brotherhood members, that is, 3338 police, signed a letter stating loss of confidence in the director of police. The action arose out of the race relations problems experienced by the MUC Police, and what the brotherhood described as the director's "near-neurotic concern with public relations." The brotherhood suggested the director was non-cooperative and adversarial, and had acted in disregard of the welfare of his employees in order to placate an irate public (*Ottawa Citizen*, August 6, 1988).

To take another example: in 1979 the Moncton Police Association, in explicit opposition to their chief, opposed the implementation of team policing, submitting an elaborate brief to the mayor and city council. In the city of Moncton the police association has been in prolonged opposition to the chief. In 1987 they passed a motion of non-confidence, in the context of a longstanding controversy over the chief's alleged misconduct in a restaurant disturbance (Montreal *Gazette*, November 27, 1987).

Other than in the RCMP, what police managers and politicians think of as the "good old days" of rigid paramilitary command have been drastically and irrevocably altered. Yet there are still efforts to limit the power of police employee groups. As we have remarked, many jurisdictions do not grant in law the right of police employees to withdraw their services as part of the process of collective bargaining or grievance resolution. On the questionable assumptions that police strikes endanger the public, and that prohibition of strikes can prevent withdrawals of service, policing is often defined as an essential service. Where the right to strike exists, frequently the government will intervene to prevent the strike. In New Brunswick, for example, twice in the period of one week in May, 1985, the provincial cabinet ordered police not to strike. In Moncton, and then in Saint John, the government in effect withdrew the right to strike, and imposed binding arbitration following a mandatory period of bargaining (*Ottawa Citizen*, May 19, 1985). In Regina, when a strike threatened in 1988, the legislature passed a bill requiring the parties to return to the bargaining table. Although the Regina police union has the right to strike, in 1988, legislators, mindful of disruptions in a 19-day 1976 strike, argued that since the current dispute was over the choice of an arbitrator, the parties should be required to reconvene (Montreal *Gazette*, May 21, 1988).

JOB CONTROL

In any organization, unions affect the relative control of the working conditions enjoyed by employees. So too in policing. In some part, therefore, this has meant maintaining the status quo, jobs and shifts as they have been in the past. Innovations, unless they are technological innovations, have often been resisted, seen as top-down. And often, in fact, they have been top-down. While police associations have been accused, for example, of resisting community policing, it is also the case that community policing (see Chapter Ten) has often been ill conceived by police managers, used as a device for economies, and not introduced on a collaborative and negotiated basis.

With police unions, police administrators found themselves having to deal with personnel less compliant with senior officers. Matters as fundamental as shifts and even unit organization became the concern of the employee organization. Non-compliant individuals are represented and protected by their union, and the union itself might seek to shape policy. This is illustrated with a decision by a Winnipeg police constable, supported by the association, to refuse to work on grounds that a personnel shortage was creating hazards to his safety. Described as "a first in Canada," the officer and the association cited the province's Workplace Safety and Health Act as granting the right to refuse dangerous work, the danger in this instance created by shortfalls in patrols (Montreal *Gazette*, July 19, 1989). Following the deaths of two OPP officers in 1983 and 1984, for example, the association argued unsuccessfully that the deaths in isolated rural areas were the consequence of an outmoded radio-communications system. Meeting with no improvements, they leaked their documentation of complaints to the press in 1986 (*Toronto Star*, February 26, 1986).

In the Ontario town of Hawkesbury, the police association had for many years publicly criticized the local police board and town council, arguing that insufficient funding had been provided for training and equipment. While it may be said that the dispute brought the force into disrepute, the association had a point. Claiming that officers' lives were in danger, the association won an Ontario Solicitor General Office's audit of the force. The subsequent finding, consistent with the association complaint, was in fact that there had been serious underfunding of basic police support. The association campaign culminated in a decision to have the town policed by the OPP, who agreed to employ former Hawkesbury police officers (*Ottawa Citizen*, October 24, 1997). With this policing contract, local police board and town council influence was reduced, and in fact, all but eliminated.

Like all unions, police associations have acted to protect the jobs of members as well as to improve their compensation and working conditions. Thus, for example, police unions have been opposed to any efforts to create parapolice or to delegate policing tasks to non-police personnel. When the mayor of Kingston, Ontario, proposed hiring civilians to deal with traffic, including speeding, thereby freeing police officers for other tasks, the Metro Toronto Police Association was quick to comment that it was a bad idea, ostensibly because the speeding violation often turns up dangerous offenders (*Toronto Star*, May 7, 1985).

In defending their employees' interests, unions have prevented measures that police managers might otherwise have employed to reduce operating costs. Once jobs traditionally assigned to police officers are protected by contract, they are difficult to transfer later to less costly civilian employees or to volunteers. Even a force such as the OPP, which has traditionally employed volunteers or auxiliaries, found itself contending with a union demand to enforce a contract prohibition on auxiliaries accompanying officers in cars after 10 p.m. (*Ottawa Citizen*, April 10, 1987). The provincial association head opposed auxiliaries as "cheap labour," and as "taking the bread from our mouths" (*Ottawa Journal*, August 22, 1980).

Significant in police association efforts has been defence of its members. Police officers had always been subject to relatively unfettered command discipline, often relating to violations of administrative rules of conduct as much as improprieties involving the public.

Police unions have been able to check what appeared often to be arbitrary discipline. Additionally, it may be said, they have been effective in supporting officers in more recent circumstances of public or civilian-based enquiries.

In Quebec, the president of the provincial umbrella organization of municipal associations, the Féderation des Policiers du Québec, opposed the practice of public hearings by the Quebec Police Commission, on the grounds that public hearings into alleged misconduct harmed the reputation of the police. In Manitoba, the Winnipeg Police Association went to court to block an enquiry from reopening a case that had ruled the fatal shooting of a native to be accidental (Montreal *Gazette*, February 13, 1989).

In another prominent case, the Police Brotherhood of the MUC Police supported a constable who was eventually dismissed following his shooting of a young black man. The brotherhood publicly criticized the dismissal as bowing to public pressure. It did not manage to reverse the decision (although reinstatement was later ordered) however, and was left to organize a modest financial fund to aid the dismissed colleague (*Ottawa Citizen*, July 9, 1988). About one-half year later, when the director of police announced his retirement, among those praising him was the president of the brotherhood. When reminded of his earlier criticisms, and especially the letter stating the loss of confidence over the constable's dismissal, the brotherhood president remarked that the disagreement was "all part of the game" (Montreal *Gazette*, January 20, 1989).

In "playing the game" the MUC brotherhood has been very aggressive, not only outspoken in its criticisms but brash in its implementation of or resistance to measures over the orders of senior management. A basis for the brotherhood's power has been its comprehensive character, including in its membership not only rank-and-file police officers but also those of supervisory ranks. In 1989, of 4500 police officers in all ranks, only 64 were excluded from the union (Montreal *Gazette*, January 26, 1989).

In 1989 Quebec police unions joined in forming a watchdog committee to protect the rights of members in response to disciplinary procedures and public criticisms. They were particularly concerned with the prevalent practice of suspensions without pay in instances of alleged offence. The unions stated that they would be closely attending to appointments to the civilian review boards due to come into place in Quebec, replacing the older police commissions (Montreal *Gazette*, January 24, 1989).

BARGAINING AND ARBITRATION

Everywhere in Canada police employee groups bargain with civic officials for their salaries. Even very small-town police usually have the bargaining representation of a provincial umbrella group, such as the Police Association of Nova Scotia. The RCMP is a kind of exception. As previously remarked, the Force has not unionized, and instead works with elected division representatives. These representatives now have a real role in dealing with the federal Treasury Board over salaries. Treasury Board, for its part, in the 1970s struck a salary level for the RCMP that has been pegged to the salaries of other major municipal police forces in the country. They worked to a weighted average of the OPP, Sûreté, Calgary, Edmonton, Montreal, Toronto, and Winnipeg police salaries. The RCMP remained competitive as they "piggybacked" on other forces' wage settlements.

The major municipal forces and the two large provincial forces all monitor salary con-tracts, and in their bargaining, take care to keep pace. Montreal and Toronto, especially, bargain against one another's contract advantage.

Most observers of labour relations favour arbitrated awards, allowing settlements to be reached (imposed in the case of binding arbitration) without job action and the associated dis-ruption. Arbitration may also be used to find a solution where a strike is already under way. In policing, where usually the employees do not have the right to strike, arbitration has been the favoured resolution mechanism. Increasingly, however, arbitrators' awards have been criticized by public representatives and management as excessive. Often, too, the arbitrator makes awards, with cost implications, that have to do with working conditions and not with salaries, arguably in the absence of any real knowledge of policing. In Toronto, for example, an arbi-trator's award secured two-officer patrols for the Metro Toronto police even when the union did not particularly want it. The consequences for the city were increased personnel needs and costs. In Quebec, the Quebec Union of Municipalities meeting in 1982 urged the right to strike for policemen, in the view that dealing with strikes would be preferable to having to accept arbitrated awards they saw to be unreasonable. Quebec police officers, naturally, were quick to react by rejecting the suggestion (Montreal *Gazette*, September 25, 1982).

In general, one would find that police employee groups have done rather well from ar-bitration awards. Yet some police union representatives have also expressed suspicion and dis-like for arbitration. In Ontario, police regret having arbitration regularly invoked, finding that it denies them the "big hammer," the strike. In the Halifax strike of 1981 the union leader asked for provincial legislation, but did not want arbitration. In Winnipeg, in 1988, an arbi-tration panel awarded a two-year contract that carried an 8.8% salary increase, raising the annual salary of a first-class constable to $41 000. Yet the police were dissatisfied, and threat-ened a work slowdown over the arbitrated award (*Ottawa Citizen*, December 14, 1988).

MILITANCY

Police militancy has been expressed in public statements, job action such as violation of dress codes, work slowdowns, and of course, in strikes in some jurisdictions. Where strikes have been legislatively prohibited, creative job actions have from time to time occurred.

In 1978 some British Columbia police reported to work in civilian clothing and without shaving to protest a breakdown in contract talks (*Ottawa Citizen*, May 13, 1978). Across the country, in Ottawa in 1981, the police also resorted to creative job action. Several wore grotesque masks while on duty (*Ottawa Journal,* September 21, 1981). A few years later in the course of a contract dispute, the mayor of the city of Ottawa and some local aldermen ob-jected to the police demonstrating in uniform and demanded disciplinary action. The police commission, however, took no action (*Ottawa Citizen*, November 8, 1984). Metro Toronto has had an aggressive police association. In 1980 the association turned down a $3000 in-crease in annual salary and began refusing off-duty assignments and reducing the number of parking tickets (*Ottawa Journal*, August 12, 1980).

Everywhere in Canada the years of the late 1970s and the early 1980s were periods of great labour conflict with police groups. From Victoria to St. John's, police resorted to job action, threats to strike, and actual strikes. Against this background, police won very sub-stantial salary gains. In Vancouver, police threatened their first-ever strike (*Ottawa Journal*,

January 8, 1980), and in Quebec and in Nova Scotia, police did withdraw services. The RCMP members began to organize for unionism, and in 1981 came close to being unified in intent when the federal government threatened to renege on an agreed retroactive salary payment as part of an overall salary agreement that kept the RCMP at the same level as major municipal forces (*Ottawa Citizen*, June 11, 1981). Threatened with a union, the federal solicitor general countered with a threat to cut the size of the Force (Montreal *Gazette*, June 9, 1981). The government, reacting to RCMP dissatisfaction and adverse editorial opinion (*Ottawa Citizen*, June 11, 1981), then acted to restore the originally agreed-upon retroactive pay (Montreal *Gazette*, June 11, 1981).

The degree of militancy in various Canadian jurisdictions has varied considerably, as has governing legislation. In some jurisdictions, such as Nova Scotia, New Brunswick, and Saskatchewan, the police have the right to strike. They have done so rarely in Saskatchewan, but frequently in New Brunswick and in Nova Scotia. In other areas—Quebec, Ontario, and Alberta—the police are prohibited from striking. In Ontario, in 1984 the OPP Association and the Metro Toronto Police Association unsuccessfully sought judicial intervention under the Charter of Rights to amend the Police Act, in order to gain the right to strike. The attempt was in part prompted by the Ontario attorney general's efforts to restrict police association bargaining (*Toronto Star*, July 12, 1984).

But police have walked out in Quebec, and they generally are regarded as among the most militant. A dispute over working conditions erupted in Hull, Quebec in 1978. Police refused to take their patrol shifts on the grounds that their radio equipment was inadequate and endangered their lives. Interference and dead spots in police transmissions were the concerns, because emergency calls for backup were being interrupted. The brief withdrawal of service ended after less than three hours when the police obeyed an order to return to work under threat of suspensions. Municipal officials, for their part, responded by accelerating installation of a new system (*Ottawa Citizen*, September 26, October 4, 1978). The Sûreté du Québec (Quebec Police Force) has also frequently been involved in job action. The Sûreté went out on strike for three days in 1975 and for six days in 1978 (*Ottawa Citizen*, March 16, 1985). In 1985 the Quebec government found itself contending with Sûreté job action, and had actually removed force members from security responsibilities for a Quebec City meeting between Prime Minister Mulroney and President Reagan. At that time it was reported that the government contemplated disbanding and breaking up the force (Montreal *Gazette*, March 18, 1985).

In 1978 the MUC Police Brotherhood membership defied and pressured its own leadership, demanding strike action and withdrawing most services in the course of a slowdown. To emphasize their dispute over work schedules, police stayed in station houses. A reported consequence was an increase in area robberies (Montreal *Sunday Express*, February 5, 1978).

Brotherhood job action also occurred in 1984 over implementation of a pension agreement. The city had fallen millions of dollars behind in pension contributions and had refused to follow a provincial public service formula. In response, for 10 days the police wore non-regulation clothing such as jeans, army pants, and a variety of hats, ignored traffic and parking violations, flashed their lights, and did not file reports or clean their cars (*Globe and Mail*, December 17, 1984). In the course of the pressure tactics, described by MUC Police management as "close to an insurrection" and "total insubordination," at least 44 officers were suspended, but refused to turn in their badges, revolvers, and identification, and remained on the job. The chairman of the MUC executive committee remarked that "the president of the policeman's union has become the boss of the police department" (*Globe and Mail*, December 12, 1984). Anticipating a possible full walkout, plans were in place to have the RCMP move in to assume policing duties, and an executive committee spokesman noted that brotherhood members would be liable to dismissal (*Globe and Mail*, December 13, 1984). The association tactics were called off after the provincial government required the city to follow the pension calculation sought by the police (Montreal *Sunday Herald*, December 16, 1984). A residue of the action was a total of at least 2500 disciplinary actions and 44 suspensions. The brotherhood demanded they be dropped as part of the settlement, and when management refused, attempting to regain control, the antagonists entered upon a new round of pressure tactics and slowdown (*Ottawa Citizen*, March 9, 16, 1985). Finally, a few days later, the city offered compensation for the suspensions and the latest round of pressure tactics was called off (*Ottawa Citizen*, March 20, 1985).

STRIKES

Whereas unions have traditionally viewed the right to strike as intrinsic to labour relations, the resort to strike action is not universally available to police employee organizations in Canada. Police officers usually express a preference for the possibility, while legislators, managers, and some impartial observers have tended to hold the opinion that strikes and other job actions by police officers are a serious threat to the nature of law enforcement and the public trust. Grant (1980:57) finds collective bargaining the occasion for a major redefinition of police responsibility, with the "right to strike and executive authority in personnel deployment and promotion policies" "the major problems" in current policing. Concern about the public reaction to police strikes as well as the alterations in control of police forces have also been remarked (Forcese, 1980). For many, despite expression of dislike from police representatives, binding arbitration seems the alternative (Fisher and Starek, 1978). At a press conference held by the president of the Quebec provincial association, the president opposed a call by municipal mayors to extend to police the right to strike. The mayors had been responding to a perception of unfavourable arbitration awards. The association, in turn, expressed its support for binding arbitration, suggesting that in strike situations the police would be routinely subjected to back-to-work legislation (Montreal *Gazette*, June 25, 1986).

In Ontario and Quebec, where the bulk of police employees work, there is some assurance of police service by virtue of police strikes being illegal. Policing is in effect considered an essential service. Yet, while the illegality is an undoubted inhibition, police strikes have occurred in Quebec. Ontario has not had major force-wide action as has Quebec. But in addition to job actions stopping short of strikes, there have been several threats of withdrawal of service, and in 1995, in the context of widespread disgruntlement over management disciplinary actions against two officers, there was a brief wildcat strike of a section of Metro Toronto police officers.

All Canadian provinces have some experience of police militancy. Not all, however, have experienced police walkouts. The most famous strike in Canada occurred in Montreal in 1969. It was brief, but illegal, and there was publicized disorder. New Brunswick experienced its first police strike in 1976 in Fredericton; it lasted for two days. The jurisdiction in which there has been the greatest number of strikes is Nova Scotia, especially in the late

1970s and early 1980s as the umbrella body, the Police Association of Nova Scotia, sought to reduce marked wage disparities in the province and between police in Nova Scotia and other provinces. The longest Canadian police strike took place in Westville, Nova Scotia in 1978. After four months, the police union and the town council agreed to binding arbitration. The force of only four men was aided in its strike action by the provincial association. While the strike was under way the town was patrolled by the RCMP (*Globe and Mail*, October 17, 1978). In most other provinces, including Canada's most populous province, Ontario, strikes are prohibited under the Police Act and there has never been a strike in this century.

Strikes, where they have occurred, have been associated with some disruption, but have not generally resulted in measurable increases in crime. In part this is attributable to the additional self-protection measures that citizens take. But also, in all strike situations, there are non-union personnel available, and the RCMP. The RCMP have frequently been used in police jurisdictions where the police have been on strike. The consequence has been animosity between the RCMP members and the striking police, to whom they are "scabs." Sensitive to the charge of being strikebreakers, the RCMP are nonetheless obliged by virtue of their contract with the provinces where they police to provide service when so ordered (Montreal *Gazette*, August 30, 1979).

A police strike in Sydney, Nova Scotia, in 1971 resulted in considerable vandalism. But in 1984, when the municipal police force of 66 again struck, 30 RCMP officers were immediately called in, and there were no incidents through the duration of the strike, from mid-September until early October, when the parties agreed to settlement by an industrial enquiry commissioner (*Globe and Mail*, September 18, 1984; *Ottawa Citizen*, October 3, 1984).

In 1979, for a period the RCMP were policing the three largest towns in northern Nova Scotia, when local police in Truro, New Glasgow, and Amherst were all on strike (*Ottawa Journal*, October 23, 1979). Strikers in Truro marched with signs proclaiming their salaries at $13 720, in contrast to the RCMP constable's salary of $21 700 (*Ottawa Citizen*, October 20, 1979). In 1980, the personnel of the Royal Newfoundland Constabulary struck for one day in protest over the appointment of a public servant, formerly an RCMP officer, as deputy chief. Two members of the constabulary, including a commissioned officer who refused to obey an order, and the president of the brotherhood, were suspended. During the brief strike the city of St. John's was policed, to the constabulary's displeasure, by the RCMP. The strikers threatened that their "blue flu" might become "scarlet fever"—an allusion to the RCMP role (*Ottawa Journal,* June 4, 1980).

In Halifax, in 1981, there was even hostility between non-striking Halifax police detectives still on duty because of their contract, and RCMP members. One on-duty police officer remarked that "We don't like them and they don't like us much" (*Toronto Star*, July 19, 1981). At one time the on-duty officers, members of the Officers' and Non-Commissioned Officers Association, bound by their own contract, asked the Nova Scotia government for a legislated end to the strike, claiming they were overworked, and that their relations with striking colleagues were being ruined (*Ottawa Citizen,* July 15, 1981). Eventually the negotiator for the police sought back-to-work legislation to break the impasse. The government, however, refused what they called this "quite unusual request," declaring that there was no threat to public safety (Montreal *Gazette*, July 8, 19, 1981).

The Halifax strike of 1981 lasted for almost two months, while non-commissioned officers and RCMP personnel policed the city. On the first weekend of the strike there was street rowdyism and some property damage. Six hours after the start of the strike, a noisy crowd gathered in front of the police station, tearing up trees, starting fires and hurling bottles and rocks at those police still on duty, while striking officers on the picket line watched (*Ottawa Citizen*, May 30, 1981). Eventually riot-equipped non-striking police dispersed the crowd, and thereafter through the strike there was little disorder or crime. Although other civic workers supported the strike, with bus drivers honouring police picket lines, there was little public concern or pressure for rapid solution, and picketing police officers, losing several thousand dollars in salary each over the course of the strike, were embittered, resenting non-commissioned officers, the RCMP, and the public whom they apparently had expected to sympathize with them (*Toronto Star*, July 19, 1981; *Globe and Mail*, July 17, 1981; Montreal *Gazette*, July 22, 1981). In the midst of the strike the chairman of the Board of Trade remarked that "We're getting the best police protection the city has ever had." Rather than sympathize, the public increasingly blamed police officers for neglect of duty and loss of business (*Ottawa Citizen*, July 23, 1981).

In 1984, when the 33-person Glace Bay, Nova Scotia police force withdrew service for 29 hours, the RCMP were again available. As in other strikes, owners took precautions, such as boarding up windows, and there were some reports of vandalism. There was no breakdown of order, however, and no outbreak of crime. Local police claimed that during the strike there were twice as many RCMP Police on patrol as during a normal shift of the Glace Bay Police (*Ottawa Citizen*, June 30, 1984; *Globe and Mail*, July 2, 1984).

The RCMP were not even required in the holiday period of 1983 when the Newcastle, New Brunswick, police force of 13 went on strike when an officer, the vice-president of the local police union, was fired. The chief and his deputy remained on duty for the 10-day period, and the town remained free of rowdyism and vandalism (*Toronto Sunday Star*, January 1, 1984). More recently, in September 1989 supervisors patrolled in Dartmouth when the police went out on strike, but the RCMP were ordered in, having been on standby in anticipation of the strike for some weeks (*Globe and Mail*, September 14, 1989). Because of RCMP intervention there were no disruptions in the Nova Scotia city (*Ottawa Citizen*, September 15, 1989).

In Chatham, New Brunswick, where there was a police strike in 1985, merchants hired security guards and stayed overnight on their premises. On two previous evenings there had been street drinking and racing and some broken windows. At one point the 11-man force briefly returned to duty to disperse a crowd of about 400 people (*Ottawa Citizen*, June 3, 4, 1985). Ironically, the chief of police blamed news photographers for the rowdiness, claiming that the crowds were provoked by the attention of cameras. He went on to threaten to jail news photographers if they persisted. Eventually the chief and his deputy were not able to work for "health reasons" and the provincial government ordered the police back to work, with binding arbitration to be invoked if there was no contract settlement in two weeks (*Toronto Star*, June 14, 1985).

POLITICS AND LOBBYING

Another consequence of police unionism has been a greater political role for police. By and large, Canadian police, unlike their American counterparts, have been detached from political participation. In most jurisdictions police are not expected to comment on political candidates, and are prevented under police Acts from themselves becoming candidates. They have also refrained from commenting publicly on public issues. But unions have pressed for changes. An explicit instance was the intervention in Hull, Quebec, of approximately 50 police officers who visibly joined other citizens to protest a proposed pay raise for city councillors. The police action occurred while they themselves were in the middle of a contract dispute with the city (*Ottawa Citizen*, September 19, 1984).

Toronto provides several notable examples of police union political power. The Metro Toronto Police Association's disagreements with Mayor John Sewell in the 1970s were well-publicized, and the association announced its explicit opposition to the mayor's bid for re-election in 1980 (*Toronto Star*, September 28, 1980). The mayor had publicly stated that the police had racist elements. The association therefore "reluctantly set ... precedent" and passed a resolution to "withdraw and reject" support for the mayor (*Ottawa Journal*, October 1, 1979). Later, the newly re-elected president suggested that it was time the association began offering block support to suitable candidates with money, campaign work, and endorsements (*Toronto Star*, October 21, 1982). In his statements Sewell advocated measures such as a more representative police commission, civilian review boards, more open and minority-oriented police recruitment, and improved police training (*Globe and Mail*, September 29, 1980). Sewell lost his bid for re-election.

An opposite intervention, in support of a politician viewed as friendly, occurred in 1989. The Ontario Police Association publicly endorsed and sought the reappointment to cabinet of a minister, Joan Smith, who had resigned on opposition demands related to her having visited an OPP detachment to enquire on behalf of a friend's son (*Ottawa Citizen*, June 15, 1989).

Another example of the power of police unions in the political context involved a libel case in Toronto. In November, 1980, a court decision was reached in a lengthy libel suit involving a police constable and an alderman. The Toronto alderman had publicly criticized two police officers who had detained him on suspicion of breaking into cars. The policemen complained, apparently with the encouragement of the chief of police as well as the union, of violation of their civil rights, and brought suit. The suit was financially supported by the Metro Toronto Police Association. Although the outcome was merely a "contemptuous" judgment of libel in the amount of $4.00 in damages, the real financial consequence was reported to total $40 000 in court costs, to be met by the alderman (*Toronto Star*, November 2, 1980). The police officers, at no financial risk, therefore, were able to react punitively to a public critic.

Police unions have also been vocal in commenting on and criticizing government policies and legislation. The Toronto Police Association explicitly affiliated with other labour organizations in 1983 in campaigning against public-sector wage controls. The association paid for a full-page advertisement in Toronto newspapers criticizing the government for failing to meet its responsibilities. The association also publicly advocated a legal ban on strikebreakers following the injury of a police member when enforcing access for strikebreakers at a strike at the *Toronto Star*. The association president stated that "it is unfortunate that police officers have to intervene while management peers out of the window watching pickets and police defend themselves" (*Globe and Mail*, October 29, 1983). Another example of a major political intervention was the Canadian Police Association opposition to the Charter of Rights. Like the Canadian chiefs, the police rank-and-file estimated that the Charter would effectively erode their authority, introducing an American-style procedural check governed by court interventions. The association was particularly concerned about the exclusionary rule of evidence provisions, whereby improperly collected evidence could result in the dismissal of a case, even where the evidence is conclusive. An association spokesman suggested that the provision left justice to the vagaries of court composition, and protected offenders and not victims (*Ottawa Citizen*, September 29, 30, 1981).

The police association has also been very critical of the treatment of offenders. Opposition to capital punishment is a major example, as is association opposition to parole procedures. Commenting upon the immunity granted to a man acknowledged to have participated in at least one murder by supplying a weapon, in exchange for his acting as Crown witness, the head of the Metro Toronto Police Association told the press that he was "full of revulsion and sickened," going on to suggest that twenty years ago, rather than being protected the man "would have been hanged" (*Toronto Star*, March 26, 1982). Similar criticisms were voiced across the county by police following the controversial deal made by the RCMP with Clifford Olsen, whereby he received payment for revealing the fate and location of his victims.

In 1979 police power was demonstrated in Edmonton. The Edmonton Police Association allied with the chief of police, to criticize the practices of the National Parole Board. Their familiar contention was that a significant proportion of offenders with whom police had to contend were persons prematurely released from prison by the board. The public criticisms brought the chairman of the board to Edmonton, and negotiations to adjust the practices of the board were initiated.

The employee group lobby for capital punishment was most vigorous in the late 1970s and early 1980s. In 1978 in Quebec City, where the Canadian Police Association was meeting, capital punishment was identified as the "most important item on the agenda." Contributions of $4.00 were fixed for each member across the country to finance a "national advertising campaign" that eventually exceeded $200 000 (*Globe and Mail*, March 31, 1979). One newspaper editorialist attacked the fund as a violation of the traditional concept of police political non-intervention, and declared that "Police should be neutral" (Montreal *Gazette*, April 12, 1979).

The theme of capital punishment, it should be noted, was no less significant at this time in other democracies. It had been identified by British researchers as the clearest and most significant indication of police politicization in the United Kingdom, as the police sought to influence national elections (Taylor, 1980). In Canada, in 1979 advertisements appeared in newspapers across the nation, paid for by the Canadian Police Association. "Bring Capital Punishment to Parliament Hill" exclaimed the large print. The advertisements went on to urge the public to measure political candidates against their stand on capital punishment. At the same time as the formal national campaign was mounted, individual representatives of police associations were outspoken. In 1980, for example, following the death of a prison guard at Dorchester, the president of the Kingston Police Association called for a strike of prison guards, and the restoration of the death penalty (*Ottawa Citizen*, October 13, 1980). Similarly, after the shooting death of a Toronto police constable, police association leaders spoke out, and the Ottawa association president called for "drastic actions" to regain capital punishment (*Ottawa Journal*, March 17, 1980).

In 1984, Canadian police associations reasserted their interest in the restoration of capital punishment following several police deaths. At the annual convention of the national Canadian Police Association, delegates agreed to urge the government to call a national referendum on restitution. The resolution called upon the government to "recognize public opinion and institute a public referendum with respect to the issue of reinstating capital punishment as an optional sentence for persons convicted of first-degree murder and that the government abide by the wishes of the people." In October a crowd of 4000 demonstrated on the Hill to honour murdered police officers and guards, two days after Prime Minister Trudeau rejected the call for a national referendum on capital punishment (*Ottawa Citizen*, October 1, 1984).

Later in the year a major march by police on Parliament Hill was intended to influence the government to restore capital punishment and to amend parole procedures. Responding to several police deaths, the demonstration was organized by the Ottawa Police Association, despite the misgiving of police chiefs. The commissioner of the RCMP explicitly opposed the demonstration, and his members were not allowed to appear in uniform. Other police chiefs reacted similarly, including the commissioner of the OPP and the chief of the Edmonton Police Force. But the chiefs of some major forces, such as Metro Toronto, supported the demonstration. Preceded by prominent advertisements in major newspapers, the march took place with an estimated 1500 police, prison guards, and civilians participating (*Ottawa Citizen*, October 25, 26, 27, November 6, 1984).

PUBLIC RELATIONS

Police unions have often sought to influence public opinion. In 1979, for example, following a police shooting of a black man, the Metro Toronto Police Association purchased a full-page advertisement in Toronto newspapers, extolling and defending the police force. The advertisement called upon the public to demonstrate their support by writing to newspapers and to government representatives (*Toronto Star*, September 13, 1979).

Associations also have inhibited measures that are possibly in the public interest, such as complaints boards, or very simple matters such as police identification tags. Not until the mid-1980s did Metro Toronto police begin wearing name tags in addition to badge numbers, and only in 1990 was the practice instituted in the city of Ottawa. In contrast, the RCMP have worn identification tags since the 1970s. In Ontario, the Ontario Provincial Police Association attempted a court injunction to block such a measure in 1987 (*Ottawa Citizen*, March 12, 1990). The association claimed that its members would be subject to harassment, whereas the government saw the requirement as an improvement in police–public relations. The court rejected the association's arguments (*Toronto Sunday Star*, May 3, 1987).

A good deal of police association attention has been given to public accusation of bias. As police forces have faced complaints of racist bias in actions against visible minorities, and as the chiefs individually and collectively have committed to more aggressive recruitment of minority persons, police associations have reacted defensively.

Responding to a provincial task force examining racism and the police, and recommendations that included lateral entry and advanced promotion for minorities, the head of the Metro Toronto Police Association exclaimed to the press: "Damn it all, it's unfair, simply unfair" (*Ottawa Citizen*, May 1, 1989).

Also in Toronto, following the announcement of charges against Peel and Toronto constables in unrelated shooting deaths of black persons, the Metro Toronto Police Association organized a mass meeting of support, criticizing the charges and demanding the resignation of Ontario's attorney general as having been politically motivated and seeking to appease black activists (*Toronto Sunday Star*, January 15, 1989; Montreal *Gazette*, January 16, 1989). The assembled police officers declared that, "We, the members of the Metropolitan Toronto Police Association, condemn the action of the Ontario government in the matter of

PC Deviney. Further, we condemn the specific actions of Attorney General Ian Scott and demand his immediate resignation" (*Ottawa Sun*, January 16, 1989). In this instance, the police union sentiments and those of police management seemed synonymous. In response to police association calls for support, thousands of people called the police department. It was later reported that a list of more than 12 000 callers was provided to an association called Concerned Citizens for Order, Peace, and Security, with the prospect of mobilizing public demonstrations (*Ottawa Citizen*, January 26, 1989).

In 1990, following another Toronto police shooting that seriously injured a black youth, the *Toronto Star*, in its aggressive and critical reporting of police actions, cited black community members describing the Toronto police as the "most brutal, murderous, police in North America." The president of the Toronto Police Association, in response, stated that Toronto police were incensed, and that they were now more apt to draw their guns because of the public outcry. He went on to claim that "if the Metro force is not the finest, then it is one of the finest in the world" (*Ottawa Citizen*, May 22, 1990).

In 1990 five Toronto police officers were facing several charges for shooting incidents involving black persons. The charge against a Metro Toronto police officer who had fatally shot a youth was changed from criminal negligence to attempted murder, upon weighing the fact that the young man had been shot twice in the back. In response, the president of the police association claimed that charges were laid only because of pressure from the black community. He went on to claim low morale in the force, and that one-quarter of the force "would leave Toronto today for lower wages" if they could find work elsewhere (*Ottawa Citizen*, June 2, 1990).

In Toronto, in the late 1970s, police association attitudes were publicly exposed and damaged the public relations of the force. Revelations of racists statements in the association journal, *News and Views*, were publicized by the press, as were opinions to the effect that police management had lost control of the force. One article in the journal, written by a staff sergeant, entitled "The Homosexual Fad," was a crude anti-homosexual polemic, which also criticized then Toronto Mayor John Sewell for condoning "acts of perversion" (*News and Views*, March, 1979; Montreal *Gazette*, March 21, 1979). A column by a retired police officer was notorious for scurrilous comments about ethnic minorities, women, and Catholics. One column included this: "If you want a laugh, drive over to Glencairn and Bathurst and see the Jews in their Oldsmobiles. It's better than a Frank Sinatra special." It went on about Catholics: "Now that they've elected a Polish Pope, we can look to lots of co-operation between the Communists and the Vatican. They both have the same ambition: World domination" (*News and Views,* December 1979:11).

In the context of the public exposé of this content the chairman of the police commission threatened an investigation. The acting chief of police remarked however, that in the absence of demonstrated bigotry in police work, there was no provision in the police code that allowed sanction of a member such as the staff sergeant. The Ontario Police Commission also concluded that there was no basis for punitive intervention, although the articles damaged public confidence in the police. They expressed the "opinion that whatever an officer's personal views may be concerning minority groups, he should avoid public expression of those views if to do so will admit or sound of prejudice, or cause concern in the general public as to the objectivity of the police force" (*Globe and Mail*, July 28, 1979).

In 1989 the Metro Toronto Police Association president complained about a women's group monitoring a case against a police officer who had shot and wounded a black woman.

The association president referred to the Women's Coalition Against Racism and Police Violence as "prejudicial bigots" and the "real racists" (*Toronto Star*, January 30, 1990). As a gesture of support the association had determined to attend each court hearing of the accused officer charged with the careless use of a firearm. The charge was laid following investigation by the OPP (*Ottawa Citizen*, December 5, 1989; *Toronto Star*, January 30, 1990).

Experience in the democracies suggest that police unionism is a conservative rather than a liberalizing influence. In France, one contrary indication of a union's liberalizing effect was reported in 1980. The leader of the major police union publicly exposed police interventions in support of right-wing extremism, such as the Fédération d'Action Nationalist Européene, whose membership included police officers (*Toronto Star*, October 5, 1980; Montreal *Gazette*, October 15, 1980). Generally, though, police have become a very effective interest group, with a conservative ideology that reinforces that of their management even as they may oppose management on interest issues (Cerda, 1977). Management and unions may differ, but they share an ideology that is protective of policing. Thus unions act to defend members against public criticism or discipline, whether from management or from civilian review bodies. Racism, for example, as illustrated in several previous examples, is generally denied, or blatantly expressed and defended.

In the United States also, conservative police attitudes have been vigorously expressed in antipathy to black populations in American cities (Reiner, 1980:379; Johnson, 1976:403) and in their opposition to effective civilian control (Halpern, 1974; Bent, 1974). The job situation of police officers inevitably places them in conflict situations with economic minorities, who in turn are often racial minorities. The job confrontations reinforce what may often be a class bias, given the working-class origins of police officers.

In the United States, Skolnick (1975) and others perceived police unionism as a move to right-wing radicalism, a defensive measure on the part of police in the face of 1960s criticism and confrontation. In Britain, Reiner (1978b; 1978c) remarks upon the "contradictory class position" of police workers and states that the contradiction resolves itself in favour of occupation or peer loyalty, as police are isolated from the larger labour movement. It is estimated that in the United Kingdom 80% of police support the Conservative Party (Reiner, 1980:405), the party that upon initial election acted immediately to increase police compensation. In Canada and the United States, conservative sentiments cannot be estimated to be different. An isolated example only, but perhaps indicative: in Ontario in the 1980 federal election, an OPP constable defied the political prohibition in the Police Act, and ran as a federal candidate for the Progressive Conservative Party. He was unsuccessful. The officer, subsequently charged with "discreditable conduct," was defended by the union, and his action upheld by an arbitration board (*Globe and Mail,* January 20, 1981).

CONCLUSION

Police associations have come to be major players in the conduct of policing, and in police relations with the public. They have been aggressive in defence of members and in their demands for benefits. They have at times advocated changes, as in regard to work week, and at other times impeded change, as in some opposition to amended patrol formats. Inevitably, as police managers and governments have sought to alter the police services, the police associations or unions have had to be a party to the changes.

The public usually reacts strongly to the ultimate labour weapon, the strike. Other militant activities also generate a negative public response. Where a union goes out of its way to use the public as leverage in a wage settlement, the reaction is most apt to be quite strong. There is little doubt that police union militancy often damages the public perception of police. The Canadian public had tended to idealize its police, seeing them as dedicated persons in an occupation somewhat apart from the rest of society. With unionism, and more particularly, with job action, public support is usually lost. Whether or not the public is directly damaged with job action there is some loss of respect and confidence in police personnel, who are seen not only as unreliable, but self-seeking like any other employee group. The pedestal is shattered, and with it, therefore, a good deal of the deference that is the basis of public cooperation.

ANNOTATED READINGS, CHAPTER FIVE

Downie, Bryan and Richard Jackson (eds.). *Conflict and Cooperation in Police Labour Relations.* Ottawa: Canadian Police College, 1980. These are the informative published proceedings of a 1978 conference examining labour relations in Canadian police forces.

Reiner, Robert. *The Blue-Coated Worker.* Cambridge: Cambridge University Press, 1978. This provocative analysis considers British police employee militancy. It offers the view of police as occupying a contradictory class position in society.

6

RECRUITMENT AND TRAINING

Organizations maintain themselves by regulating renewal. Police organizations have been quite successful in controlling recruitment and training. Public overseeing of recruit selection and recruit indoctrination has historically been slight. The police have renewed themselves, isolated from more heterogeneous publics and broadly based education. In this chapter we consider the general character of recruit selection and training for Canadian police services.

In Canada, as in Britain and the United States, policing has been a respectable occupation. Even while salaries through much of this century, until the 1960s, were not high, the job was considered to offer security and respect. It was, therefore, an opportunity for native-born working-class and rural Canadians to move upwards, and for immigrants, too, as long as the immigrants were from the British Isles and had similar attitudes to policing as an occupation as Canadians.

RECRUITMENT

To be eligible as a recruit for various Canadian police services, one must usually be a Canadian citizen, or landed immigrant and legal resident. A recruit applicant must be 18 or 19 years of age, have matriculated from high school (grade 12), or increasingly in some services, completed a two-year community college diploma, usually in criminal justice or law enforcement. Some forces will mention that they are interested in persons with a university degree. The applicant must be in good physical condition, have reasonably correctable vision, and not have a criminal record. The ability to speak French or English, as regionally relevant, is generally unstated, although specified by the RCMP. A driver's licence is also expected, with a good driving record. Some services may require other qualifications, such as typing skills. For example, Halifax Regional Police Service asks for evidence of typing skills, and Red Cross rescue skills training (see Figure 6-1). Additionally some services with remote jurisdictions, such as the RCMP, OPP, and Sûreté du Québec, may specify a declaration of willingness to serve anywhere where the service operates. Beyond the basic qualifications, all services will test and evaluate applicants physically and psychologically, as well as attempt to test for "suitability." Vancouver, for example, will require an initial written test, to evaluate spelling, grammar, reading comprehension, memory, and general mathematics, with a specified passing level of 65%. Vancouver will also require a polygraph examination.

Still evident in this inventory of qualifications is the historic recruitment expectation, the youthful high school graduate.

The traditional recruitment preference of North American police forces has been for males from the less educated, working-class population. In some American cities, especially those now experiencing difficulties in recruitment, the tendency has been extreme. In Detroit, for example, there is indication that males from the lower half of graduating high school classes dominate recruit selection. After the urban unrest of the 1960s and following from a President's Commission on Law Enforcement, the Americans introduced a Law Enforcement Education Program. The program was intended to improve the educational level of American police, with an emphasis therefore upon post-secondary education. Despite undisputed effort and a proliferation of college and university programs, results were not altogether encouraging over the 10-year period of the program. Educational standards did increase, perhaps too often in tailored programs exclusively for police, and generally with the result of more highly educated management-rank officers, while high school level education has remained prevalent for rank-and-file police (*Police Forum*, American Criminal Justice Society, January 1996). In Canada there has yet to be a major program of post-secondary basic recruit selection, nor any formal policy statement favouring post-secondary education beyond college-level training. Another traditional recruit preference, consistent with the paramilitary origins and stereotypes of policing, has been persons with military experience. Military experience in the two World Wars figured prominently, in the past, in Canadian police recruit selection, just as experience in later wars continues to do in the United States. Overall, though, in Canada military experience has been less prominent in recruiting, and may be a partial explanation for the decidedly less violent character of Canadian police. American police, in the absence of major wars, have maintained a large military establishment, and continue to show some inclination for police recruits with military experience.

In the late 1970s, 80% of serving policing officers had as their highest educational attainment high school completion. Only 4% had graduated from university (Martin, 1979:225). There has been change, however, over the past two decades. In Quebec, graduation from CEGEP (community college) is required (Coutts, 1990:99). Usually recruits will be chosen from among persons who have completed a three-year diploma program at a

FIGURE 6-1   Example of Recruit Advertisement, September 1996

Halifax Regional Municipality
Future Career Opportunity (Training)

POLICE SCIENCE CADET CANDIDATES
HALIFAX REGIONAL POLICE SERVICE

The Halifax Regional Police Service (HRPS) is inviting applications from individuals interested in participating in a police candidate selection process. The intent of this process will be to establish a list of candidates qualified to participate in provincially recognized Basic Police Science training programs. This selection process is being undertaken in order to establish a waiting list in conjunction with a long term staffing plan addressing the anticipated future police constable staffing needs of HRPS.

Qualifications:
A Canadian Citizen

Age: Minimum 19 years of age by application deadline
Grade XII Education (University Preparatory), by the application deadline. A record of marks or achievements must be supplied with a résumé.

Physical Requirements: Candidate must be in good physical condition

Visual Requirements:
Visual Acuity: Uncorrected 20/40 – 20/40
Correctable to 20/30 – 20/30
Colour vision and visual fields normal

Criminal Record: Applications will not be accepted from persons who have been convicted of a criminal offence or have received an absolute or conditional discharge unless a pardon has been granted.

Upon application, candidate must provide a copy of the following documents:
birth certificate
driver's licence
certificate of academic achievement (Grade XII certificate)
Motor Vehicle Record check (driver's abstract obtained from the Department of Motor Vehicles)
valid standard First Aid certificate
valid CPR certificate (level C)
Red Cross Survival Swimming Course/Rescue Skills certificate
Canada Safety Council Safe Driving Course certificate or equivalent
Keyboard Certificate at a speed of 25 wpm for a minimum of three minutes with no more than three errors
three letters of reference

All applications received will be reviewed. Only those applications where applicants meet the specified qualifications and which are accompanied by the specified documentation will be processed. If all basic requirements are met, applicants will be contacted by letter to verify receipt of application. Telephone inquiries should be directed to the **Halifax Regional Police Service Training Section at 490-5413.**

Interested candidates are asked to forward a résumé, all required documentation, and covering letter **prior to 4:00 p.m. Friday November 1, 1996 to:**

Halifax Regional Police Service
1975 Gottingen St.
Halifax, NS, B3J 2H1
Attn.: Recruiting Officer

Source: By permission Deputy Chief of Administration and Support Services, Halifax Regional Police Service.

Quebec community college. Ontario is also implementing a college-based program requirement from which services are to select recruits. Announced in 1997, like other programs,
it is not a general college experience requirement, but specific to a law enforcement program for a pool of basic recruit candidates. The measure has its origins in a major report,
A Police Learning System for Ontario (1992). While the report was largely ignored by
successive governments, in 1997 the Ontario government announced a change that had its
origins in the 1992 document, although perhaps as much attributable to the government's
user-pay philosophy. Persons wishing to become police officers were to be obliged, effective year 2000, to take a two-year basic law enforcement course, at their own expense,
in a community college. Following the course, they would be examined, and if successful,
be eligible to be recruited to an Ontario police service. If hired, they would then go to police college.

Generally in Canada, as in many American jurisdictions, there is now some deliberate
university-education recruitment. And in forces such as the RCMP, there is gradually increasing support for university-level training for serving police officers. Some municipal
chiefs, as in Ottawa, have repeatedly expressed in public a preference for increased numbers
of university-educated recruits; in Ottawa the chief has said that he would prefer only
university-educated, a view that has not met with police association favour. Yet the numbers
are still small, probably around 10% in North America overall, in contrast to 15 to 20% of
serving members with university education in the RCMP. In that force, the favoured approach appears to be recruitment, police training, and then higher education, rather than recruiting persons out of universities. No Canadian force, in contrast to British policy, offers
a police career headstart or rank advantage to the university educated, although there is indication that the credentials can accelerate promotion. Most significantly, relatively few
command rank police officers, especially chief constables, have themselves been educated
to a university level. In the coming decade, however, the numbers should increase, as mid-
dle-rank police managers, now more often better educated, begin to move into top positions and bring attitudes more supportive of a better educated police service. Illustrative,
perhaps, is the present commissioner of the RCMP, himself university educated and driving for changes such as minority recruitment.

There has also been some discernible influence of family tradition in recruit selection.
One relatively prominent example was the chief of the Ottawa Police Force who in the
1980s had one son serving as an officer on the Ottawa force, and two others serving in
nearby police forces (*Ottawa Citizen*, May 2, 1990). Another illustration may be found in a
1995 documentary film, *10–7 for Life*, describing the final working days of a female police
officer with Metropolitan Toronto Police. Her grandfather, her parents, an uncle, and several cousins were police officers. The film's content in part deals with the expectations and
pressures that were associated with this family occupational tradition.

Recruit selection has been very effectively controlled by the police forces themselves,
with criteria that largely have been implicit, and perhaps quite arbitrary. In Ontario, not until
1978 was it necessary for municipal forces to indicate reasons for failing to employ recruits following their probation. At that time the Supreme Court of Canada ruled on a case and declared that reasons for probationary dismissals were necessary. The lawyer acting for the
appellant suggested that hitherto, the unaccountable dismissals were a result of some police forces
using the cheap labour of probationary personnel, and then releasing them, without having to
incur the heavy costs of pensions and benefits (*Globe and Mail*, October 4, 1978). (The probationary period is one year, whereas most recruit training programs last just 12 to 16 weeks.)

Traditional selection procedures for police forces were not terribly sophisticated. Writing in 1975, Brian Grosman (1975:59) observed: "Most municipal forces in Canada have yet to develop selection techniques beyond a background investigation and a personal interview of the potential recruit. Poor selection procedure for recruits, combined with low educational requirements and a promotion only-from-within policy abets the progressive advancement of ... mediocrity ... . Rigid physical and social-cultural standards have dominated municipal recruitment."

American research also casts doubt upon the efficacy of psychological testing of recruits. Most Canadian forces do such tests, and a 1989 Ontario task force urged uniform psychological testing of recruits. But, as concluded by a former chief of police in Calgary, psychological testing is of dubious validity, and often biased. It may also be culturally biased.

In 1983 the chief of the Calgary Police Service declared that he had abandoned standard psychological testing for recruits, in the view that such tests are culture-biased and discriminate against minority candidates (*Globe and Mail*, October 24, 1983). At about the same time an Ontario chief of police was advocating the use of polygraph tests, a discredited technique, for *all* recruits. The recommendation was made by the chief of the Ottawa Police on behalf of the Ontario Association of Chiefs, who noted that the lie detectors were in use in other cities, including Calgary (*Ottawa Citizen*, November 10, 1983). Although several forces in western Canada use the polygraph to test recruits, its use is banned in Ontario (*Globe and Mail*, March 4, 1986.)

Recruitment biases in testing were confirmed in a study commissioned by the Canadian Association of Chiefs of Police, which criticized the North American Christian cultural bias of the standard psychological test, the Minnesota Multi-Phasic Personality Inventory (*Globe and Mail*, March 4, 1986). Yet, curiously, the Ontario Task Force on Race Relations referred to earlier recommendations that all forces require a standardized psychological test. It also recommended a centralized province-wide recruitment procedure as a means of hastening minority recruitment (*Ottawa Citizen*, March 10, 1989).

The conclusion of American research was that "a usefully valid and unbiased procedure for selecting police officers has not been demonstrated as yet." There is reason to believe that psychological testing is attractive to police forces because it offers the illusion of scientific precision, and lessens uncertainty, especially from the outside, about police selection decisions (Cordingley, 1979:128–129, 159). The choice of tests, their application, and their interpretation have all been found to be deficient, suggesting a symbolic importance, but also a redundancy where tests are used to justify legitimate selection decisions already made. Cordingley concluded that "it is important for Canadian police forces to realize the fallacy of claiming that the use of psychological tests is precise, scientific, or universally appropriate."

Another persisting police practice is that of refusing lateral or advanced entry. All officers begin police service at the bottom. Unlike the officer corps in the military, or the recruitment that occurs in most modern organizations, police have effectively resisted hiring persons who have not worked themselves up within Canadian policing, and indeed, often within the particular police force. By and large, only chiefs and deputy chiefs among commissioned personnel have occasionally been recruited from outside a given police organization, and then, they are persons who themselves worked up through another Canadian police force. Police management and police unions have resisted any change, insisting that without street experience management personnel in policing could not function effectively.

Following the 1989 Ontario task force there was some public discussion of lateral entry. The president of the Metro Toronto Police Association reacted with the statement that "Parachuting people into higher levels would be utter stupidity" (*Toronto Sunday Star*, March 12, 1989).

For three decades after World War II, police forces expanded their personnel numbers at a rate that far exceeded the growth in the Canadian population. Police expansion, therefore, has not been a function of some significant population or criminal growth. It has, however, in part been a response to population redistribution, as urbanization produced a population overwhelmingly concentrated in towns and cities. Before the brief downturn in police numbers in 1982 and the temporary halt in recruiting, Canadian police forces were experiencing difficulties in recruiting and training sufficient candidates. The Calgary police, for example, who had expanded during the Alberta boom years, sent representatives on recruiting trips to central and eastern Canada. In Gloucester, an expanding bedroom city adjacent to Ottawa, several recruits annually were pressed into service for periods of up to six months, armed, before being sent to police college for systematic training. The Gloucester chief defended the practice as a cost economy in his relatively small 84-man (there were, in fact, no women as the chief did not believe women were suitable for regular policing) force, and argued that the rookies were under the strict supervision of experienced non-commissioned officers. One police officer described his firearms training: "One day someone takes you out to the pits (a local quarry) and you start shooting 'til you hit 65 (out of 100) and they give you a gun" (*Ottawa Citizen*, February 11, 1982). In 1988 the Halifax Police Department, usually having taken recruits from training programs at the Atlantic Police Academy, began offering its own training over just 26 weeks in order to accelerate recruits' entry into service (*Toronto Sunday Star*, December 11, 1988).

Only in the 1980s did recruitment slow, with most forces doing little or no recruitment in the early part of the decade. The RCMP training depot in Saskatchewan, for example, trained large classes of 1000 or more in the 1970s. But only 23 graduates completed in 1983–84, and 67 of 91 staff instructors were returned to the field (*Globe and Mail,* February 13, 1984). But the pause in recruiting was brief, and police began renewing their personnel by the late 1980s, with pressure to recruit women and minorities.

Although Kelly and Kelly (1973:12) record the first full-time police woman in Canada, a woman who served with the Edmonton force for 31 years from 1900, and also the first native Indian police officer, appointed to the Edmonton force in 1909, the highly educated, visible ethnic minorities and women traditionally have been excluded from police recruitment.

The OPP, to cite another example, has traditionally consisted of white working-class males; in 1988 only about 5% of the force consisted of minorities and women, with 26 natives, 212 women, and 18 visible minority group members. In order to increase its recruitment of women and ethnic minorities, the force has been increasingly active on the campuses of Ontario universities (*Ottawa Citizen*, November 24, 1988).

Their provincial counterpart, the Sûreté du Québec, as of 1988, with 4500 members, had only 50 women officers. As with the OPP and the RCMP, the remote and isolated rural policing is often unattractive. The Sûreté's director remarked that "We're offering the North Shore, the Magdalen Islands, and Abitibi, as we must, to any newly hired officer. It's less attractive" (Montreal *Gazette*, December 15, 1988). Similarly, the RCMP has had experience of having successfully target-recruited, including affirmative selection of francophones and women, only to find subsequently that officers will resign because of remote postings and turn to policing jobs in an urban municipal service. Remote postings in these large services are a particular problem, one not shared by most urban municipal services.

The serious difficulty common to all Canadian police services in the 1990s relates to policy commitments to diversify the gender and ethnic composition of police services. Both ethnic minorities and women have had some perception of policing as a hostile, white, male-dominated occupational environment, and have not come forward readily as recruit applicants.

The RCMP have had the most determined policy of affirmative recruitment, with preferred status since the early 1980s for bilingual persons, women, natives, and the university educated. Yet the affirmative recruitment policy was supposedly abandoned in 1988. For some years there has been criticism of the preferences, especially those favouring bilingual persons, as members presumed that they discriminated against persons from western Canada. The hiring of francophones was raised in the Manitoba legislature in 1985, and brought to the attention of the federal government by the Manitoba attorney general and area members of parliament (*Ottawa Citizen*, May 30, 1985). In 1983–84 when criticisms prompted the commissioner to announce a review, 51% of RCMP recruits were from Quebec, where only a minority, about 6% of RCMP regular personnel are employed. Recruits from western Canada, where much of the criticism centred, made up only 11% of the 1983–84 recruits, although approximately 7592 regular members from a total complement of 12 622 were stationed in the West. The western complaints were underlined by the observation that although the RCMP is a federal force, because it works under contract with the western provinces for municipal and provincial policing—which it does not do in Quebec—the costs of the Force are in large part borne by the western provinces. The RCMP found itself caught between the western expectation of representative recruiting, on the one hand, and on the other, the federal government Treasury Board requirement that the Force reach 20% francophone membership by 1996, as contrasted to the present 14%. Consequently recruitment from Quebec moved from 22% in 1981–82, to 27% in 1982–83, to the 51% figure that elicited criticism in 1983–84, as the Force played catch-up to meet the Treasury Board guideline (*Ottawa Citizen*, May 8, 1985; October 30, 1988).

The Mounted Police also pioneered in native policing. The RCMP made efforts relatively early, in the 1970s, to recruit native persons as special constables. Because they would deal primarily with native peoples, the RCMP waived standard qualifications and recruited Indians and Métis to serve in the northern part of the provinces and the Territories. The practice began in 1977 in Manitoba (*Toronto Sunday Star*, April 4, 1982). As early as 1976 a Native Policing Branch was established in Ottawa to inform training as well as recruitment (*Liaison*, October, 1976).

Ethnic Recruiting

In the United States pressure for minority recruitment to the police grew out of the turmoil of the 1960s. But in Canada it was not until later that pressure was felt, as Canadian immigration began in the 1970s to include substantial members of visible minorities. Not only were immigrants becoming more apparent as part of the police officers' public, but also aboriginal Canadians. Increasingly evident, First Nations peoples not only were not being well served by law enforcement agents on reserves, but the increasingly large numbers in the major cities of Canada were virtually unrepresented in municipal policing, even in those police forces with major native policing responsibilities. In Winnipeg and in Edmonton, each of which had in 1990 about 1100 police officers, there were about one dozen natives on the respective forces. In Regina, there were 6 among 350 officers. Calgary offered 2 Indians and 1 Métis among 1230 police offices (*Globe and Mail*, April 20, 1990). While police organizations have taken steps to redress historic recruitment biases, especially in policy, few if any services are meeting their targets, even when they recruit aggressively, because the applicants are not forthcoming due to unfavourable minority views both of policing as work and policing as a career. In 1996 Edmonton Police reported qualified success—of 62 recruits, 7 were aboriginals and 9 were visible minorities; the service had sought at least 11 visible minority persons (*Edmonton Journal*, March 5, 1996).

Canadian police forces have always reflected in their composition the majority populations in Canadian society. Working-class males of British or Irish origins have long dominated in Anglo-Canada, and the presence and acceptance of other Caucasian minorities has

Montreal *Gazette*, May 20, '88 Dave Sidawa.

Constable Arlene Antoine became the first black female officer in the Montreal Urban Community Police force in 1988. (Reproduced by permission of the Montreal *Gazette*.)

varied with waves of public prejudice. During World War II, for example, police officers of Italian or of German extraction were considered undesirable; and not only were they not recruited, but officers with good reputations were dismissed. For example, Nero Brombal, a 12-year veteran of the Windsor Police Department, was dismissed because he was of Italian extraction. A letter of recommendation from his chief refers to his having "served faithfully" and that "The reason he is not a member of this Department now is on account of him being of Italian birth" (private correspondence, July 4, 1940). In December 1990, the Department made a formal apology to his family in keeping with the larger federal initiative of expressing regret for the treatment of Italian-Canadians during the War.

At present, probably fewer than 5% of police officers are distinguishably from minority groups. In a study conducted for the Canadian Association of Chiefs of Police, submitted in 1985, it was demonstrated that only four of the fourteen cooperating police forces had visible minority representation in excess of 1%. Not until 1986 did the Ottawa Police Force recruit its first Asian police officer, a former armed services corporal of Taiwanese origin. At the time of his recruitment only four other minority group persons were members of the force, two native Indians and two blacks (*Ottawa Citizen*, August 6, 1986).

In the 1980s in Toronto, the largest municipal police force in the country, fewer than 150 police officers were non-white in a total complement of approximately 5600—despite having Canada's largest urban non-white population (see Table 6-1). The first black police officer was hired in 1960, a Jamaican immigrant with experience in the Jamaica Constabulary. That same individual became the first black sergeant on the Metro force in 1982 (*Toronto Star*, October 10, 1982).

TABLE 6-1 **Visible Minorities in Policing, 1985–1987**		
Police Force	**Visible Minorities**	
	1985	**1987**
Metro Toronto Police Department	2.7	3.04
Vancouver Police Department	1.4	2.3
Halifax Police Department	1.8	1.9
Edmonton Police Department	n/a	0.7
Calgary Police Service	0.8	0.6
Regina Police Service	0.3	0.6
Montreal Urban Community Police	0.1	0.3
Ottawa Police Force	0.3	0.3
Moncton Police Force	0	0.07
Winnipeg Police Department	0.2	n/a
RCMP	n/a*	n/a
Ontario Provincial Police	0	n/a
Sûreté du Québec	n/a	n/a

Sources: Winterton, 1985; Jain, 1988. By permission of Canadian Association of Chiefs of Police (CACP).

*Although not reported in the Winterton study, the RCMP numbers are at less than 1% as of 1988 (*Liaison*, May 1988:5).

The Montreal Urban Community Police chief publicly committed his force to a minority recruitment drive in 1987. Advertisements were placed in newspapers, including the ethnic papers, and recruiters were sent to schools and community centres. In the period of little more than a month of this campaign there were 600 applications, of which 45 were visible minorities and another 46 from other ethnic minorities. From these 91 applicants, only 2 Italian-Canadians were selected, and 1 person of West Indian background (Montreal *Gazette*, October 21, 1987). The Montreal Urban Community Police publicly expressed an objective of 300 visible minority police, but recruiting that included waiving the normal expectation of CEGEP police technology programs netted a total of 8 recruits in 1986 and 1987. In 1987, in fact, all but three recruits were francophone, one English-speaking and the other two Italian-Canadians (Montreal *Gazette*, July 15, 1987; November 21, 1987).

Ironically, as late as 1988, well after repeated public commitments to minority recruitment, 2000 posters produced by the federal government for Police Week had to be withdrawn. The poster featured a photograph of Ottawa area police officers, including three women. But all were white (*Ottawa Citizen*, May 11, 1988).

In 1989 the RCMP sponsored a major national conference called "Policing for a Pluralistic Society 1989" and publicly reaffirmed its commitment to recruiting visible minorities. To do so it had been operating a national recruiting team since early in 1988. Its six members included one person of aboriginal origin, one oriental, one black, two women (one anglophone and one francophone) and one white male, university-educated (*Liaison*, May 1988:6). As individuals, sub-teams, and as a group, the team travels the nation, recruiting on university campuses and elsewhere.

At the same time, police organizations are slow to adjust their conventions, such as those related to dress; a prevalent view was that there was some inviolable merit in listing uniform codes, and that it was incumbent upon "new Canadians," and not the system, to adapt. Disputes arose, for example, over whether Sikh police officers would be allowed to wear the turbans that their religious beliefs required. By prohibiting turbans, police forces in effect prevented otherwise well-qualified Sikhs from serving. As one Montreal editorialist wrote, "the neatness of the Sikh turban would be preferable to the unkempt locks and no police cap that many officers now affect when driving in their cruisers" (Montreal *Gazette*, May 7, 1988). Major forces, such as Edmonton's, have modified dress codes, although the Sikh officers in the Edmonton service have elected not to wear turbans, beards, and the kirpans (the religiously significant ceremonial daggers). Toronto police decided to allow such changes in 1986 following a request from a recruit, although other serving Sikh officers in Toronto had not sought dress code changes. In April 1989, Canada's largest police force, the RCMP, also announced a change in its dress code to allow Sikh beards, turbans, and, if not exposed, the ceremonial dagger (*Ottawa Citizen*, April 27, 1989). The change, explicitly supported by the commissioner of the RCMP, elicited enormous public complaint, especially in western Canada, about the desecration of a "Canadian tradition." Later, in 1990, the commissioner of the RCMP also announced that native Canadians serving in the RCMP would be allowed to wear braids (*Ottawa Citizen*, October 25, 1990).

For years the turban dispute lingered on for the RCMP despite unequivocal Force policy. Former members brought a court case. Ultimately the Supreme Court of Canada refused to hear an appeal to overturn the inclusion of turbans in the official RCMP dress code (*Calgary Herald*, February 16, 1996).

While Canadian police are now publicly committed to minority recruitment, success has been slow. In Ontario, a provincial task force, one of whose members is the chief of Halton Regional Police Force, recommended in April 1989 that there be accelerated promotions and mid-rank recruitment of minority group persons in order to break the tedious slowness of minority recruitment. By May of 1989 the Ontario police associations had repudiated the recommendations, and by late June the Ontario Association of Chiefs of Police, whose president of the time was the same Halton chief who had helped shape the recommendations, rejected the proposals (*Ottawa Citizen*, June 29, 1989).

Only in the late 1970s and early 1980s did Canadian police services amend a point system (which assigned cumulative values for a range of attributes) for recruits that de-emphasized height and other physical characteristics in an effort to recruit a broader array of people to policing (*Toronto Star*, March 8, 1980; *Ottawa Journal*, March 10, 1980). To pursue the objective, some forces resorted to advertising in ethnic newspapers. The Ottawa force, for example, placed advertisements in Chinese-language ethnic newspapers in Montreal, Toronto, and Ottawa (*Ottawa Citizen*, November 23, 1985). Another basic measure was to amend recruitment criteria and review procedures. Eliminating physical requirements in favour of a point system allowed potential access for minority group members and women. By 1990 these measures had increased somewhat the applications of native persons and other visible minorities. The actual selection numbers are still slight, but an appreciable change from the past is evident. In a 1990 swearing-in ceremony of 16 recruits to the Ottawa police force, 5 were men from visible minorities. Another 4 of the 16 were women (*Ottawa Citizen*, April 26, 1990). Another innovative measure being attempted in Ottawa in order to win support is to have minority ride-alongs as paid summer employment (*Ottawa Citizen*, March 14, 1990).

In Toronto, a joint citizens and police working group prepared a report to be used as a recruiting guideline for the Metro Toronto Police and other interested forces. The working group recommended non-sensational measures such as review of application literature for biased content, recruitment speakers at community events and in high schools, television advertising, and "personalized" and "voluntary one-on-one" recruitment efforts by individual police officers. The working group also considered the interview screening, where many potential recruits are screened out, and sought qualified interviewers and unbiased testing, identifying a range of potential biases from security and reference checks to physical testing expectations (Toronto, 1986; *Toronto Star*, June 18, 1986). In 1989 a task force on minority–police relations toured the province of Ontario in the wake of several controversial incidents. The testimony was invariably critical, especially when the meager minority recruitment was discussed. In Ottawa the chief of police testified, expressing frustration at his inability to recruit more minority members. Members of the task force were critical, even sarcastic, prompting one editorial urging "patience" because of the "complex economic and sociological reasons" for slow recruitment. The criticisms were themselves criticized as "unfair and counter-productive," and resorting to "innuendo," and ethnic associations were urged "to encourage" young persons from their communities to become police officers (*Ottawa Citizen,* February 17, 1989). The Ontario Race Relations and Policing Task Force eventually offered 57 recommendations to enhance minority representation, the most controversial of which were lateral entry and preferential selection of minorities (Lewis, 1990:205–206).

It should be noted that the commitment to minority recruitment does introduce new stresses in policing. An obvious difficulty is the resentment of existing personnel who may be racist or may simply resent what they perceive to be preferential treatment, as in the RCMP members' resentment of francophone recruitment. Once recruited, the few minority group members are very conspicuous, to fellow police and public alike. They are targeted for special attention, a good deal of it negative, and experience inordinate stress in an already stressful occupational environment. Such was the case in 1981 in Toronto when a probationary police officer of East Indian background was dismissed. The probationary period, of course, is intended to assess the suitability of recruits on the job, before making a long-term career commitment. In this instance the dismissal, which moved from internal appraisal, to Divisional Court, to the Human Rights Commission, and to a binding decision confirming the dismissal by the Board of Police Commissioners, was based on failure to cooperate with other officers, improper use of a vehicle, failure to report an accident with a police vehicle, failing to give evidence in court, and improper dress. The counter allegation was racism (*Globe and Mail*, July 10, 1981).

When minority group persons, especially visible minorities, have been successfully recruited, they are placed in a fishbowl, highly visible to their peers, the public, and the media. In Quebec, the Bellmare Committee, reporting on the MUC Police, set a target of 10% visible minority representation, intended as sufficient to attain a "critical mass" that would permit "gradually dispelling stereotypes and prejudices" (Normandeau, 1990:222). In 1988 the press reported that the MUC's first police officer of Vietnamese origin began "walking the beat." On the same day a photo report marked the swearing-in of the MUC's first black female officer, having previously given front-page attention with the photograph and story of her having completed her course of training (Montreal *Gazette*, May 20, 1988; June 11, 1988). The pressures to conform, and to excel, are enormous.

Minority recruiting is subject to media attention, and sensitive to allegations of racism. In Toronto in 1989 a black female probationary constable was discharged for failing to meet marksmanship and driving standards. The constable alleged discrimination, and the Board of Police Commissioners agreed to extend her probation by six months in order to allow her to complete, without any failures, the nine-week training course at the Ontario Police College in Aylmer (*Ottawa Citizen*, February 11, 1989).

It is not altogether clear that critics or police themselves have any explicit benefits of more heterogeneous recruiting clearly in mind. At the most general level, the symbolism of more representative police forces is seen as valuable. Additionally, it is expected, perhaps, that heterogeneity will lead to a diversity of attitudes among police, and more tolerance. Also, some no doubt expect that minority police officers would be assignable to minority communities, and by virtue of their ascribed status, be more effective. Only the first expectation seems to be sound. Minority group police officers are simply too few in number to markedly alter attitudes. Nor are they apt to be assignable to minority neighbourhoods, given the nature of shift management. Moreover, often there is a disadvantage for the minority police officer in such an assignment. The minority officer will quite often not have the trust that had been expected, since for many minority groups the officer has denigrated his or her status by becoming a cop. Minority officers often explicitly prefer assignments away from their communities. This was the case in Montreal, for example, where the MUC Police's one officer of Chinese origin preferred to work away from the Chinese community (Montreal *Gazette*, September 7, 1986). Finally, too, there is no evidence to suggest—in fact, there is some to the contrary from the United States—that minority police will be less prone to abuse other minority persons. An isolated Toronto incident may serve to illustrate: a black police officer was among four chastised by a judge for the harassment of a black man (*Ottawa Citizen,* April 26, 1989).

American experience, too, has cast doubt on the assumption that minority police offer more satisfactory minority-group relations in policing. Certainly, while there may be satisfaction with the symbolic and democratic correctness of numerically proportionate police services, and perhaps even with the sense of being policed by one's own, there is no doubt that acts of misconduct or error that are often associated with police racism persist in circumstances of altered police composition. Black police officers in the United States, and native police forces such as those of the Navaho and the Iroquois nations, have themselves been involved in violent encounters and allegations of police abuse.

It has been argued that it is less important to alter recruitment composition than to alter perceived and real differential treatment of ethnic groups (Jayewardene and Talbot, 1990). The argument seems to be that minorities should not be made responsible for changing others' racial biases. In any case, since many minorities have negative attitudes regarding policing, they tend not to opt for an occupation in policing, even where there are favourable recruitment efforts.

Nonetheless the official commitments to ethnic diversity have continued to develop as policy, with the national Canadian Association of Chiefs of Police repeatedly reaffirming the practice. In 1993 the CACP published, for example, in French and in English, a booklet, *Police and Race Relations*, intended to encourage and advise all member bodies in their efforts to recruit and to retain minority members (CACP, 1993). In this "how-to" manual distributed to all police services, having observed some of the reasons why ethnic minorities might be disinclined or hostile to a policing career, recruitment strategies are offered (see Figure 6-2). They also report advice from a marketing firm following a review of five police services, consisting of advertising and marketing strategies to encourage minority recruits and good public relations, by depicting visible minorities in a diversity of affirmative roles (CACP, 1993:13). There are also succinct descriptions of career support measures to retain minority officers.

FIGURE 6-2   Recruiter's Top 10 Ideas for Improving Recruitment

1. Use qualified and trained recruiters.
2. Involve police officers who have personal and professional contacts in visible minority communities.
3. Recruit in visible minority communities.
4. Recruit in schools.
5. Use professional/community networks to identify candidates, such as career counsellors, principals, and clergy.
6. Use visible minority constables who understand equity and race relations issues.
7. Consult visible minorities about the recruitment efforts.
8. Advertise in the ethnic media.
9. Use recruitment teams.
10. Encourage civilian staff to seek employment as police officers.

Source: CACP, 1993:11. By permission of Canadian Association of Chiefs of Police (CACP).

Female Recruiting

In the 1970s and 1980s demand also grew for the recruitment of women to Canadian policing. Where, in the past, there were a few policewomen or matrons for special duties, the modern expectation is that women be recruited to serve in the same capacity as any male officer. By 1980 police services were recruiting women as full-service officers, and not as policewomen for special duties. Just as with visible minorities, as police yielded under pressure to the criticism of exclusionary physical requirements and amended expectations as to height, opportunities for the recruitment of women increased. It must be emphasized that this is a relatively recent development. Many forces were effectively excluding women in the late 1970s and early 1980s. In 1977 the press covered complaints from women, for example, turned down by the OPP and by the Ottawa Police Force on grounds of physical height and weight requirements. The requirement was 5'10" and 160 pounds. Following a complaint in 1979, the Ottawa Police Force was ordered by the provincial Board of Inquiry to change its standards in order to accommodate women (*Ottawa Citizen*, September 14, 16, 24, 1977; January 20, 1979).

Yet, by the end of the 1980s relatively few women had been recruited, and inevitably, fewer yet promoted. This experience has been consistent with the American experience whose earlier efforts at female recruitment, aided by formal affirmative action objectives, were associated with very gradual increase; some cities such as Detroit actually declined in female numbers.

In Ottawa, the first female constable, who had joined the force in 1961 as a meter maid, was promoted to detective in 1980. In Montreal, only in 1988 did the MUC Police have its first female detective. The woman, a detective-sergeant, was one of the first ten women recruited eight years previously by the MUC Police. In 1987 that sergeant became a lieutenant, the first woman to achieve that rank in Quebec (Montreal *Gazette*, May 13, 1987; June 7, 1988). Montreal also had the dubious distinction of having the first Canadian female police officer killed in the course of duty. In 1985, while investigating a report of an armed prowler, the constable was shot and killed by a rifle bullet. The tragic incident occurred as the MUC Police prepared to swear in 34 new recruits, among them 14 women, bringing to 111 the women in the MUC force (Montreal *Gazette*, October 24, 28, 1984). By 1989, when in January the MUC Police swore in 47 new constables, 12 were women. Included in the 12 was a diminutive (5 feet 2 inches) 34-year-old mother of 2 children (Montreal *Gazette*, January 25, 1989).

In Quebec, admission to the Institut de Police du Québec at Nicolet was adjudged to be fair, as is the training for women. But observers noted the continued resistance in "the marketplace," as prospective police employers avoid hiring female graduates (Montreal *Gazette*, March 11, 1989). The OPP launched a special recruitment drive in 1984, headed by a woman police officer. The campaign was reported to have doubled the number of female applicants over the previous year, based on the first six months of each year. More than 4000 female applicants were reported (*Ottawa Citizen*, July 23, 1984).

Women in policing were slow to gain acceptance, and slow to win promotion. In 1988, 18.8% of all police personnel were female, but only 5.1% of police officers were female. More than 95% of women police were constables, 4% were non-commissioned officers, and only .01% were command rank officer (*Juristat* 9, August 1989:4). In Canada's largest municipal police force, Metro Toronto, early in 1987 there were 226 female offices, in contrast to more than 5000 males. They represented, therefore, merely 4.2% of the force (*Toronto Sunday Star*, March 8, 1987).

The RCMP has been a national leader, with the Force recruiting its first female troop for Depot training in 1974 (Linden, 1984:1). But even with such early initiative in the RCMP where women had been recruited rather aggressively, numbers remained small, around 7% as of 1988, well short of the 20% target. As important as sheer numbers, the attitudes of many male force members remained negative. In part, prevailing attitudes related to the traditional expectation that policing depended upon strength and the capacity to use physical force; women were defined as too weak, and apt to endanger male officers. But in no small part, too, negative attitudes were a result of perceptions of favouritism, as is commonly found in any affirmative action program. This was illustrated by the opposition to the commissioner of the RCMP when he determined to employ female instructors at the training depot. Force members and their divisional representatives objected not to women instructors, they stated, but to bypassing normal promotions standards and procedures. Seven positions advertised were open to women only. The commissioner's action, which had been intended to appoint women where none existed previously, and to improve the environment for female recruits (there were 60 women out of 300 in training in 1988), was seen by members as violating the integrity and fairness of the system (*Ottawa Citizen,* April 6, 1988; *Liaison,* May 1988:18).

The women in police forces are subject to scrutiny, and are resented by males, especially older males with whom they did not share training. On the one hand they may be subject to rude and sexist jokes and innuendo, and on the other, to protective gestures by "fatherly-types." In 1969 the chairman of the Toronto Police Commission stated that "the woman's place is in the home with her child" (*Toronto Sunday Star*, March 8, 1987). Where a protective attitude dominates organizationally, women will tend to be assigned less onerous duties, including less demanding patrols if assigned regular policing duties.

Resistance to female police officers is strongest in smaller police forces. In 1988, for example, a modest award of $2000 was granted by the British Columbia Council of Human Rights to a qualified female applicant to the force of Matsqui. She had been rejected twice for policing, in 1980 and 1986, despite having had eight and a half years experience as a police officer in New Westminster. In 1986 she was working part time as a civilian dispatcher for the Matsqui force. Only in 1987 did Matsqui finally hire her as its first woman, after the suit, and after the complainant had been accepted by the RCMP. Explaining the attitude, she stated that "There's a lot of older males there and maybe that's why" (*Ottawa Citizen*, December 24, 1988).

When in service, women police officers report few if any difficulties in performing their duties. They do frequently report difficulties with their male colleagues, however, who react with an array of positive and negative gender stereotypes. For example, male officers tend to persist in the conviction that strength and size are intrinsic to policing. It has been a problem from the beginning to decide whether women in training should have to conform completely to standards, including levels of physical performance, despite their physical disadvantage, or whether they should be treated explicitly as exceptions (Martin, 1982:105–119).

On the job, men, especially older men, seem to believe that courage is associated with the male sex, and that women will let down male partners in a dangerous encounter. As women were recruited and experienced the concerns of all rookies, they often seemed to buy into the male presumption of the importance of strength. Ontario female police officers, in interviews in 1978, worried about perhaps having to use a gun where a man might not, because of physical inequality, or of being overcome in a physical struggle (*Globe and Mail,* September 21, 1978). One police officer, remarking on her recruit class of 13 women, said that all but 3 had left policing because of job stress, lack of confidence, or the social pressures of policing (*Ottawa Journal*, September 28, 1978). Although women, like others, may recognize the overemphasis on physical capacity and the aggressive skills and attitudes that males acquire through prior socialization, they still enter an occupational environment where such is the prevailing culture.

Incidents that appeared to corroborate this expectation tended to be well publicized while women were still a novelty in policing. A case of some notoriety in the United States was that of two black female Detroit police officers who were dismissed because of "cowardice." It was claimed that they stood idly by while a naked man beat up a male police officer. As the enquiry developed, however, it appeared that an aggressive male supervisor intervened forcefully when they were calming a distraught man. Both were eventually restored to the force (*Toronto Star*, January 27, 1980; *Ottawa Journal,* March 22, 1980). In Canada, one incident involved a female RCMP officer in Virden, Manitoba. She was shot and wounded, and later testified that she had hesitated to use her gun, first shouting a warning and then eventually firing at the gunman and missing before she herself was shot and wounded. The constable had finished her basic training six weeks previously (Montreal *Gazette*, November 16, 1978).

Fortunately, examples of successful female police officers were also well publicized, and serve to contradict the stereotyping. One off-duty Metro Toronto policewoman observed a bank holdup, tackled the bandit, fought with him, and recovered the money; the offender escaped only after pulling a gun (*Toronto Star*, February 21, 1986).

Male stereotyping of women and preconceptions as to their ability to perform the traditional tasks of policing have not been confined to rank-and-file officers. Commissioned officers in Canada were slow to acknowledge a role for female police officers, and slow to adapt their organizational practices to accommodate women. A remarkable dispute occurred in Ottawa in 1983, when the chief of the Ottawa Police Force refused to transfer a pregnant police officer to non-street duties. The police officer was one of four women hired in 1979, over the objections of the force, following a requirement by the Ontario Human Rights Commission that the force amend its physical requirements, which were sexually discriminatory. The chief, defending his decision that at three months pregnancy she be required to go on unpaid maternity leave, had stated that "Due to the economy and the restraints placed on us, we simply can't afford it. The city can't afford it. She can go on UIC if she needs the money." The Police Commission overturned the chief's decision, agreeing that she be allowed to work in the police property room in a role that had been intended for a civilian employee (*Ottawa Citizen*, November 30, 1983).

Contending with a similar situation, the Winnipeg Police Force also found itself overruled by its police commission. A police officer who was seven months pregnant had been obliged to assume clerical duties at reduced pay. Light inside duties at full salary had, until this case, been the Winnipeg practice. The Winnipeg Police Association grieved, and won an award of back pay from the commission. Thereupon the Winnipeg police management declared that in the future, pregnant constables must submit to a medical examination to determine fitness for duty, and if unfit, they would be required to take unpaid maternity leave, as had been attempted in Ottawa (*Ottawa Citizen*, November 30, 1983). A similar incident was ruled on in 1988. A pregnant police officer in Fort Frances, Ontario was refused permission to wear civilian clothes and no gunbelt during a pregnancy in 1985, and her efforts to modify her uniform were rejected by the chief of police who referred to her looking "ridiculous and stupid" and "like a clown." She was placed on unpaid leave for six months, and immediately thereafter, pregnant again, on a further five-month unpaid leave, having been refused light duties. She took her case to the Ontario Human Rights Commission, seeking compensation, and was turned down, with the denial confirmed by the Supreme Court of Ontario, ruling that the uniform and gunbelt were essential. In the same ruling, however, they also found that the force was at fault for not having offered her light duties as they would have done for a male officer on medical leave (*Ottawa Citizen,* December 3, 1988).

It should be acknowledged that police forces have generally been loath to acknowledge that there are "light duties" to which any injured or otherwise unfit sworn personnel can be assigned, men or women. In 1984, for example, an Ottawa police constable was dismissed, although he had requested light duties, because of a blood deficiency requiring regular medication. The disability only became known in the course of a physical examination after the officer was beaten by three assailants (*Ottawa Citizen*, April 28, 1984).

In 1986 following public complaints of harassment from women in RCMP British Columbia detachments, the federal solicitor general called for an enquiry. Six women complained that harassment by male colleagues was responsible for the high number of women leaving the force, a rate five times higher than for men. In a two-year period, 1983 to 1985, 69 women were hired and 68 resigned. Former officers said that sexual expectations were such that you were thought of by males as "a lesbian if you didn't or a slut if you did." The wives of male police officers were also a problem, often convinced of affairs. "They were all convinced you were sleeping with their husband. Some of the men even told their wives that to get more attention" (*Ottawa Citizen*, January 20, 21, 1986).

Another well-publicized incident illustrated the attitudinal difficulties facing the RCMP as they have attempted to lead in the employment of female police offices. In 1988 the public relations vanguard of the Force, the Musical Ride unit, was splashed over the front page of the nation's newspapers following the complaint of a female Ride member that she had been subjected to extreme hazing and that a videotape of her, including an obscene gesture, had been made while she slept on an RCMP bus. At her request the female officer was transferred out of the Ride, and 12 male officers were reported to have been disciplined (*Ottawa Citizen*, June 9, 1988). What may or may not have been no more than the sometimes ribald interaction that has traditionally characterized close-knit male units assumed a different character because of the changes associated with integrating women into the Force.

The problems of integrating women successfully into policing does seem to diminish with time, as the turnover in police forces removes the older generation of police officers who have been most opposed to female police. Male police officers were questioned in 1980 about their views of women in policing. While 30% were opposed and 20% were uncertain, 50% approved. Older officers were more likely to be opposed. Reasons cited for opposition were physical size and strength, and the inability to deal with violent situations (Vancouver *Sun*, September 13, 1980; *Ottawa Citizen*, September 15, 1980). Other reasons included the belief that they took more sick leave and were more frequently injured. Also, it was suggested that they would create marital problems, as they would be resented by spouses of male officers. This latter bias was starkly revealed in the comments of American chiefs of police meeting at the FBI Academy in 1976. The chiefs declared the need to defend the family, and opined that women police officers meant sexual relations on the job and marital breakdown. The chief of police of Dallas put the point sarcastically when stating that "If you put two women together [in a squad car] they fight. If you put male and female together, they fornicate" (*Ottawa Citizen*, October 6, 1976).

Steadily, albeit slowly, roles for women are being normalized, and they are not excluded by definition from any standard task or special unit. In 1987, for example, the first woman in Canada to join a police tactical unit joined that special squad in the Hamilton-Wentworth Regional Police (*Toronto Sunday Star*, October 4, 1987).

Through the 1980s and 1990s attitudes and tensions appeared to moderate. More women were recruited and the glare of the spotlight diminished. They were more often accepted by their colleagues, with whom they were seen to perform competently. Research data began to confirm the competence. Early American research reported that women performed equally well as men, with the bonus that they were found to be more friendly and pleasant by civilians (Milton, 1972; Bloch and Anderson, 1974; *Globe and Mail*, December 1, 1977). Persistent research in Canada by Linden on the RCMP and Vancouver police (Linden and Minch, 1980, 1982; Linden, 1983, 1984, 1985; Linden and Fillmore, 1993) indicated that women do the work as well as men, including similar arrest rates. Women do appear to take more sick days, but men are more apt to have job-related injuries. There is one striking difference: more women, almost twice as many, leave the police service to which they were originally recruited (Linden and Fillmore, 1993: 18).

Available research does suggest that female job satisfaction and the evaluation of female job performance in policing is high (Linden, 1985). Yet female attrition is also significantly higher than for males. Linden's work suggests that this had to do with internal animosity or performance problems, but is related to marital obligations. Policing is known to strain marriages for males, and there is some indication that postings or shift schedules that keep an officer from shared time with a spouse are more often judged unacceptable by the married female officer than by the male officer.

By the 1990s women, while still a minority of around 10% in policing, had achieved substantial numbers. The change has been methodical, from a mere .5% of all police in the 1960s, fewer than 200 persons, increasing by the mid-1980s to about 3.5%, and increasing more rapidly through the 1990s to 9%, more than 5000 persons, by 1994 (see Table 6-2). It may be speculated that their numbers are still so small as to have them subordinate to, and even adopt, the male subculture attitudes and behaviours of policing. As women do the work, they adapt to the attitudes of male fellow workers, male supervisors, and male managers. But unquestionably female police officers in the 1990s are doing policing. And slowly they are ascending the policing hierarchy, and moving into command positions. While there

TABLE 6-2	Female Police Officers in Canada, Selected Years	
Year	**Number**	**Percentage of Total**
1965	190	0.6
1970	186	0.5
1975	562	1.2
1980	1092	2.2
1985	1833	3.6
1990	3573	6.4
1993	4561	8.1
1994	5056	9.0

Source: Adapted from Statistics Canada, *Juristat*, Catalogue No. 85-002, Volume 16, Number 1, 1996:4 (Table 1).

were still fewer than 1% women commissioned officers in 1994 (.06%), the number of female non-commissioned officers more than doubled from 1986 (3.74%) to 1994 (8.43%) (*Juristat* 16, 1996:5), as new cohorts of female police constables worked their way up the police rank hierarchy.

Sexual Preference

The traditional police premium upon toughness or male machismo is illustrated in the attitudes to women. Another related manifestation is the police attitude to homosexuality. In several American forces, most particularly San Francisco, there have been challenges to this stereotyping. The first homosexual recruits to the San Francisco Police Department were sworn in 1979 (*Ottawa Journal*, November 15, 1979). But in Canada the concern over a role for homosexuals in policing has barely surfaced, and where it has, the issue has been in connection with the continued service of someone discovered during their career to be a homosexual. Police have been reluctant in the extreme to accept homosexuals in policing, viewing homosexuality as a compromising perversion. When homosexuality is discovered, an officer is ostracized, prevented from career advancement, or forced to withdraw from policing. Court interventions, however, are forcing a change. A former RCMP officer who had been forced to resign in 1984 was awarded $100 000 in damages in an out-of-court settlement in 1988, and reinstatement as a regular officer. Since his resignation he had been employed as a civilian member of the RCMP (*Ottawa Citizen*, July 19, 1988).

Expressive of prevalent attitudes, the attorney general of Nova Scotia addressed a convention of maritime police chiefs in 1986. He used the occasion to declare that he had cabinet endorsement of his opposition to recruiting homosexual police officers. He declared that the government would even resort to the "notwithstanding clause" in the constitution if necessary to prevent homosexual recruitment (Montreal *Gazette*, July 14, 1986). Nova Scotia political comment notwithstanding, to this day, homosexuality in policing is by and large not addressed in Canada. As in other occupations, homosexuals are not an affirmative recruitment category or group in policing, even though explicit discrimination on grounds of sexual orientation would normally be prohibited. Nor is the silent incidence of homosexuality in policing often acknowledged, although a national support group for officers is organized out of Toronto (Seagrave, 1997:99). The extent of homosexual numbers in Canadian police services is simply not known, nor is there quantitative indication of recruitment or work experiences of homosexual Canadians in police organizations.

AGE AND RETIREMENT

Another individual characteristic that has received scant attention as regards Canadian police is age. With regard to age regulations, there have been no serious attacks upon age limits in police recruitment. Consistent with its paramilitary traditions, and its emphasis upon strength and the applications of force, policing has traditionally depended upon young men. Virtually no police force will consider as a recruit any person older than the mid-20s. There is little lateral entry, even for very senior personnel. One challenge did occur in 1985. A man who had served both as a correctional services officer and as an OPP auxiliary officer had applied at age 40 to become a police officer in the Ontario town of Smiths Falls. He did not pass beyond the screening stage. An Ontario Human Rights Commission hearing was convinced that the applicant was better qualified than the two successful candidates and that there had been age discrimination. The Smiths Falls Police Commission was ordered to pay general damages of $3000. By the date of the award the complainant was employed as an officer in the sheriff's department of Sarasota, Florida (*Ottawa Citizen*, January 4, 1986).

Twenty-five or thirty years of service is the normal duration of police service, with many senior officers long since removed from routine street-level contact policing. Exit at age 55 is normal, and service to age 60 unusual. For many officers, the full pension, with the possibility of a replacement career following retirement, is usually attractive, especially in the context of a cultivated cynicism about the "job." Yet challenges can successfully occur. In Ontario, for example, a Niagara Regional Police inspector, forced by his organization to retire at age 60 as contracted, brought an appeal to the Human Rights Commission. The commission observed that mandatory retirement in the province is age 65, and irrespective of collective agreements, therefore, police service to that age may be expected. In settlement of the particular claim, the police service is reported to have paid the complainant $229 275 (*Ottawa Sun*, February 27, 1994). Also, for most ranks, the organization tends not to prepare the individual for exit. Senior police, with management experience, do have some greater opportunity to move into second careers. Chiefs and commissioners have been appointed by corporations and government departments to executive positions. In some instances, as in the case of an MUC chief, upon retirement another position as police chief is found (Montreal *Gazette*, February 23, 1989). The occupational experience for most police, however, as for most other people, becomes dominant, the basis of daily life orientation and for social networking. Faced with retirement after 25 or 30 years of service, the typical police officer finds he or she has few marketable skills for a second career, especially if exiting from a low rank, and no preparation for the post-retirement idleness and loss of social contact (Johnson, 1978; Forcese and Cooper, 1985).

One advantage in the present period for most police is decent pension income, a benefit that has been effectively negotiated by police unions over the previous decades. The benefits are associated with major police forces, and often are still not significant in minor municipal or small-town organizations. In 1990 six Montreal Urban Community Police officers went to court because the city and the Police Brotherhood representing them had failed to standardize pensions within the force. When the consolidation of Montreal area police forces occurred in 1972, the Montreal city pension benefits were superior, but the suburban officers within the MUC Police who began careers in the now-amalgamated suburban forces, will retire with significantly smaller pensions: at the rate of 22% of salary versus 69% (Montreal *Gazette*, February 23, 1989).

In light of the costs of police recruitment and training, and the non-productivity of retired persons, it may be speculated that some effort to extend service might be cost effective and—assuming the "burnout" syndrome has been avoided—useful in policing. Just as there is reason to believe that the service of a greater number of women acts to moderate police violence, it has been suggested that more senior personnel on the street would moderate conflict. Conceivably, too, more senior recruits would be desirable. Police psychologists have argued that youth is a major factor in police violence, with young officers more impressed with a forceful approach to policing, especially because they are inexperienced and insecure. But older officers are generally moved off the street, or onto day shifts, creating a circumstance where conflict encounters are more often met by young police officers (Meredith, 1984:26). In one of the most influential works of research on policing, Niederhoffer offered controversial observations about police attitudes of cynicism and authoritarianism. Stressing that these were learned attitudes, he observed that the better-educated police officer was less apt to display authoritarian views and behaviours. But such persons were promoted off the street, into administration, and out of public contact (Niederhoffer, 1967:138–140). Or they are hastened to retirement, for the conventional role conception of policing still stresses youth.

RECRUIT TRAINING

Canada, like the United States but unlike Britain, does not have uniform training curricula. Major police forces, such as the RCMP and the Ontario and the Quebec provincial police, have their own training establishments. So do some large urban forces such as Metro Toronto's, with the Charles Bick College. But the locus and the nature of police training varies across the country. In most municipal forces people are recruited, oriented, and then sent to police college for training at the expense of the province. In some cases they are recruited from community college programs, and then offered in-service training.

Most Canadian police recruit training facilities are standalone. That is, they operate for police recruits, and officers returning for additional training, in disassociation from any public educational institution. Even where there is a location within a college environment, such as the Atlantic Police College on a community college campus in Charlottetown, Prince Edward Island, or the Saskatchewan Police College on the University of Regina campus, aside from some lecturers from the community, the environment is one of police recruit students and police or former police instructors.

The isolation of police recruit training, and its paramilitary character, is most pronounced at RCMP Depot in Regina. In an RCMP-approved film, "Tall Boots to Fill," the paramilitary character of RCMP training is evident. The RCMP operate Canada's best known training establishment in Regina, Saskatchewan, with a basic recruit training course of 26 to 27 weeks. The program is introduced in the *Reference and Orientation Manual* as a "military or paramilitary lifestyle," which recruits may come to regret. There is an explicit emphasis upon drill and discipline, explained as the RCMP way of developing group solidarity. But it is also evident at the other police training establishments, such as the Quebec Police Academy at Nicolet, the OPP Academy at Orillia, or for Ontario municipal police, the OPP Academy at Aylmer. A paramilitary character exists at most police training establishments. With only police recruits present, the objective is rapid socialization to the occupation. The prevalent expectation, especially explicit in the RCMP, is that from the immediate objectives of group cohesion, peer dependency, and organizational commitment, achieved from "imposed discipline," will come a "self-discipline" needed to police effectively. In a handout for their new recruits the RCMP stated that "Self-discipline has to start from a base of imposed discipline. Recruits are involved in a semi-military lifestyle, which imposes high standards of dress and turnout, instant obedience to orders, and a requirement to abide by rules and regulations" (RCMP recruit handout, circa 1980). Yet the modern inclination in most police training is to diminish such paramilitary emphasis, especially as more attention is paid to human relations skills and new-style policing. It has been observed, in contradiction of the RCMP assumption, that paramilitary training, incorporating harassment and demeaning demands, is poorly suited to policing, which consists of intelligent discretion and problem solving (Post, 1992).

Somewhat distinguishable is the newer Justice Institute of British Columbia, which seems to offer broader training content and will include in courses persons from other non-policing criminal justice occupations (Seagrave, 1997:80). In most jurisdictions, as in Ontario, an individual is selected by a police service, and then sent for police college training, with pay. Training duration is also broadly similar, extending from about 15 to 26 weeks at different institutions, and variously divided into modules. The Quebec Police Academy, for example, offers 17 weeks of basic training, and the Ontario Police Academy 15 weeks. The 15 weeks in Ontario would be split, perhaps into 9- and 6-week periods, with field time in between, followed by several months of probationary service where training on-the-job is expected to continue. A field-trained recruit would also be expected to return to the college for additional training units.

Policing is probably one of the most demanding jobs in our society. Police have to contend with a plethora of demands, many of them dangerous and stressful, and they do so with often little time for reflection. Yet the intellectual and skills-related requirements expected of police recruits are modest. Generally the remarkable feature of police recruit training is its brevity. Were one to assume a simple occupation, with rudimentary and straightforward job demands, then training of high school-educated recruits for no more than 26 weeks—or in some extreme instances, not at all—would be acceptable. But such brief pre-service training, followed by non-systematic supervised or probationary service of six to twelve months, usually referred to as an in-service training period, is deplorable for a demanding, stressful, and sensitive job such as policing.

Where police spokespersons may speak of policing as a profession, in fact, it is treated as a trade, an activity where the prevalent view and practice is that effective job training is on-the-job experience. Everyone starts at the same level, and no one is promoted except from within the organization on the basis of normal experience. Unlike in a profession, recruits lack high standards for selection, and are "trained" in basic programs lasting weeks rather than years. It is as if physicians, selected from among indifferent high school students, were then turned loose on a public with a dozen or so weeks of crash preparation in the glamour aspects of medicine, such as surgery. In policing, persons authorized to carry and use weapons, make life-threatening decisions, and detain and arrest members of the public, are placed in positions of considerable authority. In an occupation intrinsically characterized by the exercise of discretion or judgment, police training consists of brief emphasis upon "cookbook" law and physical skills including weapons training, and cultivating a dependence upon the obedience to command, which is stressed in the paramilitary system.

Curriculum content in police basic training is very task-oriented, or "cookbook" training. The objective is to have the police novice quickly prepared to deal with work routine, while continuing to learn on the job. "Academic" content focusses upon criminal statutes and police powers. Driver training, general patrol and investigative practices, physical training, force techniques, and firearms training are other major components.

Weapons use remains a focal element of police training. Contrary to some public misconceptions, police are not trained to be marksmen, engaging in precision shooting enabling them to disable offenders. In Canadian jurisdictions police are taught to use weapons as a final resort, but once committed, they are guided by their "instinct training," where they begin shooting as they raise their weapon, and aim not for an extremity but for the torso, with emphasis upon hits (*Ottawa Citizen*, August 21, 1987). Periodically, there are demands for improved firearms training, and for training in alternatives to the use of firearms. A flurry of incidents in Ontario in 1979, for example, precipitated such an interest. In one case an Ottawa police officer shot to death from close range a burglary suspect, generating public comment and editorial opinion seeking training in self-defence and the disarming of offenders without resort to guns (*Ottawa Journal*, August 14, September 7, 1979).

The skills-related training that is presumed by the public to be well done in policing, even though general education and cultural sensitivity may be lacking, is itself not so clearly a feature of police programs. Driving skills, for example, have been notoriously poor, as will become clear in our review of police errors in Chapter Eight. So too, tactical intervention in crisis situations has been shown to be deficient, as in an example involving the OPP, where an operational breakdown resulted in the death of an innocent man. Similarly in Montreal, when Mark Lepine went on a rampage killing 14 young women at the University of Montreal, a coroner's inquest concluded that it was perhaps due to divine grace and not police expertise that there were not more deaths. The coroner wrote of the event and the assailant's suicide, "Thanks to God, he decided on his own that it was enough." He took his own life "although he was not in danger, since no police assault was under way or even obviously being prepared" (*Ottawa Citizen*, May 15, 1990). The police failure to intervene led to a decision to introduce new training courses to deal with "leadership and supervision, safe maneuvering in high risk situations, stress management, and the efficient use of weapons and communications" (*Ottawa Citizen*, May 25, 1990).

Increasingly, however, despite traditional emphases, police college curricula are attempting to dispel romantic notions that recruits bring to the training in the expectation of cops-and-robbers careers. The director of the Quebec Police Institute considers that the one of the major jobs is to deal with the stereotypes of the recruits, to dispel their "*Miami Vice* ideas of what a cop's job is all about" (Montreal *Gazette*, February 27, 1988). The remark is frequently echoed by veterans who have remained on patrol, and speak about community service and the social-work role of policing (*Ottawa Citizen*, June 5, 1982). Training in basic language skills, driving, helping activities, and multiculturalism characterize the curriculum in addition to the traditional emphasis upon physical competence and investigative procedures. There has been an increasing use of role-playing, and the use of professional actors, to simulate work experiences such as the domestic disputes to which young and very inexperienced police officers must respond.

There is new emphasis especially upon ethnic relations, yielding to the pressures of incidents that have plagued police forces in the previous two decades as the character of the Canadian population has changed. At the Quebec Police Institute in Nicolet, for example, unfortunate incidents such as the shooting death of a young black man by an MUC constable are featured in the training, and staff psychologists lecture on ethnic relations (*Ottawa Citizen*, March 12, 1988).

The military influence in police organizations has been singled out as a persisting flaw. The perceived difficulty can be summarized as a disparity between police training and organizational decision making on the one hand, and actual police duties on the other. Police training has tended to emphasize discipline and obedience to command, as in the military. The emphasis may be well-suited to most aspects of the military role, where there is a group response to conflict, and a forceful response, applied in a concentrated manner under the direction of superior officers who define the objectives. But police officers rarely work in groups; they work as individuals. They are obviously subject to orders, but the individual officer in the street does have to make his own decisions, often under pressure and with little time. There is no superior officer with whom to consult, usually only a peer of similar rank.

Policing requires the exercise of judgment or discretion, but all prior training stresses obedience. Rather than preparing the recruit for the actual field circumstances of policing, training practices stress a response that is often ill suited, except insofar as they teach some self-control. Policing and soldiering are not alike, but the structure of police, from selection through training and command structure, is based upon the premise that they are.

Another feature of police training is its isolation, an unfortunate foretelling of the isolation that is characteristic of police in service. Like the military college, or other "total institutions" in Goffman's terms (1961), the recruit is placed in a circumstance of new social dependencies, and resocialized. The recruit training and work experience that induces isolation was remarked upon in 1969 in the public report to the government of the Canadian Committee on Corrections. "The nature of police work tends to produce in the police officer a sense of isolation and to set him apart from the community" (Canada, 1969). This isolation begins in the training establishment, where the recruit is immersed in a new environment requiring total commitment, conformity, and loyalty. Thereafter, the report continues, "police policy will require him to be selective in his associations, which necessarily accentuates this isolation." It follows, therefore, suggests the report, that "To counteract this tendency towards isolation ... police training programs should be broadened with a view to developing in police officers a better understanding of their role in relation to total societal goals and a better understanding of the behaviour of particular groups."

Years after this report was made, the remarks remain all too apt. They were suggested again in Toronto by a sergeant who observed that too many police officers have known nothing but policing since they were 17 years of age. Recruited at such an early age, they resist other points of view and change (*Toronto Sunday Star*, January 25, 1981).

Unlike in the United Kingdom, where a standard national curriculum has been developed with very specific objectives, police training in Canada lacks uniformity. There is no doubt that the training begins to develop a sense of occupational solidarity, but it may also inculcate a sense of isolation and intolerance. A former police officer criticized his training as isolating, for recruits are conditioned to socialize with their peers and to avoid discussing their work with others. Veterans employed as teachers stress peer loyalty, and teach recruits to distrust outsiders in favour of the opinions of the police subculture (*Ottawa Journal*, April 18, 1979).

Difficult to accommodate in a cookbook skills-oriented tradition is course content dealing with interpersonal skills and social relations. All basic training now attempts to do so, attempting to represent the preventive and service elements of police work. As amendments are pondered in police curricula, the emphasis has been upon better incorporating these "soft" elements, whether in basic or in-service training. In 1992, for example, a major review and recommendations for police training was released in Ontario. The "police learning system" was premised upon a need for more elaborate police preparation, and the participation of public educational institutions. The report suggested 20 learning requirements for a constable, which overall represented a de-emphasis upon traditional police training content (see Figure 6-3).

In-Service Training

It is not simply that basic training is inadequate. In a sense, in any occupation or profession, including medicine and law, basic training or education is inadequate in itself, and is

---

FIGURE 6-3   Twenty Strategic Learning Requirements for the Police Constable

1. Communications skills
2. Interpersonal and sensitivity skills
3. Knowledge of human behaviour
4. Ability to adapt and work with community diversity
5. Ability to serve victims
6. Ability to initiate, promote, and facilitate community policing
7. Ability to use police-related technology
8. Analytical skills and problem-solving ability
9. Knowledge of political systems and processes
10. Knowledge of crime prevention strategies
11. Personal and organizational development skills
12. Knowledge of other agencies
13. Team-building skills
14. Ability to use crime-trend information
15. Ability to apply basic police authorities and knowledge of case preparation
16. Ability to act ethically and professionally
17. Ability to maintain a reasonable level of physical fitness and well being
18. Ability to use force appropriately
19. Officer safety skills
20. Conflict avoidance, resolution, and mediation skills

Source: Ontario, 1992:359.

---

followed by systematic on-the-job training (internship, articling, and so on). In policing, however, the brief training is followed by non-systematic on-the-job tutoring and example by other serving police officers. Beyond recruit training is a mixed bag of on-the-job coaching and peer tutoring, whereby many of the values, attitudes, and practices prevalent in the police culture are passed on. Additionally, to enhance on-the-job learning police services have resorted to an irregular muddle of courses for in-service officers. These courses are quite erratically available. Officers may be selected to attend; others may not be freed from duties to attend. From time to time some issue or operational circumstance demands a "course," perhaps no more than a lecture. Often when ordered to attend, the courses are met with almost juvenile rowdiness, or reserved skepticism, because they are inconsistent with the action ethic of the police subculture. And as the courses are often ill conceived and ill prepared, a reserved or even negative attitude may be appropriate.

Officers may be referred to courses provided "in-house" by the service, perhaps in collaboration with a community body, as has often been done with race relations. Sometimes officers may be referred to courses at public institutions, colleges, or universities; and increasingly serving officers are choosing to pursue university courses and degrees. Also there is usually an expectation that officers will from time to time return to a police training establishment for refresher courses, or advanced courses. Even where there is a specified expectation that persons return to police college following basic training and service, it may not happen. An Ontario task force reporting in 1990 noted the need to upgrade the quality of in-service training, and called for "high standards" for training and retraining of coach officers who should also be "monitored" (Lewis, 1990:208).

The recruit is taught to adapt and survive by learning the conventions of the police sub-culture, and the system of established beliefs and values is thus maintained. On the job, guided by a more experienced officer with whom he or she is assigned to work, the rookie learns to cope with the work environment, including management. Fundamentally he or she acquires a shorthand of responses to environmental stimuli. Certain environmental cues call for certain reactions, usually reactions oriented to maintaining the police officer's authority and control. Control is everything in an encounter. Disrespect threatens control. Imperfect information threatens control. Non-compliance threatens control. And the absence of control is stressful and dangerous, the police officer learns, and potentially life-threatening.

The police culture defines on-the-job training as a real world correction of academy preparation. A headline in a recent media account of the experiences of a rookie officer and her coach read: "Life on the Street Must Be Learned on the Beat" (*Ottawa Citizen*, September 21, 1997), a truism that often is exaggerated and represented as having to undo everything previously taught.

If the police academy has a few surprises for the new recruit, in-service training and occupational experience offer even more contradictory lessons for the new police officer. There has long been evidence that service acts to substantially amend academy instruction. Gradually, on the job, the novice acquires survival skills, both with respect to the street and to the organization. Research suggests that appropriate rates of work are taught, with peers and even superiors not appreciating the "ratebuster." The high motivation and zeal that may have characterized the recruit are gradually eroded to low commitment and activity, defined as behaviour less likely to get one into trouble. In the words of an American police veteran, "There's only two things you gotta know around here. First, forget everything you've learned in the academy because the street's where you'll learn to be a cop, and second, being first around here don't mean shit. Take it easy, that's our motto" (van Maanen, 1975:225).

Ultimately, of course, the quality of in-the-street coached learning depends upon the selection of appropriate coach officers. Through a policing career, but especially over the first several years, street experiences while on patrol will have a critical influence upon learned police behaviour. As police suggested in Windsor, Ontario, "high-stress incidents on patrol" were most influential in influencing police conduct (Vincent, 1990: 79).

In response to demographic changes, most major urban police forces have participated in in-service multicultural programs. The RCMP were among the earliest police to approach multicultural training in a serious manner, with a particular emphasis, in keeping with Force contacts, upon aboriginal peoples. In recruit training, lectures, films, and simulations over approximately 20 hours—admittedly a brief time—attempt to "sensitize" recruits to other cultures (*Liaison*, June 1977:7–9).

The ambitious Canadian Police College, operated by the RCMP, has made a major attempt to offer special courses to nominated officers across the country, much as in the United States, the FBI Academy has offered courses to American (and Canadian) police

personnel. The RCMP Police College in Ottawa was established in 1937 for special administrative and operations training for selected personnel from Canada's forces (Kelly and
Kelly, 1976:127). Later the Canadian Police College, Rockcliffe (Ottawa), was opened on
November 15, 1976. Federally funded and managed by the RCMP, the college is intended
for middle-management training of personnel from forces across the country. Examples of
courses include executive development, new officer training, and highly specialized technical
courses (*Liaison*, December, 1976:8).

The Police College courses, however, are available for a fee to police services. A sam-
pling of the courses available includes

Community Problem Analysis and Program Management ($150),

Multicultural Education Trainers ($150),

Native Awareness Trainers ($150),

Police Explosives Technicians ($550),

Forensic Identification ($350),

Major Crime Investigative Techniques ($225), and

Electronic Search and Seizure ($150).

For a more detailed list of the courses offered by the Canadian Police College, see their
web site at http://www.cpc.gc.ca/ccost_e.html. However, these courses are often an expense that a police manager is unwilling to bear—especially as free training is sometimes
available from the FBI Academy. Popular in-service themes, at the Canadian Police College
and on-site in local police establishments, have been courses in community policing and
race relations.

The Chief of Police of the Ottawa-Carleton Regional Police has called for greater access
to such courses, and at federal expense (*Ottawa Citizen*, January 10, 1998). He did so in
the context of stating the opinion that broad-based federal government support of policing
was needed in Canada, in training and in information services. In doing so, he remarked
the irony of paying fees for courses at the Canadian Police College, while when sending
personnel to the FBI Academy in the United States, there was no cost for the courses.

An obvious preoccupation in police in-service courses has been intercultural training. It
is obviously the case that Canada's heterogeneous population with many new immigrants from
non-Western societies, is apt to create conflicts. The inability to comprehend different views
is reciprocal; the police fail to understand persons from other social backgrounds, and the new
members of the public fail to understand the traditions and practices of policing in Canada.
As remarked in the context of an intercultural program for police and new immigrants in
Edmonton, "There are people out there who are more afraid of police than they are of crime"
(*Edmonton Journal*, March 2, 1996).

Impediments to Better Training

Yet there is no convincing evidence that such in-service courses have been successful;
rather, neutral outcomes, or even police resentment, have been identified in post-course
evaluations. The programs are characteristically met with great skepticism, even hostility,

by police officers. One such two-day seminar in Montreal in 1987 elicited reactions such as that of an officer who stated that "They're trying to solve a problem that doesn't exist. Our job is to stop criminals and we treat everyone the same. But some races are just more defensive. They are the ones who should be taking the course" (Montreal *Gazette*, February 13, 1987). Also in Montreal, one police officer took the extreme measure of booking off sick in order to avoid the race relations course, describing the course as a "political game" played by the director of police. Underlying the incident was the officer's having been named in a suit alleging racism (Montreal *Gazette*, April 6, 1988). In Toronto, a seminar for police relations with the Tamil community, sponsored by the Tamils, illustrated the attitude often perceived by police in such settings: that they are being attacked. At the particular course, the only police officer present stalked out (*Ottawa Citizen*, March 4, 1996). Evaluations of race relations programs have observed that to be effective, they need to consist of well-prepared courses that are integrated with a larger police training curriculum. To schedule occasional sessions, as has tended to be done, in effect only briefings where police officers are "talked at," and expect attitude change is exceedingly naive (von Stein, 1996:16–17). Courses attempted in many police organizations were ill prepared and taught in a manner that tended to reinforce ethnic biases rather than alter them. The Bellmare Committee recommended that such career-long training continue, but that in the multicultural awareness sessions "more material" and improved "educational methods" be incorporated (Normandeau, 1990:223).

Examples of similar experiences are to be had from Britain, where a participating female staff sergeant observed, politely, that the racism awareness course in which she had participated was discursive and insufficiently fact-oriented. The police students indicated in the post-course evaluation, when asked what they had learned, that "nothing had changed." Moreover, the instructor remarked upon suspicion and hostility, police resentment of criticism, and a greater solidarity in response to the criticisms. The police insisted that they treated everyone fairly and the same, and that difficulties were attributable to minority group members whose own attitudes towards the police were unreasonable, and whose ignorance of policing procedures resulted in police being "hampered by the unreasonable behaviour of some" (Bainbridge, 1984:168). Generally similar observations were discreetly put 10 years later in an evaluation report prepared for the British Home Office, concluding that there was a need for better preparation and, ideally, integration of racism awareness training into the basic training of recruits in police procedures (Southgate, 1984). Yet earlier evidence had made clear that attempts to alter attitudes were prone to failure, tending often to reinforce prejudices instead of altering them (Great Britain, 1975). Such findings, quite well established in social science, suggest a need to emphasize behaviour control when dealing with established bodies of personnel.

In the United States, where well-meaning people have been meeting, holding conferences and symposia, and arranging training programs for many years, evidence long available suggested the limited efficacy of race-relations training in the absence of fundamental institutional change. Where attitudes might change, at least according to some measures, behaviour may not, if the person does not know in what precise way behaviour should be altered or is offensive, or thinks that alteration would not be supported by peers and superiors (Chesler, 1976:44–46). It follows, therefore, that training programs must be reinforced by organizational or environmental features to support the precise behaviour desired.

Also, research indicates that race relations and intercultural training, if well designed, are most effective for recruits, as part of the initial occupational socialization. On the other hand, older in-service officers tend to be most negative, viewing the training as a waste of time (Gould, 1995).

Another very irregular aspect is access to university courses and degree programs for in-service police officers. This has tended to be access for senior personnel, especially junior and senior management-rank officers. But constables and non-commissioned officers have increasingly been found in university classrooms, sometimes at their own initiative, sometimes with the cooperation of their service, but rarely with financial support and release time from their service. Nowhere in Canada is there a policy, or a provision in a collective agreement, of supported in-service university education.

One of the benefits of higher educational requirements for the police officer, in addition to whatever skills may be acquired, is to alter values and to break down occupational insularity that sustains undesirable behaviour. The demand for better-educated police officers is premised upon the expectation that the brevity of police training is inconsistent with job demands. It also implies an expectation that better-educated police officers will be more sensitive to their public, and have support networks other than their police colleagues. The police officer educated in a public institution will develop views other than those of the occupational group. A review of one Canadian college program in law enforcement and community relations found participants to have a better self-image, to be less likely to believe the public to be hostile, and to be more interested in the helping role of policing (Stebbins and Flynn, 1975).

The evidence on the value of higher education is not, however, unambiguous. American reformers, spurred in particular by the President's Commission (1967), have tended to assume that the better-educated police officer will be less prejudiced, less violent, and generally more sympathetic to the public (Saunders, 1970). But the experiences of an American criminologist, George Kirkham, who trained and served as a police officer, suggest that the liberal sentiments of education are rapidly overcome by the harsh stimuli of the police environment (Kirkham, 1974, 1976). He writes that his "personality began to change slowly ... as my career as a policemen progressed," as he experienced the stresses of policing, and the critical views of non-police, especially media reports and judicial decisions. Although Kirkham was exceedingly well educated, and had the additional advantage of being able to retreat regularly to his previous academic environment, the experience of the police role changed his attitudes and conduct.

Evidence suggests that higher education is not a panacea. It expands the range of opinion and experience brought to policing, and the more general the education the better. Research suggests that where police higher education is too vocational, and itself isolated, the effect of police experiences supersedes any expected attitude change arising from education (Weiner, 1974; 1976:34–38). General education in a public setting, where the police officer is working with and testing ideas with a wide range of other persons rather than in the isolation of the police service or the homogeneous police science courses at community colleges and police academies, is the circumstance in which the greatest benefits are to be expected.

CONCLUSION

In the past 15 years, there has been a shift in expectation regarding the composition and, to a much slighter extent, the training of police personnel. The current expectation is that police service members must be more representative of society, as regards gender and ethnic makeup. There has been progress, but it has been far slower than reformers had hoped. Once recruits are selected, training is expected to incorporate content sensitive to the diversity of Canadian society, and also to recognize a preventive mode, as opposed to a traditional reactive mode of policing.

Good, broadly based recruitment and basic recruit training are integral to quality policing. But they are not sufficient in themselves in the absence of in-service education in public institutions that permits contact and exchange between police personnel and other members of the public. In order to achieve the self-renewal of serving police officers, to deter the distortions of viewpoint associated with isolated policing, and generally to assist in a genuine professionalism that deters error and misconduct, open police education of a continuing nature is a social necessity.

ANNOTATED READINGS, CHAPTER SIX

Harris, Richard N. *The Police Academy: An Inside View.* New York: John Wiley and Sons, 1973. The author offers a sociological analysis of the socialization process of the police academy in the United States. The segregation of the recruit and the subsequent career isolation of police officers is a major theme of the book.

Jayewardene, C.H.S. and C.K. Talbot. *Police Recruitment of Ethnic Minorities.* Ottawa: Canadian Police College, 1990. This essay considers the extent and the consequences of more heterogeneous police recruitment in Canada. It offers the conclusion that employment equity in itself will not alter the perceptions of segments of the public in regard to police conduct.

Sherman, Lawrence W. *The Quality of Police Education.* San Francisco: Jossey-Bass Publishers, 1978. This book considers the "quick fix" approach to police problems of the 1960s in the United States, that stressed improved police education. The author urges broadly based curriculum rather than narrow specialist and police-based education.

von Stein, J. *Race Relations in the Police Curriculum in Canada: A Content Analysis.* Ottawa: Canadian Centre for Police–Race Relations. The Centre has published numerous little monographs examining aspects of police–race relations, and may be usefully consulted. This monograph in particular is a realistic review of the literature.

POLICE WORK

The front-line work of policing occurs in the street. Infrastructure and support activities may be considerable, but patrol and investigations are the important activities for ordinary Canadians. This chapter discusses factors associated with police work and behaviour, including stress.

Policing is an occupation, a job. Persons selecting and selected to perform the job are ordinary Canadian men and women. They are attracted to the job for ordinary reasons—chance, whim, career security, interest in helping, a desire for excitement. Like any job, it must be learned. To be a police officer, one must be socialized: formally and informally acquire the attitudes and the behaviours expected of the occupation. Ideally the expectation that the public has of an occupation and those of the practitioners are closely related. In any event, both the public and peers will influence subsequent behaviour.

Socialization may, in some sense, begin prior to entering the work of policing. Arguably persons seeking to be police officers have previously acquired, albeit imperfectly, some information and values inclining them to the job. They might also have adopted what they think are appropriate skills and behaviours. It would be wrong, however, to account for police conduct by reference to pre-socialization or some recruitment bias.

ON THE JOB

Subculture

Previously we have remarked on the organizational character of police services. The paramilitary origins and training have been reflected in a precise rank hierarchy. Within that structure command prerogatives have been stressed, along with a style that has attempted to implement command-down policy and micro-management. While the work of policing depends upon individual worker discretion, the organizational model is one that has its origins in the command direction and unit action of the military. The history of policing may in a sense be viewed as an ongoing tension between organizational command and discipline, worker subculture, and public accountability and control. In the 1990s there are indications that emphasis has been placed on public accountability (see Chapter Nine), while management has had command control moderated because of police unions (see Chapter Five) and more decentralized community policing (see Chapter Ten). A peer subculture of shared experiences and learned responses continues to be a powerful shaper of police conduct.

Police, like any occupational group, develop an organizational culture, with characteristic values, norms, and beliefs. Police are an especially cohesive working group, so they have cultivated a suspicion of outsiders, including media reporters and researchers. A sociologist who had worked for two decades with police in the United States remarked upon the secretiveness and the unwillingness of rank-and-file officers, and especially command officers, to share information with him. One command rank officer complained of the police being overstudied (Baldwin, 1977:9–11). Resentment and hostility to research, and the presumption that any external observation will be critical, have characterized police attitudes (Bent, 1974:xii).

The environment they share, from recruit training through the range of job experiences, creates officers' attitudes and behaviours. There is a social type, not a psychological or personality type, which is selected for policing and produced by policing. There is a literature that speaks of an authoritarian personality, or even a pathological personality selected for policing. But the evidence suggests that such dramatic characterization is absolutely unsound (Lefkowitz, 1975). The personality syndrome that is quite consistently identified in the research literature, and even in fiction, displaying defensiveness, secrecy, cynicism, suspicion, conservatism, and even violence, is socially determined in the context of the occupational experience and not inborn (Skolnick, 1975; Niederhoffer, 1967; Kirkham, 1974, 1976; Genz and Lester, 1976).

In a very illuminating account, an American criminologist related his academic view that there was a personality type, rather authoritarian, that self-selected into policing. But when he himself trained and worked as a police officer, he found that his academic liberalism translated into on-the-job conduct much like that of his fellow police officers. Socialization, the occupational subculture, peer influence, and the environmental contingencies of policing, not prior personality, were determinant (Kirkham, 1974; 1976). Whatever one's prior personality, at least within some range of so-called "normality," a control-oriented authoritarian inclination is created. "The police system transforms a man into the special type of authoritarian personality required by the police role," concluded Niederhofffer in 1967 (Niederhoffer, 1967: 125–126).

The authoritarian character of modern policing may be exaggerated. There is, though, evidently an emphasis upon control among police officers, and as a group, a commitment to "conservative" attitudes and values. These do vary, of course, with individuals, despite group effects, and by subsets of persons in policing. Older police officers are more apt to be conservative, and while the evidence is unclear, perhaps male officers more than female officers. Generally, too, the frequency and the nature of police interaction with citizens will affect police conduct. The style and working conditions in the organization also matter. Police officers must cope not only with the job on the street and their encounters with members of the public, but with organizational rules and regulations, and with supervisors and managers. On the job and in the street, they work quite different neighbourhoods, and consequently deal with somewhat different incidents and contacts with citizens. And also, irrespective of the general patrol conditions in which an officer works, he or she can be influenced by the idiosyncratic experiences of the job, the particular incidents experienced, and, especially, crisis situations where violence is involved (Roberg and Kuykendall, 1997:318–319).

The police culture or subculture may be understood as shared meanings and behaviours, reinforced and maintained daily by peer influence, reinforcement, and experiences. This worker culture, as well as the reality of most police work occurring in a situation not subject to observation or supervision, has sustained discretionary behaviours particular to police officers. Policing, with origins in isolated training that stresses conformity and group solidarity, and subsequently relatively unique and often alienating experiences, is characterized by a distinguishable set of attitudes and behaviours.

The behaviour that is learned and expected by the subgroup is adapted to the job experience, whether the adaptation is that which the public would wish or not. Attitudes such as cynicism may be dysfunctional from the public's perspective, but for the police officer may be "functional aids" (Wilt and Bannon, 1976:44). It seems undeniable that, given the complex range of demands with which today's officer is encumbered—from straightforward street crime and crime detection, to highly charged social service and public order demands—he or she must develop certain survival skills to cope with a job that is unimaginably stressful, often demeaning, and isolating.

As officers gain experience, they gradually render their working environment manageable and develop an inventory of cues and a mental image of the physical or ecological environment and its inhabitants. In an empirical study of police in St. John's, the police conception of crime and city area was shown to influence definitions of appropriate police response (McGahan, 1984). In part, the image is but a mental mapping of the social classes police define as troublesome; but there is also an awareness of environmental features that create problems of crime, such as poorly lit parks and high-rise buildings.

The naive, sometimes idealistic expectations of the recruit are steadily modified in the course of a police career. Friends from outside of policing diminish in number, as friends shy away from interpersonal disagreements. Cynicism increases, with an unwillingness to trust outsiders. There is a decline in expectations of "having a personal impact," a recognition of the public relations or symbolic content of policing, and vocational objectives are displaced in favour of concern with promotion. Finally, as the career progresses, there is a concern with the personal cost associated with the job (Cooper, 1982). Despite the moral tone and dedication with which police present their role, they adapt to the occupational organization, and conform to behaviourial expectations that enhance careers rather than serve ideals. Vincent (1979:39) quotes a Windsor police officer: "To do well in the police force almost requires total time and dedication to playing the game. The commitment is not necessarily to good service but rather heavy involvement with the internal political game."

Conceived of as public servants—albeit as public servants doing society's "dirty work"—they become alienated from the public they are to service. Self-isolation, even from their own families, and cynicism—a sense of the "incurable" wickedness of human character—will mark their lives. The reality of dealing with a public in trouble or making trouble, or of simply being the one who always brings the bad news, will set them apart psychologically and socially. An officer of the French national police invoked the concept of the "police ghetto," suggesting the isolation from the public and the commitment to the police organization in and of itself (*Liaison*, July–August 1980:9–13). Vincent (1979:81) in his study of the Windsor Police Force, found that "The longer the men were in police work and the higher their rank, the more they tended to associate only with other police."

While they may be committed, and view themselves as the last line of defence, the "thin blue line" against social disorder, they do not really expect to change things. They will be politically and socially conservative, perceiving themselves as the bulwark of upstanding values. Police, isolated from the public, since they tend to interact on and off the job with other police officers, learn to be suspicious, and not to trust anyone except other police, and especially their partners. From suspiciousness, isolation, and the experience of other people in trouble and making trouble, they become cynical. Not trusting others, and with information as a survival and success commodity, they become secretive, hoarding information. They learn a cookbook of responses and "craft rules" (Reiner, 1992:111) and any idealism, as Niederhoffer put it (1967), comes to be replaced by an operative pragmatism. They cultivate an "action" orientation, and thrive on adrenaline rushes (Reiner, 1992:111), such as those to be had from high-speed chases. Part of the isolation and separateness is found in insider language, epithets, and jokes. The jokes are often racist and sexist. Illustrative is the joke circulating in Los Angeles following the horrendous incident involving the police and Rodney King: the new police motto, replaying a version of "To serve and protect," was to have become "We treat you like a King."

Separateness becomes self-fulfilling, and is reinforced by the remote mode of policing which depends upon cars and separateness from local communities. Like other alienated subcultures, the police will have a strong sense of group identity and loyalty, and will be most comfortable and trusting among their own. The peer allegiance itself becomes a pressure for conformity, where the complexity of the job may demand initiative. A sense of non-support from the public, secrecy, sensitivity to criticism, and defensiveness eventually become part of the complex attitude-set of police officers. And when the generally supportive public do in fact express the odd critical and hostile judgment, the police self-defence tactics are reinforced, and the "blue veil of secrecy" becomes paramount.

One psychologist has described the peer cohesiveness of police officers as an "adolescent stage" that "keeps ... [police] from growing up." The police "subculture retards the social development of individual officers" (Meredith, 1984:23). The people with whom the police officer works daily, not the public, not recruit training, and not the superior officers whom the police officer must please but to whom he is relatively invisible, shape the police officer's behaviour (Vincent, 1979:42–54).

Within the context of peer pressure and ill-defined or impractical departmental guidelines, each officer must come to terms with the job; must cope, get by, keep the lid on. Unable to respond to all demands, unable to deal effectively with all violations, he or she must pick and choose from among offences, engage in trade-offs, even violate the law, in order to "keep the peace" in a manner that he or she judges practical. As James Q. Wilson (1969:130) remarks, "What many policemen were doing even when they were thought of as crime fighters was not so much enforcing the laws as maintaining order." The police are "reinforcers" a much as "enforcers" of behaviour (Sykes and Bent, 1983:28), legitimating and defining moral behaviour. The police function has always been keeping the peace, and that leaves little time or resource for crime. A 1988 survey of police functions calculated that 58% of police officers' time was dedicated to patrol and general duties, 10% to criminal investigation, 3% to drug enforcement, and 11% to administrative duties, with the remaining time spent on sundry duties such as public relations and court-related duties (*Juristat* 9:1989:5).

Part of the subculture, too, is an exaggerated maleness or machismo. This has been seen to be associated with a pattern of heavy drinking and sexual activity. Historically police officers have been males. And historically these males have been expected to be tough. The first few women in policing tended, therefore, to be segregated and were used for auxilliary tasks such as custodial duties for female prisoners or parking enforcement. They were often distinguished by uniform dress. As recently as 1960 a female police officer in Ottawa wore white uniform dress and not blue (*Ottawa Citizen*, November 1, 1997).

When women began to be recruited to regular policing, the resistance of men was pronounced. The male police officers presumed that they were not strong enough, not tough enough, could not fight and were unlikely to use their weapons, and were probably a risk to their male partners. Yet researchers have consistently failed to find measurable differences in job performance, except perhaps, an indication that female officers were less likely to initiate incidents than were males (Linden, 1993:103). Some American findings also suggested that women were somewhat more effective in "talking down" a volatile situation and less apt to be complained about by members of the public. And, in respect of the subculture, a very distinct finding was that women tended to leave policing in greater numbers (Linden, 1985;1993), often because of marital obligations, especially in the RCMP where diverse postings were a problem. Women, too, have often been the object of harassment, including sexual harassment in this male-dominated subculture. In 1996, for example, an internal RCMP reported that 60% of female RCMP officers reported some form of sexual harassment, including 10% reporting sexual touching (*Globe and Mail*, September 22, 1996).

Work

Police are asked to perform complex tasks. It is expected that they provide a diversity of services to the public, from general assistance and protection to crime fighting. They are expected to deal with local by-laws, such as those related to noise or to traffic, and with criminal violations, whether break-and-enter or acts of violence. To prepare them for these tasks, police officers receive relatively scant training. Much of their training is preparatory to learning the tradecraft of policing on the job.

The daily round of police work for the police officer has often been described as boring. Traditionally police work has been incident-driven, or reactive. That is, police are out and about, until a member of the public initiates a call for service. Rarely does an officer simply come upon a serious incident requiring intervention, a crime in progress. Moreover, as police officers have for decades mostly worked in patrol vehicles, rather than on foot patrol, they do not even have the benefit of humanizing and monotony-breaking ordinary or benign contacts with members of the public. "This separation from the community essentially limited police contact to victims, suspects and offenders" (Murphy, 1992: 5). Isolation is reinforced by motor patrol, and the skewed contacts with the public reinforce police isolation, dependency upon a partner and fellow officers, and traits such as suspiciousness and cynicism.

As most police officers work on patrol, they are expected to randomly be available in a patrol area or zone, and to react to calls for service or to incidents that come to their attention. Random patrol historically has been assumed to be preventive, that is to deter civil or criminal violations, and therefore to be an effective use of police time. Yet research has suggested that modifying patrol intensity or volume does not affect crime rate or public satisfaction. The famous Kansas City (Kelling et al., 1974) experiment fundamentally called into question the common-sense view of patrol effectiveness, and found that increasing or decreasing motor patrol tended not to have an effect.

An historic expectation in reactive patrol policing also has been that rapid response is important. Repeated work, however, suggests that rapid response is rarely relevant, except in the attitude of the public who in crisis expect urgent police response. Initial critical work on response was also done in Kansas City (Van Kirk, 1977). Research on police response time documented a significant time delay in citizen reporting of crime, and consequently despite public expectation, rapid police response was not effective most of the time.

Patrol officers are in constant reach of radio and/or computer communication and therefore poised to respond to dispatch when a call for service reaches a police facility. Most of the time on most watches or shifts, a police officer is not responding to a call for service. And when responding, most of the time the occasion is not crime-related or serious. Most of the time, therefore, rapid response is not relevant. Rarely does an officer on random patrol stumble upon a serious crime in progress. And rarely is a response to a reported crime sufficiently prompt as to permit police attendance, no matter how rapid, while the violation is in progress. During much of a shift, unless one is engaged in the relative rarity of a foot patrol beat, the patrol officer infrequently engages a member of the public.

The number of officers on patrol tends to be much less than the public expects, and their response much less rapid than they expect or think necessary. Increasingly police have systematically prioritized responses to calls, knowing that rapid response does not usually matter (except for public impression-management) and because there are too few police officers to do otherwise. These "differential police response systems" having systematically defined priority responses, will then require less serious complaints, including break-and-enters, to either have a much delayed police response, or even, as has become prevalent, that the complainant report by telephone, come in person to the police building, or perhaps have the complaint detail taken down by a responding civilian volunteer (Lewis-Horne and Forcese, 1993).

One British estimate calculated the disposition and availability of patrol officers in a police service of 2500 officers. In a so-called typical British town it was estimated that 10 patrol officers at any one time would be normal, allowing for police in supervisory/management tasks, detective work, special assignment, off-duty shifts, court-time, and illness (*Sunday Times*, September 15, 1996). American research has similarly calculated a "Ten for One" rule, suggesting that to put one officer on the street, ten have to be employed (Bayley, 1994). In Canada, many Ontario towns and rural areas, for example, have their OPP stations unmanned at night. While the "graveyard" shift, midnight to 8:00 a.m., can be very demanding in some jurisdictions on some nights, often there will tend to be very few police officers on patrol. The heaviest shift tends to cover evening hours before midnight.

Working in shifts of 8, 10 or 12 hours, and organized in watches or platoons, police officers therefore populate, usually by automobile, a sector of a jurisdiction. Officers may rotate shifts from a day to an evening to a night shift, and the shifts are often lengthy, 10 to 12 hours becoming somewhat more common than 8 hours. In some jurisdictions, as in Ottawa-Carleton, the patrol officer works alone, and in others, such as Metro Toronto, there are two-person patrols. Some number of patrol officers for some periods of time may have dedicated responsibility for aspects of traffic enforcement. This is but part of the generalized capacity to respond to events as they present themselves while a police officer is on duty.

Because random patrol is often tedious, even though police officers may generally appreciate having safely completed another shift, there is also some tendency to revel in occasional excitement. A problem in policing everywhere, remarked in Chapter Eight, are high-speed pursuits. Research suggests that officers are aware that they enjoy the excitement, the "adrenalin rush" of the chase. In one sample of over 800 police services in the United States, the researcher found that 84% of the officers acknowledged excitement (Alpert, 1997). There is a consequent reluctance to break off the pursuit activity to which they had committed, and lose the game. Evidence suggests that many, perhaps most chases, are for relatively minor infractions, such as auto theft, often involving youth. And because of the excitement, if the offender is finally pulled over and confronted by the police officer, the probability of violence increases. Most police agencies therefore attempt to regulate chases, with policy guidelines in respect to seriousness and risk, and also attempt to have a control officer in communication with the pursuit officer, able to command that the chase be broken off.

While random patrol may be less effective than assumed, more proactive measures do seem to have some utility. It has been found, for example, that traffic stops at police initiative are a remarkably good tool for dealing with other offences, such as burglary, drug, alcohol, and firearms violations. Offenders use cars. And traffic enforcement appears to be as or more effective in arrests of such violators than specialists' work, including detective investigations. Whether random stops, or stops in response to some vehicle or driver anomaly, the effectiveness occurs (Marchment & Mackay Limited, *Canadian Market Digest* [company newsletter], July, 1993: 3–4).

After time devoted to random patrol, work time relates to social service or helping tasks, court duty, and traffic control, and not to investigative or "crime-busting" activities. General social control, or maintaining public order, is also an integral task of policing. This is accomplished generally by police officers simply being present rather than by overt action. These diverse tasks engage highly paid personnel, even when, like much court duty, they are not overtly functional. In the city of Ottawa, for example, 1987 salary costs associated with police being in court for testimony were $1.2 million. A deliberate program to reduce costs in 1988, involving an assistant Crown attorney assigned to coordinate between lawyers and police, helped reduce the figure to a still staggering $981 900. In each year approximately 80% of the officers subpoenaed and paid never testified (*Ottawa Citizen,* January 10, 1989).

Only a small component of policing requires detective work. The bulk of activities, such as by-law enforcement (traffic, pet control, etc.), patrol, and social service, are banal. The social service role consists of all manner of social problems, from domestic disputes to calls for emergency assistance. Because of their 24-hour service, police are often called upon to meet needs that might properly be met by other service agencies. An American estimate put up to half the calls received by police as relating to domestic problems, most of these from non-middle-class families (Bard and Berkowitz, 1967).

Yet police do stress control of criminal activity as their most important task, especially violent crime. In work examining Canadian police chief estimates of crime seriousness, wherein 321 police chiefs or commanders responded, Goff and Kimm (1987:4–7) compared Canadian views with American, using a list of offences initially developed in the United States. They found no significant differences, with both Canadian and American chiefs rating crimes of violence, of aggression, and involving death as most serious. Both ranked "assassination of a public official" as first in seriousness. They remark on four items of notable difference, varying by ten or more places. Canadian respondents rated "beating up an acquaintance" and "mother-son incest" as more serious than did their American counterparts. Conversely, they rated "deserting the army in time of war" and "selling pep pills" as less serious than did American police commanders. Even as community-based policing becomes the fashionable concept, police, in defining their roles and their raison d'être, will rank crime fighting as of primary importance.

The public and the police share misconceptions about policing. Police recruits are attracted by the glamour of law enforcement that is featured in film and television. Yet the law enforcement they will be called upon to perform is far more often minor by-laws enforcement, not criminal law. They will be dealing with the ordinary citizen in an adversarial way. Yet police wish their time to be devoted to the regulation of crime. In the prestige hierarchy of police forces, detective rank is highly valued, and patrol rank undervalued. Ironically, patrol officers are the most effective in responding to crime. Foot patrol is especially low in regard, as are "inside jobs" and cellblock duties. Sergeants still assigned to patrol responsibilities appear to be especially dissatisfied with their work (McGinnis, 1985a:270, 279).

Hour after hour spent isolated on motor patrol, which removes the patrol officer from contact with members of the public, is extremely tedious. Paperwork and court appearances are almost equally monotonous. The tedium may, of course, be dangerously and unpredictably interrupted at any time; this is what creates the constant tension that permeates policing. The consequence is high absenteeism, estimated recently in Montreal as high as 20% at any given time (though this included absence due to court appearances) (Montreal *Gazette*, September 12, 1988).

Naturally, some shifts, such as Friday nights, are notoriously busier than others. One published estimate in Winnipeg states that police responded to 500 calls on an average Friday night in the period from 10:00 p.m. to 4:00 a.m., dealing with drinking offences, rowdiness, fights, and similar disturbances, most of them in the inner city (*Winnipeg Free Press,* August 7, 1988). But calls are but a fraction of the police time on the job, and even they do not deal exclusively, or even in the majority, with criminal acts. In 1981 the Ottawa Police Force responded to 132 282 calls, of which only 40% were related to criminal offences (Monteiro, 1982:23). Police are somewhat intolerant of service demands, believing that they simply divert scarce human resources from "true" law enforcement. In Montreal, the director of MUC Police cited the statistic that 80% of the 1.2 million calls in 1980 were service related, and, as a way of coping with budget cuts, proposed to refuse to respond to such calls (Montreal *Gazette,* June 4, 1981). In Montreal and in Quebec generally, the press suggested that the high rate of traffic accidents and fatalities was in some part attributable to a police attitude. It was argued that because traffic enforcement was not seen as worthy, it was not pursued vigorously by police, allowing a high number of infractions. A Montreal police constable was quoted as stating that drivers "just don't expect us to enforce the law as strictly as they do in other provinces." This is because "There's a general feeling among police officers that traffic is demeaning. You're only half a cop when you're on traffic. Cops are supposed to take care of crimes" (Montreal *Gazette*, June 2, 1979).

Police training programs do try to impart the routine nature of policing to recruits. An inspector teaching at the Quebec Police Institute observed that recruits seem to have a concept of policing derived from American television, and expect constant action dealing with criminals rather than engaging in social services for the public (*Ottawa Citizen*, March 12, 1988). But basic training is brief and itself encumbered with traditional conceptions of policing. Most police behaviour is learned on the job, as officers learn to contend with their occupational environment.

Police tend to be ill prepared by formal training, and by disposition, to deal with many service demands. Domestic disturbances, for example, are viewed as dangerous and ambiguous, in which it is difficult to determine offender and victim. Because of this, many police forces have begun to employ social workers and family crisis experts to assist them, as well as to develop a routine referral service. One of the first such attempts in Canada was in London, Ontario, where a Family Consultant Service was established in 1973. Police officers were taught about the various service agencies available in the city, and were able to share and to engage in referrals, freeing themselves for other activities.

Most police officers spend a career in patrol. All police officers in Canada begin their work in this fashion, and some are promoted out of the street.. Although in most police forces detective work is very senior and prestigious, the job tasks of the patrol officer are more complex and sensitive. It is ironical, therefore, that they are usually performed by the least senior personnel or those evaluated as least deserving of promotion. Detectives deal with events after the fact, events that are generally agreed by police and public to be serious. Patrol officers have to contend with ambiguous events, and deal with victims and suspects in demeaning circumstances in which it is difficult to clearly justify this or that explicit action. They are active, as Piliavin (1973:3) reminds us, in general order-maintenance or peacekeeping activities, where no crime may have been committed. The uncertainty in the event is itself one of the causes of mental stress.

Few police officers wish to stay permanently in patrol; most want to be detectives and seek a career path into the CID, the criminal investigation department, while others seek advancement in administration (McGinnis, 1985a:255, 261). But career advancement is not usually possible at the level of direct service to the public, or patrol.

A promotion that historically has been much sought after is to detective branch. Detectives will tend to be more senior, and generally hold a rank equivalent to sergeant or higher. To be a detective has usually meant that one has greater discretion to pursue serious incidents. A patrol officer reacts to an event, but passes an investigation on to a specialist, a detective. Detectives may specialize by offence type. Some may be associated with so-called major crime, such as murder or armed robbery. Others may be attached to investigative and regulatory units dealing in morality crimes or vice, such as prostitution.

An interesting implication of detective work has to do with its effectiveness. While few people would dispute that follow-up investigations are necessary, there are indications that detective work is not very productive. In a famous and controversial RAND study in the

United States in the 1970s, looking at 200 detective units it was found that information collected on site, potentially by the responding patrol officer, was crucial to the great majority of investigations. Subsequent "detection" largely consisted of reviewing information (Greenwood and Petersilia, 1975;1977).

The extended investigations of detectives yield a relatively low pay-off, especially when considered relative to the number and seniority of the personnel (Chappell et al., 1982). The detective function as it evolved in Britain, the United States, and in Canada is a form of career elitism that diminishes the role of the patrol officer. The existence of a detective branch in large police organizations limits the uniformed officer's engagement in the community, and also limits job satisfaction. As police organizations attempt to introduce community-based policing, it is logical for investigatory functions to be distributed among all members rather than reserved for a detective elite. Arguably, too, there is a "symbiotic relationship ... between detectives and corruption" as the specialized body is removed from supervisory and community scrutiny. The anonymity of detectives and perhaps also their persisting contact and immersion in criminal environments and networks permits corruption (Byrett, 1989:261–271).

In Canada, a now well-known study of detective work in the Peel Regional Police suggested the familiar theme that detectives in following through on cases are selective and make decisions regarding follow-up on the basis of estimates of "investigative pay-off" (Ericson, 1981a:vii). The author further observed that detectives are especially free of supervision, and have the very considerable discretion that allows them to pick and choose, to ignore or to emphasize, and ultimately to "make crime." These propositions and some of the illustrations offered by the author offended the police, who claimed breach of trust and unfairness. The police commission exercised the right, agreed upon when the research had been approved, to published a rejoinder appended to the book (Ericson, 1981). Contrasting realities were at play. The researcher, observing that all offences were not enforced at all times and with equal vigour, chose to present as a thematic point that the "freedom of choice" of police detectives was a process of shaping, defining, underlining, and making crime and criminals. The police, for their part, presented themselves as impartial and professional, with organizational control effectively in place. The symbolic interactionist interpretation of the researcher not only was not accepted by the police, it was perceived as a criticism and a distortion of reality.

Also featured in police work are various special units and roles, sometimes temporary and sometimes more enduring. Prevalent today, for example, are special tactical units, designed variously for crowd control and emergency response (Tactical Units, SWAT or Special Weapons Attack Teams, Emergency Response Teams). Depending on the size of the force, a single unit may be intended for these diverse special functions, or there may be specialized units. And they may also, when not responding, be engaged in some regular duties, usually patrol. These highly paramilitary units have tended to be very prestigious. They are viewed as highly skilled, and associated with stimulating and exciting work. Within such units, there will be specialized roles, such as that of the sniper, or that of the negotiator. In Ottawa, not atypically, the tactical unit is available to act, following initial police response and assessment, to high-risk calls ranging from domestic disturbances to hostage-takings.

Other special units may also be found. Most police service have full-time personnel devoted to sexual offences. Calgary Police, for example, operate an innovative sex crimes unit (*Globe and Mail*, November 22, 1997), and Ottawa offers a sexual assault and child abuse squad that also deals with Internet pornography (*Ottawa Sun*, November 16, 1997). The Ottawa police also offer a rather unique bias crime unit or so-called hate squad to deal with offences against racial, sexual, or religious minorities" (*Ottawa Citizen*, March 12, 1996). In Toronto, the police have from time to time operated forms of ethnic squads, intended to deal with crime associated with a distinguishable minority group, such as their Combined Forces Asian Investigative Unit or the Black Organized Crime Squad (*Toronto Sunday Star*, January 28, 1996). These latter units may be greeted with criticism and suspicion, as stereotyping entire communities, or as treating crime as associated with a class of peoples; the Toronto Black Crime Unit was shut down in 1997 following intense public pressure (DiManno, 1996: A7). A more familiar form of specialized police action relates to traffic enforcement, whether through temporary assignments to "blitz" particular violations or areas, or by creating more enduring traffic specialists, such as the Ontario Provincial Police TMOs (Traffic Management Officers) (Forster, 1997: C1, C4).

Other police officers are promoted to the ranks of management. Some non-commissioned and commissioned officers assume roles that are related to public contact, as in public and media relations. Others are assigned to supervise specialized functions, such as communications. Virtually all Canadian police forces find their operational managers, those who direct field operations associated with patrol or crime-response, from within the ranks. Everyone, including the chief, must work their way up. Everyone must be thoroughly imbued in the police subculture. Everyone is expected to have started with street encounters.

ENCOUNTERS

An instance of a police officer interacting with a member of the public may be designated an encounter. An encounter is interactive. Each party influences the other. The outcome is a function of the interaction, that is, the behaviour and perceptions of behaviour of two or more parties. Social psychologists, especially those working from the viewpoint of symbolic interactionism, have long insisted that human behaviour is a response to cues. A psychologist in the behaviourist tradition would make a similar observation, but would speak of stimuli. Subgroups within a society develop a repertoire of shared meaning or definitions of their reality, a bag of familiar stimuli, and learn to respond in certain ways to these environmental features. Occupational training is intended to sensitize the novice to the group's definitions and responses. It is not remarkable, therefore, to find that police respond in patterned and predictable ways to environmental cues or stimuli.

The learned and shared responses of police officers are a practical adaptation to working situations. Most police would observe that they learn to recognize the cues and to develop their "cookbook" of responses not in the basic recruit training establishments but in the streets. There they acquire the occupational survival kit. They will learn to recognize suspicious demeanour or dress as indicators of danger, criminal behaviour, or sometimes simply control-threatening disrespect. The cues may sometimes be rightly construed by outsiders as prejudices, as when the police respond to a black man in a white neighbourhood, or a shabbily dressed man in a wealthy suburb. But they have been taught to police officers as being associated with high probability of misbehaviour requiring their intervention. An apt concept is that suggested by Skolnick (1975:45–46), who speaks of "symbolic assailants," persons who for one reason or another attract the cultivated suspicions of police officers.

Other observers have argued that a considerable part of police response to cues constitutes a learned need to defend self-image and authority. In his work, Westley (1970) found that police officers reported that lack of citizen respect in an encounter was sufficient reason to take action, whether that action was some form of caution, arrest, or violence. Lack of deference by a citizen, especially by young people, was found to be a provocation to police intervention.

Chevigny gives similar examples from New York City, and argues persuasively that police respond negatively to disrespectful demeanour or citizen behaviour that is not submissive and respectful. Violence by police officers is often elicited in such encounters, and justified by the police because the disrespectful citizen is labelled a "troublemaker" (Chevigny, 1969:138); he becomes one of Skolnick's "symbolic assailants." The more blatant or visible the cue, the greater the probability of a forceful encounter (Stark, 1972:95). The officer is always inclined to act in such a way that his authority itself overawes the subject of his intervention. If he does not act in this self-protective way, and someone questions or defies his authority, by taking his badge number for example, it can have dire consequences for his career. The vigour of the police response, too, will be associated with learned expectations of danger and violence, predicted by the officer on the basis of the citizen's group membership.

The police officer's interpretation of what is a threatening or disrespectful cue is biased by class and ethnic group membership. That is, majority group, middle-class Canadians are apt to respond to police with deference and acceptance, even when having committed an offence for which the police have intervened. Objections will tend to be polite. Serious objections, too, will carry the possibility of serious follow-up because middle-class persons are not powerless, and the police response may tend to be restrained. Working-class persons, and some minority groups with learned hostile or suspicious attitudes to police, may react without the expected deference, and will be known to be less likely to follow up with formal complaints or suits. Generally, persons will respond to police on the basis of perceptions or stereotypes learned in their social environments. Naturally, when persons who feel mistreated, and police who have preconceptions of what their behaviour is likely to be, act out their antagonisms in public encounters, they mutually reinforce the harmful stereotypes already at play.

Most police responses, about 75%, are initiated by citizens. But no matter at whose initiative the encounter, the police officer then attempts to take over (Lundman, 1980a). A police officer's immediate objective in an encounter, whatever the occasion, is to establish control. Whether responding to a break-and-enter, a public disturbance, or a domestic dispute, in order to do the job and to protect his- or herself, the police officer needs control.

Police are potentially always in harm's way. They deal with individuals who may or may not comply with police directions, may or may not be violent, and may or may not have to be restrained. Police therefore learn various indicators and techniques, and are expected to exercise good discretionary judgment in assessing a situation and weighing responses. While on the job, at whatever level, a police officer has considerable discretion. Although there is frequently resort to after-the-fact evaluation and criticism, in the course of action the police officer is generally acting without supervision or opportunity to consult.

Throughout an encounter, intent upon controlling the situation and averting personal harm, a police officer must assess risk. And often a situation unfolds rapidly, and may even afford the officer no opportunity for control, and few options in response. An example is that of use of deadly force, a last resort. There is some evidence in the United States and from research in British Columbia that often police shootings occur in circumstances where a distraught and possibly suicidal person confronts a police officer and forces a deadly police response (Howard, 1996: A3).

It is necessary in an encounter that the citizen cooperate, and that there is compliance with the directives of the police officer. Part of such public compliance is suitable expression of respect, deference, and docility. Failure to comply is an indication of danger or risk for a police officer, and words or gestures that are not respectful are cues that the citizen is not compliant. Overtly threatening speech or actions, or the mere presence of a weapon, are even more obvious indicators of risk to the police officer. Stark (1972) and others write of the citizen being subjected to an attitudes test by police in an encounter. Rubinstein (1973) observed and wrote of "cop rules" and the "principal concern" of the police officer to physically control. Failure to express suitable respect and deference has been shown to be related to police harassment and violence. Passing the test allows the police officer to "normalize" the encounter, allowing the police officer some security, and also permitting the citizen to influence the police officer in determining discretionary outcomes.

Because the police officer has learned to establish control, and to look for indications that show whether or not control can be established, the behaviour of the citizen is a factor in police actions. If it is the case, as it is, that persons from differing social backgrounds react differently to police officers, then it is also the case that outcomes are also apt to be distinguishable by social type. Middle-class persons, for example, are apt to be more polite and deferential to a police officer than working-class persons; native-born Canadians are more apt to be deferential and polite than those from abroad with a different tradition of policing. Not only is an encounter then distinguished by the specific cues in a specific encounter, it becomes the case that police officers come to learn group-associated cues, and develop expectations of citizen behaviour on the bases of evident physical indicators of group membership. Whether assessing clothing, speech, or skin colour, the police officer is quickly assessing the evident information which he or she has learned to be associated with different outcomes. In so doing, the police become vulnerable to allegations of systematic bias— for they have in fact learned to be biased. This is a dilemma of policing: even as it may be stressed that police must be impartial and objective, the police officer is an ordinary human being attempting to do a job and survive in a real world. And he or she has learned to dislike some people, to distrust some people, and to recognize indicators that he or she is dealing with such people. To change police behaviour, therefore, in some measure one has to change the behaviour of citizens.

An officer's seeking to take charge is not usually problematic, especially if the encounter is unrelated to some actual or potential violation, a non-threatening call for assistance. But in a risk-laden encounter control is all the more important. Generally, the very presence of a police officer is intimidating for any member of the public. Some research suggests that aspects of police appearance, such as the military-style uniform and equipment, can be a provocation to members of the public. A participant in the 1996 public service demonstration in Toronto, for example, in a letter to the *Toronto Star* (January 25, 1996) remarked upon the OPP riot squad's appearance as "threatening" and an attempt at "intimidation." But the individual officer's appearance can also be intimidating, the mere presence of a police officer, the uniform, the weapons, and the police vehicle.

Beyond mere presence, the police officer will have learned a hierarchy of techniques to elicit citizen compliance, all based upon a calm and somewhat intimidating demeanour. A police officer begins with words, with persuasive directives or commands. This verbalization can become firmer and harsher if citizen response is inadequate. From verbalization the officer may proceed to physical techniques, such as firm grips, not painful, such as taking hold of a finger, wrist, or shoulder. Pain compliance is a next step, as in come-along holds, such as an arm-lock. Up the hierarchy of police response are then impact techniques that are painful and even incapacitating but not supposed to be life-threatening, as in use of a baton. A controversial impact technique is the choke hold, controversial because it has caused loss of life in the United States and Canada. In addition to the police baton the officer will have non-lethal tools, usually pepper spray, or devices such as stun guns. Restraining devices, such as the handcuff, are to be used as an aid where there has not been voluntary compliance or there is other serious prospect of escape and threat. Ultimately, use of deadly force, the police gun, is available (Skolnick and Fyfe,1992:38–41).

Ideally, in the public expectation, and also in the police officer's expectation, compliance will occur at a low threshold along the hierarchy. It is in everyone's interest that in an encounter there is non-violent cooperation. By the time violence intrudes, an encounter has deteriorated, controlled normalization has not been achieved, and danger of physical harm and stress have been introduced into the police officer's work.

STRESS

A prevalent view of policing is that it is dangerous and very stressful. Yet the data regarding stress and behavioural symptoms for police officers in Canada is exceedingly scant, and no real estimates can be confidently made of the incidence of stress among police officers. Some literature reviews, in the United States and Canada, suggest that stress in fact is less prevalent among police officers than other occupational groups (Hart et al., 1995).

The presumption of unusual rates of police stress tend to be associated with the perception of policing as dangerous. This presumed relationship is propagated by the media (see "Officers on the Edge," *Time* Magazine, September 26, 1994), but widely shared by others, including the police themselves. When a police officer is seriously injured or killed, the press coverage is extensive. The police themselves mark the events with elaborate ceremony. Dress funeral processions are the norm, often with participation from police forces everywhere in Canada, as in a 1978 funeral with 1000 marchers for a Toronto constable shot to death when responding to a domestic dispute (*Globe and Mail*, September 20, 1978; *Ottawa Citizen*, September 23, 1978). Several days after the Toronto funeral, a massive ceremony was initiated by the Ottawa Police Force, with the participation of 800 uniformed police from across the country. The demonstration was defined as a commemoration of police deaths. With the Ottawa Police Chorus and the Ottawa Police Pipes and Drums leading a dress parade from the Supreme Court Building to Parliament Hill, a crowd estimated at 2000 attended, and observed the widow of a police officer killed in the course of duty escorted on Parliament Hill by a colour guard. The Ottawa chief of police declared that "being a policeman or prison guard is one of the most dangerous professions in the world. And the opportunity of getting hurt or killed is much greater than anywhere else." Therefore, the chief continued, police are "heroes" and "are the people we can trust." The police denied that the ceremony was in any way part of a police lobby for restoration of capital punishment (*Ottawa Journal*, September 25, 1978; *Ottawa Citizen,* September 25, 1978). He also suggested that the ceremony should be an annual event.

Prior to the free vote in the House of Commons on capital punishment in 1987, the shooting of a police officer would invariably elicit demands for the restitution of the death penalty. This happened, for example, after the shooting death of an RCMP constable in

Calgary in 1987 shortly before the parliamentary vote. This was the first police shooting death in 1987 after an alarming spate of deaths from 1984 through 1986 (Montreal *Gazette,* January 27, 1987).

Statistically, it is true that police are less apt to be injured on the job than persons in many other occupations; nor is the mortality rate exceptional. An RCMP study in 1977 found that the fatality rate for the RCMP was less than that for the construction industry (Savage and Ault, 1995). In a 20-year period, 1961 to 1980, 44 municipal police officers, 16 RCMP officers, and 13 provincial police officers (8 from the Sûreté and 5 from the OPP) were murdered in Canada (*Juristat* 2, June 1982:1). This rate, .155 per 1 million population per year, was more favourable than the United States with a rate of .408 per 1 million population, but less favourable than other western democracies such as England, at .020 per 1 million population. The year 1984 was a tragic year for police officers, with nine police deaths in the course of duty, six in shootings. Of the six, five were in Ontario, a record number. In the space of four days in 1984, three police officers were shot to death, a Montreal and an OPP officer in a re-lated incident, and a York Regional Police officer. It was later determined that the OPP of-ficer received his fatal wound from a police rifle bullet (*Ottawa Citizen,* October 15, 1984). Extending the time frame, in the 30-year period 1961 to 1991, 103 Canadian police officers were murdered while on duty. The incident category most frequently associated with the murder of a policeman was responding to a robbery (Stansfield, 1996:123). The rate over 30 years is quite stable, suggesting no increase in risk for police officers; in the period 1961 to 1970 there were 36 police deaths, from 1971 to 1980 there were 37, and from 1981 to 1990 there were 27. As Stansfield (1997: 123) has observed, the police kill more Canadian civilians than there are police killed—itself no doubt a circumstance of severe "critical inci-dent stress" for police officers.

However moderate the statistics, police are, in the nature of the job, sometimes deliberate targets of violence. It is known that in the United States they are more apt to be murdered than a person in the general population. And in the course of their work, they do put themselves at risk, sometimes unexpectedly. While policing is not statistically very dangerous com-pared to many other occupations in terms of the risk of serious injury or death, the necessity for police to expose themselves to a variety of unpredictable risk in the course of routine, un-eventful boring duty, does create stress.

Events need not occur frequently to create stress. A remarkable event, such as most cit-izens would not experience, such as a shooting, may stress a working police officer despite years of experience. Possibly, too, some of the lifestyle features of the job, such as the shift schedule, the secretiveness, the need to be seen as tough, and a propensity to "wind down" with drink, may be associated with police stress symptoms. And because of the strong male peer pressure, gay police officers are apt to be stressed. Even the demands of the organiza-tion, with its rules, regulations, paperwork, and court appearances, can stress the police of-ficer. Of the public sector contacts, the court system seems to rank high as a stressor for police officers.

In fact, work conditions are often cited by police as the most disturbing, as was noted by Vincent (1990). It has been suggested that the serious stressors of police are poor pay, poor equipment, inadequate numbers of personnel, and poor supervision (Standfest, 1996). There are also indications that these affect women more than men, and that new officers (one to five years) are more stressed than older officers (Silbert,1992:661–663). "Officers who have been on the force longer take their work less seriously," and put greater emphasis upon life away from work than do younger officers (Silbert, 1992: 662–663).

The uncertainties of policing, the nature of shift work, the unpleasant encounters with the public, the threat and danger, and the prevailing daily experience of boring routine, isolate and stress the police officer (Vincent, 1979:80–90). Insofar as policing is organized into large centralized operations and removed from benign contact with the public, the perceptions of solitary responsibility, non-support, and the associated stresses are reinforced. One observer, Pierre Turgeon, has referred to "burnout" or "emotional exhaustion" as a feature of police lives (*Globe and Mail,* September 15, 1984).

A comprehensive inventory of stressors in policing was offered by Perrier and Tower (1984). External stressors, which we have mentioned in previous chapters, include dissatisfaction with the court system, unfavourable and allegedly unfair media reporting, unpleasant minority group relations with the attendant non-support and criticism, generally unfavourable public perceptions and excessive expectations, and poor community resources. Stressors internal to the police organization include poor training, supervision, equipment, pay, incentives for performance, peer support, managerial support, and poor policies in general. Associated with these external and internal factors are those intrinsic to the police role: the numerous demands; heavy workload; job fragmentation; exposure to suffering and human beings in unpleasant contexts; irregular hours with the attendant disruption in eating, sleeping, and personal activities; and periodic boredom, fear, anger, and danger. Finally, characteristics of the individual police officer may create stress, as with the female officer, the minority group officer, or the person insecure about ability or bravery, or personal, medical, or interpersonal problems.

Some work also indicates, not surprisingly, that police stress is not limited to field personnel. Police managers also experience stress, perhaps especially in an environment of downsizing. Taking disciplinary action and accounting for department actions to the public appear to be the most significant stressors for police managers (Standfest, 1996:2).

The tensions arising from policing have been associated with three major occupational pathologies: suicide, divorce, and alcoholism. These, of course, are not at all unique to police. But they are significant occupational hazards that have been recognized, and in more progressive forces, treated. The tensions endemic to the job are translated into cynicism, suspiciousness, unwillingness to talk about the job with outsiders, including the police officer's own family, and even self-dislike; together, these symptoms are characterized as "burnout." In turn, burnout affects performance because it is "accompanied by physical exhaustion, vulnerability to disease, or by psychosomatic systems (for example, ulcers, back tensions, headaches)." Behaviours such as alcohol abuse, violence, and marital conflict, are derivative. So is the decline in job performance, as "burnout can contribute to low morale, impaired performance, absenteeism, and high job turnover" (Maslach and Jackson, 1979:59).

Whether these pathologies are more prevalent among Canadian police than other population sectors is simply not demonstrable in Canada, even though there are some indications from the United States that they are a peculiar policing problem. For example, in the United States there are data suggesting a rate of alcoholism among police officers that is higher than the general population. One estimate has it that while 10% of the general population who drink become alcoholics, for police officers the rate is 23% (*Los Angeles Times,* March 6, 1994).

Research suggests that drinking and alcoholism are related to the incidence of police suicide. A study of Buffalo police found that suicide was a far higher cause of death than homicide (Violanti, 1995:19). It is reported that among New York City Police, suicide has been the leading cause of death for several years, and that male police officers in the United

States had a higher rate of suicide than 36 other occupations as measured in 1950, or three times higher than the general population as measured in 1986. The American Association of Chiefs of Police has estimated that in the United States there are about 300 police suicides each year, or about twice the number of suicide deaths as there are police killed in the line of duty (*Los Angeles Times*, February 5, 1995).

The Calgary Police Service employs a full-time psychologist to attend to these and other problems associated with the police workplace. This decision followed a rate of suicide in the 1970s in the Calgary Police Service that was the third highest in North America (*Maclean's* Magazine, March 5, 1979). Estimates place suicide at as high as six times the national average, with a greater risk of a police officer's death by suicide than in an encounter in the line of duty (*Toronto Star,* November 23, 1986). Other illnesses such as heart disease are also attributable to the job and the associated lifestyle. The average life span of a police officer is 57 years (*Toronto Star,* November 23, 1986).

Jon Shearer, a psychologist who has taught at the Ontario Police College, studied four major municipal police forces, and estimated that the rate of marriage breakdown was from 52% to 67% (*Ottawa Citizen*, August 23, 1982). The brotherhood of the Montreal Urban Police Force have for several years urged attention to the problems of marriage and policing, and did win management's consent to a program of spousal "ride-alongs" to address the problem of the fear and tension in a marriage related to the spouse's uncertainty and lack of knowledge of the police officer's job. Similarly, in July 1990, the Nepean, Ontario police implemented a ride-along program for spouses.

Because police have been wary, however, of voluntarily acknowledging that they were experiencing difficulties, many problems do not receive attention and the "code of silence" prevails. In 1988 the press reported that an RCMP officer in Burnaby shot himself with his revolver, becoming the eighth RCMP member stationed in British Columbia to commit suicide over the previous six years. Four of them had been in Burnaby. While under review by a staff psychologist, an RCMP spokesman promptly stated that "Any relationship to a duty factor has been ruled out or eliminated totally" (*Ottawa Citizen*, May 7, 1988). The RCMP, intent upon their public image as an elite force, have been reluctant to acknowledge psychological factors. If acknowledged at all, they are recorded as a disability (Kankewitt, 1986:135). In order to attend to police suicide it is probably necessary to amend both the public and the police self-image of toughness. As an American journalist put it, "Cops cry," suffer emotional crises, and require support and assistance (*Toronto Star*, November 23, 1986).

In Winnipeg, in the course of a major investigation of the shooting death of a native leader by a police officer, an inspector due to testify and previously in charge of the internal investigation, committed suicide the day before he was to testify. His widow stated to the press that stress treatment for police officers must begin early in their career and that police must learn not to be afraid to ask for help. An inquest following the suicide advised the police department to provide stress treatment services. In related testimony, a female police officer, who was the partner of the officer who had shot the native victim, testified that she and her partner sought private psychological help, because none was forthcoming from the police department. The officer who had fired the fatal shot ultimately entered a psychiatric ward and testimony stated that he was suicidal (*Ottawa Citizen,* August 26, November 8, 1989). He did eventually testify at the hearing under heavy sedation (Montreal *Gazette,* September 5, November 2, 5, 1989).

A 19-year veteran of the Sûreté, now trained as a social worker, served for a period as an instructor at the Quebec Police Institute, and later travelled the province speaking to police officers about stress. His lectures emphasized the extraordinary expectations of police performance, and their stressing effects. He speaks of policing as a "... dog's job. Statistics show that—on average—we get six seconds to make important decisions in our work. That can mean six seconds to decide whether you shoot or get shot. And then others take months to rule on the legality of your act." Or, "Other people are presumed innocent until they are found guilty. When a policeman makes a mistake he gets suspended without pay. That stresses the hell out of me." He also states that the job changes people. "I became a repressive, potentially dangerous policeman. For a while, I lost the ability to laugh." He continues: "Our work makes us intolerant, insensitive, cynical ..." (Montreal *Gazette,* December 19, 1987).

Despite some such attempts at support measures, there remains a prevalent sense that stress symptoms are a sign of weakness and unsuitability. Forces often seem unwilling to assist a stressed officer by making adjustments in their rule-bound procedures. A dramatic instance was reported in 1986. An RCMP officer stationed in Kelowna, British Columbia, was posted out of the country to accompany a witness in a drug-related case. He and his family received death threats, and after the trial, in fear for their lives, he sold his house and kept his family in the United States. He claims to have expected RCMP support, both with respect to housing and living expenses in the United States, and compensation for his time. He also had requested a year's leave, after using up holiday time to stay with his family. Instead, a board was convened to rule on his dishonourable discharge, and he resigned under protest six years short of his full pension. A commanding officer stated to the constable's wife that "The Force has no obligation to you or the children" (*Ottawa Citizen,* December 4, 1986).

Police organizations have generally been slow to respond to these kinds of problems, for reasons that are not altogether clear. The attitude appears to be that the incidents are sufficiently isolated, and related only to persons manifestly unfit for the job of policing. Often suicides, for example, are simply dismissed as "not job-related." In fact, rather than offer stress-relief programs, Canadian police forces seem more often unsympathetic. In Ontario, for example, a Durham Regional Police Force officer was pronounced not "psychologically fit." The officer, a 19-year veteran with 5 commendations for bravery and outstanding work, had been twice injured on duty. He twice suffered broken jaws, was on extended sick leave, and had requested "light duties." The police commission decided to dismiss him (*Ottawa Citizen,* November 11, 1989).

In the United States there appears to have been far more attention to stress and stress-related dysfunction than there has been in Canada. One of the better known stress programs is the Boston Police Stress Program, founded and operated by a former Boston police officer, Bill Donovan, who had himself contended with alcoholism, divorce, and suicidal impulses (Kankewitt, 1986). Donovan and two officers working with him met widespread opposition, even from the police union. But the program was officially operational in 1974, working largely with volunteers. Donovan himself was involved in much of the counselling, and in lecturing about stress at police academies, an approach that he favoured as preventive.

The U.S. National Institute of Justice, under provisions of the federal government Crime Act, annually funds numerous research investigations and projects intended to moderate stress problems. In 1996, for example, almost $1 million was made available for family support and stress reduction programs (*National Institute of Justice Bulletin,* July, 1997).

In contrast, in Canada there is virtually no public funding, and many initiatives have tended to be at the urging of police unions rather than managers. The Montreal Brotherhood has also been outspoken on the problem of alcohol abuse. In 1982 the head of the Brotherhood stated to the press that fully one quarter of MUC police officers have a serious drinking problem, and at least as many depend upon tranquillizers and other drugs. He attributed the abuse to job stress, and stated that the consequences were hazardous to the public. He claimed that in the previous three months several officers were in hospital for treatment arising from alcohol abuse, several were on the verge of suicide, and at least five had committed suicide related to stress and alcohol. Claiming that few if any received help from the force—and, in fact, instead were apt to receive poor job ratings—the spokesman urged that the force study the problems and implement assistance programs (Montreal *Gazette*, December 14, 1982).

Police forces, however, in the 1990s do operate employee assistance programs, and stress is now at least explicitly recognized. In Metropolitan Toronto, for example, it is stated in a policy statement co-signed by the Chief of Police and the President of the Police Association that "The Metropolitan Toronto Police Force recognizes that it is in the best interest of the Members and the Force to provide a *confidential assessment/referral service* for those members experiencing personal problems relating to marriage, finances, alcohol and drugs, psychological or emotional disorders, or critical incident stress" (Schaer, 1994). Many police services now also post explicit bulletins to members encouraging attention to stress-related matters, especially family support. The RCMP, for example, printed a work by a staff psychologist stating that "stress and marital problems take the heaviest toll on our members' emotional health" (Black, 1998).

CONCLUSION

Police officers are products of their social and occupational environments. Much of what they learn is deliberate and formal, and a good deal more is informal. Their attitudes and behaviours are learned, sustained, or modified in interaction with others. Historically, police social interaction has been dominated by contact with other police officers, and their shared experiences of a somewhat distorted and non-representative public, that is, members of the public causing trouble or in trouble.

Subject to the mix of organizational characteristics, individual experiences, and the subculture of policing, mistakes occur. Police make errors, as do any workers. In policing, as in any workplace, an objective is to reduce mistakes to some practical minimum. Organizational policies, supervision, individual training and retraining, support systems, general public and media scrutiny, and accountability procedures are all intended to reduce errors, as well as to prevent outright deliberate misconduct. Errors and misconduct are the subject of Chapter Eight.

ANNOTATED READINGS, CHAPTER SEVEN

Rubinstein, Jonathan. *City Police.* New York: Ballantine, 1973. This book is the best, simply the best. A detailed ethnographic account by a keen observer of the life of a street cop. Adjust for the American setting, and you have no richer source other than being on the job.

Skolnick, Jerome H. *Justice Without Trial: Law Enforcement in a Democratic Society* (2nd ed.). New York: John Wiley and Sons, 1975. This is another book that should be viewed as a classic in the police literature. It is a successful attempt to comprehend police behaviour in the United States as a function of police conceptions of order and their exercise of discretion in interaction with the public.

Vincent, Claude. *Police Officer.* Ottawa: Carleton University Press, 1990. This slightly revised version of a book published in the 1980s is a straightforward account of policing as an occupation. The work uses a symbolic interactionist theoretical framework, and the fieldwork is in Windsor.

BAD POLICING

Bad policing refers to unsatisfactory police conduct. The unsatisfactory conduct may be error, or it may be deliberate. Also, the improper conduct may be idiosyncratic, that is, occasional and the act of an isolated individual, or it may be attributable to some group practice in policing. It may be of a serious nature, or trivial misbehaviour, such as improper dress. Inappropriate pursuit, excessive force, and corruption are serious instances of police improper conduct occurring in the course of police duty. This chapter considers the nature and extent of improper police actions.

Bad policing happens. It need not always happen because of bad police officers. Often it is the satisfactory worker who, sometime in the course of a career of very satisfactory work, commits an error. The extent to which the errors are significant varies. The errors of the surgeon versus those of the philosopher, for example, are obviously of differing import, at least with respect to immediate human consequences. An error by a surgeon on the operating table can have obviously disastrous results. Similarly, an error in judgment by a police officer can be extremely hazardous to the officer and to the public, and be extremely visible. Absolute elimination of error is not the goal, for such would be impossible; but minimization of error is certainly important.

ERRORS

Recruit selection, training, and retraining, operational guidelines, and support are all intended to optimize the quality of police discretionary decisions, and to avert error. Nonetheless, in doing the work of policing, as in doing any work, there are numerous reasons why errors might occur. Haste, overwork, illness, faulty equipment, or simple honest misjudgment may all affect an action sometime in the career of a working police officer. Even when the officer's record is otherwise sound, errors may occur; the errors need not be chronic, although undoubtedly some unsuited persons do work as police officers. As police often must respond quickly to rather unpredictable and sometimes hazardous events, errors may occur— even if those errors only become apparent afterwards, possibly when more information is available than at the time the police officer was determining the action.

While the individual commits the action, it is pertinent to consider whether there are police routines or practices that are unnecessarily prone to error. It is also necessary to note a fine and often indistinguishable line between police error and police misconduct. To the extent that it can be identified, unacceptable behaviour that is deliberate is misconduct. Unacceptable conduct, on the other hand, which is the consequence of limited capacity, limited time for judgment, stress, or a number of other related factors, can be viewed as error, an individual's error, as opposed to the faults in the structure or system responsible for improperly placing the individual in such error-prone circumstances. Unacceptable behaviour that arises from general attitudes such as racial prejudice, or from organizational policy or tradition, may affect judgment unwittingly. In such instances the line between error and misconduct is extremely difficult to discern. Organizational flaws, for example, may be expressed in poor internal communications, or poor communications and coordination among police forces.

There is often a difficulty in coordination between the numerous police forces in Canada, and even within some large forces. A shared access to computer information has assisted police. But at times command link breakdowns, and jurisdictional jealousy inhibit effective police action. A notable example was that of the bus hijacking in April 1989. A Greyhound bus was commandeered in Montreal and ended up on Parliament Hill. RCMP officials in Ottawa were caught unawares, despite police action in Montreal and notification of area police forces and at least three U.S. police forces (*Ottawa Citizen*, October 30, 1989). In another, far more tragic incident, internal miscommunication apparently delayed the action of Montreal Police at the University of Montreal and led to the shooting deaths of female engineering students. Delays and fouled communications were featured in a report later filed by the police director. Lack of initiative and leadership were also cited (Montreal *Gazette*, January 26, 1990). Police reported in consequence that their directives or guidelines for responding to hostage-taking crises were being revised in the view that they were probably too restrictive and inhibited initiative on the scene (Montreal *Gazette*, March 21, 1990).

In considering police errors and misconduct, consider, as discussed in Chapter Seven, that public attitudes to police are influenced by direct encounters, whether as victims, complainants, or offenders. The quality of the encounter, with respect to the police officer's manner, politeness, and effectiveness, shape the citizen response and evaluation. Most encounters, especially those which are stressful, will be with young, and generally male, patrol officers, the persons on the front-line of enforcement and police response. It is the younger police officer who is most apt to be insecure or uncertain of appropriate conduct, and apt to be aggressive and authoritarian.

It is also the case that an encounter with a police officer is, to state the obvious, an interaction, that is, there is a two-way flow of cues and communications. The quality of the encounter, therefore, is affected not only by the police officer but also by the citizen (Wiley and Hudik, 1980). Police behaviour, therefore, is itself influenced by citizen behaviour, and vice versa. The police officer will act to establish control in the encounter (Rubinstein, 1973:267–277), but the citizen does influence the interaction. In exercising discretion, a police officer will be mindful not only of departmental procedural guidelines and priorities, but also of public definitions of priority and the particular reactions of individuals in an encounter situation (Lundman, 1980a:22–24). Moreover, in that much police behaviour is reaction, that is, a response to citizen calls for action, the public affects enforcement and the definition of the extent and seriousness of violations (Black, 1980), even though ultimately it is the police decision whether or not to intervene, and in what manner, that officially records or defines crime.

Two major manifestations of police error, each expressing elements of personal misjudgment or poor discretion, and of imperfect organizational directives and control are chases and excessive force.

CHASES

Police driving has historically been a matter of difficulty. As long as police and public believe that speed is intrinsic to effective police response, problems occur. Persons have been injured and property damaged as police respond to a call, disregarding traffic, safety regulations, and often police service guidelines. High speed "hot" police pursuit of offenders is the frequent occasion of controversy.

Chases are not the only difficulty; police often disregard basic traffic procedures, unnecessarily and illegally, in responding to calls, and have been subject to internal as well as court discipline. Thus, for example, in 1986 in one weekend in Ottawa two separate crashes involving police cars left one woman killed and eight injured. In one instance, a police car responding to a domestic dispute ran a red light and collided with a car, killing the driver and seriously injuring her daughter.

Police driving deficiencies have been found to relate not only to high speed encounters, but generally to inadequate training. In Ottawa, for example, the RCMP Division "A" found that too many officers were colliding with stationary objects, including the pillars in their underground garage. The force introduced a supplement to an Advanced Driving Course already being taught, and reduced the number of accidents (*Ottawa Citizen,* September 26, 1981).

Police instructors readily concede that among the notable deficiencies of recruits are driving skills. Accordingly, police academies are spending an increasing amount of time on driving courses to impart basic skills such as methods of steering, skid control, accident avoidance, and alternatives to high-speed chases. Until 1982 there was virtually no driver's training for police in Ontario, nor in most other Canadian jurisdictions, despite the nature of police duties. The difficulties often appear to be related to attitude as much as to skill.

An editorial in the *Ottawa Citizen* in 1981 noted 3 deaths and 124 injuries arising from police chases in the last 6 months of 1980. It went on to note that many police accidents also arise from rushing to respond to a call, and have even occurred in the police garage. "Many police officers have no special training in driving, and are no better prepared to drive a car at 150 kilometres per hour through urban streets than the average motorist. The cruiser itself will be equipped with a special police vehicle package, but the driver is essentially un-skilled" (*Ottawa Citizen*, October 5, 1981). In 1980, following a rash of incidents, the Ottawa Police instituted a course to correct the bad driving habits of police, which were producing more than 200 police vehicle accidents annually. As there were no Canadian training materials, the Ottawa force purchased two American driver training films for police, and modelled their program after that of the Peel Regional Police. At that time only Peel and the RCMP were offering driver instruction for police. The first students were those on the Ottawa force with an accident record (*Ottawa Journal*, February 4, 1980; *Ottawa Citizen*, February 5, March 17, 1980). The first driver instruction course at the Ontario Police College in Aylmer, one week long, was started in October 1982, and employed a former racing dri-ver and other instructors seconded from police forces in the province (*Globe and Mail*, October 12, 1982).

The practice of police resorting to high-speed driving still seems endemic. The cases that come to public attention with deserved notoriety often involve police action for trivial offences, generating a risk and sometimes outcomes out of all proportion to the incident or offence that first attracted police attention. Often a high-speed pursuit is a risky action, a risk that may be not in keeping with the importance of the violation. Questions arise regarding the judgment on the part of the participating police officer, and the policy guidelines of the force. Both questions imply the absence of successful efforts to develop alternatives to the vehicular chase.

Too often the results of a chase are the deaths of innocent people, or of the offenders, often young people committing a relatively minor infraction. Such was the case in 1987 in Ste. Foy when the MUC Police chased a car at high speeds; a collision occurred at an intersection with another automobile, and four young people were killed (Montreal *Gazette*, September 9, 1987). A similar tragedy occurred in Toronto in 1984, when during a high-speed chase a car being pursued by a Metro Toronto police car collided with a motorcycle, injuring the driver and killing his companion, a 23-year-old mother of three (*Toronto Star*, May 20, 1984). Similar accidents have occurred for years, and in all jurisdictions. In 1980, in New Brunswick, several police forces, including the RCMP, chased a car driven by a 19-year-old who failed to pay for $12.00 in gasoline. The offender crashed into a road block, and was killed (*Maclean's* Magazine, August 11, 1980).

Police officers are themselves often among the victims of chases that they initiate, as in Saskatchewan in 1980 when an RCMP officer and two others were killed in an accident arising from a high-speed chase. Two other RCMP officers were injured (*Ottawa Journal*, May 28, 1980). In Ontario the OPP and the local police from Goderich, near London, were in high-speed pursuit of a car. The OPP had pulled the vehicle over when the Goderich car came over a hill, collided with the car, and killed an OPP officer standing beside it (*Toronto Sun*, September 26, 1983).

Police chases seemed especially out of control through the 1970s and 1980s, with a plethora of incidents that eventually led to some greater control. In Alberta, during a two-month period in 1989, six people were killed in separate high-speed chases involving the

RCMP. In the period January 1987 to August 1989 there were 20 chase deaths in Canada, of which 11, excluding the 6 mentioned above, were in Alberta. In the face of criticism and anonymous death threats (*Ottawa Citizen*, September 22, November 1, 1989), police representatives insisted that they had to resort to chases to do their jobs. Following the deaths in Alberta resulting from police chases, a provincial task force was struck. It reported in October 1990 and merely recommended a $500 fine for failing to stop for a police officer, and an immediate suspension of licence. The Alberta government rejected both recommendations. It accepted a weak recommendation to fix guidelines for all police detachments, without any legislative weight. The guidelines, ostensibly serving to encourage "consistency," allow an officer to set upon a chase when it is judged that there are "reasonable and probable grounds to believe that the serious nature of the offence outweighs the danger of pursuit." The guidelines call for a senior officer or superior to control the chase (*Calgary Herald*, October 5, 1990). In effect, no significant curtailment of chases was imposed by the government.

Almost daily the newspapers reported police high-speed chases through heavily populated areas. Monitoring the press over a 10-year period turns up regular reports, and regular expressions of editorial indignation and calls for mandatory restraints. Such was the case in 1979, when Ottawa papers reported the injury of a boy who was a passenger in a car struck by an Ottawa Police cruiser, responding at high speed to an alarm. One editorial referred to police driving tactics as "hooliganism," and suggested that chases must become very rare events, and police too "must obey the law" (*Ottawa Sunday Post*, September 9, 1979). The police officer involved in the Ottawa incident was charged with going through a red light, consistent with regulations requiring police vehicles to come to a full stop even with lights and siren on, before proceeding through a red light (*Ottawa Journal*, September 4, 8, 1979). The police officer was charged with dangerous driving, and was convicted (*Ottawa Citizen*, September 12, 1979; January 26, 1980; March 30, 1980).

The question of police chases was brought up in the Ontario legislature following deaths in Burlington and Port Colborne. In each case, innocent third parties were killed as police chased minor offenders—a speeder and a car thief (*Ottawa Journal,* November 10, 1979). In February 1980, the legislature heard about chases again, following what was described as a "Starsky and Hutch-style police car chase" in downtown Hamilton, during which seven shots were fired at the car by police (*Toronto Star*, February 4, 1980). Some months later, still in 1980, police from Gatineau, Quebec, and Ottawa chased a car at high speeds on both sides of the river. In the course of the chase at least one shot was fired by a Gatineau police officer before the car was finally halted. An Ottawa resident protested "endangering lives for this sort of thing" (*Ottawa Journal*, April 28, 1980). A Toronto newspaper editorial, following yet another discussion in the legislature after a chase-related injury, again invoked the comparison of police reality and television policing, and called for legislators to "end high-speed police chases" (*Toronto Star*, May 17, 1981).

A citizens' group in Toronto suggested in a brief to the Ontario solicitor general that all high-speed chases except in instances of serious crime be banned. In their statement it was estimated that in 1983 over half of the chases in Ontario related to traffic offences, and that only 22 of 1648 chases related to serious criminal acts. They further itemized 7 deaths, 130 injuries and $831 196 in property damage arising from the chases in Ontario (*Toronto Star*, May 10, 1985). Earlier, in 1981, an Ontario Police Commission survey itemized 1015 police chases in the last 6 months of 1980, with 3 deaths and 124 injuries. Only 18 of the chases involved persons presumed to have engaged in serious crime (*Ottawa Citizen*, June 11, 1981). Public figures indicate that in 1987, 8 people were killed and 269 injured, including 82 police officers, in the course of 1346 police chases in Ontario. Estimates placed the 1987 Ontario property damages arising from chases at $1.7 million (*Ottawa Citizen*, August 24, 1988).

In Montreal, the Public Security Commission was informed that in 1988, despite years of public concern, the number of high-speed chases had actually increased by 8% over the previous year. There were 88 chases at high speed, resulting in 1 death and 20 civilian and 11 police injuries. The commission also learned that in 1987 40% of accidents involving police vehicles were attributable to officers with fewer than five years of experience. Twenty-three percent of the accidents involved officers with less than one year of service (Montreal *Gazette*, March 3, 1989).

To date there have been no large civil awards arising from injuries sustained in the course of a high-speed chase, but the prospect looms. In the United States in 1985, a man who lost both legs in an accident caused by a police chase five years previously, as police pursued a bank robber, was awarded $5 million compensation. The original theft involved $3000 (*Ottawa Citizen*, January 15, 1985). In the United States, police pursuit driving has been described as "one of the most controversial and litigated topics in policing" (Alpert et al., 1997). In British Columbia, in what appears to be the first award of its kind, an RCMP officer was ordered by the British Columbia Supreme Court to pay one-quarter of the costs associated with injuries to a motorcyclist injured when, while being chased at high speed in the Victoria area, he collided with a car in a roadblock. The payment was about $4500. The man was being pursued only for speeding, in violation of Force guidelines, which call for high-speed chases and roadblocks only in instances of serious criminal violations or serious danger to persons (*Ottawa Citizen*, January 6, 1987).

Police are loath to simply forbid such chases as dangerous out of proportion to the incident being policed, so high technology alternatives are often considered. In 1984, for example, following an in-depth television report, the Ontario solicitor general considered the rather expensive alternative of helicopters such as were reportedly being used effectively in Baltimore (*Ottawa Citizen*, September 22, 1984). An absolute ban on high-speed chases is in place in Baltimore, with police depending upon surveillance, including helicopter surveillance, to apprehend the offender safely by summons. According to local legislation, a range of traffic offences do not require stopping the vehicle. Police officials claim an 80 to 90% success rate in the ultimate apprehension of the offenders (*Toronto Star*, November 2, 1981). In Calgary, chases are routinely broken off after two minutes, and a guideline for officers states that "no member will be criticized if he elects in the interests of safety not to pursue or continue to pursue a vehicle which refuses to stop." In Calgary, too, a police helicopter has been reported as useful as an alternative to ground pursuit.

Prevalent police practice is to have in place a control officer in communications with a pursuit vehicle, who can monitor, authorize, or call off a chase, subject to some inevitably imperfect, remote assessment of public risk. Chases involving injury are subject to subsequent investigation in Ontario by the provincial Special Investigations Unit. Police also continue to develop blockade techniques and stopping devices. Helicopters, budgets permitting, will no doubt also become more prevalent. But essentially, the error of inappropriate chases will most nearly be resolved by clear priorization of offence and risk, and rigid enforcement of guidelines.

Police find themselves in pursuit for diverse reasons. Police learn to recognize cues, indicators of illegal conduct. Vehicular stops often lead to significant arrests, and so too, a fleeing vehicle is sometimes associated with a more serious offence. It has also been suggested that the challenge to authority represented by a fleeing vehicle is a provocation. Police officers will acknowledge a difficulty in restraining themselves from pursuit of an offender, and may note the "buzz," the adrenalin rush, the challenge, and the excitement of a chase during an otherwise tedious patrol shift. All of these factors relate to some incidence of force, including shootings, in association with a chase.

Some incidents illustrate the dangers both of chases and of weapons use. A "retired businessman" was pursued at high speeds by Toronto police in 1982, related to a drug investigation. When he was stopped, an officer placed a gun through the window. It went off, possibly when the victim grabbed it, killing him (*Toronto Star*, November 14, 1984). In 1990 a black teenager ran a radar trap, was pursued, and was shot and seriously wounded by a Toronto police officer (*Ottawa Citizen,* May 15, 1990). In Quebec in 1985, two Quebec provincial police officers attempted to pull over a car driven by a woman whom they knew and whose residence they knew. Rather than finding her at her home later, they pursued her truck at high speeds, attempted to take out a tire by firing a service revolver, and then resorted to a shotgun. The woman was hit in the head and severely injured by the shotgun fire (Montreal *Gazette,* April 7, 1985).

EXCESSIVE FORCE

Individuals

A recurrent complaint against police is that from time to time they use excessive force to intervene or to make an arrest. These incidents may involve individuals and police officers in an encounter, or, massed police in a crowd control situation. At issue will be the appropriateness of the level of force used, and whether it was necessary to the police intervention or, as was long ago found to be a factor in the United States, a response by police to public disrespect (Westley, 1970). Deciding what may have been appropriate force, especially where an injury has occurred, may then be left to the courts.

Such a case occurred in Montreal where a man was arrested and handcuffed despite indicating an arm injury, and consequently had his arm fractured (Montreal *Gazette*, March 7, 1989). Beatings and the use of handcuffs are frequent components in allegations of excessive force. A Montreal policeman, for example, sued his own colleagues on grounds of excessive force and wrongful arrest in having handcuffed his 17-year-old son for four hours, hands behind his back, when arrested for underage drinking (Montreal *Gazette*, December 30, 1987). A different kind of complaint about police use of force, overlaid with charges of racism, has been the use of police dogs. In Regina for many years the police patrolled with unleashed police dogs. In the period 1981 to 1982, 85 people were bitten, 59% of them native persons (*Globe and Mail*, September 20, 1983).

Also in Montreal, police surrounded a slightly built man armed with a knife. Witnesses who observed the confrontation in the man's backyard claimed that the man was armed, but not threatening. He was shot dead by a MUC Police constable, described as "young and nervous" (Montreal *Gazette*, January 4, 1989).

Montreal has had the reputation as a city in which armed crime and armed police response is prevalent. In that context, it is difficult to establish an acceptable benchmark for police use of guns. Given the size of the city and its police, and the number of encounters, a 1988 statistic of 26 shots fired by MUC Police might be viewed as slight. This figure was a reduction from 60 shots in 1980. Yet enquiries into the shootings established that half were unjustified (Montreal *Gazette*, March 3, 1989).

The Montreal police have acquired a reputation for forceful encounters, and have especially been criticized in the English-language Montreal *Gazette*. In 1989 two MUC Police officers were convicted by a jury of assaulting an English-speaking McGill University student in 1987. One conviction was for assault causing bodily harm, and a second for simple assault. The officers had been attempting to disperse a celebratory crowd outside a nightclub following a Stanley Cup victory, and were convicted following testimony that they had slammed the student's head against the side of their automobile (Montreal *Gazette*, June 18, July 2, 1989). The officer convicted of bodily harm was sentenced to six months in jail, and the *Gazette* applauded the sentence in a lead editorial, citing the conviction and sentencing as a welcome change from the tendency to overlook police violence.

Crowds

In analyzing crowd behaviour and control in the United States in the 1960s, Stark (1972:128–129) noted the poor preparation and inadequate organization of police personnel in contrast to regular military units. The discipline and fire control of military paratroopers contrasted with Detroit police unreliability and resort to weapons use. Police misreaction or misconduct associated with crowd control situations were described by Stark as a "police riot."

Stark's observations were profoundly relevant when observing Quebec police, RCMP, and Canadian army conduct in Quebec in 1990 when dealing with the Mohawk protests. The Sûreté apparently were ill equipped to respond in an effective and disciplined manner, and especially in the opening encounter, showed little weapons control. They resorted to tear gas, night sticks, and charges in dealing with Châteauguay residents protesting the Mohawk blockage of the Mercier Bridge (*Ottawa Citizen*, August 13, 1990). Police were reported to have reacted throughout the prolonged siege with verbal and physical harassment, and earned unpopularity with the Mohawk and other Quebec protestors (*Ottawa Citizen*, September 9, 1990). The soldiers, in contrast, were regarded as disciplined even in the face of provocation.

Police difficulties sometimes seem to occur as a function of their very presence and paraphernalia—a form of self-fulfilling prophecy where the attempted preventive action incites future incidents. A striking example was that of the native peoples demonstration on Parliament Hill in 1974. On September 30 of that year approximately 200 demonstrators, men, women, and children, many of whom had trekked from British Columbia in a "native peoples caravan," marched to Parliament Hill. Police barricades and RCMP officers met them, with their tactical force in full riot gear. This was the first time this trendy unit had been deployed. The demonstrators were driven off the Hill, and police spoke of a native riot. The demonstrators spoke of a police riot.

An earlier example was that of the so-called Gastown Riot in Vancouver in 1971. The urban area had become somewhat avant-garde, and was viewed by police and others as an area of heavy drug use. A protest against enforcement turned into a three-hour battle with Vancouver city police, including mounted police, with several citizen and police injuries and 79 arrests (Bourne and Eisenberg, 1972:36–46).

A major instance of police difficulties occurred in Montreal following the first referendum on sovereignty association. The police apparently lost control and reacted violently
to the crowd. A subsequent police commission enquiry concluded that the riot squad committed "illegal acts," that the head of the squad and 56 members should be transferred to other
duties, and that two divisions of the riot squad should be dismantled (*Globe and Mail*, July
19, 1981). And in 1988 an orderly demonstration by students protesting inadequate government support of universities met with forceful police action. The Quebec City Police
cleared demonstrating university students while in full riot regalia (*Ottawa Citizen*, November
3, 1988). Similarly, in Montreal 33 students were arrested and several injured when MUC
Police in riot gear intervened in a university student protest against a tuition fee increase
(*Ottawa Citizen*, March 29, 1990).

Another notable case of police problems in crowd control, doubly interesting because of
the lessons to be drawn concerning police–minority relations, was the object of a Manitoba Police
Commission enquiry. In 1983 a demonstration of approximately 700 people in front of the
Manitoba Legislature was protesting the United States' invasion of Grenada. Counter-
demonstrating militia members attempted to disrupt the demonstration, and fighting broke
out (*Globe and Mail,* November 23, 1983). Television and news reporters witnessed police
beating demonstrators with nightsticks following the arrest of one person who was a Chilean
refugee. In the enquiry it was indicated that many of the demonstrators, with experience of
demonstrations and police action in Chile, were terrorized by the police action. The Winnipeg
police, as do others, have policies governing the policing of demonstrations. The emphasis is upon
peacekeeping, using photographs of the crowd for later action when circumstances are not
volatile, and there are clear instructions to ignore taunts and other provocation. The nightsticks
are to be used only for self-defence or to protect a citizen. But the police lost control, and especially
overreacted to the frightened Chilean demonstrators, while the militia personnel who had initiated the violence escaped arrest (*Globe and Mail*, June 23, 1984). In 1985, a Manitoba Police
commission report to the Manitoba Attorney General concluded that Winnipeg police had used
"excessive force" in clearing the demonstration (*Ottawa Citizen*, April 10, 1985).

As discussed elsewhere, police in Canada have frequently been called upon to intervene massively in industrial disputes, and routinely are present to patrol strikes. In maintaining
order and public access where picket lines are up, the police frequently become the objects
of frustration and violence, even when they act with restraint. As the interaction develops,
arrests occur. The police are themselves often reluctant to be present. In 1978, during a
Canadian Union of Postal Workers strike, a Metro Toronto Police decision was taken not to
police the pickets, in order to avoid generating conflict. In response, a CUPW spokesman referred to the cooperative attitude of the police in this uncommon decision (*Ottawa Citizen*,
October 19, 1978).

Policing strikes is an extremely uncomfortable situation for police. They are obliged to
maintain order and access, but are thereby defined by strikers as aiding management and
strikebreakers. In the emotion of a strike, the police themselves become the accessible object of anger and violence and, of course, often reciprocate. A tragic instance occurred in 1986
when Quebec Provincial Police pinned a union demonstrator with a choke hold. The man died,
apparently having choked on his own vomit (Montreal *Gazette*, October 28, 1986).

When the police are called upon to intervene in demonstrations, for example, or in
picket lines during strikes, they often find themselves in a controversial role, no longer
"neutral" intervenors, but appearing to protect one side more than the other. They are being
required by the authorities to limit or to prevent the actions of persons engaged in more or

less legitimate actions. The police then become themselves the object of hostility. Picket line clashes are the best illustration of being "caught in the middle." In the violent Gainers Meatpackers strike in Alberta in 1988, police were required to enforce a court injunction limiting pickets. They arrested dozens of strikers and generated union protests against police tactics. One union spokesman went so far as to say that if the police had not been present there would not have been "scabs" breaking the picket lines and the company would have had to negotiate seriously. A member of the police commission defended the police actions, noting that "There is a statutory obligation on the part of police to enforce the law" (*Winnipeg Free Press*, June 4, 5, 1986).

Prompted by the Gainers strike as well as other incidents in the country, the clearest expression of labour attitude to the "statutory obligation" of police was put by Shirley Carr, then President of the Canadian Labour Congress. Claiming police brutality in a speech to delegates to the annual convention of the Ontario Federation of Labour in Toronto, she suggested that workers consider not paying taxes. "We are paying salaries to police who brutally beat us on the picket lines—we don't have to pay taxes to someone who beats us up" (*Ottawa Citizen*, November 26, 1986).

When police fail to respond quickly or effectively to public disorder, they also incur public criticism. A prominent instance was the post-Stanley Cup disorder in Montreal in 1986, when police took two hours to react effectively after the first several police cars withdrew in the face of the crowd. In the interim, widespread vandalism and looting occurred (Montreal *Gazette*, May 27, June 14, 1986). Police spokesmen later suggested that they were cautious in their response for fear of criticism for overreaction as on referendum night in 1980 when police used excessive force on a crowd on Mount Royal. In a scathing editorial the Montreal *Gazette* concluded that "A trained, professional police force is supposed to know the difference between a harmless crowd letting off steam and vandals running amok. It is supposed to know the difference between zealous overreaction and inexcusable inaction" (Montreal *Gazette*, May 30, 1986).

Deadly Force

Not surprisingly, the use of arms by police has always been the most contentious aspect of police conduct. From the inception of our policing tradition in Peel's England, the dangers of a civic paramilitary force were feared. Ultimately, Britons conceded uniforms and a paramilitary structure; but to this day they do not generally concede their police the right to bear firearms in the normal conduct of their duties. In Canada, however, as in the United States and virtually everywhere else in the world, the police are routinely armed and trained in the use of firearms. A Canadian exception is the Newfoundland Constabulary, Canada's oldest police force, which was founded in 1872. Like their British model, the constabulary served unarmed until 1998, although weapons were available as needed. Only one member of the constabulary has been killed on duty during the history of the force, and that was in 1959 during a labour dispute (*Ottawa Citizen*, November 24, 1988).

In Canada there have generally been stricter controls than in the United States upon the use of weapons by police officers. But, inevitably, incidents occur that prompt public concern about apparent errors or unnecessary use of deadly force by Canadian police. Yet, despite numerous instances of controversial application of deadly force, no police officer in Canada has ever been convicted of killing or wounding a civilian in the line of duty (*Toronto Sunday Star,* October 28, 1984).

An interesting comment by the president of the Canadian Police Association was re-ported by the press. It was suggested that police treat animals better than they treat human beings, in that they are more apt to incapacitate an animal whereas they will shoot disturbed people. It was suggested that rather than relying on heavily armed tactical units, police de-velop weapons intended to immobilize rather than to wound or kill. In fact, police in New York City are now equipped with stun guns and water pressure canisters (*Ottawa Citizen,* March 3, 1990).

Since police are armed and do deal with dangerous situations, police must be expected to use their weapons. But questions must be asked, not only about the basic assumption of arming all police officers, but also with regard to the nature of the arms, and the nature of the training in arms use. Deadly force is the ultimate police intervention, and especially in a society that proscribes capital punishment, it is the most serious form of intervention, es-pecially when there is a chance of mistakenly harming innocent parties. In fact, determin-ing error, as opposed to police intent, or police carelessness, becomes part of the issue. The questions become even more complicated and serious in connection with the actions of non-uniformed police who are not easily identified as law enforcement officers, and in-deed, are often dressed to appear as undesirable people. This latter difficulty, as well as race relations problems, may be illustrated by a Mississauga case involving two police of-ficers from the Peel Regional Police Force.

Two black teenagers were driving a stolen car. Two police detectives in jeans appeared in the street in front of them. They later testified that they attempted to stop the car, but the driver attempted to run them down, and so they had acted to protect themselves. The teenage passenger testified that he did not recognize the men as police officers, and considered them threatening. The 17-year-old driver was shot in the back of the head and killed (*Toronto Sunday Star*, December 11, 1988). Later it was established that police were using hollow-point bullets which have greater "stopping power," as they expand on impact, but which were prohibited by the Police Act (*Ottawa Citizen*, December 24, 1988). Sometime later the Ontario solicitor general, having initially dismissed the use of "hot-point" bullets as al-ready under control, ordered Ontario police chiefs to enforce the ban, making the bullets available for police use only in specifically authorized circumstances, under the authority of a chief (*Ottawa Citizen,* January 2, 1989).

In Toronto especially there were instances of the use of deadly force by police in the 1970s and 1980s that marred the relations of police with visible minority populations, underlined perceptions of police racism, and ultimately led to a public review board.

The police shooting of a black man, Albert Johnson, in 1979, the eighth shooting death by police in a year, has become almost a benchmark (*Ottawa Journal*, September 19, 1979). Police had responded to a complaint of a disturbance, and shot the man as he descended the stairs of his house brandishing what appeared to be an axe but was, in fact, a lawn edger. The two police officers responsible were eventually acquitted of manslaughter charges in court. But despite assurances of amended responses, the problems persisted through the 1980s, underscored by another incident where a black man, Lester Donaldson, was shot and killed by police in 1988. Within a week of the charges against the Peel Police officers, a Toronto police officer was charged with manslaughter in this shooting death. The black com-munity response was to label the police as "racist" (*Maclean's* Magazine, September 24, 1981; *Toronto Star*, August 23, 1988).

An internal police enquiry found no fault, but charges were laid on the basis of an Ontario Provincial Police investigation (*Ottawa Citizen*, January 12, 1989). The officer had indicated that his partner was being threatened by the victim armed with what appeared to be a knife. In reaction, numerous Toronto police officers declared that they would cease to wear their guns, and thereby cease to patrol, as regulations required that they be armed. Others responded only to emergencies. The protests died out during the course of the day of January 12, when the arrest and charges became known, and Police Association spokespeople took up the cause. The Police Association president made it clear that he believed the charges unfair, and a response to public pressure. He attributed the action to the pressure of black activists, called for public support, denied racism in the Toronto Police Force, and went on to declaim that "if this city wants to be run by a very small group of black activists, then what you're going to end up with is another Detroit" (Montreal *Gazette*, January 12, 13, 1989). The Chief of Police made a statement indicating that the investigating force, the OPP, had to his knowledge not recommended charges, but that the decision was made in the Office of the Attorney General. The *Toronto Star* reported that the chief considered the decision to have been political (*Toronto Star,* January 14, 1989; *Ottawa Citizen*, January 18, 1989).

The consequence of the succession of events involving Toronto police and black citizens has been a loss of the public collaboration upon which police depend. In May of 1990, a team of Toronto police officers, male and female, was attacked by a crowd when they attempted to arrest an armed man (*Ottawa Citizen*, May 22, 1990). The crowd response, within days of a Toronto police shooting of a black youth, was indicative of a deterioration in the traditional compliance of the public with police actions.

An incident in Montreal precipitated a crisis in police relations with minority communities. In 1987 an experienced police constable shot in the back and killed a fleeing black youth, following his arrest after the complaint of a taxi driver who claimed that his fare was not being paid. The officer, contending that his gun discharged by accident, was suspended, eventually tried for manslaughter, and acquitted. He was, however, dismissed from the force on the recommendation of a discipline board on the grounds of negligence (Montreal *Gazette*, July 1, 1988; Ottawa *Citizen*, July 9, 1988). In the view of the constable's colleagues, he was a scapegoat, and the brotherhood criticized the MUC Police director for pandering to public opinion.

Approximately one full year after his acquittal, the Crown made it known that it would file a request to appeal the verdict before the Quebec Court of Appeal (Montreal *Gazette*, March 7, 1989). Yet a Quebec labour arbitrator, hearing the case brought forward by the police brotherhood, ordered that the constable must be reinstated to the force on the grounds that the shooting was an accident. In response the Montreal black community immediately began to lobby the force in opposition and the Crown appealed to the Quebec Superior Court. The court ruled in favour of the officer, and in January 1990 the officer was returned to work, assigned to the electronic surveillance division, out of uniform, unarmed, and away from the public (*Ottawa Citizen,* August 24, 28, November 23, 1989; January 23, 1990).

In western Canada, police shootings with racial overtones most often involve native people. In Winnipeg in 1988, an enquiry cleared a police constable of any fault following the shooting death of a native man who was a member of a tribal executive council. Reports suggest that the victim was stopped by the police constable who had been involved in the chase of two car theft suspects, after the constable knew that the suspects were already in custody. The victim approached and was recognized by the police officer as a native person. He was asked for identification, refused, there was a scuffle, and he was shot and killed with the police officer's revolver. One journalist, writing of the incident and the enquiry, described it as arising from mutual cultural distrust, with native persons accustomed to and expecting harassment from police they consider to be "racist and violent" while police, for their part, view native persons as dishonest troublemakers, "alcoholic and violent." A current police joke was "How do you wink at an Indian?" The pantomimed response was the gesture of pulling the trigger of a gun (Gillmor, 1988).

Even though objective review has found no evidence in Canada of discriminatory use of force by police against minority persons, the perception is well entrenched that such discrimination occurs, perhaps because there is evidence of verbal abuse (Stenning, 1994). Moreover, in a nation where police shootings are relatively rare, there has been a flurry of well-reported incidents extending over at least two decades. A lawyer for a family in Toronto has claimed that in Toronto 24% of fatal police shootings involve blacks, putting Toronto ahead of major United States' cities such as Detroit, New York City, Chicago, Los Angeles, and Miami (*Globe and Mail*, September 28, 1996).

Tactical Units

A development that illustrates the extremity of the problem of police management of deadly force has been the Canadian copying of the American fad of tactical squads. Every police force seems to require such a unit, even those in environments where demand for such a unit is improbable. In the suburban, Ottawa-area city of Nepean, for example, a riot squad with riot gear was established even in the absence of any historical need, and with other area police forces already having such specialized units in place. Exaggerating the military "special forces" character of policing, these units were intended to deal with the extremely unusual, whereas policing generally is concerned with the banal and usual. Critics have suggested that these forces, having been created in the absence of genuine need, are then applied unnecessarily, simply because a use and justification must be found. Often, they seem to be plagued by coordination and communications breakdown.

Dramatic and tragic credence is lent to these criticisms by incidents in southern Ontario. In 1984 in Woodstock, Ontario, provincial police tactical personnel were called in to apprehend two suspect murderers. Before the operation was concluded, a 27-year veteran of the force had been shot and killed. The subsequent inquest testimony indicated that there was a breakdown in information regarding the positioning of the tactical squad, allowing the victim to be caught out of position attempting to evacuate residents (*Toronto Star*, February 22, 1985). Further evidence indicated that the officer, although wounded several times by the criminals, was actually mortally wounded by a bullet fired from a police rifle (*Ottawa Citizen*, October 15, 1984).

On August 14, 1988, the OPP called in their special tactical unit to deal with a reportedly suicidal young man. There was not evidence that the man was a danger to persons other than himself, but he was undoubtedly armed with a rifle. Local police, known by the young man, were removed from the situation, and the heavily armed tactical squad were told in a briefing of the extreme danger of the situation. The OPP apparently were never provided with an accurate description of the suicidal man. In the confusion, where ranking officers apparently misunderstood the location of the tactical unit and the man, an innocent person, terrorized by the presence of armed intruders, was shot to death in his yard. The subsequent inquest showed that the squad went into action six minutes after having been inexplicably ordered by their senior officer to "take out" the suspect on the grounds that he "is going to try to take one of them out" (Montreal *Gazette*, September 28, 1988). The suicidal man was later wounded and detained by the OPP squad when they learned of his correct location; meanwhile his girlfriend had been in continuous conversation with an OPP negotiator (*Globe and Mail*, October 12, 14, 19, 1988; *Toronto Star*, October 18, 1988).

The tragedy was reconstructed in a well-reported inquest through the autumn of 1988. At the inquest, the widow testified that she was in contact by telephone with police twice, telling them of armed men in the yard. Audio tapes confirmed the calls. Local police were told of the calls by the civilian dispatcher, who, however, was unable to reach the OPP. After her husband was shot to death, the woman remained in the basement with her child, with police on site apparently unwilling or unable to tell her of the shooting, according to an OPP sergeant testifying at the inquest. He had finally told her of the accident. The pathologist who performed the autopsy testified that 2 fatal police shots struck the man when he was down on the ground, and that the victim was shot a total of 13 times, resulting in 25 wounds. He went on to remark that in his seven-year career, which included one month in the Detroit area, he had never seen so many gunshot wounds (*Globe and Mail,* November 8, 18, 1988; *Ottawa Sun*, November 8, 1988; *Ottawa Citizen,* November, 8, 10, 1988).

In retrospect the errors are manifest. A hyped-up, heavily armed police squad, poor command coordination, a distraught 19-year-old with a rifle defined imprecisely as a dangerous target, an innocent man frightened by the present of an armed band in his dark, rural yard—all contributed to a tragic conclusion that probably would not have occurred with a more traditional police approach. The heavily armed police engaged in a frenzy of shooting that could have had little purpose other than to "take out" the victim. The family, failing to reach an agreement for compensation, filed a suit against the OPP for $7.65 million, alleging excessive force and the use of hollow-point bullets (Montreal *Gazette*, January 19, 1989).

Another instance of tactical unit error may be had from Quebec. In 1987 MUC SWAT team members battered down the door of a Montreal apartment where a man, his wife and 18-month-old infant were eating dinner. They entered firing automatic weapons, wounding the woman and the man, who bled to death, untreated. The raid was promoted by an arrest warrant for attempted murder, arising from a fight in a restaurant between the victim and an off-duty police officer. In a civil suit the widow was ultimately awarded approximately $250 000 in damages (Montreal *Gazette*, February 25, 1988). In the same month of the court award, with other major damage suits against the MUC pending, the chief of the MUC Police suggested that no more than 4 or 5% of police use excessive force and "that the media place too much emphasis on such cases" (Montreal *Gazette*, February 3, 1988).

A notorious instance of unnecessary and gross error in the use of deadly force unfolded in Quebec in 1984. Two Sherbrooke police detectives had been intent upon tracking down a fugitive. Acting on information, they burst into a motel, machine guns firing, and shot to death a totally innocent man; another innocent man in the room was seriously wounded. In an adjacent room a man and his wife cowered on the floor as bullets pierced the wall above their bed. The fugitive was not in the motel. A coroner's inquest concluded that "the incomplete and too cursory checking and planning, the lack of reflection and the rashness shown before the police action shows ... that they acted with serious negligence" (*Ottawa Citizen,* September 13, 1986). Subsequently, they were acquitted by a jury of any wrongdoing, having been charged with manslaughter and weapons charges (*Toronto Sunday Star*, October 21, 1984; *Ottawa Citizen*, October 22, 1984). The acquittal prompted the premier to order a review with respect to a possible appeal. While on trial the police officers had remained on duty, but unarmed. Two days after their acquittal they were given back their guns (*Globe and Mail*, October 23, 1984). Despite the acquittal, the Quebec Police Commission recommended that the officers be demoted to patrol constables for at least three years, but the recommendation was rejected almost three years later by Sherbrooke City Council and the three police officers escaped all sanction (*Ottawa Citizen*, September 13, 1986). "Dodge City lives on in Sherbrooke," concluded a newspaper columnist (Montreal *Gazette*, September 10, 1986). Finally, in 1987, in an out-of-court settlement, the City of Sherbrooke paid the estate of the man killed the sum of $8000 (*Ottawa Citizen*, August 8, 1987).

Police tactical squads seem to have glamour appeal for the media as well as for the police. In Quebec, a few months before the tragic Ontario incident, the front page of the *Sunday Gazette* featured a large photograph and a feature article on "swat cops," with the headlined theme, "They let the bad guys decide—whether to live or die" (April 17, 1988). Where the correct tradition of Canadian policing is to prevent and to apprehend without violence, SWAT teams and other similar special tactical squads are premised upon massive firepower and violent, indeed deadly, intervention. And the media apparently endorse this radical departure. In the text of the feature article, the author wrote approvingly that when the SWAT police "come calling, they slow you down with tear gas, open the door with a battering ram, and enter with Uzi submachine gun, M–16 automatic rifles, semi-automatic pistols and sawed-off shotguns." The team leader is then quoted as stating, "with a hint of a smile," "that we're geared to make war" (Montreal *Gazette*, April 17, 1988). The primary concern of the British public when the notion of a domestic police force was first broached, that it not be a domestic army licensed to violence, is brought to mind by the alarming portrait of the Montreal team. Although the lengthy feature went on to indicate that the team, referred to by the team leader as "the gang," had as its priority the safety of the public, the impression left is probably the reality: a police unit trained for and expecting to resort to violence.

In Toronto, a full-page photo spread was featured in the *Sunday Star* describing the Metro Police Emergency Task Force, with the dominant photographic emphasis upon weapons and the Special Weapons Team. Unlike the Montreal story, however, the Toronto feature stressed the evolution from its founding in the 1960s as a "tough and ready crew" to one now trained "to avoid violence." The brief text concluded by noting that "they're trained to negotiate, rather than shoot, and usually end explosive situations through talk" (*Toronto Sunday Star*, January 7, 1982).

Yet, for all the skilled use of negotiation and the timely application of precise force, tactical units continue to pose difficulties, perhaps just because they have become so much more common. Forceful raids on homes and buildings have become frequent, associated with suspected motorcycle gangs and drugs. With faulty intelligence, the incorrect site may be raided, with enquiries going on for several years. Such occurred in a 1991 drug raid in Ottawa where an innocent man was shot and killed, when a home was incorrectly targeted (*Ottawa Sun*, February 20, 1994). Near Toronto an OPP tactical unit battered their way into a farm home looking for a wanted person, and in an RCMP raid in British Columbia the emergency response team forced their way into the wrong house in Surrey (*Toronto Sun*, February 21, 1996; *Ottawa Citizen*, January 21, 1996). Police tactical units, as used for crowd control, have elaborate equipment that may be provocative in contrast to normal police attire. Their very presence or deployment also may create expectations of violence and use of force. They are controversial among police and public alike.

And crowd control remains, apparently, a police weakness. The Ontario Provincial Police Riot squad, whom many observers, including Metro Toronto Police, believe should never have been called out to police demonstrating public servants in Ontario in 1996, engaged in well-reported and rather shocking violent interventions. A Metro Toronto police officer was reported as referring to the OPP squad as behaving "like animals." Another observer remarked that the police "looked like stormtroopers out of a Star Wars movie" (*Toronto Star*, March 19, 1996).

Controls

It is true that in Canada the weight of police armament has been more moderate than in the United States, just as violent crime has been more moderate. Where American police support more arms because their's is an armed society—and they continue to oppose, by and large, gun controls—in Canada the police have recognized public arms restrictions as a basic measure to protect themselves. In Canadian jurisdictions, especially in Ontario, the discharge of a firearm by a police officer is a very serious matter, and subject to mandatory enquiry. Prohibitions upon the resort to weapons are strongly reinforced in Canada, although arguably much less so in Quebec. In the Ottawa metropolitan area, for example, the OPP stopped a speeding car and in the course of the encounter, a passenger, who had moved into the driver's seat, was shot in the hand. Following investigations by the Ottawa police, in whose jurisdiction the incident occurred, and the OPP, in whose jurisdiction the chase began, the Ottawa police charged the OPP constable with aggravated assault, using a firearm in the commission of an offence, careless use of a firearm, and pointing a firearm (*Ottawa Sun*, November 21, 1988).

Police defend members who have used weapons, pointing out that real or perceived jeopardy cannot always be appreciated after an encounter. In 1982 a Montreal detective-lieutenant apprehended a man who was then convicted for 11 bank robberies. In the course of his action, he fired a warning shot in the air after shouting "Police, stop" several times. The fugitive had his hand in his pocket, suggesting the possibility that he was armed. For firing a warning shot, against a force directive that a gun be used only when an officer or citizen is endangered, a reprimand was entered on his personnel file. Calling the warning "a very dangerous precedent," the brotherhood grieved the sanction, unsuccessfully (Montreal *Gazette*, January 7, 1982).

Mandatory investigation any time a weapon is used has not, however, prevented improper use in Canada. In the Winnipeg incident resulting in the shooting death of a native leader, witnesses reported that several police officers in pursuit of youthful car thieves whom they had no reason to believe were armed, were running with drawn guns; police denied the reports, claiming that witnesses were mistaken and actually saw walkie-talkies in their hands (Gillmor, 1988). More clearly, in Toronto the press editorialized about at least five occasions where the public were endangered by stray police shots, in incidents such as firing at fleeing vehicles (*Toronto Star*, March 29, April 3, 1984).

As in the Quebec and Ontario incidents, evidence shows clearly that most police shots miss their target. The police response in training has been to attempt to teach police officers to shoot without aiming, that is, to point and fire, to avoid jerking the weapon in stress (*Toronto Star*, November 27, 1988). Yet the public would, by and large, prefer that if their police are to be armed, they have the capacity to shoot accurately.

When incidents occur, there are demands for better weapons training, and for more organizational prohibitions or controls upon police use of arms. Occasionally there is even the suggestion that police require more training in unarmed combat, thereby providing them with an alternative to gun use. In an encounter in Kingston, Ontario, an OPP officer stopped a man for impaired driving. The man assaulted the officer, and ignored a warning, following which the officer shot and killed him to defend himself. The OPP made known that the constable when approaching the driver had neglected to carry a nightstick. Noting that it is not mandatory for an officer to carry the nightstick, the spokesman observed that "We've been issued just recently with these sticks. They're not a thing we've been carrying for years. They're there to disarm people to prevent possible use of firearms" (*Globe and Mail*, January 8, 1985).

A countervailing demand has been that of the police, often through their employee groups, for more and more powerful weapons—ostensibly in response to more armed and more dangerous offenders. The demands rise to a strident level whenever a police officer has been shot. In Vancouver in 1983, for example, the president of the police union called for better weapons training, but also for shotguns in every police car (*Toronto Star*, January 3, 1983). In the Mississauga case of the 17-year-old shot and killed by the police, the banned bullet was used because of its stopping power. An unidentified police officer remarked to the press that the bullets are used despite the ban "because in a shootout with a criminal they want to be sure it is them and not the bad guy who goes home to his wife and kids that night" (*Ottawa Citizen*, December 24, 1988). In 1987 the 10-member equipment advisory board of the Ontario Police Commission and the commission unanimously advised the solicitor general to authorize the hollow-point bullets, on the grounds that they have greater stopping power without fragmenting and causing extensive damage, and are less likely to pass through a body and do other damage. The solicitor general refused (*Ottawa Citizen*, January 29, 1987). The bullet is now used by most police forces.

While the police do lobby for improved weapons, and protective equipment, it is also the case that they have urged the development and the availability of devices as alternatives to deadly force. Ironically, devices such as stun guns and pepper spray have themselves caused serious injury, and prompted charges of police brutality, as in 1997, in a crowd control situation, when the RCMP are alleged to have unnecessarily used pepper spray on demonstrating students at the University of British Columbia during the Asia-Pacific Economic Cooperation meetings (*Globe and Mail*, November 29, 1997).

Whether or not police should be armed is rarely a topic of serious debate any longer in Canada. Where the British police have persisted, albeit imperfectly, in maintaining the tradition of unarmed uniformed police, in Canada we have historically accepted the frontier-like expectation, influenced no doubt by the United States, that our police be armed. The only exception was the Newfoundland Constabulary, until 1998 the only unarmed police in North America, and there police demanded successfully that the Constabulary be armed, as are the RCMP, the CN Police, and the Ports Authority Police in Newfoundland (*Toronto Star*, March 14, 1986). The absence of guns was by tradition, not law, and the Constabulary carried only batons, with firearms in reserve if necessary. The Newfoundland officers, like their British counterparts, used to back off and await support where a situation threatened to require firearms. While they waited for their arms, as a police spokesperson acknowledged, sometimes the situation would moderate (Montreal *Gazette*, January 29, 1989).

MISCONDUCT

Errors and misconduct have their origins in the same complex web of factors including improper recruit selection and training, and ineffective organizational control.

Again, there is a need to distinguish between different categories of actions. Some forms of misconduct discussed below are of little or no consequence for the public. Rather, they are violations of the regulations of the police organization, and have only a vague possible consequence of some diminishment of police organization efficiency. Such misbehaviour can be distinguished from serious misconduct: abuse of powers of arrest, brutality, corruption, or illicit financial benefit. Somewhat distinguishable from corruption, which tends to refer to benefits as a police officer, is when police officers engage in thefts and robberies, on duty or off, that are not directly related to their role. Some police misconduct has detrimental consequences for the public, and possible profit for police officers. Corruption ranges from the petty to the grand, as does police abuse of power. Sometimes power is abused to protect the police officers. On other occasions it may be resorted to out of a misguided sense of duty, what Richard Henshel referred to as "offences in pursuit of vigilante objectives" (Henshel, 1981).

Each of the above forms of misconduct may be limited to one or a few individuals, the "bad apples," or they may derive from the basic character of a police unit and involve widespread collusion. This latter serious form of misconduct is a function of the character of the policing organization, environment, and subculture, what Shearing (1981) has referred to as "organizational police deviance."

Police misconduct is therefore a concept encompassing an array of behaviours. An American observer, referring to corruption, seeking to illustrate the pervasiveness and the gradations of corruption or misconduct, itemized the following deviant behaviours (Stoddard, 1974:286–287). "Mooching" is receiving minor benefits such as free coffee or meals, or discounts without explicit police favours in return. "Chiseling" consists of a police demand for benefits such as meals or admission to events. "Favouritism" consists of obtaining privileged treatment for oneself and family members by identifying in some way that one is a police officer. Stoddard also considers "prejudice" to be a form of deviance, wherein some groups, such as homosexuals or visible minorities, receive less service or more offensive actions that others. "Shopping" is the police officer's helping himself to items such as minor foodstuffs, when encountering an unlocked store. "Extortion" is defined as demands for support, such as the purchase of tickets for police events, in exchange for implied or explicit favoured treatment. "Bribery" is the payment to police of benefits in exchange for explicit favoured treatment, such as avoidance of prosecution. A "shakedown" is a more serious form of "shopping," with police taking major items from premises that are unprotected, such as during the course of investigating a break-in. "Perjury" is collaborating to create stories or lies or silence that police may engage in to protect their peers. And finally, Stoddard noted "pre-meditated theft or burglary."

Manifestations of police misconduct seem never-ending. It may be argued that misconduct is inevitable, not merely in a statistical sense with regard to the large number of police officers, but with respect to the nature of police duties and organization. Charged with the complex tasks of law enforcement, maintaining civil order, and performing service, while yet limited in their responses under law, and at the same time acting much of the time without observations or supervision, police misconduct must occur (Cain, 1979:147). The factors that permeate the policing experience and lead to corrupt acts also include: the latitude for discretionary behaviour—which some seek to limit because of corrupt practices; infrequent on-site supervision—a problem that management has historically always sought to correct; long periods of isolation from the public with irregular social contacts that proffer opportunities for misconduct; group solidarity and secrecy extending to supervisory levels; and a sense of under-appreciation, in prestige and remuneration (Sherman, 1974:12–14).

Misbehaviour

Police may find themselves in difficulty for behaviour that might be described as "conduct unbecoming a police officer." Some of the misconduct appears peculiar to a police organization's performance or disciplinary code. Other behaviour will be such as is generally considered improper, but not necessarily serious by the general public.

An Ottawa case where it was alleged that a senior officer had frequented a massage parlour, not an illegal act, was a serious matter of investigation and reporting, because it called into question the moral authority of the police officer (*Ottawa Citizen*, November 12, 1997). It also placed enormous pressure upon the police officer and his family while the investigation proceeded. Subsequently the officer was exonerated fully, as it was definitively established that he was not the person named as a client of the massage parlour (*Ottawa Citizen*, February 14, 1998). In the nature of policing as a public service dependent upon public respect and confidence, the allegation was not only newsworthy, but a significant matter for the police organization and for the individual.

Relatively innocuous conduct by police may bring down discipline, even when that conduct will not be perceived as discreditable or undesirable by the public. For example, a constable with 13 years service and 10 citations of merit on the Niagara Regional Police Force was dismissed for discreditable conduct. His offence was to operate a travel agency for the International Police Association on his own time and without personal gain (*Globe and Mail*, November 13, 1978). A Vancouver policeman was brought before a discipline hearing because while off-duty he sang with a rock group. He was suspended without pay and recommended for dismissal for persisting in his singing over orders to desist, and for talking with the press about the matter (*Ottawa Citizen*, February 18, 1988). A similar case had surfaced in Ottawa several years earlier. A constable assigned to the crime prevention section, had also worked as a singer. His police role was prominently featured in his singing, with a first album called "Off Duty." He was accused of singing in an area club before completing a tour of duty, and charged and found guilty internally of discreditable conduct and neglect of duty (*Ottawa Citizen*, October 2, 1981). Similarly, a Toronto police officer went to court in a four-year long dispute concerning his having been convicted internally of insubordination and misconduct in refusing an order to trim his moustache. The officer lost his case, as the court took the view that the force had the right to set and enforce internal regulations (*Globe and Mail*, March 12, 1979; *Ottawa Citizen*, January 9, 10, 1986). A member of the Waterloo Regional Police Force was found guilty of insubordination for refusing to shave a full beard. He lost 10 days leave for insubordination, and 5 days pay for neglect of duty, in a judgment given by the Waterloo Regional Police Commission (*Toronto Star*, July 7, August 20, 1982). In Toronto a police sergeant was charged with violating regulations for playing dominoes with constables and refusing orders to break up the game (*Montreal Gazette*, March 2, 1987). In an American case, a female police officer was fired in 1983 from the New York City Police because in 1980, one year before she became a police officer, she had posed nude for a men's magazine. She was reinstated in her job with full back pay by the state Supreme Court in 1998 (*Ottawa Citizen*, April 10, 1985).

In another curious incident, an Ottawa police officer with a reputation as a practical joker used a black raincoat and a wig to impersonate a judge while police were interrogating a mentally disturbed 17-year-old for break and enter. The Crown recommended no criminal charges against the police officer, but an internal discipline hearing resulted in a reprimand and the loss of 14 days paid vacation (*Ottawa Citizen*, October 25, 1984). Another inventive action by an Ottawa police constable with a curious sense of class consciousness earned a reprimand and the loss of eight days of paid vacation for discreditable conduct and neglect of duty. The constable, over a period of months, had been taking vagrants from downtown Ottawa and depositing them in the upper-class community of Rockcliffe, policed by the OPP under contract to the village (*Ottawa Citizen*, April 16, 1986).

The misbehaviour may be sufficiently serious as to constitute negligence, as in the case of a Montreal police detective whose unmarked car collided with four others. The officer did not have permission to take the unmarked car beyond MUC territory, but apparently, while on duty, he had been returning from the opening reception of a firm in Laval. He had twice the legal limit of alcohol in his blood, and was killed in the collision as he failed to stop at a red light (Montreal *Gazette*, May 23, 24, June 14, 1986).

The policeman's role may create a circumstance in which the officer cannot meet his job obligations, and therefore commits an offence. Such was the case of a Metro Toronto constable who refused an order to guard an abortion clinic. His "pro-life" commitment from religious conviction prompted his decision, and in seeking his dismissal before a police commission appeal board, a police spokesperson argued that "When you volunteer to join this police force, certain rights go out the door." The Staff Inspector's testimony continued, "He chose God over his police chief. That's not what he was hired to do" (*Toronto Sunday Star*, December 11, 1988).

Drunkenness, public disorder, consorting with a prostitute, and even petty theft, do not constitute corruption in the usual sense of the word. But they are illegal and will bring the police into disrepute, and invoke disciplinary action against the police officer. A common view is that police officers must be exemplars in their personal conduct, and not be in a position of having to enforce laws which they have themselves violated. A Nepean police officer with 10 years service, for example, resigned rather than face internal disciplinary action following his conviction in court of having assaulted his young son. The assault did not occur in the course of the police officer's duties, but was viewed as discreditable conduct under the Police Act (*Ottawa Sun*, November 29, 1988). In Ottawa, a police sergeant resigned under protest after having been ordered to quit for having been found guilty of having sexual relations with a prostitute. Found guilty of discreditable conduct, the sergeant's adventures had taken place while he was on duty in the morality squad that is responsible for policing prostitution in downtown Ottawa (*Ottawa Citizen,* May 14, 20, 1987).

Some incidents have involved very senior officers. The deputy chief of the Saskatoon police force was forced to resign after being publicly exposed as having been found with a prostitute (Montreal *Gazette,* June 25, 1988). In the small town of Southampton, Ontario, the chief pleaded guilty to discreditable conduct, having been fined in the previous year for fish poaching by using an illegal dip-net. He was demoted to constable (*Toronto Star*, March 4, 1986). The chief in the town of Lakefield, Ontario, was demoted to constable after being found guilty under the Ontario Police Act of discreditable conduct: he had been found guilty and fined on two counts of indecent assault against women, having in one instance kissed a woman against her will, and in another placed a ruler down a woman's blouse front. The demotion imposed by a district court judge cited the higher standards of conduct expected of police, and especially of a chief of police (*Globe and Mail,* June 22, 1985). In contrast, the chief of police of Nepean, Ontario, was arrested by Ottawa police for purchasing a prostitute's services. Citing depression arising from overwork, he pleaded guilty to violating the Police Act. He was not demoted, however, and retained his position, while the force was authorized to appoint an additional deputy chief to relieve the chief of some of the workload (*Ottawa Citizen,* June 16, 29, 1981).

Another senior police officer, the chief of the Moncton Police Force, found himself in difficulties in 1982, and the controversy lingered for several years. Reports of the chief having been drinking in a restaurant, hurling dishes when refused service, and leaving without paying his bill attracted nation-wide press attention and an eventual New Brunswick Police Commission enquiry following charges of cover-up. Previously, a routine police report had been filed, with no action; the town council had dismissed allegations; and the Police Association, which was opposed to some of the chief's policies, had pursued the issue, eliciting threats of dismissal from the chief for insubordination. The case was complicated by longstanding adversarial relations between the chief and the union, and the town council and the union. The association eventually passed a motion of non-confidence in the chief, with 89.2% voting in favour. Persisting allegations of cover-up and the resultant publicity led the solicitor general to order the Police Commission to re-open their enquiry in December, 1987 (Montreal *Gazette*, November 7, 27, December 17, 1987; *Globe and Mail*, November 14, 1987).

In a curious incident with racial overtones in British Columbia, an Esquimault constable at the Victoria Essential Services Club performed an impromptu striptease during ladies night. Two Victoria police officers, one an East Indian Canadian and another a Chinese Canadian, witnessed the display. The East Indian constable attempted to intervene, argued, and was grabbed and thrown down some stairs, suffering a broken arm. The other Victoria constable confirmed the incident, also noting that the Esquimault constable was sworn at during the altercation (*Toronto Star*, March 4, 1986).

In one interesting case, police misbehaviour influenced a court decision. Persons in Edmonton accused of running a common bawdy house, having been arrested in a police raid, were acquitted by a judge on the grounds that the establishment was widely frequented by police officers. Police patronage of the establishment, concluded the judge, suggested that there was nothing wrong with it (*Ottawa Citizen*, June 9, 1986).

Misbehaviour may also occur as a thoughtless remark by an officer. A legendary tale, perhaps apocryphal, has to do with an RCMP officer on a traffic stop, asking the driver for his passport, because the driver was Asian. There was a similar case of a Toronto police officer who was found guilty of misconduct after having reportedly stated to a Muslim driver in a traffic accident that he should find another more convenient religion. The officer made the quip, one would infer, in exasperation, while trying to solve a problem of tired children and the need for the parents to provide witness statements, only to be told that the driver was unprepared for religious reasons to allow his wife to be alone with other men, police officers (*Ottawa Citizen*, January 19, 1996).

Misconduct may arise from working relationships. An RCMP corporal was tried, and acquitted, when he used his service revolver to wound an RCMP constable with whom he had longstanding antagonistic relations and was fighting. The corporal, head of the Oakville, Ontario, drug unit, claimed that he used the revolver to stop the fight and not with intention to wound. The fight occurred after an evening of drinking. Two others, both staff sergeants, were charged with obstructing justice, having failed to report the shooting incident to Halton Regional Police. The two antagonists had been suspended with full pay pending trial outcome, and the two sergeants transferred (*Toronto Star,* June 26, 1985).

Finally, too, misbehaviour of police officers may occur as an aspect of worker–management relations, as in any workplace. Insubordination occurs as a problem in the paramilitary police services, and such charges usually are a barometer of police association–management relations. In 1996 in Toronto, insubordination charges were reported to have doubled, matters of refusing to obey orders or to complete paperwork (*Toronto Star,* February 23, 1996). The same Toronto report indicating increased insubordination also found that cases of off-duty criminal conduct increased over the year, from 23 cases in 1994 to 33 in 1995, an increase of 43.5% (*Toronto Star*, February 23, 1996).

Crime

Police officers may also commit offences, more or less serious, that are crimes and not mere violations of police regulations. That is, they are criminal code violations that do not depend upon privileged position as a police officer. These criminal acts are not intrinsic to the police role. Misbehaviours, as we have considered them, are minor violations of police regulations. And other misconduct we will consider, such as corruption or even on-duty theft, are instances of taking advantage of the police role. But a police officer may steal or attempt murder while away from work and not under the protection of the police role. These are violations by a citizen who happens to be a police officer. But because the person happens to be a police officer, there are additional consequences to those provided in law, for in effect, the police officer will have disqualified him- or herself as a sufficiently upstanding person to continue in policing.

The instances of police crime are as diverse as criminal opportunity is for the general public. Drugs afford a particular opportunity. In 1994 an RCMP officer in the Montreal area, who stated that he was tired of being poor, was convicted of drug trafficking. Drugs, and other smuggling opportunities, can appear very lucrative. Two RCMP officers on an anti-smuggling task force along the St. Lawrence River were caught and resigned because of several thefts (*Cornwall Standard-Freeholder*, January 31, 1996). Another case of police crime was reported in Montreal. In this somewhat bizarre case, an off-duty police officer was fleeing police in a car filled with stolen toys (*Ottawa Citizen*, December 29, 1997). In Mississauga, two Peel Regional police officers, one of whom had been honoured as Police Officer of the Year and held the Ontario Medal for Police Bravery, were charged with a forceful house-invasion robbery (*Toronto Star*, January 27, 1996). In Toronto, a police officer, apparently in uniform, was one of three men in the armed robbery of an armoured truck (*Globe and Mail*, January 20, 1996).

An Edmonton police officer was convicted of collaborating with his lover in the attempted murder of his wife. He had manipulated his lover into actually committing the attempt, and was sentenced to 10 years imprisonment (*Toronto Sunday Star*, December 11, 1988). Also in Edmonton, a police constable charged with sexual assault of a female police constable in a police lounge shot and killed his wife—also a police constable—and himself (Montreal *Gazette*, April 8, 1989).

Abuse of Power

A critical form of misconduct is the abuse of police powers in an encounter with a citizen or in the course of investigation or legal procedures. The abuse does not consist of personal financial benefit (corruption) nor does it involve inappropriate or excessive force (brutality).

Often it consists of verbal abuse, such as name-calling, including racial slurs. False charges and improper arrest are other manifestations of abuse of power, sometimes used to cover an officer's indiscretions (Brodeur, 1981:154). And sometimes the distinction between abuse of power and brutality breaks down, when there is an escalation to violence.

An example of misconduct for the selfish interests of the officers involved comes from Ottawa. Two Ottawa police constables were disciplined—one resigning and the other delayed in promotion—when they brought false charges against a mentally disturbed man, claiming that he had damaged their police car, covering up their own accident (*Ottawa Citizen*, August 19, 1988). Another example of police misconduct arising from public abuse occurred in Ottawa during a peaceful street demonstration by citizens seeking a controlled road crossing; a man was injured by police who used excessive force in arresting him. The man had been verbally abusive, and the police responded forcefully. The injured man later won a $57 000 award in a civil suit (*Ottawa Citizen*, May 24, 1985).

A case in Toronto evoked a 30-minute criticism of 4 police officers by a judge who acquitted a black man facing several charges, including assaulting police and dangerous driving. The judge accused the police of lying, fabricating evidence, collusion, and harassing the man—who had complained about police at least 25 times in about 3 years. One of the four police officers was black (*Ottawa Citizen*, April 26, 1989).

A large proportion of citizen complaints about police arise not from encounters with criminal offenders, but from routine enforcement with law-abiding citizens on such matters as traffic offences. Altercations may occur because of real or perceived lack of cooperation by the offender, rudeness, or inadequate deference. Several years ago John Chevigny (1969) wrote of how the New York City Police systematically resorted to making "cover charges." When the police became involved in an altercation with a citizen, and perhaps overstepped their authority, they would cover their error or misconduct with a charge against the citizen, such as creating a public disturbance or assault, which, if true, would have justified their forceful intervention.

The lack of proper deference, or any challenging behaviour, however legitimate, is frequently taken by the police as abuse. Failure to comply immediately with an instruction, for example, may elicit a serious response, as control of an encounter is vital to the police. A request by a citizen to have a badge number, an action that many would think of as fundamental, is often interpreted as threatening behaviour, and may elicit violence and/or charges. Such appeared to be the nature of a Toronto incident where a man enquired as to why a friend was being arrested, and then when he too was arrested, requested a badge number. In a complaint filed afterwards it appears that he was beaten at the time of arrest and afterwards. When the man asked why he was being charged, the police officer "pulled out his billy and began hitting at me and going crazy. It was like a nightmare." Beatings continued, from at least four police officers at the station, with one officer reported as stating "This is our law" (*Toronto Star*, October 29, 1984).

Another type of misconduct is motivated by a sense of duty or responsibility, whether purely an individual interpretation or in some way sanctioned by the organization. Such would be the practice of illegal wiretaps, and other actions such as were disclosed in the course of the McDonald Commission enquiry into the RCMP (discussed below). The police, developing their own perceptions of justice and their own rules of conduct, and often with firm opinions of guilt even in the absence of judicial evidence, attempt to meet what they believe are their legitimate objectives, even if illegalities are involved. It may be argued that this form of misconduct is intrinsic to policing, with its maze of demands and restraints working at cross-purposes (Ericson, 1981a:101–102; Brodeur, 1981:152–153). Brodeur writes of a fundamental contradiction, in that as police are more rule-bound, they will violate restraints more frequently in order to perform what they understand to be their job, to fulfil their sense of duty. Like Ericson, he attributes the problem to a diffusion of policing tasks, and argues that a solution may be a more precise and limited definition of policing tasks.

Police perjury is an abuse of the police role often engaged in under a perverted sense of justice. It is probably correct that most people, including members of the judiciary, are inclined to believe the testimony of a police officer. Police may take advantage of this. In New York City, a program of seminars was introduced in truth telling for experienced police officers. This occurs in the context of frequent police perjury to gain convictions, a practice that police view as helping balance the system (Associated Press, March 23, 1996).

A well-publicized Toronto incident, in which a stock promoter was being tried, featured video tapes of Metro Toronto Police officers in conversation discussing instances of police lying, police brutality, political interference, and judicial corruption (*Toronto Star*, November 18, 1982). Also in Toronto, in 1986, after lengthy investigation it was concluded that a Toronto police officer was guilty of perjury. In court, the officer had earlier denied threatening a witness. The witness produced audio tapes, however, having hidden a recording device on his person during meetings and telephone conversations with police (*Toronto Star*, May 15, 1986). Without the tape recordings, one might speculate, the police officer's credit would have prevailed over the testimony of a much less reputable person.

Again in Toronto, a judge found that a man was a victim of assault, false imprisonment, and malicious prosecution, and awarded him $8200 in damages for the unwarranted arrest and charges. The police had been in search of some streetfighters when they found the victim in his van, grabbed him, and threw him from the van. The judge also found that the officers had altered their notebooks before appearing in court to testify (*Globe and Mail*, November 15, 1983).

The Toronto police did not have a good year in 1983. Another case found a judge ruling out police evidence as false and presented in bad faith. Charges against four men were withdrawn when the judge concluded that following an illegal search, a police officer lied about having had permission. He also ruled out a statement by an accused suspect on the grounds that it was obtained under duress (*Globe and Mail*, November 8, 1983). In 1985 the Metro Toronto Complaints Board commented upon having "serious concerns about the reliability of ... police witnesses" (*Toronto Star*, August 30, 1984), following an enquiry into a citizen complaint of assault. The panel found for the complainant, and suggested that other officers testifying had contrived to present false testimony. A newspaper editorial remarked critically, and itemized four other recent instances of questionable police testimony (*Toronto Star*, August 30, 1984). In response to the panel's comments, the president of the Toronto Police Association speculated that officers might have a basis for a civil action (*Toronto Star*, August 30, 1984).

Another illustration comes from Ottawa. The RCMP were engaged in a drug surveillance operation downtown, and arrested a man employed at the adjacent National Arts Centre. The man had been on his way to the Centre to pick up a paycheque when he was seized and searched, with nothing found. Following complaints about the arrest and police comments, in a civil suit the judge criticized police for destroying the actual photographic record of events in order to be able to make insinuations against the man (Montreal *Gazette*, November 15, 1985).

In Hull, Quebec, following a police chase in which an Ottawa motorcyclist was killed, expert RCMP testimony at a coroner's inquest suggested that a Hull police recording of radio transmissions during the chase was deliberately erased. The expert implied that the blank tape was produced to protect the police in the enquiry (*Ottawa Citizen*, February 12, 1986).

A curious transnational instance of abuse of police powers occurred in British Columbia in 1984. Two Vancouver police officers detained a man wanted in Florida and transported him to Washington State, where he was jailed. Eventually the man was released on orders of the state governor, and the two Vancouver police officers were charged with unlawful confinement and conspiracy to transport the man to the United States without lawful authority (*Toronto Star*, October 2, 1984). Like other instances of police abuse of power, the case suggests that police act as a law unto themselves, not satisfied to endure due process. Such direct "justice" and the associated deceit to prevent the actions from coming to light make up a major element of abuse of power.

A notorious instance of police abuse of power, probably in collaboration with other persons in the justice system and government, was the case of Donald Marshall in Nova Scotia. The young native was convicted in 1971 on the basis of Sydney police evidence that was later shown to be false, whether due to incompetence, racist bias, or the determination to gain a conviction. When the RCMP sought to investigate, they were prevented by the Nova Scotia attorney general (*Toronto Star*, October 19, 1984).

Finally, an illustration of job-related "playing the system" which, if not misconduct, verges upon corruption. It comes from police manipulation of charges and court time. As remarked elsewhere, police have considerable discretion, and have the opportunity to load a number of charges. Sometimes this is in order to sanction the alleged offender, or to "cover the waterfront." In Ontario, in Peel Regional and in Ottawa, police and town officials concluded that officers were loading charges in order to increase their court time and overtime income. Thereby police added to the large problem of court backlog. In Ottawa the solution was Crown–police collaboration in order to pare charges and costs.

Corruption

The social location of police is such that corrupt conduct is virtually inevitable, even though in Canada it has been considered an abnormality. Recruited from relatively disadvantaged economic strata, with wages below those of most middle-class and many working-class counterparts, and yet called upon to suppress lucrative illegal activities, the corruption of police personnel is not at all remarkable. More remarkable, in fact, is the strong ethic in Canada that has restricted such corruption to the status of aberration.

Corruption is, for our purposes, the acceptance or extortion of benefits by police, and the use of their position to engage in crime for profit. One writer defines corruption as "police behaviour that results in private gains at public expense" (Shearing, 1981:1). Corruption, therefore, is distinguishable from other forms of misconduct in that it consists of personal benefit for the police officer. In some part, corruption has its seeds in plausible trade-offs in which police engage to maintain order. The exercise of police discretion, requiring the collaboration of law-abiding citizens and of offenders, offers circumstances in which favours are exchanged. Similarly, the respect, or fear, the public has for police will generate privileges, from free coffee and doughnuts to the proffering of expensive commodities. Economic opportunities, therefore, from the petty to the grand, are part of the policeman's lot.

In Toronto the newspapers publicized free meals apparently received by police officers at local fast food restaurants. Free cups of coffee, meals of a few dollars' value, or substantial discounts, were reported by managers of several of the largest franchise chains. Except for one restaurant outlet too near the police station, and therefore generating too high a volume for free items, the managers were not dissatisfied with minor free items or discounts comparable to those for employees, arguing that they were thereby receiving better police service or at least the protection afforded by frequent police presence. The chief of police, however, ordered the practice stopped following the publicity (*Globe and Mail,* August 10, 1976).

Another illustration may be taken from Winnipeg, where city police were accused of fixing traffic tickets in exchange for free restaurant meals. As a consequence, one sergeant was tried and found guilty by the Police Commission, but allowed to continue in service on one year's probation (*Globe and Mail,* June 3, 1985). In Alberta, the investigation by the RCMP into possible fraud by the American-based Royal American Shows while operating in Alberta, and the subsequent Laycraft enquiry report found that at least six Calgary policemen had received gifts, including cash payments of between $50 and $300 (*Ottawa Citizen*, July 25, 1978).

A minor form of corruption consists of police violating by-laws relating to traffic, while in the course of duty or not, and taking advantage of the relative immunity afforded them by their uniform. An ironic illustration may be taken from the Montreal *Gazette* who awarded a "brickbat" to a constable in Montreal for parking his personal automobile in a No Parking zone while consulting his lawyer. He was consulting his lawyer in regard to his acquittal on the previous day for a charge of assault against a man who had complained about his having blocked traffic by double-parking his patrol car outside of a grocery store. That altercation had been videotaped by the shop's security camera and broadcast in January 1986 on television news throughout Canada and the United States (*Globe and Mail*, January 11, 1986; Montreal *Gazette*, June 14, 1986).

In Thunder Bay, Ontario, some police officers had been receiving benefits from the operators of two local brothels. When a massive raid was planned by Thunder Bay City Police and the OPP, they attempted to interfere with the execution of the warrants in order to protect the brothels. Three officers were arrested and charged with "conspiring to obstruct justice" (*Toronto Star*, March 27, 1983).

Sometimes police use the protection, or the information, afforded them by their role to engage in crimes such as breaking and entering, and robbery. In 1986 a Ste. Foy police officer admitted to having committed over 300 instances of robbery or vandalism while on duty, beginning in 1969 with a fellow police officer and continuing until 1985. His crimes came to a tragic end in 1985 when he was convicted of shooting to death two Quebec City police officers who caught him in the act of committing a break-in (*Ottawa Citizen*, June 12, 1986; Montreal *Gazette*, June 12, 1986).

A similarly violent outcome was associated with the actions of a pair of Winnipeg police officers who were engaged in a series of thefts. Believing that they were being informed on, they killed a man in 1981, and were convicted of second-degree murder (*Ottawa Citizen*, March 5, 1989). A rather prominent case was reported in Vancouver in 1987, involving a police officer who was the son of a former Vancouver police chief. While on duty investigating a burglary he stole a ring valued at $60 000. The family, as the police officer expected, believed the ring to have been stolen during the burglary. The police officer advised them to offer a reward, and that informants would be liable to turn up the ring for the investigating officer. The officer then accepted the $6000 reward for the return of the ring (*Ottawa Citizen*, April 3, 1987).

Another sort of corruption involves using the contacts and information gained as a police officer to engage in illicit behaviour. One of the more lucrative opportunities relates to drug enforcement, where major scandals have occurred in police forces in the United Kingdom, the United States, western Europe, and Canada. An elaborate case involved a Montreal police officer who was serving as head of the drug squad. Following an investigation by a team of Montreal and RCMP officers, a detective captain was arrested for stealing drugs from the squad vault and selling them to a contact, a former MUC police officer. He was later convicted of theft, possession, trafficking and conspiracy to sell drugs, and sentenced to 14 years (*Globe and Mail,* November 26, 1983). A short time later an RCMP officer who worked on the narcotics squad in Montreal was convicted on drug possession and trafficking charges. His sentence was five years, a lesser term than the Montreal officer because the RCMP member had not been head of his enforcement section (*Globe and Mail*, June 27, 1985).

Whatever the offence, once detected and made known, the police officer's special status has been tarnished, perhaps ruined. In Ottawa, while on duty and having the presumed immunity of police uniform, an officer with 16 years experience stopped at an automated bank machine. A customer at an adjacent machine left his card, and the officer used it to withdraw $200. Detected by a security camera, he was charged. Charges were dropped in favour of a "diversionary" program, and he was found guilty internally of discreditable conduct and eventually ordered to resign. The police adjudicator's statement summarizes the police and public standard: "(His) usefulness as a police officer on this police service, in this community, has been diminished to such an extent that he cannot be retained in that position" (*Ottawa Citizen*, January 16, 1998).

Brutality

Throughout the history of policing there have been incidents involving police and excessive use of force. Why the police should engage in brutality has occasioned considerable speculation. It has, in part, been attributed to the character of police recruiting, with the emphasis upon ill-educated working-class males who come from an environment that is characterized by male aggressiveness and violence. Further, where there is an emphasis on prior military experience, and when training stresses the use of force, the propensity for violence is reinforced. The daily working environment of the police is also pertinent, where their frequent occupational contacts consist of violent persons who might, given a chance, do them harm or fail to show them respect.

The Montreal *Gazette* reported that in 1987 lawsuits against the police totalled $5 million in claims. The police director considered that "at least half the suits are frivolous," and argued that while there are "rotten apples" on the MUC force, police "gratuitous violence" is infrequent. He did also acknowledge, however, that improper use of force "is a problem that is there and will always be there and it is up to us to ensure that it does not go beyond acceptable limits" (Montreal *Gazette*, November 12, 1987).

Because police work in a stressful environment and have learned to anticipate danger in apparently innocent circumstances, police conflicts with citizens often arise from very routine events. The very first Toronto Civilian Complaints Board decision, which found police misconduct, was handed down in 1983. A businessman had been stopped for a traffic violation. He attempted to leave the police car, a scuffle ensued, and in subduing the man and his wife, some force was used. The businessman claimed that he was later assaulted while in custody. No action was taken on the complaint following an internal police enquiry, but the Complaints Board found for the citizen following a public hearing. He had been charged with assault and, the hearing suggested, correctly so; but it ruled that at the same time the police officer had imposed his own on-the-spot punishment, consisting, according to a doctor's report, of 13 injuries consistent with kicks and punches (*Toronto Star*, July 15, 1983). Again in Toronto, an incident arose from a traffic violation. A lawyer who was arrested for driving under the influence of alcohol claimed that he was beaten by police officers, having refused to blow into a breathalyzer. He too was charged with assaulting a police officer (*Toronto Star*, May 17, 1984). In Ottawa an OPP officer shot and wounded a man who was the passenger in a car that had been speeding, driven by his wife. The incident occurred as the man shifted to the driver's seat and attempted to move the vehicle (*Ottawa Citizen*, November 19, 1988).

Police brutality does, of course, also arise from police criminal investigations. These are instances when the police may react excessively to perceived threat, or may seek confessions. A case came to light from rural Quebec in 1988. A young man was arrested in 1984 by two officers from the Maniwaki detachment of the Quebec provincial police. They had arrived at his home convinced that he was responsible for two robberies. The police drove him to an isolated sand pit and beat him in the back of the parked car, urging him to confess. He was then released. A police commission hearing, following a complaint from the man's brother, recommended brief suspensions for the two officers, and the Sûreté refused to make public the sanctions that were finally imposed. As the victim remarked following the enquiry: "It's more dangerous to meet a police officer than a criminal. At least with a criminal you can defend yourself. You can't with a police officer—they're the law" (*Ottawa Citizen*, March 24, 1988).

In Montreal in 1986, in an incident previously mentioned, a store camera captured a police officer manhandling a person who had objected to the police officer having double-parked. When the individual complained, the officer demanded identification. The incident escalated as the man refused, and in turn took down the police officer's badge number, whereupon the officer grabbed the man by his hair and dragged him into the store. The police then charged the man with assault. Eventually the civilian was acquitted of charges, the police constable suspended without pay, and tried for assault. Five months after his suspension without pay, the constable was acquitted in court of assault and other charges by a jury that was apparently influenced by the well-publicized videotape and accompanying audio that included evidence that the complainant may have fabricated aspects of the alleged assault (Montreal *Gazette*, June 11, 1986). The officer was acquitted in a jury trial and the acquittal upheld on appeal. Two civil suits were then brought against the constable by the civilian (Montreal *Gazette*, May 21, 24, 1986; November 25, 1989). Public sentiment and press comment expressed disappointment in the acquittal. One columnist wrote of "the inclination to give a policeman every benefit of the doubt" as the explanation of the verdict. He argued that if, in face of evidence such as the videotape, a conviction could not be gained, citizens will be unwilling to come forward unless next time there is at least a "smoking gun" (Montreal *Gazette*, June 12, 1986). The constable was suspended without pay for

30 days by the force director—half the length recommended by the MUC disciplinary board—and obliged to take a course at his own expense on police powers of arrest (Montreal *Gazette*, February 13, 1987).

A bizarre incident was uncovered in Toronto in 1979. A police officer disguised his appearance by wearing a bunny suit, and proceeded to beat a prisoner in custody in order to force a confession (*Globe and Mail,* March 12, 1979). Also in Toronto, four policemen were jailed following court convictions for beating a young man while off-duty. The incident involved a constable, a sergeant, and three others. The court appeared to react to the subsequent cover-up as much as to the original incident. The officer in whose home the beating took place, was sentenced to 3 years in prison for assault and for obstructing justice, while one of the officers received 18 months and the two others 12-month terms. The conviction depended upon the testimony of a policeman who revealed the cover-up to a superior officer and then testified in court. He later resigned from the police force because thereafter he was "ostracized socially and professionally" (*Globe and Mail,* May 30, 1987; Montreal *Gazette*, September 15, 1987).

Also in 1987, an incident involving brutality reached the courts in Ottawa. In June of that year, 10 police officers raided a house where a party was under way. Apparently some of the party-goers had made insulting remarks to police officers when they responded to earlier complaints. The group of police returned later and illegally entered the home and beat several people with fists and batons. Four of the occupants were then charged by police, but acquitted by a judge who found that they had been denied their rights. As in the Toronto case, the police then faced internal procedures and civil lawsuits (*Ottawa Citizen,* August 1, 1987).

In Quebec following the first referendum on sovereignty association, the MUC Police used excessive force in controlling crowds demonstrating on Mount Royal. Several persons were injured, including a CTV cameraman who was beaten unconscious by the police (Montreal *Gazette*, December 11, 1980). A police commission enquiry harshly condemned the police actions, calling for the disbandment of the riot squad divisions responsible for the mayhem. The enquiry concluded that "the police have contributed to loss of public confidence, have tarnished the image of the Montreal Urban Community Police, and have so abused their power and authority that they cannot be allowed to continue to hold a front-line position" (*Globe and Mail*, July 18, 1981).

In 1990 the Quebec provincial police riot squad intervened in a university student demonstration protecting fee increases on the steps of the National Assembly in Quebec City. Earlier in Montreal, MUC Police had intervened to quash demonstrations, most notably by junior college students at the Montreal Stock Exchange, and had been accused of excessive force (*Globe and Mail*, March 31, 1990). In a street demonstration by students, the MUC riot squad moved in with nightsticks. Several people were struck several times, including some who had already dispersed. Illustrative of the class-based resentment that can affect police actions, a police officer was quoted as referring to the demonstrators as a "bunch of welfare recipients." He went on to state that "they should try working at McDonald's instead of complaining. That's how I got through school" (Montreal *Gazette*, March 17, 1990).

The most extreme expression of excessive force is, of course, the improper resort to weapons. As we have already seen, there are instances where police use their weapons unnecessarily, or ineptly, resulting in the death of citizens. In Cornwall, for example, in 1981, a police officer was charged with second-degree murder in the shooting death of a young man who had previously broken a pane of glass on the door of a beer hall (*Ottawa Citizen*, July 29, 1981). The shooting generated a flurry of allegations in the Ontario town about police misconduct, and revealed a widespread adversarial attitude between the police and many residents of the community (*Ottawa Citizen*, August 27, 1981). Related to the shooting, two other police officers were charged and convicted of public mischief when the morning following the shooting death, they arrested the two brothers of the victim. All three officers were found guilty of discreditable conduct under the Police Act and ordered to resign as a "matter of public credibility" (*Ottawa Citizen,* September 17, 1983).

INSTITUTIONALIZED MISCONDUCT

Our discussion thus far has dealt with misconduct by individual police officers that is an aberration or abnormality within the police force. The Lac Brome incident, described below, although involving a very small force, illustrates the existence of an even greater problem, where an entire force or some significant element of the force, including senior officers, participates in or tolerates misconduct. In such instances the misconduct may be thought of as institutionalized or normalized. In Canada this extreme of widespread participation in the misconduct, a form of "organizational deviance, has, arguably, been rare (Shearing, 1981).

In the absence of a strong ethic or tradition deterring the acceptance of benefits, the exploitation of criminal opportunities, or the excessive use of force, misconduct will occur on a widespread basis. In some instances, as in periods of the history of the New York City Police, the misconduct becomes almost "normal." A recent investigation in Canada illustrates the possibility of the thorough corruption of a police force. In 1988 an Ontario royal commission was struck to enquire into the conduct of the Niagara Regional Police, following an investigation by the OPP. It became apparent that there were extensive ties between the police, from command rank personnel to the rank-and-file, and motorcycle gang members involved in a variety of illegalities from drug dealing to gambling and prostitution. The case uncovered financial payments to police, and the suppression or delay of investigations (*Ottawa Citizen*, October 21, 1988).

An example in a major force that comes very close to the concept of institutionalized corruption came to light in 1987 and also involved the Niagara Regional Police in Ontario. An internal report by a special investigative team concluded that in the 750-person force, the sale of seized weapons had been routine. The revenues were then used by the force to finance its own purchase of weapons. In February 1987, 500 prohibited weapons were found in the closet of the former chief of the force (*Ottawa Citizen*, November 24, 1987). Reports of the internal investigation were passed on to the Ontario attorney general in June 1987, and a decision was taken against laying criminal charges. A Niagara Regional Police sergeant who had worked on the investigation, fearing a cover-up, leaked material to the *Globe and Mail*, and on the following day a royal commission of enquiry was announced. The sergeant was consequently brought up on internal charges, pleaded guilty to breaching his Ontario Police Act oath of secrecy, and ordered to forfeit eight days of paid leave. The ruling judge, though, commended the sergeant as a "credit to the force" (*Globe and Mail,* December 3, 1988).

Detective work, perhaps because of the anonymity of the job and the intensity of contact with criminal behaviour, seems especially prone to serious misconduct, whether excessive use of force or receipt of pay-offs. Major illustrations are to be had from abroad as well as from Canada. In 1972, for example, there was a major investigation and clean-up of New Scotland Yard, with their commissioner resorting to rotation of detectives into uniform duty in order to break the CID network. Similarly, in 1972 in New York City, the Knapp Commission revealed massive detective corruption, celebrated in the revelations of "Serpico" (Bryett, 1989:268–269; Maas, 1973).

In Ste. Foy, Quebec, a Police Commission enquiry into misconduct learned of police protection of one of their colleagues suspected of burglary, including an order from the chief, according to the testimony of a sergeant, to stop any investigation (Montreal *Gazette*, May 23, 1986).

A Canadian example of police brutality that gained national notoriety involved two police officers from the Quebec town of Lac Brome. The six-member force had a controversial record, with several cases of alleged brutality eventually coming before the courts. In 1982, a man residing in British Columbia visited relatives in the town. He was arrested as a burglary suspect, and according to the testimony of a police officer, was tortured for five hours by police, who punched him in the face, struck him in the kidneys and legs with nightsticks, and ignited tear gas in his mouth, before releasing him in woods near town (*Ottawa Citizen*, May 29, 1985). The beating, intended to elicit a confession to break-ins, was undertaken by the chief and other officers, and was additionally described as "beating him, burning his genitals and handcuffing him barefoot outdoors to a steel pole in freezing temperature for more than an hour." The chief and the constable principally involved resigned in 1985, but charges were brought and both were convicted of assault. They were, however, initially given lenient sentences of three months and $1000 fine, and one month and $1000 respectively, later increased by the Quebec Court of Appeal to two years and one year respectively (Montreal *Gazette*, March 29, December 8, 1988). Following the incident with the British Columbia man, there was a Quebec Police Commission investigation, generating numerous charges against all members of the small force for forcible confinement, assault, and theft. In December 1988 the former chief was convicted of three counts of assault involving other persons, and sentenced to five months, two months, and two months, to be served concurrently with the prior two-year term. The former constable was convicted on two counts and given a sentence of two months and one month, to be served concurrently with the prior sentence of one year (Montreal *Gazette*, December 8, 1988).

Also in Quebec, in Trois-Rivieres in 1982, the Quebec Police Commission enquired into the 100-man police force. The enquiry followed an incident in 1981 when a local police detective was convicted and sentenced to 10 years in prison for shooting out windows in the house of a town official and for attempting to have a woman killed. Other revelations followed, as witnesses complained of extortion, sexual intimidation, such as forcing women to undress during questioning and having topless dancers perform on desks in the police station, setting up robberies in order to arrest the thieves to improve arrest records, and perjury. The local police association attempted to block the enquiry. Before the enquiry began, two officers were fired; eventually the chief of police, following the commission's findings that problems in the force were attributable to his "abdication of responsibility and an almost complete neglect," was ordered by city council to resign or be fired (*Ottawa Citizen*, December 9, 11, 1982; June 3, 1983). In its findings the Quebec Police Commission recommended that 39 charges be laid against 20 current and former police officers for offences such as armed robbery, assault, extortion, intimidation of witnesses, fabrication of evidence, theft, forgery, obstruction of justice, and perjury (*Globe and Mail*, August 23, 1983). It was recommended that another seven officers be suspended without pay for several days each.

In 1984 the Nova Scotia Police Commission released the report of a year-long enquiry into the conduct of the Kentville, Nova Scotia, police force. The Commission examined police relations with the town administration and the conduct of the police following cases of mistreatment of citizens. The chief was described as having misled the local police commission and having tolerated misconduct. In examining the complaints, and accepting their validity, the commission noted beatings, racist remarks directed at blacks, entrapment, unnecessary body searches, and unjustified use of mace. The commission recommended that the chief be fired or forced to retire. A constable involved in numerous citizen complaints was also identified as deserving dismissal, while two others, including a sergeant second in the command structure, and a constable who was head of the local police union, were recommended for demotion (*Globe and Mail*, July 28, 1984).

The enquiry also called into question the conduct of the police union. The demotion of the union head was ordered because of evidence that he had used the police computer to supply union lawyers with information on complainants. It was also learned that the constable dismissed for brutality had been protected by the union from dismissal three years earlier. At that time, while still a probationary constable, the union hid the man for several days so that he did not receive his official notice of dismissal until after the completion of his probationary period (*Globe and Mail,* July 29, 1984).

Canada's largest municipal police force, Metro Toronto, was accused of harbouring a "rogue squad" in the early 1980s. A citizens' group of area lawyers, aldermen, and community association representatives, which was formed in July 1981 to challenge internal police complaints procedure (*Globe and Mail*, July 14, 1981), accused Toronto police of torture and beatings in two reports submitted to the Toronto Police Commission. The reports of the Citizens' Independent Review of Police Activities presented documentation from medical records and photographs, with corroborating testimony from defence lawyers and one former Crown attorney, of 29 cases of brutality, including indication of frequent resort to suffocation by placing a plastic bag over individuals' heads. The Citizens' Committee, an aggressive element of the lobby for a civilian review process in Toronto, argued that offences seemed common in one division and in the hold-up squad, where they suggested that "brutality has become a deeply rooted habit among detectives" (*Ottawa Citizen*, October 24, 1981). Thirteen complainants cited by the committee eventually signed a statement indicating that they would not cooperate with an internal police investigation, but would fully disclose evidence in a public enquiry (*Globe and Mail,* October 29, 1981).

In legislative committee hearings that eventually led to the establishment of a civilian review procedure for Toronto, evidence was given that suggested frequent mistreatment and brutality by police, with persons unwilling to come forward to complain out of fear and distrust of the internal police investigations system. One physician testified that he was familiar with 19 persons with injuries consistent with allegations of police mistreatment. He testified of allegations that one person was held upside down over a bridge, another's head was forced into a toilet bowl, another was put through a mock execution, and seven were threatened with death by police. The witness also observed that 15 of the 19 men were members of ethnic minorities (*Ottawa Citizen*, October 8, 1981).

One of Canada's most famous instances of widespread police misconduct in the name of duty occurred in the 1970s when the RCMP engaged in mail tampering, break-ins, theft, and arson in their attention to the separatist movement in Quebec. Mann and Lee (1979:19) describe the police actions as "structured deviance." The security service of the RCMP was responsible for the actions, as the senior and leading element of investigations that also involved a combined anti-terrorist task force of the RCMP, Sûreté, and MUC Police. Not only did the revelations of misconduct generate public criticism and tarnish the image of the entire force, it also reinforced some of the resentment that many Force members had of the security service. Regular members found them arrogant, and regular managers resented having personnel skimmed off from regular policing duties (Sawatsky, 1980:17–18). As a consequence, two major commissions of enquiry were conducted, the Keable Commission in Quebec and the federal McDonald Commission.

The misconduct became public when Robert Samson, an RCMP corporal, disclosed a 1972 break-in at the Agence de presse libre de Québec (APLQ) at his trial on an unrelated matter in March, 1976 (*Globe and Mail*, May 27, 1977; Fidler, 1978). As a consequence, the province of Quebec established a commission of enquiry into the break-in under the chairmanship of Jean Keable, and then extended the commission's mandate to other RCMP "irregularities."

The Keable Commission found itself caught up in questions of provincial rights, and was found to have exceeded its authority and to have violated the Official Secrets Act in enquiring into RCMP actions. When the commission sought a Supreme Court ruling with the support of five other provinces, the Court ruled that the provincial commission did not have the right to enquire into the RCMP as an organization, or to require testimony or documents from federal ministers (*Ottawa Journal*, October 31, 1978). In effect, the provincial commission was limited to the investigation of individual RCMP members, without access to much of the necessary material. Subsequent information gained by the federal McDonald Commission made it clear that the illegal acts could not be understood simply as individual actions.

The McDonald Commission investigation of the G-4 squad, the unit of RCMP Security Service responsible for monitoring FLQ activities, exposed a host of illegal acts from illegal break-ins to phony warrants. The revelations were to earn them the appellation of "dirty tricksters." They operated with enormous autonomy, preparing their own job descriptions and not reporting to headquarters (*Ottawa Journal*, September 28, 1978). Among the revelations was that of two RCMP sergeants who testified of having burned down a barn in rural Quebec that the police believed was being used for meetings by FLQ members. They testified that they considered they had no alternative as they were incapable of "bugging" the barn (*Globe and Mail*, September 12, 1978). One of the witnesses declared that he had no reservations about the action, never expecting that his career would be harmed, never considering that he should refuse an order. Two others of the four participating in the incident testified that they had been unaware of the nature of the evening's work before they set out (*Ottawa Citizen*, September 13, 1978). Later testimony revealed that one force member had stolen dynamite from a construction shed, and that he considered the act to be appropriate, "covered under his job description," with protection under the Police Act, and that he was "simply doing my duty" in obeying an order to obtain the explosives. The staff sergeant who headed the section responsible for FLQ activities in the early seventies denied the order, although he did accept responsibility for the car-burning and other activities as the senior non-commissioned officer. By 1972 he was in dispute with Ottawa headquarters over his initiatives. He testified of impatience with the slow actions of his superiors, describing his immediate superior as a "philosopher." He criticized "text book commanders" in Ottawa, slow to act and not understanding field problems (*Ottawa Citizen*, October 5, 1978). He was dismissed from the RCMP in 1973 (*Globe and Mail*, September 20, 1978; *Ottawa*

Journal, September 20, 1978; *Ottawa Citizen*, October 4, 1978). The mounting testimony suggested a high degree of licence allowed to field operatives, with only the vaguest guidelines on reporting to superiors.

The RCMP actions were loosely related to the paranoia over the October crisis of 1970. In 1971 the field personnel of the RCMP Security Service attempted to create dissention in the FLQ and to publicly discredit it, by releasing a fraudulent communiqué. The fraudulent release was apparently even accepted as genuine in RCMP headquarters (*Globe and Mail,* January 10, 1978). The RCMP indicated that the APLQ break-in of 1972, ordered by the head of the security services in Montreal, and the removal of files, were intended to thwart a violent "anniversary celebration" of the James Cross kidnapping (*Maclean's Magazine,* July 11, 1977; *Ottawa Citizen*, October 3, 1977). A 1973 action, when the RCMP stole dynamite from a Montreal construction site and set fire to a barn in Ste. Anne de Rochelle, was intended to prevent the radical American Black Panthers from meeting to instruct the FLQ members in kidnapping techniques (*Ottawa Citizen*, October 31, November 2, 3, 1977). Less obviously related to political extremism were RCMP investigations and surveillance of the Parti Québécois and the New Democratic Party. In 1973 RCMP personnel broke into a Montreal printing office and removed computer tapes containing Parti Québécois membership and financial information, an action apparently authorized by the director of the Security Services (*Globe and Mail*, November 1, 1977). The leader of the NDP, Ed Broadbent, charged that the RCMP also broke into NDP headquarters in Ottawa in 1972 (*Ottawa Citizen,* November 13, 1977).

It would seem accurate to consider that RCMP actions, although illicit, were correctly perceived by operatives as consistent with government and the will of the general public. Even organized labour seemed to approve, for in its brief to the McDonald Commission the Canadian Labour Congress agreed that police surveillance of the labour movement was a good thing, in order to deal with communist and separatist influences (Fidler, 1978:18).

In the publicity surrounding the "dirty tricks," a lengthy history of "irregular activities" came to light in the RCMP defence of national security dating back at least to the 1950s. Under the codename "Operation Cathedral," for example, mail had been illegally opened since 1954, with the cooperation of postal officials (*Ottawa Citizen,* November 10, 18, 1977). Another series of break-ins, known as "Operation 300," also dated back to the 1950s. In response to the Gouzenko spy revelations of 1946–47, "Operation Featherbed" was mounted, the covert surveillance of at least six senior civil servants (*Ottawa Citizen*, November 17, 1977).

A former RCMP Commissioner, William L. Higgitt, testified that a policy had evolved in the Force allowing an RCMP officer to refuse an order to perform an illegal act. He would not be disciplined, but he might be transferred. Further, if an officer was caught committing an illegal act for the Force, he would be defended, with lawyers, fines, and salary paid for by the Force, and even re-employment if the officer were convicted of an offence and jailed. He declared that "this was the policy from the time I was a constable and it was well known throughout the force" (*Globe and Mail*, October 26, 1978).

As the McDonald enquiry unfolded, the federal government of Pierre Elliott Trudeau attempted to win closed sessions and to curtail public knowledge of the RCMP actions. Eventually, as the RCMP tried to defend its actions, the government sought to regain cabinet documents and minutes of cabinet discussions during the 1970 crisis, which the Force had obtained for its defence. Commissioner Higgitt in effect chose not to be the scapegoat in a situation where the RCMP actions had apparently been tacitly condoned, if not required, by political authorities. He indicated that three solicitors general were aware of illegal actions such as mail openings. "There was no secret of the fact we were doing it and it was not withheld from the ministers." Later evidence suggested that the documentation provided by Higgitt was less explicit than he had implied, outlining an RCMP agenda rather than explicitly indicating actions. The former director-general of the Security Service, John Starnes, testified that the cabinet had discussed the illegal acts, and had considered what would be done if the illegalities came to be known. He contended that the actions were justifiable, and had been understood as occurring with the blessing of the cabinet who chose not to pay attention (*Ottawa Citizen*, October 5, 6, 27, 1978; Montreal *Gazette*, October 25, November 9, 1978, November 30, 1979; *Toronto Sunday Star*, October 29, 1978; *Globe and Mail*, November 8, 1978). The enquiry became not just an examination of police, but more fundamentally, of public and government control and responsibility for policing.

The major consequence of the McDonald Commission was a recommendation that the RCMP be divested of its security/intelligence functions and that a separate agency be established. The recommendation was acted upon and a civilian agency was formed in 1984, the Canadian Security Intelligence Service (CSIS).

PEER PRESSURE

Even where it may be impossible to find institutionalized or normalized misconduct, almost invariably one finds a collegial loyalty. Police are reluctant to suspect fellow police officers and reluctant to investigate them, and where they have evidence of misconduct or of errors, they often take measures to protect them, from elimination or suppression of evidence to perjury. In the incident involving the Ste. Foy police sergeant who had committed numerous burglaries over an extended period of time, there was apparently a willful turning away from disturbing facts. In fact, there were suspicions for at least five years, according to testimony by the Ste. Foy chief before a Quebec Police Commission hearing. The chief had apparently put aside data provided by a police statistician demonstrating that there were three times the number of burglaries when the sergeant was on duty (Montreal *Gazette*, May 22, 1986). The chief had, apparently, been fearful of creating disruption and resentment among the other police officers in Ste. Foy by initiating an investigation or charges.

The extent of resentment and loyalty may be illustrated by another Quebec situation. A Sûreté officer testified before the Quebec Police Commission that he was drugged, beaten, and harassed by his colleagues because it was known that he was investigating another officer suspected of involvement in prostitution and drugs. He was so badly injured that he required medical leave for more than a year (Montreal *Gazette*, May 22, 1986).

In Ottawa in 1983, an RCMP officer testified that he had adapted his testimony in order to avoid revealing that a murder investigation had been bungled when fingerprints were not taken at the scene. The murder investigation by the Gatineau, Quebec, force was reviewed by the Quebec Police Commission. The RCMP officer testified that he discussed with the Gatineau police officer what he would say at the trial on the question of fingerprints (*Ottawa Citizen*, November 10, 1983).

The peer pressure need not be overt. Individuals in policing have been socialized to depend upon and be loyal to other officers. The infamous "code of silence," arguably not peculiar to policing, will prompt officers to avoid having to damage the career of another police officer, even though they might disapprove of actions. Illustrative is an Ottawa-area case that dragged on over years, in a succession of enquiries, findings, and appeals. A young man walking alongside a highway was killed by a hit-and-run driver. The driver, it was eventually determined, was an undercover OPP officer. He had apparently been drinking. In an extended defence, eventually leading to dismissal, he claimed that he drove on thinking that he had hit a deer. Meanwhile, another officer, from another police service, was later implicated for having failed to respond properly at the scene, having failed to attend to the young man. In the public view the implication of clumsily attempting to protect another officer was as serious as improper police response, further calling into question police integrity beyond the initial crime.

POLICING THE POLICE

Police misconduct, in all its forms, has precipitated numerous efforts by the public—most of them unsuccessful—to establish more effective control or investigative access to their police services. Characteristically, the police have been allowed to investigate themselves, in the presumption that misconduct is rare, and that the investigative resources necessary for an enquiry require police expertise. The public, however, have frequently mistrusted police self-investigations. Practices have frequently changed over recent years. For example, investigation (see Chapter Nine) of alleged misconduct by outside agencies called in by the Chief of Police, or by a professional provincial Special Investigations Unit, are presently provided for in Ontario. But civilian commission reviews of complaints have, after several years of province-wide operation, been discontinued.

Although more active sectors of the public, such as the media and ethnic interest groups, have pressed for greater control over the police in the conviction that the police cannot be trusted, the police in Canada continue to enjoy the support of the general public. A striking instance involved the case of Constable Gosset, dismissed from the MUC Police after he shot and killed an unarmed black youth. Appearing on a radio call-in show 10 months after his dismissal, Allan Gosset was greeted by a majority of callers who viewed him as a victim of unfair dismissal, a sacrifice to the black community (Montreal *Gazette*, September 9, 1988). Resolute in their conviction that Gosset was an innocent scapegoat, the Police Brotherhood honoured him with a plaque and a cheque for $12 000 at an event months after his dismissal (Montreal *Gazette*, November 5, 1988).

CONCLUSION

The continuum stretching from individual police error and accident through poor judgment, to intentional misconduct and illegality, represents the most dramatic and the most frightening aspect of police encounters with the public. The parallel phenomenon of group or institutionalized error and misconduct highlights the need for effective supervision of police forces. Citizen recourse in the face of police abuse often runs headlong into second-level misconduct: having committing the original error, the police then resort to perjury, further threats, destruction of evidence, or other illegalities in order to cover up the first one.

The police, by the nature of their role, have a privileged position and the trust of influential persons in society. When misconduct occurs, it will often be police actions against less influential members of society. Complaints from such persons may be perceived as falsehoods, and malicious; and sometimes they are. The police officer's interpretation of events, whether accurate or false, will usually prevail. Where police are found guilty, sentences are often light.

Ultimately, the best citizen protection is a competent and honest police force, well-selected, well-trained, well-managed, and regularly monitored and scrutinized by the public. The sheer scope of policing makes it inevitable that some abuses will occur. Their minimization, if not their total elimination, is the realistic public objective.

ANNOTATED READINGS, CHAPTER EIGHT

Bourne, Paula and John Eisenberg. *The Law and the Police.* Toronto: Ontario Institute for Studies in Education, 1972. It is unfortunate that this little book was not updated. It is intended as a study aid for high school and university students analyzing the limits and the abuses of police authority.

Shearing, Clifford D. (ed.). *Organizational Police Deviance.* Toronto: Butterworth and Company, 1981. This anthology offers analyses with the prevalent theme that police misconduct in Canada is attributable in some part to the complexity and ambiguity of the modern police role.

Sherman, Lawrence W. (ed.). *Police Corruption: A Sociological Perspective.* New York: Anchor Books, 1974. A good many works have been written describing police corruption in the United States, including many since this anthology was published. The book does offer, however, a good cross-section of narrative account, theory, and analysis of police deviance in the United States.

Stark, Rodney. *Police Riots: Collective Violence and Law Enforcement.* Belmont, CA: Wadsworth Publishing Company, 1972. Stark's account, dependent upon the American crisis in policing arising from the 1960s, offers what is still the most convincing analysis of the role and organizational flaws in policing with regard to crowd control and unit behaviour.

CONTROLLING
THE POLICE

The police are limited fundamentally by legislation. There are several means to enforce these limits. Police are subject to indirect pressure and control by way of general public surveillance, usually by way of the media and occasional legislative enquiry. Of interest to us in this chapter are direct measures intended to regulate policing. Court proceedings, government-appointed police commissions, and internal organizational controls are the most prevalent. More recently there have been attempts to employ external civilian agencies to examine police conduct.

While virtually all police forces are organized after a military-bureaucratic model, police services are delivered largely by individuals. At the symbolic level, we find the military model prevalent in style of uniforms and in rank designations. These elements reflect the traditional organizations, though moderated by the effect of police unions and professional training, wherein police officers are intended to be subject to a well-defined hierarchy of command. Obedience to such command is stressed in training, where the recruit is subject to constant parade-ground demands, often petty and meaningless. But this command extends only imperfectly to the street. On the job, behaviour and decisions are a matter of an individual's judgment or discretion.

DISCRETION

The police officer lives with significant contradictions. For purposes of organizational control, it may be argued, soldier-like discipline, and impartial, almost impersonal treatment of the public are essential. The military style is contradicted, however, by police employee associations, by the professionalism that is now influencing the police services (especially with increasingly better educated personnel), and by the street level demands upon police officers. Police duties and professionalism stress individual skill, judgment, and autonomy. Working alone, or with a single partner, often under stress, the police officer must exercise intelligent discretion in encounters with citizens. Yet recruit selection, training, command structure, peer association, and even, sometimes, the general public and the media, expect conformity and routine behaviour.

On the job, despite motorized transportation and high technology communications, the police officer makes independent decisions. Often this is all the more true in serious street encounters where there may be little time to refer to superiors for instructions. As noted in the Ontario Task Force on Policing (Ontario, 1973:12), "The fact is that the vast majority of significant decisions in a police force are made by the constable in the daily course of his duties. These decisions, which reflect his concept of role, affect the rights of citizens and the safety of the community. They are most frequently taken without consultation with superior officers and very often under conditions which do not permit deliberation or reflection."

Through most of Canada's modern history, there has been general acceptance of the idea that police must have discretionary power. The public confidence in police allowed the exercise of judgment without a sense of unfair treatment, and also reflected a sense of realism, that police behaviour could not be rule- or administration-bound (Grosman, 1975). An Ontario task force (1973:14–15) could speak of society expecting "constables to exercise some degree of judgment in deciding when to invoke the criminal law process." The task force continued, "we can see little advantage and many dangers in systematic attempts to codify criteria for the exercise of ... judgment. We favour emphasis on the training and education of officers, and in the processes of supervision within forces, which address themselves directly to issues of judgment and which prepare each officer to exercise the power of judgment wisely."

Lately, though, the whole question of police discretion has become confused. Current interest in increased public and judicial control now seems to contradict the traditional expectations.

Legal prohibitions, administrative and procedural controls, review bodies—all means to control police conduct, inhibit police judgment, and reinforce police solidarity. But resorting to excessively codified behaviour will inevitably be inadequate. The greatest assurance of good service from our police is in quality personnel recruitment and training, integration into the community, and commitment and capacity to engage in effective, professional self-policing, not to the exclusion of external or internal administrative controls, but as their necessary foundation.

The police in Canada are defined as agents of the public. They are therefore responsible to the public, and presumed to be controlled by the public through its duly elected or designated representatives. It would simply be nonsense to deny that the definition has, by and large, been met in Canada. The police have acted as agents of society, or at least, of government, in maintaining order, and have not sought policy autonomy. It is also true, however, that they have enjoyed considerable operational autonomy or discretion, from the level of the corporate organization to that of the individual officer.

POLITICAL CONTROL

Acceptable police conduct, however, has largely depended upon police conformity to the democratic norm or definition of police as a subordinate body of very special civilians, usually armed, charged with the tasks of enforcement. Such control as the public has explicitly exercised has been sporadic and imperfect. Generally, the controls on police may be distinguished as internal and external. The former refers to the internal organizational procedures and regulations that are enforced through chain of command. The latter refer to direct interventions by persons or bodies who are not themselves part of the police organization. The former would include internal investigations and discipline, as well as investigations by other police forces, and the latter would include police commissions and civilian review boards. Table 9-1 shows the continuum from internal to external control. It should be noted that such bodies' functions range from investigative to adjudicative.

How control is exercised, through levels that mediate between the public and the police, is a most basic concern of all citizens. Generally, actual control is mediated through government, and government-appointed (non-elected) bodies. All Canadian police are regulated by legislation. Some are directly responsible to local government, others are controlled by police commissions; virtually none are directly controlled by local community groups, although as community policing is implemented, there is some opportunity for increased direct community influence. Government control, which is often remote but sometimes also too intimate, may fail to avert police misconduct.

The RCMP faced a major crisis in the 1970s. Under the Trudeau government, which was contending with radical separatists in Quebec, the Force found itself responding to imprecise cues from its political masters (*Ottawa Journal*, June 6, 1979). Its security service was discredited by 1981 as the public learned of illegal acts that preceded and followed the separatist movement and the October crisis of 1970. Both organizational control, as well as governmental control over the intelligence gathering and counter-espionage units (Montreal

TABLE 9-1	Controlling the Police		
Internal	**Quasi-internal**	**Quasi-external**	**External**
Command/ management supervision	Other police investigations	Police commissions	Ombudsman Courts Standing commissions
Internal affairs		Municipal provincial, federal governments	Civilian review
Discipline board			Judicial review
			Task force or Royal Commission

Gazette, April 4, 1981) appeared to have broken down. One restrained critique concluded that there were "fundamental failures in control and accountability ... demonstrated in the RCMP ... and in its relationship to ministers" (French and Beliveau, 1979:3).

The police in Canada are expected not to engage in politics, but in turn, they wish to be free of overt political interference. Neither condition has been perfectly met. But by and large, devices such as commissions have in most jurisdictions served to insulate police from political interference. Exceptions are mostly likely to occur in small communities where police are subject to the direct control of local councils. Too frequently this has been a feature of policing in Atlantic Canada, but also in other small communities, with "independent" police forces. An advantage of having the RCMP or one of the large provincial forces serve such towns is that it provides the necessary autonomy from local political interference, albeit sometimes at cost of suitable local responsiveness.

The McDonald Commission into wrongdoing in the RCMP (Royal Commission of Inquiry into Certain Activities of the RCMP under Mr. Justice David McDonald, created by Parliament in 1977) raised the possibility of a police service, or a section of it, the security service, having been too entangled with the political objectives of a government. Consequently, following commission recommendations, the Canadian Security Intelligence Service (CSIS) was proclaimed by Parliament in 1984 (*The Canadian Encyclopedia*, 1985; Mann and Lee, 1979). Another instance of political interference occurred in Alberta, where police were required by the Alberta government in 1983 to seek government approval before proceeding in any investigations involving government personnel. The guideline stated: "In cases where an offence is alleged to have been committed by an employee of the Government of Alberta while on duty or in respect of his employment, notification is required prior to the commencement of any investigation [if] having regard to the circumstances overall, the matter is perceived to be sensitive in nature and/or one which may attract media attention or generate public controversy." The police, and the Canadian Bar Association, urged the government to withdraw the guidelines on the grounds that they compromised the police and constituted political interference (*Globe and Mail*, September 15, 1984).

Government does have a responsibility to be active in monitoring police conduct. Sometimes they refuse to accept the responsibility, even when urged by police agencies. In 1984, a report following an Ontario Provincial Police (OPP) investigation of the Hamilton-Wentworth Police (a young man had allegedly been beaten to elicit a murder confession), was not pursued by the solicitor general (*Ottawa Citizen*, November 8, 1984). In Edmonton, the police commission declined to proceed with an enquiry into police brutality. Police had been accused of breaking the fingers of two persons arrested in a domestic dispute. They were acquitted of all charges and cleared in an internal investigation, but accused of excessive force and cover-up by a presiding judge. The provincial government refused to pay half of the costs (the other half having been volunteered by the Edmonton Criminal Trial Lawyers) (Montreal *Gazette*, December 8, 1988).

Police, too, have at times declined to enforce legislation, effectively nullifying government legislation. When amended seat-belt legislation was introduced in Quebec in 1990, provincial police argued that the public had not been properly informed. They then refused to enforce the law. Soon thereafter full-page advertisements paid for by the government appeared in the Quebec newspapers "explaining" the amended legislation. As was remarked upon, the police had in fact declined to enforce a law (Montreal *Gazette*, January 6, 1990).

Ultimately, of course, governments fix the legislative limits of policing. The Police Acts or other legislation defining police powers are the product of the representative bodies of the public. And the legislators can choose to amend such powers as they have granted. They also may choose to initiate investigative processes, either through ad hoc investigations or via standing investigative bodies. The extent to which governments choose to intervene generally depends upon public pressure.

The size and operations of police forces are most directly controlled by budget. The extent to which municipal authorities are willing to authorize spending drives police recruitment, the size of the police establishment, and the range of police services. Police chiefs are continually engaged in convincing their immediate authorities—municipal councillors and police commission members—that more monies are needed because of the enormous demands upon police.

Historically, the tactic has been to stress crime in the community, although there is a negative consequence in this tactic: the possibility of creating a perception of police incompetence. Usually, however, the crime-fighting tactic of lobbying has been effective. For example, in the early 1990s, Canadian police, like their American counterparts, were pressing for budget and personnel increases in order to combat drugs.

The public through their representatives also have a measure of control in the appointment of the chief executive officer of police forces. The appointment of chiefs of police derives from commissions or municipal councils. By participating in and ratifying a chief's appointment, and thereafter by fixing salary and other benefits, the civil governing bodies have a major input into the policing operation. An interesting example is that of the former chief of the MUC Police, who had asked that he be allowed to take his pension of approximately $88 000 a year, for which he was eligible at age 53, and also be paid a salary of approximately $100 000. The city refused, he retired, and then was hired by the city of Ste. Foy, with council's approval, at a salary of $85 000 per year. Where formerly he had previously managed the MUC Police force of 4500 officers, he now moved to direct the small Ste. Foy police force of 150, collecting his pension plus salary (Montreal *Gazette*, February 16, 23, 1989).

While the police have had to contend with their supervising commissions, local municipal politicians have struggled with a different problem: they bear the costs, while the province appoints the commissioners. Such was a Toronto complaint in 1984 when a local controller argued that the police should be controlled directly by a council body (*Toronto Star*, October 17, 1984). A similar objection arose in Ottawa in 1980, when city council voted to request the province to eliminate the police commission following their approval of a 14% pay raise for senior officers (*Ottawa Journal*, June 8, 1980). Again in 1984, Ottawa City Council and the police commission were visibly in conflict; council ordered a cut in the police budget, and the commission refused (*Ottawa Citizen*, June 12, 1984).

Ironically, where councils have dealt with police as in the Atlantic provinces, the absence of a neutralizing or insulating body appears to have generated overt conflict and interference. One alderman anticipated this consequence in opposing the council resolution and predicted "a political finger in each operation of the police" (*Ottawa Journal*, June 8, 1980).

The police chief, as the chief executive officer of the police enterprise, has to contend not only with public representatives but with police associations. With police unionism, the salaries of personnel, the major cost in policing, have risen dramatically over the last two decades. Each new contract threatens to deplete the budget to the extent that the number of personnel hired will be inadequate. Yet, rarely is the chief directly engaged in contract bargaining. Even the political authorities paying the bills often have very limited influence, as it is the commission, or an arbitrator, who deals with the union. The chief is left to manage the outcome. In 1986 Regina's chief of police resigned, after the Board of Police Commissioners reduced his budget by about half a million dollars, rather than manage his operation with this restraint (Montreal *Gazette*, May 20, 1986). In New Brunswick, a Police Act introduced in 1987 was intended to give police managers and municipal government more control over police conduct, attempting to recapture some of the prerogatives presumed to have been lost to police unions. In response, the Saint John police considered strike action (*Ottawa Citizen*, November 5, 1987).

Since all police forces are effectively organized in employee groups labelled brotherhoods, associations, or unions, it follows that everywhere in Canada major police organizations find themselves regularly in wage-bargaining situations as contracts come up for renewal. Salary disputes have been the most frequent occasion of conflict and strikes in Canadian policing. Just as police commanders have found it difficult to accept the diminishment of their authority in the face of unions, so politicians have often found it difficult to accept that police salaries can no longer simply be imposed. Even where the mechanisms of wage settlement are accepted by the bargaining parties, political representatives have balked. For example, in 1988 a contract settlement was reached for the MUC Police by arbitration award. In the MUC Police, where agitation has been frequent, resort to binding arbitration rather than job action should have been seen as progress. The arbitration award made the MUC Police one of the highest paid in the country. The salary advantage over the Sûreté and the RCMP was cited by municipal authorities as "immoral" and unacceptable, and it was determined that the arbitration award would be appealed (Montreal *Gazette*, September 28, October 3, 4, 1988). Significantly, editorial opinion was very critical of the appeal decision, in the view that arbitration was a desirable alternative to job action, "a sensible, civilized alternative to the strike."

INTERNAL REVIEW

In most Canadian police forces management is given great latitude in the internal disposition of resources, force policy, and implementation. The pressures for an internal role in controlling police organizations have focussed not on finances but on behaviours that we have described as misconduct, where the public have expressed a distrust of internal disposition of such complaints. In the traditional police force the chief has been the ultimate decision maker, imposing a discipline when he sees fit with the assistance and advice of subordinates in the chain of command. As police have come under pressure to implement public enquiries, most Canadian police forces have resisted, generally embracing the view that the public should have confidence in police professionalism.

Moreover, it could be argued that police managers have reacted to allegations and public criticism by imposing harsher sanctions. Chiefs have not been immune to public and media demands. In Ontario, for example, Peel Regional police shot and killed a young black man in a stolen car. Charges of police racism and demands for action followed. A black officer in another police force defended Peel police in letters to two newspapers, arguing that the racism charges were "self-serving" and made by "self-appointed" leaders of the black community. The Waterloo Regional Police officer was himself criticized for expressing his opinion, and his chief stated to reporters that his remarks could be investigated (Montreal *Gazette*, December 31, 1988). In the Peel incident, charges of manslaughter were laid against the police officer by the Crown. Within the same week, charges of manslaughter were laid against a Metro Toronto police officer for the shooting death of a black man several months earlier, despite an internal police investigation finding no fault.

We discussed in the previous chapter the problems associated with self-policing in instances of major misconduct. It may be noted here that in keeping with the paramilitary structure of the police, and some of the stereotyped images of police propriety, internal control is often devoted to petty offences that relate to violations of internal organizational rules such as those related to the dress code. Policemen generally have been subjected to limits upon their behaviour that are not true of the general public, with the inhibitions codified in Police Acts. For example, police have generally been prevented from engaging overtly in politics or other forms of social protest. A police constable in Toronto was ordered to resign because he disobeyed an order to patrol outside an abortion clinic. The insubordination charge arose from the Police Act, which allowed no room for the constable's decision of conscience (*Toronto Star*, January 31, 1988).

Police commanders, however, cannot control the opinions and related actions of their personnel. Especially with strong police unions, police officers have more and more often been individually and collectively expressing views that are not consistent with the policy position of a police department. The controversial case of a constable in Montreal, previously discussed, illustrates the point. The MUC Police Brotherhood aggressively objected to the dismissal of the constable, and publicly criticized their chief and his relations with the ethnic communities. Eventually, without the permission or knowledge of the chief, they raised monies to assist him (Montreal *Gazette*, November 5, 1988).

The public presumption is that the police do not and cannot attend to misconduct within their own ranks. A survey for the Montreal Urban Community Police in 1986 "found that six out of ten Montrealers think that it does no good to complain about brutality, racism, or false arrest by police because the offending officers will go unpunished" (Montreal *Gazette*, September 10, 1987). A damning report by the Quebec Human Rights Commission, following two months of hearings, was provided to the Quebec justice minister in 1988. It concluded that existing police disciplinary boards were "biased" and "incapable of treating with any justice citizens' complaints," with decisions on whether or not to investigate a complaint often determined by the ethnic origin of the complainant (*Ottawa Citizen*, August 18, 1988). Accordingly, civilian review boards should be established, argued the report, to hear citizen complaints, while police should be allowed the right of appeal.

When an internal investigation is required, a force may pursue the case itself, with specialized personnel. Or it may call in an outside police force as an investigative agency. The latter course is frequently followed in Ontario, with the OPP acting in enquiries into municipal forces. In Quebec, similarly, the MUC Police and the Sûreté du Québec have a reciprocal agreement calling for investigations of one another when a person dies in custody (Montreal *Gazette*, November 12, 1985). But there is no systematic agreement regarding investigation of municipal forces in Quebec.

Explicit information statements to the public regarding complaints procedures are becoming more common. A pamphlet made available by the Ottawa Police Force, for example, while including a "caution" to the public that false complaints are a violation of the *Criminal Code*, includes specific instructions (see "How to Make a Complaint").

In Canada there has not been the development of elaborate police-within-police structures, such as the famous Internal Affairs Unit of New York City. Rather, police chiefs have tended to assign investigative tasks to available investigators in whom they have confidence, or to go outside. Increasingly, however, services will now have in place a standing internal investigations unit. In Ontario, for example, a professional standards section might have a section dealing with public complaints, that is, externally initiated enquiries, and another dealing with internal affairs. A commissioned officer, probably of inspector rank, would head the section, with senior staff sergeants directing the sub-units.

In some instances the police are demonstrably incapable of policing themselves. Such may be instances not of lack of will, but of such widespread misconduct and mistrust that an internal investigation is impossible, or at least appears to be. The chief of police of Ste. Foy, suspended in January 1986, testified before a Quebec Police Commission enquiry that he feared that investigators from the force would be recognized by suspects. He therefore employed a firm of private police to investigate several incidents (Montreal *Gazette*, May 6, 1986).

How to Make a Complaint

Complaints about a member or members of the Ottawa Police Force or the quality of service it provides may be made in the following manner.

In person

1. At the Ottawa Police Station, 474 Elgin Street, at any time, by outlining the circumstances to the duty staff sergeant or a sergeant authorized by him and by signing the official complaints form (the complaint will be received in private),

or

2. By contacting the officer in charge of the Internal Affairs Section at 236-0311, extension 563 on weekdays between 8:30 a.m. and 5:00 p.m., for an appointment to make the complaint in person but away from the Ottawa Police building.

By Correspondence

Address correspondence to the Chief of Police or the Ottawa Board of Commissioners of Police outlining the circumstances of the complaint.

Notification

In all cases, the Internal Affairs Section will investigate the complaint and as soon as possible inform the complainant of the result of the investigation and of the action taken.

Source: Pamphlet, Ottawa Police Service, 1990.

Generally, cases are reported only where the sanctions appear to the public to be inadequate. Stories of attempted police cover-up also occur, creating the impression of greater misconduct than may be actual. In 1982 a police sergeant in Tillsonburg, Ontario, admitted in court that during a 1974 trial he had lied to protect a fellow police officer charged with assault. Only in 1980, with the entire Tillsonburg force under investigation by the OPP, did he admit his perjury (*Toronto Star,* November 18, 1982).

In Winnipeg, the police enquiry and public inquest into the shooting death of a native leader exonerated the police officer involved of all blame, without even raising the question of whether or not the officer's intervention was justified in the first instance. Witnesses stated that at the scene of the incident an older police officer advised the offending constable to state that his gun had misfired accidentally. The shooting scene was rapidly cleaned, and the probable weapon never fingerprinted (Gillmor, 1988:50–51). The inquest's only recommendations were to arrange a study seminar for provincial court judges on inquest procedure, a program for police to recruit more native persons, and additional training for ambulance attendants.

Just as there was suspicion in Winnipeg that police and authorities conspired to obscure the investigation, in Hull, Quebec, the enquiry following the death of a man pursued by police in a high-speed chase found that police had erased a tape recording of the chase (*Ottawa Citizen*, March 9, 1987).

While there are, undoubtedly, instances of police protection of peers, as occurs in all organizations, it must also be recognized that there is often a very vigorous and even harsh police response to misconduct. A police officer may lose an entire career, in addition to whatever penalty a court may impose. Thus, in 1984, an Ottawa police constable with 18 years service, who was charged with discreditable conduct, was fired after having been convicted of theft of $97 (*Ottawa Citizen*, November 3, 1984). In 1988 an Ottawa constable who, while off-duty assaulted another man with a pocket knife in a traffic altercation, was charged with "discreditable conduct" under the Police Act. He was found guilty by a police tribunal and ordered dismissed despite 13 years of service, on the basis of this incident and awareness of two previous findings of discreditable conduct involving weapons (*Ottawa Citizen*, August 18, 1988). It should be noted that police officers may find themselves disciplined, and even dismissed for alleged misconduct, that is, charges of which they have been acquitted in a court of law. A Vancouver policemen, for example, was fired in 1981 after having been charged with possession of stolen property, despite his acquittal. In 1988 a British Columbia Supreme Court ordered his reinstatement with full back pay plus interest (*Ottawa Citizen*, November 26, 1988).

In 1988 it was reported that two MUC Police constables were fired, and a sergeant demoted, for roles in the beating of a black man. The director of police noted that two years previously 10 police officers had been dismissed for misconduct, without fanfare (Montreal *Gazette*, June 1, 1988). Yet, the Montreal *Gazette* also discovered that of 14 police officers in Montreal against whom the courts awarded civil judgments to the sum of $224 000, only one had been disciplined by the MUC Police. The awards related to assaults, racism, and false arrests in the period 1981 to 1985. The one officer further sanctioned received only a reprimand (Montreal *Gazette*, July 24, 25, 1987).

In Quebec, when serious allegations are made against an officer, the normal management response is suspension without pay. Even when the officer is later exonerated, compensation for lost salary is not routine, and often depends upon the union filing a grievance. This was noted in a newspaper editorial deploring the automatic suspensions as an infringement of the right to be presumed innocent. The newspaper was prompted by the case of an MUC Police constable who had been accused by United States customs officers of smuggling currency, and the charges were later dropped (Montreal *Gazette*, June 1, 1987).

The editorial remarked that "if the police system treated members of the public as guilty before they were convicted of any crime, civil libertarians would be sure to raise a clamour" (Montreal *Gazette*, January 26, 1989). The editorial went on to support the representations to the Quebec government of four police employee groups, the MUC Brotherhood, the Quebec Federation of Police, the Association of Quebec Provincial Police, and the unrecognized RCMP group seeking union status. In exchange, however, the editorialist suggested that the government should act to reduce the power of the MUC Brotherhood, specifically by removing supervisory officers from the union (Montreal *Gazette*, January 26, 1989).

In 1987 the Supreme Court of Canada ruled in a unanimous 7–0 judgment arising from arguments from an Ottawa and two Toronto police officers. In separate incidents the officers had been disciplined; they argued before the court that internal hearings were unconstitutional because the police force puts, hears, and judges charges. The court ruled, however, that the constitutional guarantee of an "independent and impartial tribunal" did not apply to the police, nor to the disciplinary hearings of other professional groups such as physicians and lawyers. The court did allow, however, that the guarantee extends to disciplinary hearings of the RCMP because a consequence within the Force under the RCMP Act is imprisonment for a serious offence (*Ottawa Citizen,* November 1, 1987). In 1985 an RCMP constable with 16 years of service who had been forced to resign as a consequence of an internal disciplinary hearing was ordered reinstated by the Federal Court of Canada on grounds that he had been previously acquitted in court of a charge of shoplifting (*Toronto Star*, June 18, 1985). In the course of the McDonald Commission enquiry, an RCMP member complained of internal disciplinary proceedings. Statements are mandatory, and lawyers are not provided. "The Catch-22 aspect of it is objectionable" (*Ottawa Citizen*, September 29, 1978).

In Ontario in 1984, delegates at the general meeting of Ontario Police Associations considered court action to require independent disciplinary hearings. The associations deplored the power of police commissions, and suggested that they (lower ranks) were vulnerable to arbitrary discipline. Instead, they favoured independent arbitrators or panels (*Ottawa Citizen*, February 17, 1984). The associations were not clear as to how such bodies would differ from the civilian review bodies that they had often criticized, but it was clear that some of the rank and file distrusted internal proceedings as much as some members of the public. Despite police opposition, however, in 1989 the Ontario government introduced legislation to amend the Police Act, and particularly to establish a province-wide commission headed by a civilian to investigate complaints against the police. Disciplinary procedures were also to be standardized with a greater burden of proof, thereby offering some protection to officers from internal investigations and sanctions (*Ottawa Citizen,* December 21, 1989).

POLICE SERVICE BOARDS

In 1974 an Ontario task force on policing stated, as a basic tenet, that they were committed to the concept of municipal boards of police commissioners. Such boards, observed the task force, "foster a balance between politically independent judgment and linkage to local government" (Ontario 1973:1). The 1976 report on Metro Toronto, however, contradicted this sensible proposition, reflecting the frustration of local politicians who perceived themselves as lacking control over policing. They recommended instead that organizational and financial responsibilities for the Metro Toronto police be assigned to the metropolitan government, who may then choose to create, or not, something like a board of commissioners (Ontario, 1976). A similar recommendation was made by a Waterloo commission of enquiry, arguing, in the context of a troubled police force, that local politicians must have direct control of the police, and therefore recommending that the Board of Police Commissions "be eliminated" (Ontario, 1979). The Waterloo enquiry resorted to rather strong language, characterizing the reasons for commissions—to keep politics out of policing—as "fraudulent," and described the provincial process of appointments as entirely political. Such political challenges, generally motivated by fiscal considerations, as well as concerns about complaints procedures that have increasingly led to civilian review boards, have challenged the authority and the legitimacy of police boards (Stenning, 1981c:100–121).

Local police commissions, boards charged with the task of overseeing policing and police training, are appointed by provincial governments. Municipal boards have been required in Upper Canada since 1859. In 1962 Ontario established the first provincial police commission, followed by Quebec in 1968 and Alberta in 1971 (Kelly and Kelly, 1976:45). After the early Ontario example, Manitoba established mandatory commissions for Winnipeg by 1886, as did British Columbia for Vancouver in the same year; a province-wide commission was created by 1893. By 1907 and 1908 there were boards in New Brunswick and Saskatchewan, but not until 1938 in Prince Edward Island. Alberta took until 1951, and not until 1974 did Nova Scotia have such a body. Except for the Public Security Council which governed the merged MUC Police in Montreal, there has been no municipal public body in Quebec (Stenning, 1981b:174–175).

Thus, the commission has not been universal. The Ontario model has been adopted in the western provinces, and boards have come into operation in Nova Scotia. But in Nova Scotia the municipal councils have retained budget and other control over the police that in other provincial jurisdictions is held by commissions (Sewell, 1985:168–169). In Nova Scotia, therefore, as in Quebec, police–public relations have tended to be more political and more confrontational than elsewhere in Canada. Local decision-makers have not suffered the frustration expressed by many Ontario politicians who complain of paying the bills without a role in overseeing the disposition of the monies. But because of the absence of police commissions, which have an insulating effect, the negotiations with police employee groups have often been more bitter and volatile. One can infer a relationship between the council role and the high frequency of police strikes in Nova Scotia. The Police Act and commission in Nova Scotia followed years of labour strikes. Once belatedly established, the provincial police commission faced the distrust of a very militant provincial police association. In 1984, following the commission enquiry into police conduct in Kentville, the association passed a motion of non-confidence in the commission for delays and "questionable" investigation (*Ottawa Citizen*, April 17, 1984).

In jurisdictions where there are both municipal and provincial commissions, there is some ambiguity as to who has authority where. Both levels have served, undoubtedly, to remove direct community control; this is especially the effect of the Ontario Police Commission, established in 1961. Especially for small towns, the provincial commission is of great influence, responsible for the OPP, and police discipline province-wide. In effect, local authorities do not have power to oversee conduct, especially to discipline and to dismiss (Brockenshire, 1985).

One of the reasons for vigorous public interest in review boards, other than suspicion of internal police investigations, is the failure of government and police commissions to visibly and knowledgeably exercise their rights of police governance.

Commissions have never been representative of the public, with government appointees usually drawn from the ranks of the law profession, who then participate as they may on a part-time basis. In Ontario, not until 1982 did legislation require at least five-member boards for jurisdictions of 25 000 or more. Previously, three was the number, with only the mayor representing local government. When expanded to five, one of the two additional spaces was reserved for a member of the area municipal council (*Ottawa Citizen*, August 23, 1983). The additional political representation was a concession to municipal governments who regularly objected to their scant control over police operations, and perhaps more to the point, police costs. Councils, therefore often resent the boards, and public interest groups find the non-representative commissions remote and non-responsive. Such was the nature of problems in Toronto in 1979, when council attempted a motion of non-confidence in the Metro Toronto commission that had been formed in 1956 (*Toronto Sunday Star*, September 16, 1979). Not until 1987 was there a black person appointed to the Metro Toronto Police Commission, a businessman of Jamaican origin (*Toronto Star*, March 8, 1987).

Commission proceedings in Canada, with a few notable exceptions such as Calgary, have not been open to the public. In Ontario, public meetings were recommended in the 1974 task force report, without any impact (Ontario, 1973). Nor are their deliberations and actions routinely reported by the media. As remarked by June Rowlands, who was appointed chairman of Metro Toronto Police Commission in 1988, commissions have allowed control to rest with police management (*Toronto Star*, June 4, 1988). Moreover, the appointments are not subject to public scrutiny, and are by and large drawn from the ranks of the law profession and majority ethnic groups. A notable change in this regard occurred in 1987 when a Chinese Canadian architect was appointed to the Ottawa Police Commission (*Ottawa Citizen*, August 25, 1987).

Commissions have, for the most part, been intent upon upholding the authority of the chief of police. An Ontario case illustrates this point. In Gloucester (Ottawa), upset with the chief's inaction over dissatisfaction in the force, the president of the police association forwarded documentation to the local police commission and the Ontario Police Commission, bypassing the chief. He was thereupon charged with discreditable conduct, insubordination, and breach of confidence (*Ottawa Citizen*, January 5, February 11, 1982). The document did not challenge or criticize the chief overtly, but suggested changes to improve morale and efficiency. The chairman of the police commission eventually upheld the charge of insubordination, but also criticized the chief for his failure to respond to constructive suggestions, and acknowledged a morale problem throughout the force. No action, however, was required of the chief or recommended. The commission and the city mayor hastened to back the chief, even though they were aware of and acknowledged major difficulties in the force.

Police commissions, however indifferent, have been called upon to intervene in incidents of alleged police misconduct, especially where the allegations are well publicized. A controversial case in Moncton, New Brunswick, prompted the provincial solicitor general to order a commission investigation. It had been alleged, with much publicity, that the Moncton chief of police had in 1982 been drunk and disorderly in a Fredericton restaurant. Additionally, it was alleged that there was a police cover-up. The New Brunswick Police Commission concluded that the allegations were without foundation (Montreal *Gazette*, February 27, 1988).

Public agencies exercising their responsibility to control policing may themselves be challenged in legal proceedings. An infamous case is that of Syd Brown. He was fired as Chief of Police in 1979 by the Waterloo Regional Police Commission following an Ontario Police Commission enquiry into police violence. Chief Brown resisted with court action, and at one point won back his title and salary, but not the right to resume his duties, since they were already filled by another man. The region was left paying two chiefs. Only in 1985 did the Ontario Supreme Court confirm on appeal the decision that he could not be reinstated. In the meanwhile Chief Brown was engaged in additional court action to win back fringe benefits, including an automobile stripped from him earlier (*Toronto Star*, April 4, 1985), and to oppose mandatory retirement from the position that was nominally his. To that date legal proceedings were estimated to have cost the Waterloo regional government and the Ontario Police Commission approximately $1 million (*Toronto Star*, May 7, 12, 1985). Finally in 1986, a settlement of $310 000 was accepted, with the former chief agreeing to retire at age 60 (*Ottawa Citizen*, June 19, 1986).

CIVILIAN REVIEW

In the United States from about the 1960s, and in Canada, much later, in the 1980s, there began attempts to implement civilian bodies to review and to sanction police behaviour. Such bodies have a mixed success, and interrupted lifespans, as they have been disliked and lobbied against by police officers, and deemed costly and inefficient by many politicians. They are attempted, however, because some significant segment of the public is skeptical of internal measures to control the police. In the view that the police cannot police themselves, there has been pressure for external investigations and external adjudicative bodies. Estimates in Ontario suggest that convictions of police officers are at about one-third the rate of civilians (*Ottawa Citizen*, December 5, 1997). It is perhaps ironic that the widespread public confidence and trust in the police may itself relate to a low incidence of police convictions for offences, and thereby contribute to the negative public view that the police get away with too much in a system dominated by internal procedures and court proceedings.

Recently in Canada (as had developed with imperfect results decades earlier in the United States), there has been some public demand for more direct public input and control intended to render the police more accountable for their actions. Most particularly, there has been concern that the police be more accountable for their misconduct, and that the police not be allowed to police themselves. Arising out of incidents in Toronto, Montreal, Vancouver, and other cities, there is nation-wide interest in non-police investigative and review bodies that have the authority, hitherto resting exclusively with police management and commissions, to review and to sanction alleged police misconduct. Police themselves have been very hostile to such bodies.

In the United States, opposition to civilian review in cities such as New York became a major stimulus for increased police politicization. In New York City the Policeman's Benevolent Association won a court order requiring a referendum to eliminate the review board that had been established in 1966. They then financed the opposition to the board, actively campaigned, and decisively won the referendum (Reiner, 1980:383–386).

Although public opinion is divided, there is a determined and organized core of persons in most jurisdictions who increasingly have been insisting upon civilian review. Usually the demands are associated with visible minority groups. The vigour of the demands varies with the occurrence of unpleasant incidents, but when police find themselves in a controversial encounter with a minority group member, almost inevitably, even in the absence of facts, there is presumption of misconduct by the police, and demand for external review. In Ottawa, for example, a black man was shot and wounded by an OPP officer. An enquiry followed, conducted not by the OPP but by the Ottawa police. The Ottawa police found no racial motivation for the incident, and the victim himself stated to the press that racism was not a factor. Nonetheless, a group known as the Ottawa Advisory Committee on Visible Minorities called for a procedure of civilian review, on the grounds that "when the police investigates itself, there is a perception that justice is not being done" (*Ottawa Citizen*, November 29, 1988).

In 1977, following a royal commission, the Ontario provincial government introduced legislation that provided for a civilian review board anywhere in Ontario. They abandoned the proposed legislation in the face of unanimous opposition from the chiefs of police in Ontario (*Ottawa Journal*, September 19, 1979). But in the jurisdiction of Metropolitan Toronto a civilian complaints board was established in 1981, and became operational in 1982, on a three-year trial basis. It consisted of a chair and 24 members appointed by the attorney general of Ontario, with 8 chosen by that office, 8 by the Metro Toronto Police Association and the Toronto Police Commission, and 8 by the Metro City Council. The enabling legislation in Ontario called for an initial police investigation when a complaint is registered, with the complainant having the right to bring the matter before the civilian review board if dissatisfied with the police investigation (*Toronto Star,* December 20, 1981; October 13, 1982).

A three-person panel from the board heard its first case in the autumn of 1982 (*Toronto Star*, October 13, 1982). Since then there have been doubts raised, not only by police, that the relatively uninformed persons sitting on the committee, who are not bound by usual legal rules of evidence, may in fact come down with decisions that would not have been reached in a court. Yet undoubtedly there was public confidence in the procedure. In an editorial anticipating the departure of the board's first head, criminal lawyer Sidney Linden, the newspaper stated that "a public complaints commissioner serves two functions. By giving the aggrieved citizen a place to go to complain about the police, he protects the public. He also protects the police from unfair and unwarranted allegations against them" (*Toronto Star*, June 9, 1985).

Up until mid-1985, in its trial period, the board in its rulings only handed down suspensions where it found misconduct. In that year, however, it required a police officer to resign for assaulting a civilian and other acts (*Toronto Star*, June 14, 1985).

In 1986 the Ontario Association of Chiefs of Police sent a telegram to the provincial premier opposing the establishment of Toronto-style civilian review boards elsewhere in the province. In the view of the chiefs, whatever the troubles of Toronto, the system of internal self-policing had worked well (*Ottawa Citizen*, June 26, 1986). Ignoring these representations, Ontario introduced such boards throughout the province by 1991. The province went on to develop a very elaborate system. A government-appointed Commissioner of Public Complaints had authority to initiate or to review complaints. The commissioner had the use of an investigative arm, the Special Investigations Unit, whose members could not be police officers, and whose findings could require sanction by police service management. Also established were civilian public enquiry boards, who could affix blame and penalty. There was also greater emphasis upon internal police organization professional standards and internal investigation, and the continued practice of the use by a chief of investigators from outside a force. In sum, over and above the historic control measures, an elaborate new layer was put in place. It rapidly was seen to be very slow and cumbersome, and never gained the support of the police, nor much confidence from the public. In fact, very few members of the public had any awareness or understanding of the process. In 1997, a new government passed amendments to the Police Act that revoked the Public Complaints Commissioner's office and the review boards. The Special Investigations unit was left in place, and as it had done, would continue to investigate all police actions where serious injury has occurred. Otherwise, more authority seems to have been attached to the chiefs of police, as the police themselves wished, and to police service boards. The government estimated a savings of $3.8 million (*Ottawa Citizen*, December 5, 1997).

The on-again, off-again history of civilian review, as experienced in the United States, seems therefore to be well into replication in Canada, although it is yet to be seen whether similar revocations occur in other provinces. In the general context of Canadian regard for their police, it has also been the case that the opinion on civilian review has been divided, with strongest favourable opinion in the Atlantic and in Quebec. Older Canadians were less likely to perceive a need for such a control procedure. In 1981 a Gallup Poll asked Canadians "is there or is there not a need for ... a civilian review board in your community?" The results are summarized in Table 9-2.

TABLE 9-2	Canadian Opinion on the Need for Civilian Review Boards 1981, in Percentages		
	Yes	**No**	**Don't Know**
Region			
National	50	40	10
Atlantic	56	31	13
Quebec	55	34	12
Ontario	47	45	8
Prairies	51	40	9
British Columbia	41	49	10
Age			
18–29 years	57	33	10
30–49 years	50	40	9
50 and over	42	48	10
Communities			
Over 100 000	51	38	11
10 000 to 100 000	55	38	7
Under 10 000	46	45	9

Source: The Canadian Gallup Poll.

In Montreal there had been strenuous lobbying for such review boards, modelled after the Toronto example, allowing the police to act first, and the complainant if dissatisfied to follow up to a complaints board (Montreal *Gazette*, May 14, 1987; September 10, 29, 1988). Declaimed one editorial: "Montrealers have had enough of a system in which the police police themselves." Up to 1990 in Montreal, a seven-person complaints review board, with three civilian appointees and four police officers, heard complaints from civilians and from police and made disciplinary recommendations, with no aspect of the process, including the findings, in public (Montreal *Gazette*, March 6, May 12, 1987; *Toronto Sunday Star*, February 5, 1989). The possibility of full-scale civilian review became most explicit in 1987 when a report to the MUC Security Committee recommended a Toronto-style civilian review process to hear citizen complaints. The report, prepared by a city councillor and an area mayor, examined the review process in Toronto and in 19 American cities.

The prevalent view among Quebec police managers was expressed by the director of the MUC Police, who argued that while the public must have a role, authority for discipline must not be delegated to "an ad hoc group of people" (Montreal *Gazette*, September 28, 1988). The contrary view, as editorialists have stated, is that such review boards render the police more "accountable," where it is commonly assumed that they cannot adequately police their own ranks (Montreal *Gazette*, September 10, 1987; *Ottawa Citizen*, October 3, 1988).

A Quebec Police Ethics Committee was established in 1990, and by 1996 the MUC Police submitted a report complaining of cumbersome and time-consuming procedures. Of interest, however, while police managers wanted a return to internal control, the MUC Police Brotherhood referred to their proposals as a "huge step backwards" (Montreal *Gazette*, October 17, 1996).

On a national basis, the RCMP were provided by the federal solicitor general with a complaints board of 13 civilian members. The board, however, which began operations on September 30, 1988, was established with its recommendations subject to the decision of the commissioner of the RCMP, and the board will not act unless a complainant is unsatisfied with an investigation first conducted by the RCMP themselves (Montreal *Gazette*, September 27, 1988). In reviewing a report from the Complaints Commission, the commissioner of the RCMP must advise the solicitor general of the action following, if any, and the reasons (*Liaison*, October, 1988:8).

An External Review Committee of four persons was also created for the RCMP, reporting to Parliament and intended to offer a similar independent but non-binding review of internal administrative decisions. Its first chairman, former judge René Martin, noted that this dual structure amended the concept of an ombudsman, first recommended for the RCMP by a 1976 commission (*Liaison*, April 1987:4–10; Canada, 1976). The independent, nonbinding character of the Complaints Commission and the External Review Committee, however, while perhaps a compromise, retains some of the flavour and advantages of the ombudsman concept.

Just as police findings in internal investigations are often met with suspicion and hostility by the public, the findings of public bodies are often met with suspicion and hostility by the police. In Toronto, for example, in 1985 the complaints board ruled that a Metro Police officer had assaulted a suspect. Following unsuccessful appeals of the commission ruling before a divisional court and the Ontario Court of Appeal, the police officer was forced to resign, prompting a week-long police slowdown in protest. Following discussion within the police association, Metro police then charged the former officer with assault, with his agreement, in order to have a court trial, which they expected to clear him (*Ottawa Citizen*, January 19, 1988). Previously, a meeting of the association attended by an estimated 1500 police officers voted unanimously to boycott the board, with their president remarking that "this case has confirmed our worst suspicions that the citizens' complaint process is incapable of treating police officers fairly" (Montreal *Gazette*, January 12, 1988). This in turn elicited a counter-threat by the Metro chairman that police would be charged under the Police Act if they were to follow up on their threat. All political parties in the province supported the board, and the premier intervened in a public statement supporting the commission and the concept of independent review. Adding to the controversy, the chief of police appeared before a meeting of the association, put on an association hat, and declared his opposition to the Public Complaints Board (*Ottawa Citizen*, January 15, 26, 1988).

Another interesting expression of ongoing tension and challenge to public control bodies is the case of three RCMP officers. They had been investigated, and in fact eventually cleared by the Public Complaints Commissioner, of allegations arising from the 1992 Yellowknife mine dispute. The members have nonetheless brought a defamation and malicious prosecution suit, seeking damages of $1.5 million (*Ottawa Citizen*, October 4, 1996)

Running through the debate over public review is the police perception that they are targetted for over-zealous and duplicative investigation and sanction, versus a public view, probably a minority public, that the police get away with too much. It is also the case that among police themselves, there is also wariness of too much power being placed in the hands of their own managers. While police unions can assist their members, they are not yet so powerful that they can deter a plethora of charges and sanctions. Moreover, in the RCMP in particular, there is no union protection, and the internal disciplinary hearings have been closed. Ironically, flying in the face of police concern about the media and the Charter of Rights and Freedoms, media challenges to closed disciplinary hearings in the RCMP have recently forced the RCMP to change its practice and to open the hearings, following a judge's ruling that the closed hearings violated the Charter of Rights and Freedoms (*Ottawa Citizen*, November 28, 1997). Public bodies, while seeming not to ever have won police confidence, do at least afford the police officer recourse, even the ability to appeal an internal decision. Unfortunately the public bodies that have been attempted have never been perceived as neutral.

PUBLIC ENQUIRIES AND OMBUDSMEN

Periodically, municipal police forces have been subject to public enquiries, sometimes prompted by allegations of misconduct, as with the Toronto police in both 1977 and 1989, or by public interest in reorganization, as with the commissions in the province in Ontario in the late 1970s that led to regional police forces in most urban and suburban areas of the province.

When allegations of police misconduct or inadequacy occur, public hearings by separate quasi-judicial bodies have been convened. The most notorious example was the Manitoba enquiry into native justice following the shooting of native leader J.J. Harper by a Winnipeg police officer. The widely publicized hearings were resisted strenuously by the police force and the police association, as sensational allegations were made that allegedly demoralized the police.

The stress associated with the enquiry was focused when a senior police officer committed suicide hours before he was due to testify. Suicide notes indicated that the officer, an inspector, shot himself with his service revolver because he feared public humiliation arising from what he considered a botched investigation into the shooting. Testimony at a subsequent inquest identified the incident as typical of police stress (*Ottawa Citizen,* November 31, 1989).

The public enquiry has the great disadvantage of sensationalism. It is highly visible and produces impressions not subject to rules of evidence. Ultimately, they seem far more damaging to police organizations and individuals than the civilian review boards so universally feared and despised by police officers.

There is a rarely considered alternative to both enquiries and review boards. Lost in the rush to civilian review and judicial enquiry is an office that permits a measure of objective and widely respected enquiry. The concept of the ombudsman is one that has never been genuinely tested in Canada, in particular with respect to police services.

This possibility was explicitly raised in the 1970s—a "watchman" to resolve complaints involving the RCMP. The recommended ombudsman would have "full powers of enquiry," be able to initiate enquiries and hold hearings, review complaint resolution following internal investigation, and require changes, working in cooperation with attorneys general, and report publicly through Parliament (Canada, 1976:91–108; Marin, 1980:142–143). The advantage of the ombudsman is primarily perceived to be his or her ability to review decisions impartially, with all evidence before the quasi-judicial hearing, in an "informal and non-accusatory" fashion. The ombudsman would offer an independent investigative and resolution mechanism that is much less negative and adversarial than civilian review. Both police employees and the public would resort to ombudsmen, and the office would not challenge and diminish management responsibility for the proper conduct of police members.

The concept, however, has been lost. Where it was relatively fashionable to conceive of an ombudsman role in the 1970s, the changes that have occurred in policing have, in fact, been far more adversarial.

THE COURTS

Police are, like any other citizens, subject to criminal charges arising from their misconduct, and are tried in courts of law. Police have found themselves treated rather favourably by the courts when they are brought forward on charges. Harsh punishment is more apt to occur within the organization than at the hands of the court. In the view of some members of the public, the court responses are a function of the difficulties in putting a case against the police officers. Not only is there general public support and predisposition to credit the testimony of the police, it is also the case that evidence is dependent upon the investigative efforts of other police officers (McQuaig, 1981:53–54).

Another restraint upon police is the possibility of civil suit. A citizen may sue a police officer, seeking damages where there has been abuse of police power, whether or not there has been internal police disciplinary action. If the court proceedings are civil, then the cost may deter the citizen, while the police officers have the support very often of their association. There is also the prospect of counter-charges, and counter-suit, as was apparently being practised in Toronto for a period by the police force, police association, or the municipal authorities. In 1980, for example, the Metro Toronto association brought suit for libel against two aldermen who had been critical of police actions (*Toronto Star*, December 2, 1980).

Successful court action against police officers has not been frequent in Canada. There has, for example, been the implication that police are immune from prosecution for negligence in actions arising in the performance of their duty. Such was precisely the defence in a 1990 case in Ottawa. But in 1997 a judge ruled that there was no such immunity, and the lawyer acting for the complainant, who claimed to have 20 such cases pending, declared one less obstacle to the successful prosecution of police (*Ottawa Citizen*, December 23, 1997).

The Montreal *Gazette*, which has been regularly reporting upon and criticizing the conduct of the MUC Police, has conspicuously published reports and cost inventories of suits brought against the police. For example, in 1985 an off-duty police constable pointed his gun at another motorist in the course of a traffic dispute. The motorist was actually arrested and charged with assault, having reached for an iron bar in his truck when faced with the gun. He was subsequently acquitted, and then won a total of $11 000 in damages, consisting of "$5000 for the trauma of the arrest and damage to his reputation, another $5000 in exemplary damages, and $1000 for the inconveniences of the assault prosecution" (Montreal *Gazette*, March 4, 1988). In the first three months of 1988 alone the MUC Police, who met the costs of successful suits against on-duty officers, faced approximately one dozen civil suits with claims totalling about $2 million. To that date, courts had found against the police in three judgments with damages totalling $284 000 (*Ottawa Citizen*, March 11, 1988).

In Dartmouth, Nova Scotia, in 1980 a man died from a heart attack when he was beaten by police. The incident rose out of a dispute at a toll bridge. One of the two policemen involved was convicted of manslaughter while the second was acquitted. The angry widow, left with two dependent children, fought a civil suit for damage, frustrated by an estimated $400 000 spent by the city in court costs for the police officers, while she was refused compensation (*Globe and Mail*, February 13, 1984).

Redress for citizens is often impeded by the action of the elected representatives responsible for the control of police forces. In the infamous Quebec City incident where two innocent carpet layers were shot by bungling police detectives, the mayor refused to discipline the officers on the grounds that he was backing his police. In other instances, since the costs of civil suits are ultimately borne by the municipal government, the elected political bodies will spend enormous sums of money defending against suits brought by members of the public, rather than use the money for compensation.

Intervention of another sort, however, made case history in Quebec in December, 1988. Two police officers who had taken a coffee break instead of responding to a suicide call had been suspended without pay for five days by the town council of Farnham. The officers, with the support of their union, appealed the suspensions. The labour arbitrator expressed the view that council had acted with "too much leniency" and increased the suspensions to a month each. An increase in penalty rather than mere confirmation, decrease, or even dismissal of penalty, was unprecedented (Montreal *Gazette*, February 1, 1989).

CONCLUSION

Overall, the police are subject to a multitude of imperfect and intermittently applied controls, both internal organizational checks, and external public quasi-political ones. No single one works adequately. Perhaps all may be necessary. There is disagreement, both among segments of the public, and to a lesser extent, among police themselves, on what are the most effective, objective, and fair controls. The weight of evidence suggests that the most effective assurance of satisfactory performance, as previously remarked, is to be had by competent recruit selection and training, and in the correct selection of properly trained and skilled managers. External bodies can respond to periodic, large-scale cases. Only an organization that is truly professional in all respects can respond to the myriad routine demands in a way that properly weighs and balances the powers of individual police officers.

ANNOTATED READINGS, CHAPTER NINE

Grant, Alan. *The Police—a Policy Paper.* Ottawa: Law Reform Commission of Canada, 1980. This widely read and influential monograph went through several editions. It considers the nature of democratic policing and relations of police organizations to democratic control and responsible social service.

Skolnick, Jerome H., and James J. Fyfe. *Above the Law.* New York: The Free Press, 1993. Dealing only with the American situation, this book offers a cogent analysis of police brutality. It also offers a realistic discussion of police accountability, including a discussion of the merits of civilian review boards.

Stenning, Phillip. *Police Commissons and Boards in Canada.* Toronto: University of Toronto Centre of Criminology, 1981. This is the most comprehensive account available of the power of police boards and commissions in Canada.

COMMUNITY POLICING

Contemporary policing and community policing have come in the 1990s to be uttered in the same breath. Reform, cost-effectiveness, and sensitivity are conveyed in the concept. Community policing in operation, however, means different things to different people. At times, it is mere public relations. Often it is just a superimposition upon traditional policing structure. But ideally community policing is a transformation of the police role and their relationship to the public.

Policing as we have been considering it has been around for about 170 years. The numbers of police officers have increased hugely, and they are no longer exclusively males. And the technologies have changed, permitting mobility and communications beyond the wildest conception of Peel's police. But the organizational format, and the conception of police work, has been remarkably consistent. The idea lodged initially with Peel's London Metropolitan, of police as part of viable communities, and not a band of enforcers foraying forth from Fort Apache, is essentially the notion that has motivated a reform sentiment that has touched all police services in Canada: community policing.

By the 1980s community policing had become the buzzword for reform-oriented policing. Some have criticized it as mere rhetoric and deception, a politically correct concept that is used, as Goldstein has put it, "without any concern for substance" (Herman Goldstein, in an address quoted by Kaminer, 1994:112). Others who are more prepared to concede that community policing represents a substantive change are concerned that it is a sinister development, a means whereby police extend their control, especially information control, under the guise of flexibility and partnership (Ericson, et al., 1993; Ericson, 1994; Ericson and Haggerty, 1997).

What, then, is all the fuss about? What is community policing? Why do "progressive" police services all profess a Community-Oriented Policing (COP) program? Has community policing been oversold? Does community policing consist of a thoroughgoing alteration of police organization and services, or is it some enhanced version of community relations, with show programs tagged onto the basic organization? Can community policing improve relations with the public, including minorities, and better realize the historic ideal of representing all of the public? Or is it an improved means to co-opt the public, and for the police to define and control events and information? And can community policing improve crime fighting, as has been claimed in complex jurisdictions such as New York City?

CONCEPT AND THEORY

The concept of community policing has become a sort of mantra, a symbol, and a philosophy, as well as a design and method for changing police organization and services. Commonly one encounters the notion that community policing represents a "paradigm-shift," a change

Ottawa Citizen, Bruno Schlumberger.

Bicycle patrol teams were introduced in Ottawa in 1990. (Reproduced by permission of the *Ottawa Citizen.*)

in the fundamental conception, vision, priorities, structure, and processes of policing (Gandz, 1990; Huey, 1991). Attempts to define community policing may appear rather hackneyed.

For example, numerous services in the United States and Canada have circulated an inventory of questions and answers intended to illustrate the differences between community and traditional policing. The answers, unfortunately, are pious and non-specific (see Table 10-1; see also Sparrow, 1988).

TABLE 10-1   Traditional vs. Community Policing: Questions and Answers

Question	Traditional Policing	Community Policing
Who are the police?	A government agency principally responsible for law enforcement.	Police are the public and the public are the police: the police officers are those who are paid to give full-time attention to the duties of every citizen.
What is the relationship of the police force to other public service departments?	Priorities often conflict.	The police are one department among many responsible for improving the quality of life.
What is the role of the police?	Focusing on solving crimes.	A broader problem-solving approach.
How is policy efficiency measured?	By detection and arrest rates.	By the absence of crime and disorder.
What are the highest priorities?	Crimes that are high value (e.g., bank robberies) and those involving violence.	Whatever problems disturb the community most.
What, specifically, do police deal with?	Incidents.	Citizens' problems and concerns.
What determines the effectiveness of police?	Response times.	Public cooperation.
What view do police take of service calls?	Deal with them only if there is no real police work to do.	Vital function and great opportunity.
What is police professionalism?	Swift effective response to serious crime.	Keeping close to the community.
What kind of intelligence is most important?	Crime intelligence (study of particular crimes or series of crimes).	Criminal intelligence (information about the activities of individuals or groups).
What is the essential nature of police accountability?	Highly centralized; governed by rules, regulations, and policy directives; accountable to the law.	Emphasis on local accountability to community needs.
What is the role of headquarters?	To provide the necessary rules and policy directives.	To preach organizational values.
What is the role of the press liaison department?	To keep the "heat" off operational officers so they can get on with the job.	To coordinate an essential channel of communication with the community.
How do the police regard prosecutions?	As an important goal.	As one tool among many.

Source: Ottawa Police Service, 1990.

Policing became progressively centralized through the century, and successfully appealed to the public for funding by stressing a crime-fighting role. But this traditional reactive crime-control model of police service was challenged for some years. Ideas concerning an amended policing, one that engaged police in a constructive fashion in the community and that took some initiative in preventing instead of simply reacting to crime, began to develop. Related concepts had been part of the policing vocabulary for many years: team policing, zone policing, village policing, problem-oriented policing, and storefront policing all have had currency. Especially Goldstein's work (1990) on problem-oriented policing has stimulated the development of the alternative model.

Arguably the police are at the limits of conventional enforcement and prevention except as there are coordinated public responses to social problems; and the police are being invited, de facto, to assume a leadership role in this coordination. Very explicitly, for example, in the Netherlands, a National Police Coordination Centre representing the Netherlands' police services has stressed the front-line role of police in acting with government and other agencies in crime prevention (Horn, 1991:129).

Some conspicuous failure in police ability to curtail criminal violations in major urban centres, coupled with fiscal pressures, perhaps left the police themselves looking for a new angle. Relatively rapidly, over a period of perhaps 20 years, the notion of community-based policing spread through North America and abroad. In part, in the United States, there were conspicuous crises, as in Los Angeles or New York City, that prompted the adoption of a reform slogan, if not a reform methodology. But even in the absence of major crises in Canada police agencies have embraced the concept. It possessed cachet, the aura of fiscally responsible change.

Police services were not immune to public and political sentiment, promoting at one and the same time improved service and reduced costs. In Canada and the United States private and public organizations, from IBM or General Motors to Ontario Hydro or any of our universities, have had to appraise and amend organizational and management structure, product, and service. Many of the changes stress client needs and satisfaction and the empowerment and "skilling" of employees; so too does community policing. The organizational shift to community policing in the city of Halifax in the late 1980s, for example, was approached in the philosophical or theoretical context of "quality of working life" (QWL) for police personnel as well as improved relations with the public (Clairmont, 1990:18-21).

Conservative opinion, traditionally supportive of policing, was definitely pressing for something other than the same old thin blue police line, and in a sense, conservative and liberal opinion met in community policing. Where problem-oriented policing invoked rather liberal notions of prevention, local sensitivity, community development, and general "community wellness," more conservative critics of the justice system stressed attention to social disorder and "broken windows." Problem-oriented policing (Goldstein, 1990) and zero tolerance broken windows policing (Wilson and Kelling, 1982) converged. Dealing with the evident signs of disorder, such as vandalism, graffiti, and street prostitution—the broken windows—which were being ignored by police as petty and not real crime fighting, not only would serve some of the priority needs of disadvantaged communities, it also would oblige police to get back into those communities.

Conceptual shift or revolution, however, not to mention real organizational change, are easier stated and sought than achieved in altered tasks and organization, and the vaunted shift to community policing has lacked a precision in operation. Accordingly there is considerable variance in the extent to which the concept is grasped, attempted, and evaluated in Canadian police services (Kennedy, 1991:280–282), as is also true in the United States (Moore, 1992: 127–139). Undeniably, even as there have been monitored programs in community policing in Canada (Normandeau, 1993), such as Edmonton (Koller, 1990; Hornick et al., 1993), Victoria (Walker and Walker, 1989; Walker et al., 1992), and Halifax (Clairmont, 1990), there persists some lack of specificity in the very idea, its implementation, and the results.

The easiest thing about community policing, it often seemed, was for police managers to say it was being done. But while senior managers, as in the RCMP, might proclaim community policing, members would remain skeptical, or even hostile (as internal surveys showed), and existing bureaucracy and procedure would inhibit the innovations necessary. In a serious statement that might be read as self-parody, in the RCMP Commissioner's 1996–1997 "Directional Statement" to members, it is stated as a success that the Force has been "removing the barriers to community policing and to individual decision-making." This was done, apparently, in the course of policy review begun in 1995, which had reduced 13 000 pages in manuals to 11 900 pages (RCMP Web site, January 12, 1998)!

Community policing has found its way into many police mission statements, such as those of the RCMP and the OPP; the latter speak of community partnerships, communication, and prevention. In Ontario, uniquely, community policing is vaguely suggested in the Police Services Act, where it is stated that there is "the need for sensitivity to the pluralistic, multiracial, and multicultural character of Ontario society" and "the need to ensure that police forces are representative of the communities they serve" (1993:5). In Ontario police services, therefore, even as there may be some uncertainty as to precise legislated intent, the imperatives of multicultural and community sensitivity encouraged police administrations and boards to at least state that they are doing community policing.

An inventory of basic features of a community policing organization could include: targeting identifiable neighbourhoods or communities; striking a balance between reactive "crackdown" policing and collaborative preventive policing; stable, full-time assignment of police officers to the community; empowering these officers to make police and operational decisions as to how to use and prioritize their time; frequent consultation, informal contact, and "partnerships" with community residents and agencies; familiarization of police with community residents and features; using citizen volunteers; police personnel with interpersonal and speaking skills; a proactive or problem-solving agenda, and, least often found, department-wide commitment and implementation, including deployment of most field personnel within a decentralized community policing system. To achieve these, community policing will almost certainly also involve foot patrol, and local police "storefront" stations. Not often mentioned or found in Canada, and yet a remarkably simple device to accommodate the realities of motor patrol and community foot patrol, is the advantage of "park and walk," whereby a police patrol vehicle becomes a mobile platform or station. Additionally, because of the local preoccupation, also needed is effective support by the larger police organization in collecting, sharing, and analyzing information on the community, from basic "scanning" of community demographic characteristics to incident reports (Greene and Mastrofski, 1988; Murphy and Muir, 1985).

In fully implemented community policing, the street-level or community police officer has broad responsibilities within the community, including opportunities to fashion priorities and to pursue investigations rather than turn them over to detectives. Yet, on the other

hand, when community policing does not develop beyond an add-on to the traditional policing structure, community officers tend to be viewed by their peers as doing "soft" and non-
prestigious policing.

None of this means that police would not also continue to do much of what they have previously done. That is, while the community policing literature tends to be critical of less
than department-wide patrol decentralization, it is not clear that such thoroughgoing decentralization is necessary. The balance to be found is between centralized coordination
and resources, and local flexibility and adaptability. There is also a balance to be found between inevitable reactive crime-control policing, and proactive and service-oriented policing. There is no use pretending that traditional reactive functions will disappear, although
priorities and responses will alter. Community policing is not itself a panacea; it is, though,
a strategy or model for change.

In a basic sense, for police to engage in community policing, not only must the police organization and the work of police officers change, the police must discover and even in-
vent or reinvent the communities, whether understood as locales or social subgroups! This
statement is not intended to be cute; it must be seriously considered that police, perhaps
rather more implicitly than explicitly, are singled out as the service agency in our society with
the highest profile and public confidence-level and also the best organized. The police are
therefore called upon to take a point-position in what is in effect social reconstruction or social integration (Forcese, 1993; 1994). Despite some police perception of being unremit-
tingly subject to harsh public criticism, it may be recalled that to a degree not experienced
by other occupations, professions, or organizations, police are held in very high and measurable public regard, and accorded a good deal of confidence in their ability to intervene socially.

IMPLEMENTING COMMUNITY POLICING

Some of what passes today for community policing has been around for a long time.
Community relations programs and police-initiated nominal partnership programs with communities have been in place since the 1960s. At first, as the concept of community policing
began to circulate, the community relations efforts were trotted out as illustration that "we're
already doing it." All municipal police have operated outreach or community service programs,
usually as sub-unit operations within the organizational structure. Initially these were, by
and large, packaged programs, that is, standardized measures that had been attempted in the
United States, and were mimicked in Canadian jurisdictions. These programs have allowed
police to avoid basic reorganization of service, and have been implemented with varying
vigour and success. Although they encourage community organizing to a small degree, by and
large they are sensitization or simplistic educational programs that do not alter the degree
or nature of contacts between community members and the police.

The Ottawa Police Force, for example, in 1985 listed 25 special programs of a preven-
tion or public service character. The list included Neighbourhood Watch, Operation
Identification, Residential Security Evaluations, Business Security Evaluations, Armed
Robbery Prevention, Operation Bike Identification, Cheque and Credit Card Fraud advice,
Operation Provident, Block Parent Program, Protection for Senior Citizens, Shoplifting lec-
ture, Vehicle Security advice, Police Venturer program (with Scouts Canada), Law Awareness
Program, Missing Children and Youth Programs, Bomb Threats advice, High Rise Security,

Alarm Systems, Vandalism advice, Internal Theft awareness, Victim Service/Crisis Intervention, Youth Patrol. Youth Intervention, Sexual Assault Awareness, and Environmental Design, most of which were presented in pamphlet form. Other public relations events, such as Police Week, Crime Prevention Week, and performances by the Police Chorus and the Pipes and Drums Band, were also identified.

In 1983 the solicitor general of Canada declared November 4 to 10 to be annual National Crime Prevention Week. In 1984 that federal office published in news insert format an item entitled "Good Neighbours: Looking Out for Each Other," and a handbook for interested persons who wished to do something in the way of crime prevention. The initiatives were intended to elicit community participation in self-help. In the paper they listed existing crime prevention programs: Block Clubs, a neighbourhood group designated to receive crime prevention information; Block Parents, probably the most familiar and successful measure, where residences are identified by a conspicuously placed card as havens for neighbourhood children; Watch programs, wherein block "captains" and other residents or apartment dwellers are urged to attend to features of their environment, noting hazards and unusual features for police or residents' attention; Neighbourhood Directories, with full address information for block watches; Street Observation, consisting of systematic patrol of neighbourhoods by residents and/or police, looking for occasions of risk or crime; identification programs such Operation Identification, where possessions are inscribed with an identification number to facilitate tracing in cases of theft, with notice of the inscriptions displayed to deter theft; Special Volunteer Service, with "trained" volunteers accompanying seniors or crime victims (Canada, 1984a:2).

The effectiveness of such programs was never properly measured. Crime prevention benefits are asserted, and public relations benefits are assumed. The programs are relatively well defined, as they have had the problems ironed out, and do not intrude upon the basic character of police personnel utilization. Similar efforts of a more reactive nature, such as Crime Stoppers, where public appeals and rewards are announced for information leading to the arrest and conviction of an offender, are also stubbornly defended by police. A recent Canadian research enquiry found that there is no convincing statistical evidence that the program leads to solving of crime. The "crime of the week" was often sensational and a popular item with viewers, but the reward system may have delayed spontaneous imparting of information in anticipation of financial reward, concluded the researchers, even while the overall solution rate attributable to the program was very slight, probably well under 8% (Carriere and Ericson, 1989). Yet police persist in the program; in Ottawa, while admitting that as many as 30% of informants in the program would have reported the crime in the absence of the reward system, police insisted that the research findings were incorrect and that the program would be retained (*Ottawa Citizen*, March 18, 1989).

As programs such as these were being publicized and attempted, research suggested that a majority of Canadians believed that crime was on the increase in their cities, although a minority, about one-third, believed there to be an increase in their own neighbourhoods only (Canada, 1984d:2). Large numbers of Canadians also reported being fearful of walking alone in their own neighbourhoods after dark, especially in the cities of Montreal, Halifax/Dartmouth, and Winnipeg—even where the rate of personal crime was not consistant with the proportion of persons expressing fear. For example, Montreal is popularly perceived as a crime-ridden city, but the rate of personal crime is among the lowest of Canadian cities. Women have a greater fear of victimization. The elderly are one-sixth as likely as other adult Canadians to be victims of crime, but were more fearful. Segments of the population obviously feel vulnerable, and generalize from secondhand and media images of crime (Canada 1984d: 3–5; 1985a: 1–5; 1985c: 1–5). It is reasonable to infer, then, that community self-help programs, with the usual attendant publicity to increase awareness, increase fear of crime and of personal safety. Yet research suggests that media publicity does not mobilize community members in prevention programs; rather, police attempts are most successful when working with established leaders and organizations.

Some more programs have been attempted. One was PRIDE (Prevention, Respect, Identification, Determination), operated in Gravenhurst, Ontario, with the assistance of the OPP to reduce vandalism. A committee of citizen volunteers worked with school children, and local business and voluntary associations, with the result of a reported 40% reduction in vandalism over the first year of operation (Canada, 1984a:3). Similar programs have been implemented in other communities such as Brantford, with teens employed to patrol parks, as well as attending in-school educational programs.

In Edmonton, a "Cooperative Policing Program" has worked since 1982 to achieve collaboration among retailers and security personnel in shopping malls. Pertinent elements of the program include monitoring offences, information exchange, and more generally, effective dependence upon security personnel rather than upon police for reports and investigation; costs and police investigation time for shoplifting have been reduced (*Liaison*, January 1986: 9–12).

In Calgary the Citizen Police Academy was inaugurated in 1986. For three hours in the evening over ten weeks Calgary citizens attend the Calgary policy training facility or accompany police officers while on duty. The program, a novel element of the Calgary community-based policing commitment, is managed by the Community Service Section and intended to enhance citizen understanding of policing in Calgary.

Another affirmative illustration of an innovative preventative program to be had from the city of Calgary deals with seniors. Responding to the problem of real and perceived threat to seniors, the police have developed a Senior Liaison Program. The program, consisting of lectures and the training of seniors for self-help, deals with abuse, suicide, home security, and other matters of common concern (Montreal *Gazette*, June 5, 1988).

Some police services initiated family consultant programs, as in the London Police Force. Civilian personnel are available to help with some domestic problems. The concept is premised upon the rapid intervention provided by police services, with the all-hours availability of police personnel. Once the immediate crisis is attended to, a family consultant may be called in, and in turn, a referral to a social service agency is possible.

These local initiatives began to feature in more thoroughgoing attempts to implement real community policing, as contrasted to community relations and packaged crime prevention. Such improvisations and experiments were useful, because what came to be called community policing never had a firm template. In fact, real community policing must allow for local customized options, built upon a core conception of community and community needs.

Doing community policing depends upon an informed definition of community. Existing political boundaries may be too arbitrary. In delivering community policing, collecting information (community intelligence) or "environmental scanning" is an elemental process; so too in the set-up phase, in defining communities, the quality of information regarding so-called communities is elemental to the designation of areas and the appropriate police services plan. If community is understood to be geographic, the space and the inhabitants have to be mapped, or if community is taken to refer to a social subgroup, such as an ethnic population, the population and cultural characteristics must be mapped. The two tend to coincide. The Canadian Association of Chiefs of Police have noted that community policing is especially important in improving contacts with members of visible minority communities (CACP, 1992). The CACP, as have most major police services, has developed "how-to" manuals that stress means to encourage citizen participation, although they tend to stop short of addressing major alterations in their own organizations.

In committing to community designations, sheer size must be weighed as a factor. The size of a jurisdiction and the perceived sub-communities, the extent of differentiation, and the nature of the political and non-political local organizations, will affect any police attempts to deliver community policing. A community for purposes of a policing zone must be manageable.

Community profiles need to be developed (Ontario, 1991) and the correct identification of community leaders and influential citizens for purposes of co-planning and service consultation is itself a critical matter for careful contemplation and action. If the community partners are arbitrarily or superficially designated on the basis of "squeaky wheel" local prominence, or perhaps the local business person willing to donate space and equipment, representative community contacts might not only be missed, but barriers erected.

In Halifax, for example, the Halifax Police Department was deployed to police three "zones," and inevitably there was a high degree of differentiation or heterogeneity within the "communities" that affected the ability of police to coordinate effectively with residents. The more homogeneity, the greater is the ability to integrate the police service. The downtown area, with a more transient population, was less evidently a successful community zone than suburban areas. So too in Edmonton, community policing is more evidently successful in residential areas (Hornick et al., 1993:90).

In Victoria, for example, five areas or "communities" were identified. In each of Halifax and Victoria, one area incorporated the city core of transient residents, commuters, businesses, and entertainment sites; that is, an area not generally constituting community as the concept is usually understood, and probably not as amenable as more stable residential areas to the techniques of community-based policing. Community policing cannot transform the management of problems in high intensity urban core areas with a high proportion of transients or persons who are in no sense residents or members of a local community (Walker et al., 1992:97).

Urban areas are distinguishable and call for distinguishable police responses. In general, community policing must allow for variance in police response, as all community areas are not created equally. As recognized in Victoria, in urban core areas not only might there be unique police responses and programs, a practice fully intended in the decentralized community policing model, there probably need also be distinct evaluative measures (Walker and Walker, 1989).

Given reasonably designated communities, it is generally agreed that the necessary components of community policing include stable police assignment in the definable geographic territory or community; a focus upon community relations in the sense of interactive communications, consultation, and cooperation; an emphasis upon crime prevention and proactive policing; a decentralization of police organizational authority and the traditional bureaucratic hierarchy; fewer role specializations; and a greater use of the front-line police officer as a generalist, whose tasks include criminal investigation (Wasson, 1975: 22–25; Ontario, 1991; Kennedy, 1991; Forcese, 1993:118–122, 286–287).

The community policing expectation of stable assignment of police personnel mirrors the intent to know and to work with local area residents. That is, the police officers in an area are expected to become familiar with a zone and its inhabitants, and vice versa. The police themselves are not to be transients. It is also desirable to have stable and readily identifiable police offices or buildings in the local area, rather than minor ancillary facilities, characteristically ad hoc and often uninviting, especially in the start-up phase of decentralized community policing.

Moreover, in this stable capacity, the police are expected to have decentralized responsibility for the area. That is, the highly specialized and centralized police organizations are to be altered by way of more local responsibility, and more authority and responsibility, including some investigatory, vested in the police constable or patrol officer. The individual officer has more responsibility, but additionally in the community area, the officers are expected to work within a cooperative local team definition or structure.

Organization problems therefrom arise for traditional management, but also for traditional police job expectations, including, perhaps above all, for detectives and criminal investigations units, although it is not evident that these should or can be displaced. The above characteristics—decentralized control and the generalist role—are intended to enhance communications and the quality of contact and work with members of the public, a nostalgic reinvention of the precinct system of policing, as there is also a reinvention of the often idealized community. Parenthetically it may be remarked, there is some (much less than unanimous) opinion that to make the quality community contacts, the community area officers must, in greater frequency, be on foot patrol rather than committed to vehicular patrol (Greene and Taylor, 1988).

Community policing depends upon enhanced police–public communications and other contacts. The implication generally understood is of police personnel in more frequent benign and consultative communications with members of a "community." The contacts are to be at all levels, with front-line personnel and not just command-rank personnel engaging members of the community, and interacting with persons other than elected political representatives, offenders, or victims (Roach, 1986:86). This engagement or communication may occur not only in the street, but in the committee and boardrooms of corporate and civic organizations within the communities. Related to enhanced communications, preventive policing will involve greater police participation in municipal policy-making and the activities of other public services. Examples include participation with educators, or with urban and social planners (see Lunney, 1989: 204–205). Police participation in youth education and immigrant education, in building design, and in client referrals to support agencies would all be expected to become frequent and normative. Thoroughgoing police engagement in the policy formulation and services of the community is intended to meet the basic community policing expectation of more preventive policing and general assistance to the public, as distinct from law enforcement and criminal investigation.

In part, in community policing police are doing more at the same time as they are diverting workload to other persons and agencies. Not only do community officers refer problems to other "helping professionals," they also employ citizen volunteers. Volunteers relieve police officers of some of the administrative burden of the job, such as complaint and report taking. The volunteer has become integral to community policing and to many Differential Police Response systems, wherein calls for service are prioritized, and often receive the attention, especially initially, of a civilian volunteer rather than a police officer (Lewis-Horne and Forcese, 1993).

The police–public contacts and communications are expected to be two-way or interactive, with public views influencing the police service as contrasted to a circumstance where segments of the public are passive recipients of police-derived information. There is reason to state that this is one of the most difficult conditions to meet. Even as patrol-level contacts and speaking engagements may increase, there is a tendency for the public to defer to the police as "experts," and for police themselves, accustomed to being in control, to be impatient of discussion, advice, and criticism. Also the police organization may not have in place the resources and skills to collect, collate, analyze, and disseminate information available from public participation (Seagrave, 1992; Tremblay and Rochon, 1991). A deliberate program of environmental scanning, with analysis of available information such as that from local media, and the generation of additional representative information though means such as information surveys or polls, appear as requisites to enhance other routine information gathering.

Returning to the idea of paradigm-shift and the rhetoric or language of community policing, as the policing task becomes more service- and client-oriented, some of the terminology of traditional paramilitary policing, in reference to the public and perhaps in regard to internal organization designations of ranks, or of the community zones or areas themselves, should become "civilianized" and convey the objective that has been called "total quality service." To illustrate, perhaps trivially, one American police force deleted from its motto the conventional reference "to protect" in order to highlight "to serve" (Galloway and Fitzgerald, 1992:5). Or to illustrate the absence of such a language shift, in Halifax the three community policing zones are encumbered with the paramilitary labels Alpha, Bravo, and Charlie, failing to symbolize for the public any community identification through labelling.

Given all of the above, the essence of the change to community policing is the downloading of tasks to the front-line police officers who are associated with the designated communities. Consider the conventionally agreed upon police functions of response, enforcement, crime solving, prevention, referral, and public education. Where in the traditional policing mode only the first two of these functions will be associated with the traditional front-line patrol officer, in community policing all six functions are part of the job (Clairmont, 1990: 42). In particular, the community police officer becomes more than a reactive "complaints-taker." For decades there has been speculation, largely wishful, about the police officer as "professional," wherein actually, in traditional policing, the officer, and especially the patrol officer, in doing very limited and segmented work, has been rather more like a piece-worker than a professional. Community policing, however, does genuinely allow for, and require, the front-line police officer to be a professional.

RESULTS

The results from community policing, indicated in some field experiences, are tentative and inconclusive. There are informal indications of some short-term successes attached to local police–community initiatives. In Toronto, for example, Division 51 of the Metro Police, referred to as "the valley of career death," is a notoriously difficult multi-ethnic working-class area. The police have been viewed by residents as racist, and there have been overt conflicts, including a brawl with police in August, 1996. Also, following an incident involving two young black men, television reporters, and two Division 51 police officers, and a deputy chief's decision to charge the officers despite a favourable report by the provincial Police Complaints Bureau, the police assigned to the division went on strike for eight hours in protest. Subsequently a new officer was put in charge, professing a commitment to community policing, and talking with and respecting residents. Describing community policing as old-style policing, the new command officer has been credited with improved police–public relations, as the literature on community policing would suggest, and there is apparently renewed confidence and satisfaction among the police officers in the Division (*Toronto Star*, January 27, 1996). As reported in the research literature, "police forces under local community control are more effective in meeting demands for neighbourhood police protection than is a large city-wide controlled police department" (Friedmann, 1992:69). Community policing in a sense attempts to reintroduce local control within a large department. In this extreme circumstance, a change in command philosophy and style, under the banner of community policing, has apparently achieved some affirmative results. Yet it cannot be concluded that there are substantive changes that will endure.

A similar indicator that at least suggests an aspect of community policing philosophy in action is to be had from Montreal. In a slum area of the city, Centre-Sud, plagued by prostitution, gangs and drug-dealing, neighbourhood residents and police have collaborated in efforts to clean up the neighborhood—to repair the "broken windows." Two MUC Police have been assigned to the neighbourhood full time, a stable assignment as is expected in community policing, and work the area on foot. Again, scant indicators of success are to be had, but there is some greater community cooperation, despite skepticism by other police and by residents (*Globe and Mail*, September 9, 1997).

Similar illustrations can be found in the United States. In Aurora, Illinois, it is reported that two police officers, assigned full time, working door-to-door, helped organize residents in a community to resist drug-dealing gangs. Similar planned police–resident cooperative efforts in cities such as Georgetown, Texas, Kansas City, and Reno appear also to have met with some short-term success (*USA Today*, January 26, 1996).

These are, however, merely indications of benefits associated with a community program, and not illustrative of benefits of general community policing. There is a disconcerting lack of systematic evaluation of the piecemeal attempts to implement elements of community policing, although some serious evaluations have been attempted in the United States, and in Canada. Findings tend to be a hodgepodge. In part this is because there have not been well-conceived formal evaluation measures of outcomes, or because too little time has passed with community policing in place. In part, too, tentativeness in regard to findings relates to not really knowing whether police services have really gone far enough in the changes to have achieved genuine measurable effects.

Aggregating information from several Canadian cities, one observer reports that community policing does improve public attitudes and reduce fear of crime, and also actually reduces crime (Normandeau, 1993). There is also some guarded information as to increased police job satisfaction, but also findings suggesting that officers may cling to their self-conception as crime fighters, as found in Halifax four years after city-wide community policing (Perrott and Taylor, 1995). In a city that has led in community policing, Victoria, with a system of community stations modelled after a program in Detroit, there is weak evidence of improved public satisfaction and reduced fear of crime (Walker and Walker, 1989; 1992). Edmonton has arguably become the leading influence in Canadian community policing. The police work from four divisions and twelve community stations, with an emphasis upon foot patrol. Some fairly detailed findings are available, highlighted by evidence that neighbourhood foot patrol officers (NFPs) reported higher job satisfaction, and had more citizen contacts, including time spent with volunteers and representatives of other community agencies, than did other patrol constables. The community officers spend a smaller proportion of their time dealing with specific offence incidents, suggesting that they were more preventive than reactive in their work (Hornick et al., 1993:78–89). Insofar as impact on crime, the Edmonton police themselves estimate a major reduction in violent crime and in property crime, and claim a crime rate reduction twice as great as that of 10 major Canadian cities (Edmonton Police, *Annual Report*, 1996).

Some key outcome areas should be anticipated from a general review of North American literature. In the first instance, public satisfaction with policing may be expected to improve, including public perceptions of safety (Kennedy, 1991:282–287; Peak et al., 1992; Walker et al., 1992:67–70). The cooperative and consultative relations with residents, including targeted subgroups such as seniors, should favourably influence perceptions.

Secondly, the preventive orientation of community policing, along with the consultative relations and inter-agency cooperation, may be expected to influence crime rates and solutions (Walker and Walker, 1989:10–23). However, any shift in reported offences and clearances poses a somewhat complicated problem insofar as indicators of community policing success. Generalist constable investigators, for example, especially in the earlier phases of a community-based system, may suffer from lack of training, inexperience, and problems in overall workload management, in turn potentially adversely affecting public confidence and willingness to report offences. Alternately, reported offences may increase rather than decrease, in that the closer contacts of community policing and increased public confidence may be expected to encourage greater public willingness to report violations (Clairmont, 1990; Kennedy, 1991:282–283). As well, offence rates may increase as a reflection of the "expanded police mandate" (Koenig, 1991:35) that is a feature of contemporary policing and particularly associated with community policing. Police, as a consequence of better community-based information, may "clear" more reported violations by laying charges; or they may, because of better coordination with community-based social services, refer more persons for assistance rather than invoking the criminal justice system.

Third, community policing may be expected and has been shown to result in increased police job satisfaction (Clairmont, 1990; Walker et al., 1992). The decentralization and broadening of responsibilities associated with community policing constitute a "skilling" of the front-line police officer, and an extension of professional responsibilities. Increased job satisfaction should be most pronounced among younger constables, as greater task responsibilities are provided. There is no avoiding the fact that the increased satisfaction will vary with factors such as age, time in career, and in some measure, by rank and present job function. As some number of specialized roles are eliminated, new career opportunities—and new prestige opportunities—have to be made available, and eventually be referenced into collective agreements.

Probably indicative of increased satisfaction has been a finding of reduced sick leave days. Yet, it must fairly be noted also that there is some indication that the greater emphasis upon proactive and generalist work, while appreciated by most, and especially by "beat" or foot officers in more frequent public contact, if not reinforced with an effective system of evaluation, recognition, and promotion, may be found to be insufficiently exciting or rewarding.

Lastly, there is reason to acknowledge that the community policing system can initially be paper intensive, especially in the absence of established new procedures: more contacts, more notes, more reports. New demands for coordination and communication occur, taken up at least temporarily by a flurry of meetings, memoranda, guidelines, and reports. Workloads may increase, or be perceived to increase, as new tasks are assumed by front-line personnel. It is not unusual to find demand for additional personnel, and there is evidence of some increase in civilian employees in support roles. In addition there is experience of some increase in the number of non-commissioned officers, and a comparable decrease in commissioned officers, as local coordinating needs are associated with the decentralized duties assigned to front-line officers (Clairmont, 1990:76–78).

REFLECTIONS

Characteristically, in Canada and in the United States, the rhetoric of community policing has been an aspect of police public relations. It suggests reform, progressive management, and community sensitivity. Isolated measures, such as community meetings, storefront stations, bicycle patrols, even some number of foot beats, have met with some approval. And more thoroughgoing community policing is reported to increase public and police satisfaction. But generally too little has been implemented to really have been evaluated, or even noticed, by the public.

In the United States, dramatic credit is attached to community policing in New York City, where crime rates have been declining. Yet, there is no reason to accept such claims, especially as other factors are as convincingly evident, such as zero-tolerance policing or even the stabilization and normalization of the drug trade. Across the continent, in Los Angeles, with a police force at odds with a reform chief, the introduction of community policing was adjudged a failure—a failure because in contrast to the previous aggressive policing style fewer arrests were being made (*Globe and Mail*, March 16, 1996).

Even as community policing has been essentially superficial, and perhaps partly explaining the tentative implementation, most police officers do not genuinely believe in the model. It is "soft" policing. As senior managers attempt to implement it, rank-and-file and junior officers resist. In Canada a report leaked to the media indicated that many RCMP officers, and especially senior officers—older members—considered community policing "soft on crime and overrated," and as diverting resources from "crime control" (*Ottawa Citizen*, September 16, 1996). The resistance in part is rational, as middle-management jobs are often at stake as the organization is "flattened" to allow decentralization, while patrol officers find their jobs change and new skills are required. Hence the resistance, and conflict with chiefs of police becomes more prevalent.

Police are being challenged to be more open, more collaborative, and more professional (Sparrow et al., 1990). Yet somewhat ironically but inevitably, as the police services accept the more or less explicit invitation to assume a leadership role and to be service, information, and policy proactive in their communities, they open themselves to new criticisms, or at least, new versions of old criticisms, such as that of political meddling or, as has recently been argued by Ericson (1989; Ericson et al., 1993), of information control and manipulation. Academic opinion, which had almost unqualifiedly been advocating community policing, begins to assume a more traditional critical role. There is also concern that with decentralization, police will become less accountable to the general public, and perhaps in their local zeal become less rather than more professional (Moore, 1992:103).

The practice of community policing hangs in the balance. Substantive changes and benefits, for citizens and for police personnel, have to be demonstrated. If not, the promise of community policing will dissipate. Presently there is no great groundswell of public awareness or support. And internal police opinion is divided, with nominal management commitment, and union reservation if not hostility. Most police jobs are still as they have been; that may not alter.

ABORIGINAL POLICING

Community policing was conceived for urban settings. But it has been adapted, as is readily possible, to rural areas. One of the most promising expressions of community policing is probably what is being attempted in many Canadian native or First Nations communities. Historically policing of native persons in their own communities has been assigned to the state police, such as Quebec's Sûreté, the OPP, and elsewhere the RCMP. Canadian history is replete with crises. And more generally there has long been awareness of the very high rate of incarceration of native peoples, usually for minor public order offences.

For decades there have been attempts to develop appropriate on-site policing models, and they are presently in transition. As early as 1973 the RCMP attempted a Special Constable Program, with indifferent success. In 1978 a Native Policing Branch was created at RCMP headquarters in Ottawa to coordinate programs for native policing (*Liaison*, 1976:4–7). Native persons were trained by the RCMP to police reserves under the control of the local RCMP detachment, and therefore did not have local autonomy. By 1990 about 300 communities in Canada (except New Brunswick, Quebec, and Ontario) had the experience of about 250 RCMP special constables (Canada, 1990:29). And in 1990 the program was discontinued.

By the same period, in Ontario, about 65 communities were served by 132 native constables, responsible for by-law enforcement and for the criminal code, under the authority of the OPP. The Indian Special Constable Program in Ontario was started in 1975 (Canada, 1990:29). Similarly, in Quebec an Amerindian Police Program worked 23 communities with about 73 constables. Additionally, a native Peacekeepers program has operated since 1968 in Kahnawake, and another since 1985 in Maniwaki (Canada, 1990: 32–41).

In all of these programs the native constables were subject to the authority of the senior police force, and tended only to be responsible for local by-law or band law enforcement. The personnel were selected by the senior force, and trained by them, and sometimes have had regular policing experience.

Increasingly more powers are being assigned to native police in Canada, including considerable federal/provincial cooperation in Quebec. In 1996, for example, the federal and Quebec governments signed an agreement with the Huron First Nations. Policing a small community in the suburbs of Quebec city, the former native special constables were given full policing powers; costs are shared between Quebec and the Government of Canada (*Ottawa Citizen*, January 19, 1996). Significantly, too, Oka, the site of a major crisis in 1990, now operates a Mohawk police force, also paid for by Quebec and the federal government (*Ottawa Citizen*, November 2, 1997). By 1998 at least 49 native communities had signed agreements with the Quebec and the federal governments to provide community policing, under the auspices of a community Public Security Committee (*Relations: A Bulletin from the Canadian Centre for Police-Race Relations*, November 1997:3). And in Ontario, effective April 1998, a vast northern region of the province was assigned to a 100-person aboriginal police service. The territory policed was reported to be the largest in the world for which an aboriginal police service had responsibility (CBC National Radio News, April 2, 1998).

In establishing more autonomous aboriginal police, an original intent of "culturally sensitive policing service" (Canada, 1990:23) is realized by providing sworn community members in collaboration with community residents. This is an expression of what in Canadian urban communities is being described as community policing.

CONCLUSION

Generally much more has been claimed for community policing than can demonstrably be proven. Most jurisdictions have merely implemented one or a few community-oriented programs, such as storefront offices, superimposed upon the traditional police organization. While Edmonton and Victoria may be remarked as exemplars in Canada—and certainly former Edmonton personnel have been almost missionary in their work—it would not be possible to claim department-wide community policing implementation in Canada. Nor, therefore, can it be said that department-wide community policing would be an improvement.

It just feels like it should be.

ANNOTATED READINGS, CHAPTER TEN

Canadian Centre for Police–Race Relations. *Community Policing: Interesting Practices*. Ottawa, 1994. This monograph does not attempt to distinguish full-service community policing from standalone preventive and community-based programs. But it does inventory programs attempted in police services across the country, with particular regard to race relations. It includes contact persons and addresses and a decent bibliography.

Rosenbaum, Dennis P. (ed.). *The Challenge Of Community Policing: Testing The Promises*. Beverly Hills: Sage Publications 1994. The 20 papers in this book allow an appreciation of the community policing concept versus implementation and achievement. Most of the work described is from the United States, but there is also a chapter reviewing progress in Canada.

ISSUES AND CHANGES: A POSTSCRIPT

This brief concluding chapter is a form of postscript. Unresolved tensions and developments in policing are briefly contemplated, grouped under the thematic headings of privatization, education and technology, and organizational style. Some future developments are posed. There are many unresolved issues and changes arising from policing as described in the previous chapters. We have selected some of these as portents of future developments, and group them as issues of privatization education/technology; and organizational style. Within these broad headings we can revisit the basic police–public tension between representative and accountable policing and relatively autonomous and special interests-based policing.

Several thousand words ago this book began with a discussion about the idea of public policing. And throughout there have been frequent references to the theme that the police are our agents, our public servants. They are granted considerable latitude, and must be monitored and directed; they are an imperfect attempt to represent and to protect the interests of all persons conforming to the laws of Canadian society. The "public" in "public police" is of vital importance.

The most severe challenges facing public policing are not the ongoing problems associated with police–citizen interactions, nor the continually renewed efforts of the public to regulate police conduct. These are, in a sense, normal challenges. There is no crisis of police conduct in Canada, no crisis of public confidence. In fact, there is a broadly shared consensus among police and public as to appropriate behaviour, even though there may be some disagreement about regulatory procedure. Ongoing tensions are an expression of the major challenge: the preservation and renewal of the very concept of the public police.

So much of what we have considered in policing, whether regulatory procedures, recruit selection and training, or community policing, has to do with attempts to enhance, if not perfect, the police as public servants. Sometimes, however, the introduction of new practices may undermine that quite special social institution.

PRIVATIZATION

A pervasive theme in our society through the 1990s has been cost reduction. At times in history the police have seemed to be immune from normal fiscal restraint, because of an insatiable public demand, fuelled by police rhetoric, for more law enforcement. But in the 1990s the police, like other institutions large and small, have had to attend to cost effectiveness. Arguably, this encouraged some rather friendly innovations that might otherwise have been resisted, such as community policing. But hand in glove with economies have come some possibly dysfunctional changes, such as forms of privatization. Privatization may be considered first in its association with the actions of the public police, and second in the continued development of private policing in Canada.

Public Police

There has long been a practice of off-duty police officers being employed by some organization (such as a football club), to provide uniformed security service. Most police contracts now recognize and delimit such work. Usually such off-duty policing appears innocuous, perhaps even in the public interest; yet at some point questions of propriety and conflict of interest occur. An off-duty stipend for policing a public event such as a football game perhaps can be differentiated from working for a particular client to investigate individual members of the public. In British Columbia, insurance companies have paid off-duty police to run impaired-driving spot checks (*Toronto Star*, January 25, 1996), which may have a general public interest, but was certainly calculated as having a business value to claims-paying insurers. Moreover, off-duty compensation can raise the question of what really is being bought, and slip from legitimate fee for legitimate service to corruption and betrayal of public trust. Even such a perception is damaging.

It is not just individual police officers who have established the practice of ancillary fees. In some degree our public police organizations have turned to offering special services for fees, just like other public institutions. And with fees for service comes the implication that all members of the public are not equal, in that the delivery of service is associated with the willingness and ability to pay. Fees have been creeping into police budgets, both as budget supplements and as a means of regulating calls for service. Police services, for example in Toronto, now can charge fees for criminal record checks for job applicants and for reports on stolen passports (*Toronto Star*, February 23, 1996). Sometimes there is controversy, as in Ottawa when the police introduced an annual fee for household alarm registration, suggesting that without registration there could be no assurance of police response; following public protest the fee was amended to one-time only. More often, the fee goes unremarked or unprotested, as another cost that somehow does not seem to have as negative a connotation as a tax increase, even though with a fee system there is the implication that one may be denied a basic public service.

In addition to fees for service to the general public, police have tested the entrepreneurial waters by charging special interests for special work. Some police representatives have argued, for example, that police can spend an inordinate amount of time pursuing insurance frauds, and that insurance companies should expect to pay. The notion is that the offence is part of doing insurance business, and investigations might therefore be viewed as a cost of doing business. The same reasoning, of course, can apply to many types of criminal acts; the crime would not have occurred if the offended party had not been going about his or her activity or business, whether attending an event or owning property. How to draw up the criteria for policing for a fee is extraordinarily unclear.

Even community policing provides the opportunity to seek new resources. To implement so-called community policing, police services have resorted to fundraising and donations of equipment and space. This raises the concern that donors will be the "squeaky wheels," inordinately influencing the police as representatives of the community, and claiming disproportionate police service. But for police managers, it is a way of supplementing their budgets, just as other public institutions, such as universities, have routinely resorted to such appeals. With frozen budgets and a commitment to community-based reform, the opportunity to do something by way of community policing with donations is difficult to turn away. For the general public, determining whether or not the donation is a genuine act of philanthropy and public spirit, or the indicator of a special relationship, may be sufficiently difficult to jeopardize a community policing initiative.

Private Police

Private police services have been around longer than genuine public police, and have never ceased to operate in Canada and the United States. But their growth at a time of public police retrenchment is remarkable. As our public police have had difficulty contending with an increasingly complex, heterogeneous urban environment, private policing has become a growth industry in Canada, as elsewhere in the western world (Shearing and Stenning, 1981: 198–203). Individuals annoyed with police inaction, municipalities displeased with police service, corporations lacking confidence in police abilities not only for internal security but also with regard to complex financial crimes, have increasingly resorted to private security firms. Though some of them are highly skilled, they often employ ill-educated and ill-trained persons, and the industry is poorly regulated. In Ontario, private police are licensed, even in the absence of effective standards of recruitment and training. Licences are for investigators, security guards, or cover both areas. It is the security sector that is by far the largest. As in Britain and the United States, in Canada a few large companies dominate, with the largest personnel concentration in Canada's major cities, especially Toronto (Shearing et al., 1980).

Ultimately this "privatization" of law enforcement threatens to destroy the system of publicly accountable policing. Yet, its prevention orientation is a redeeming character.

Private policing exists to protect persons and property, and to prevent offences from happening, but not to apprehend offenders. Shearing and Stenning (1980) argue that in a sense, therefore, private police bear a resemblance to the initial nineteenth century concept of policing. The growth of private policing may have contributed to the pressure upon pubic police to change into the community-based mode.

As early as 1970 it had been estimated in the United States that private police outnumbered public police, with an estimated two out of every three law enforcement personnel privately employed (Spitzer and Scull, 1977:18). In Canada, the ratio would be very similar. The growth has been attributable to dissatisfaction with public policing in the urban environment, but also, arguably, the growth in private policing is a function of private sector (i.e., corporate) interest in having more control over law enforcement, for greater protection and increased responsiveness. White-collar crime, invisible crime in contrast to the overt criminal behaviour of the working classes to which police have been trained to respond, has not been well-attended to by the public police. Fraud, embezzlement, crime in the workplace, and elaborate, computer-based commercial crimes have outpaced police forces where the majority of personnel still lack a basic university degree, let alone specialized training.

Corporations hire their own services or personnel, as do universities, and there is increasing pressure to give these workers peace officer status, and even to arm them. In the United States, university campus police, for example, are more often than not allowed to carry firearms. American practices often track into Canada, and it is therefore noteworthy that fully three-quarters of U.S. colleges and universities have sworn police officers, and about two-thirds of all campus police are armed (U.S. Bureau of Justice *Statistics Bulletin*, December 1996).

As sectors of the public seek protective and investigative services in a complex world, services responsive to their very particular needs, privatization has expanded and threatens to eventually displace the public police. Such businesses offer tailored services, and in contrast to the public police, often much less costly ones. With the inevitable public dissatisfaction with public police, entire communities may seek private police service supplements or even replace public police completely. An American example, that of Sussex, New Jersey, may be noted, where the police force was fired and a private security firm employed (*Ottawa Citizen*, June 23, 1993)—a solution pondered by local authorities in an Ontario jurisdiction near North Bay in 1997. The Ontario decision makers decided against the action because the private services would have been less comprehensive, and later opted to contract with the OPP. But in New Jersey the difference in service levels was more than tolerable, as the local council compared a cost of $285 000 annually for the police service to $48 000 for the security firm.

When pubic police were organized in the democracies, one intention was to protect the public and to maintain order, which involved preventing crimes and apprehending criminals rather than simply retrieving stolen property (Spitzer and Scull, 1977:21). Private police never disappeared, but were supplemented by a more broadly oriented "peacekeeping" role, which included industrial interventions. In Canada the role of the state in economic development reinforced reliance upon a public police. Now, in the late twentieth century, public police have become expensive and relatively non-responsive to private interests, encouraging renewed and increased use of private law enforcement.

One encounters the view that the growth in private policing will abate, and that in fact it must be integrated with public policing. Stenning (1989), for example, argues that, subject to suitable ethical and political control, an integration will generate innovation in public police service. Such integration is already under way, as illustrated by the many prominent former police officers who take management positions in private security firms. Stenning also suggests that private police, from plant security guards to shopping centre security personnel, encounter Canadians in person more often than do the public police. Similarly, at a 1990 International Crime Prevention Conference in Ottawa, an RCMP deputy commissioner recommended explicit cooperation with private police in order to more adequately deal with property crimes and by-law enforcement (*Ottawa Citizen,* October 19, 1990).

Private policing contradicts the conception of a public service; they serve not everyone equally, but only those who can pay for it. Such policing is a form of retainer to large corporate interests. It has arisen in large measure because public police have been perceived to be inadequately responsive. The challenge to Canada's future police is to re-establish a local legitimacy, trust, and a public control and integration of our public police such as to obviate the need for a domestic secret, or private, police establishment.

EDUCATION AND TECHNOLOGY

Education

Private police tend to be people who perform rudimentary tasks at a low cost, such as security guards. However, if the public police are not sufficiently skilled or do not have the resources to respond, private personnel will be depended upon to deal with intricate financial and computer crimes. The public police collectively are facing an upgrading in education and skills, not only to deal in a sophisticated way with the demands of community-based policing, but to hold market share in crime solving.

More and more university education will be expected of police recruits as well as the continuing education of serving police officers. There will undoubtedly be some attempt to segregate police education, perhaps by developing accredited programs at universities exclusively for police officers. This has tended to be the American experience. Alternately, and more desirably, police officers will be expected to have been educated at public institutions in company with other members of the public.

For major police services, such as the RCMP, education will also be the means to assume a leadership position in the provision of infrastructure or support services, from computing and information skills to forensics. That influence might yet develop nationally and internationally, as perhaps foretold in an agreement now in place between the RCMP and Carleton University to offer a 10-day forensic institute each summer (*This Week*, November 20, 1997). But in Canada there is still no institution with the credentials, resources, and influence of the FBI Academy in the United States. The Canadian Police College's role now, in offering some curriculum nationally and internationally, might be expected to evolve as a much-needed support for Canadian police services.

Technology

Whenever there is pressure on an organization to reduce costs, and to enhance general efficiency, communications, and coordination, organizations will resort to technology. Technology is the substitute for employees. Technology is the way to more rapid and effective response. Technology is the ability to extend management control.

Through the history of policing, technological innovation has been seized upon to extend the reach of policing. The automobile, radio communications, and now computer-based communications, are conspicuous examples. Arms are another, with periodic demands for more police firepower; in Los Angeles police are already provided with assault rifles so as not to be "out-gunned" (*Globe and Mail*, September 17, 1997). Trickling into the police inventory are special armoured vehicles and aircraft. Calgary police, for example, as Los Angeles has done for many years, operate a helicopter, found to be especially useful in police chases; a helicopter has also been authorized for Metro Toronto Police (*Toronto Star*, February 5, 1996).

A major area of technological development will relate to information. Information technology, for example, has been adopted in London (England) because of government demand that all services coordinate and because of the perceived need to police financial and terrorist crime. A new high-performance network is intended "to meet the requirements for rapid and up-to-date information, connect the stations together, as well as support the National Strategy for Police Information Systems ..."(Newbridge *Mainstreet News*, July, 1997:22). Similarly, in Canada, ever more elaborate information bases will grow from the existing CPIC system.

ORGANIZATION

As police organizations are pressed by political authorities to reduce their costs, police managers have had to try various tactics, including the obvious hardline bargaining over wages and salaries, reducing or eliminating recruiting, using volunteers, making referrals to other agencies, charging fees for service, prioritizing services, and just opting out. Not least, merged organizations have been promoted as an economy. Such responses have not failed to produce tensions with police employees. Insofar as changes are perceived to be motivated merely by cost-cutting and job reduction, police unions—already inclined to be wary—will resist otherwise useful innovations.

Employee Conflict

With about $6 billion a year spent on policing in Canada, about 80% on salaries, pressure will continue for police organizations to moderate employee costs, even as police unions press for increased compensation and job protection. Chiefs of police are under pressure to reform: to provide cost-effective and accountable policing. This tends to bring them into conflict with local elected politicians, and with the personnel with whom they worked as they moved up through the ranks.

Already chiefs of police in Canada, from Edmonton, Winnipeg, Ottawa, Toronto, and elsewhere are under severe public criticism by police association representatives (see Bercuson and Cooper, *Globe and Mail*, November 15, 1997). The demands for accountability, which translate into pressure to investigate public complaints against individuals and to control the payroll for expensive police personnel, have exacerbated tensions between chiefs and rank-and-file police officers. Police associations, therefore, will no doubt be increasingly aggressive in representing worker interests, and perhaps in so doing, be less inclined to be swayed by traditional appeals to essential public service. And even though ideologically police union representatives may have more in common with their commissioned officers and chiefs, having all experienced similar occupational socialization, than they do with other sectors of Canadian organized labour, there is likely to be increased police worker collaboration with other Canadian employee groups. Greater numbers of police officers with higher education will in fact probably encourage such affiliation rather than discourage it, if the recent history of union expansion through the middle-class public-sector workplace is any indication.

A good deal of the pressure for the centralization of policing was the expectation that there could be economies of scale. Similarly, and not really contradictorily, community policing has been seen by police managers in no small part as an opportunity to supplement resources. The use of civilian volunteers, for example, to take on tasks formerly performed by sworn officers, affords an economy under the guise of community involvement. Some police services now consider requiring volunteer work of anyone wishing to apply for a job as a police officer!

For decades civilian employees have featured in Canadian police organizations. Their numbers have tended to expand, and will likely expand yet more, not only as an economy, but also because civilians can bring specialized skills, as in computing, to a police service that cannot arrange or afford to fully educate and train sworn members in very specialized fields. The use of cadet officers in active service, as has been done in Metro Toronto, and the greater use of volunteer auxiliaries are related practices, layering the police service with lower-cost service providers. Whether civilian employees, volunteers, or auxiliaries, there will be opposition from police unions, who will act as responsible unions must, to protect jobs for their own members, resisting extensive departures from the historic utilization of sworn personnel.

Centralization vs Decentralization

Despite all the economies and downsizing, Canadian police services are large organizations, and growing larger. Not only has urbanization throughout this century led to larger and more complex policing services, so too have organizational and economic assumptions. In expectations of improved cost effectiveness—expectations not well supported by available research—governments have pressed for the merging of smaller police organizations. Regionalized police services have therefore become prevalent in Canada, even in suburban and rural areas. This is unlikely to be undone.

Yet, as we have seen, there is also a pervasive sentiment in favour of some renewed localism. Community policing, while an attempt to respond to the limits of conventional policing, has also in a sense been an exercise in nostalgia, a longing for a rather mythical past when policing was local and community sensitive. It can permit a greater sense of community public ownership of a police service, breaking down the social distance and anonymity characteristic of large mobile police services. For the public, community policing of some sort is apt, therefore, to be a persisting inclination, provided that it is associated with demonstrably effective service. The public may wish to know their police, but they also wish, probably above all else, to be protected and served by their police. Traditional police preoccupation with crime control is also a public preoccupation.

Conceivably community policing can generally provide better policing. Police need not react arbitrarily or indiscriminately, but tailor their reactions to legitimate community priorities. Police need not in fact be a thin blue line, but can enlist not just the generalized approval and support of the public but also explicit assistance and volunteer time. And as

bliography

rving (ed.) 1974 *On Strike: Six Key Labour Struggles in Canada 1919–1949*. Toronto: Lorimer & Co.

n, Raymond 1987 "Police force communication: member perceptions." *Canadian Police ge Journal* 11:233–272.

on, Charles 1980 *A History of the London Police*. London: Phelps Publishing Co.

n, John 1975 "People, government and the police." Pp. 7–15 in J. Brown and G. Howes), *The Police and the Community*. Westmead, England: Saxon House.

n, John 1979 *Policing Freedom: A Commentary on the Dilemmas of Policing in Western ocracies*. Plymouth: MacDonald and Evans.

Geoffrey 1997 "Pursuit driving." *Police Forum* 7: 1–12.

G., D. Kenney, and R. Dunham 1997 "Police pursuits and the use of force." *Justice rterly* 14: 371–385.

dney H. 1968 *Police Authority and the Rights of the Individual*. New York: Arco Publishing.

dge, Christine 1984 "Pilot study of racism awareness training." *Police Journal* 51:165–169.

Mark 1985 *Cops: Their Lives in Their Own Words*. New York: Pocket Books, Simon & uster.

n, Roger 1977 *Inside a Cop*. Pacific Grove, CA: Boxwood Press.

Michael 1964 *The Policeman in the Community*. London: Tavistock Publications.

Michael 1973 *Police Community Relations*. London: Collins.

orton, and Bernard Berkowitz 1967 "Training police as specialists in family crisis intertion: a community psychology action program." *Community Mental Health Journal* III:315–317.

Dannielle, and Nicole Berand 1981 *Etude Historico-Juridique: Organization et Pouvoir a Police*. Ottawa: Solicitor General of Canada.

n, Greg 1977 *A Planning, Implementation and Organization Theory Guide to the Team icing Model*. British Columbia: Ministry of the Attorney General.

David, and Harold Mendelsohn 1968 *Minorities and the Police: Confrontation in America*. w York: The Free Press.

David 1971–1972 "The police and political change in comparative perspective." *Law and ciety Review* 6:91–112.

David 1976 *Forces of Order*. California: University of California Press.

David 1977 "The limits of police reform." Pp. 219–236 in David Bayley (ed.), *Police and ciety*. Beverly Hills: Sage Publications.

David 1994 *Police for the Future*. New York: Oxford University Press.

effective policing depends upon public cooperation, it thrives upon information. Community policing, with enhanced community contacts and familiarity, can result in improved police intelligence for crime control purposes. In fact, as some fear, the potential for information control by police as information gatekeepers in a so-called "information age," through community and transnational linkages, raises yet again the spectre of oppressive policing (Ericson, 1994; Ericson and Haggerty, 1997).

Historically, however, the police have shown quite limited capacity in developing or managing information. This is particularly evident in the matter of information collection, beyond that which is incident driven; systematic community scans and research are rare. There are only a few texts or manuals, for example, devoted to offering instruction to police in research and information collection and management, although they may be portents of things to come (see Eck and LaVigne, 1994; Eck and Weisburd, 1995; Block et al., 1995). Information collation and access systems are better developed, and appear to be a police priority. The national police information service in Canada (CPIC), intended for all police services and other criminal justice agencies, is being upgraded. Its development also relates to transnational policing, for a Canadian computerized information system can hook up with other national police data banks, such as the United States Justice Information system.

Ominous as these developments might appear (Ericson and Haggerty, 1997), if policing services are to be effective, they must depend upon coordinated information collection, dissemination and analysis, among themselves and with the public and its agencies. Effective and rapid communications, intelligence gathering and analysis, and police and agency coordination is to be expected and required. So too is a police initiative or leadership role. The same demands for information are a feature of policing at every level of operations. If, on the one hand, localized community policing, expressed at the street level, is to develop further in the direction of the ideal model, the communities have to be well understood. But data and data analysis, both incident and group-related, will have to be coordinated beyond local community boundaries. Problems and violations are not delimited by community designations. And police response cannot be limited to community, provincial, or even national boundaries.

In offering skilled services, police in Canada will have to find the means to effectively coordinate across existing jurisdictions. There will be increasing demand for national services, perhaps under the auspices of the RCMP, to support local policing. And there will be increasing demand for the improved means, again probably by way of the RCMP, for Canadian police to extend enquiries beyond the borders of Canada.

Transnational Policing

To date the major impetus for international policing has been drug enforcement (Nadelmann, 1993). Policing international terrorism and computer-related and financial crimes could also benefit from enhanced transnational policing. In a sense, not only has policing not kept up with the rapid transnational flows of capital and goods, it has failed to keep up with the international mobility of people. If national states, especially the United States, developed effective transnational policing, they would be beginning to catch up with the flow of capital, goods, and labour around the world. An important and vital component of this transnationalization would be sophisticated information technology.

Such police development may be warranted for effective[...] lic, but it may also be sinister. It brings to mind not only ima[...] haps more potently, the possibility of police conduct being[...] most probably those of the United States (Nadelman, 1993; [...] cerns suggest, perhaps ironically, how great the need is for[...] agency in Canada in order to participate in transnational polici[...] populations and policy interests, and not those of others.

Another sinister implication of transnational policing is in[...] that is often used, the "war" against drugs, the "war" against[...] crime. If in fact transnational policing comes to be American-[...] of police actions might become increasingly violent and oppre[...] to have high impact tactical teams, after a military fashion, a[...] as American-style crime suppression (in contrast to crime preven[...] also affect community relations in our stratified societies, as enti[...] targeted for crime suppression. The necessary counterbalance [...] velopment of local community policing.

CONCLUSION

There are no conclusions. Policing is as complex and demanding[...] a practice. Police in Canada appear to be in transformation, but mor[...] are needed before real transformation can be demonstrated. Me[...] that policing will not go away, we can perhaps all be intent up[...] Canadian policing.

ANNOTATED READINGS, CHAPTER ELEVEN

Richard Ericson and Kevin Haggerty. *Policing the Risk Society.* Toronto: [...] 1997. A daunting but rewarding book, for its thoughtful attempt to [...] police reform. The authors ponder the role of police in defining realiti[...] tionally, by acting as information gatekeepers in the post-modern wor[...]

Beare, Margaret 1985 "The politics of policing: selling policing in metropolitan Toronto (1957–1984)." Unpublished manuscript.

Beaudoin, Gerald, and Ed Ratushny 1989 *The Canadian Charter of Rights and Freedoms* (2nd ed.). Toronto: Carswell.

Beausoleil, Gilles 1974 "History of the strike at Asbestos." Pp. 143–182 in Pierre Elliott Trudeau (ed.), *The Asbestos Strike*. Toronto: James Lewis and Samuel.

Belson, William A. 1975 *The Public and the Police.* London: Harper & Row.

Benson, Garry 1991 *Developing Crime Prevention Strategies in Aboriginal Communities.* Ottawa: Solicitor General Canada.

Bent, A.E. 1974 *The Politics of Law Enforcement.* Lexington, MA: Lexington Books.

Bent, Alan, and Ralph Rossum 1976 *Police, Criminal Justice and the Community.* New York: Harper & Row.

Berkley, George 1969 *The Democratic Policeman.* Boston: Beacon Press.

Bittner, Egon 1975 *The Functions of the Police in Modern Society.* New York: Aronson.

Black, Donald, and Albert J. Reiss, Jr. 1970 "Police control of juveniles." *American Sociological Review* 35:63–77.

Black, Donald 1980 "The social organization of arrest." Pp. 151–162 in Richard J. Lundman (ed.), *Police Behavior.* New York: Oxford University Press.

Black, Judith 1998 "The police couple." *RCMP Quarterly*: 1–2.

Blake, J.A. 1981 "The role of police in society." Pp. 77–84 in W.T. McGrath and M.P. Mitchell, *The Police Function in Canada.* Toronto: Methuen.

Bloch, Peter, and Deborah Anderson 1974 *Police Women on Patrol.* Washington DC: Police Foundation.

Block, C., M. Dabadoub, and S. Fregley (eds.) 1995 *Crime Analysis Through Computer Mapping.* Washington: PERF.

Bobb, William J. 1971 *The Police Rebellion.* Springfield, IL: Charles C. Thomas.

Bourne, Paul, and John Eisenberg 1972 *The Law and the Police.* Toronto: General Publishing Co.

Bowden, Tom 1978 *Beyond the Limits of the Law.* Harmondsworth, England: Penguin.

Bowes, Stuart 1966 *The Police and the Civil Liberties.* London: Lawrence and Wishart.

Boydston, John, M. Sherry, and M. Moelter 1977 *Patrol Staffing in San Diego: One- or Two-Officer Units.* Washington Police Foundation.

Braiden, Chris 1986 "Community policing—a personal view." Pp. 23–27 in Donald Loree and Chris Murphy, *Community Policing in the 1980's.* Ottawa: Solicitor General of Canada.

Briar, Scott 1964 "Police Encounters with Juveniles." *American Journal of Sociology* LXX:206–214.

Brillon, Yves 1984 "Les attitudes des Canadiens vis-à-vis de la police." *Revue Canadienne de Criminologie* 2:133–146.

Brillon, Yves, Christiane Louis-Guerin and Marie Christine Lamarche 1984 "Attitudes of the Canadian pubic toward crime policies: pilot enquiry." Ottawa: Ministry of the Solicitor General.

Brockenshire, John 1985 "Police enquiries—a better way?" *Municipal World* 95:292–293.

Brodeur, Jean-Paul 1981 "Legitimizing police deviance." Pp. 127–160 in Clifford D. Shearing (ed.), *Organizational Police Deviance*. Toronto: Butterworths.

Brown, Lorne, and Caroline Brown 1978 *An Unauthorized History of the RCMP* (2nd ed.). Toronto: Lewis and Samuel.

Brown, Michael K. 1981 *Working the Street: The Dilemmas of Reform*. New York: Russell Sage Foundation.

Bryett, Keith 1989 "Police specialization: a reassessment." *Canadian Police College Journal* 13(4):260–272.

Buckley, Leslie, James McGinnis, and Michael Petrunik 1993 "Police perceptions of education as an entitlement in promotion." *American Journal of Police* 12: 77–100.

Buckner, H. Taylor 1967 *The Police: The Culture of a Social Control Agency*. Berkeley: University of California (Doctoral dissertation).

Burpo, J.H. 1971 *The Police Labor Movement*. Springfield, IL: C.C. Thomas

(CACP) Canadian Association of Chiefs of Police 1993 *Police Race Relations: The Recruitment, Selection and Retention of Visible Minorities*. Ottawa: CACP.

(CACP) Canadian Association of Chiefs of Police 1992 *Police Race Relations: Raising Your Effectiveness in Today's Diverse Neighborhoods Through Community Policing*. Ottawa: CACP.

Cain, Maureen 1973 *Society and the Policeman's Role*. London: Routledge and Kegan Paul.

Cain, Maureen 1979 "Trends in the sociology of police work." *International Journal of the Sociology of Law* 7:143–167.

Canada 1969 *Report of the Royal Commission on Security* (The Mackenzie Report). Ottawa: Information Canada.

Canada 1976 *Report of the Commission of Inquiry Relating to Public Complaints, Internal Discipline and Grievance Procedure Within the Royal Canadian Mounted Police* (The Martin Report). Ottawa: Information Canada.

Canada 1980 *Perspectives Canada III*. Ottawa: Statistics Canada

Canada 1981 *Report of the Auditor General of Canada to the House of Commons*. Ottawa: Supply and Services.

Canada 1983 "Victims of crime." *Canadian Urban Victimization Survey Bulletin* 1:1–10.

Canada 1984a *Report of Proceedings of the Symposium on Policing in Multicultural/Multiracial Urban Communities*. Ottawa: Minister of State for Multiculturalism.

Canada 1984b "Good neighbours: looking out for each other." Ottawa: Ministry of the Solicitor General.

Canada 1984c "Reported and unreported crimes." *Canadian Urban Victimization Survey Bulletin* 2:1–13.

Canada 1984d "Crime prevention: awareness and practice." *Canadian Urban Victimization Survey Bulletin* 3:1012.

Canada 1985a "Female victims of crime." *Canadian Urban Victimization Survey Bulletin* 4:1–12.

Canada 1985b "Costs of crime to victims." *Canadian Urban Victimization Survey Bulletin* 5:1–8.

Canada 1985c "Criminal victimization of elderly Canadians." *Canadian Urban Victimization Survey Bulletin* 6:1–11.

Canada 1986 *Crime Prevention is ... Good Neighbours*. Ottawa: Solicitor General.

Canada 1988a "Patterns in property crime." *Canadian Urban Victimization Survey Bulletin* 9:1–11.

Canada 1988b "Multiple victimization." *Canadian Urban Victimization Bulletin* 10:1–10.

Canada 1988c *Report on Police Salaries in Canada: Current and Historical Data 1966–1988*. Ottawa: Statistics Canada.

Canada 1990 *Indian Policing Policy Review Task Force Report*. Ottawa: Indian and Northern Affairs.

Canadian Encyclopedia 1985 Edmonton: Hurting Publishing.

Carpenter, G.J. 1989 *Police Officer Performance Evaluation Systems*. Ottawa: Canadian Police College.

Carr-Hill, R.A. 1979 *Crime, the Police, and Criminal Statistics*. New York: Academic Press.

Carriere, Kevin, and Richard V. Ericson 1989 *Crime Stoppers: A Study in the Organization of Community Policing*. Toronto: University of Toronto Centre for Criminology.

Center for Research on Criminal Justice 1977 *The Iron Fist and the Velvet Glove*. Berkeley, CA: Center for Research on Criminal Justice.

Cerda, Ray 1977 "Police militancy." *Crime and Social Justice* 7:40–48.

Chambliss, William J., and Robert B. Seidman 1971 *Law, Order, and Power*. Reading, MA: Addison-Wesley Publishing Co.

Chappell, Duncan, Robert Gordon, and Rhonda Moore 1982 "Criminal investigation: a selective literature review and bibliography." *Canadian Police College Journal* 6:13–64.

Chappell, Duncan, Robert Gordon, and Rhonda Moore 1983 "Experiments, innovations and future directions in criminal investigation: a survey of Canadian police departments." *Canadian Police College Journal* 7:161–205.

Chesler, Mark A. 1976 "Dilemmas and design in race education/training." Washington, DC: Second National Symposium on Race Relations Education and Training.

Chevigny, Paul 1969 *Police Power: Police Abuses in New York City*. New York: Vintage Books.

Clairmont, Donald 1987 "Work innovations in a public sector organization: a case study." Hamilton: Learned Societies.

Clairmont, Donald 1990 *To the Forefront: Community-Based Zone Policing in Halifax*. Ottawa: Canadian Police College.

Clark, Gerald 1975 "What happens when police strike?" Pp. 440–491 in William Chambiliss (ed.) *Criminal Law in Action*. Santa Barbara: Hamilton.

Clarkin, L.P. 1979 "Centralization vs decentralization: an analysis." Ottawa: Ottawa Police Force.

Clift, Raymond E. 1970 *A Guide to Modern Police Thinking: An Introduction to Policing* (3rd ed.). Cincinnati: W.H. Anderson Co.

Coffey, John F., and Mark Chesler 1976 *Race Education/Training*. Washington: U.S. Government Printing Office.

Coker, Abayomi 1985 "Report on the police/community education program held at the Ottawa Police Department and the Chinese United Church, May–June 1985." Ottawa: Unpublished paper.

Cooley, J.W. 1978 "The social aspects of crime prevention." *Canadian Police College Journal* 2:382–389.

Cooley, J.W. 1981 "Police discretion and public attitudes." Pp. 186–196 in W.T. McGrath and M.P. Mitchell, *The Police Function in Canada.* Toronto: Methuen.

Cooper, H.S. 1981 "The evolution of Canadian police." Pp. 37–52 in W.T. McGrath and M.P. Mitchell, *The Police Function in Canada.* Toronto: Methuen.

Cooper, William H. 1982 "Police officers over career stages." *Canadian Police College Journal* 6:893–112.

Cordingley, Paul 1979 "Psychological testing in Canadian police forces." *Canadian Police College Journal* 3:126–161.

Cordner, Gary W. 1978 "Open and closed models of police organization: traditions, dilemmas and practical consideration." *Journal of Police Science and Administration* 6: 22–34.

Courtis, M.C. (assisted by I. Dusuyer) 1970 *Attitudes to Crime and the Police in Toronto: A Report on Some Survey Findings.* Toronto: University of Toronto Centre for Criminology.

Coutts, Larry 1990 "Police hiring and promotion: methods and outcomes." *Canadian Police College Journal* 14:98–122.

Cox, Barry, John Shirley and Martin Short 1977 *The Fall of Scotland Yard.* Harmondsworth: Penguin Books.

Cox, Stephen M., and Jack D. Fitzgerald 1983 *Police in Community Relations: Critical Issues.* Dubuque: Wm. C. Brown Co.

Crank, John 1998 *Understanding Police Culture.* Cincinnati: Anderson Publishing Co.

Daley, Robert 1985 *Hands of a Stranger.* New York: Simon & Schuster.

Das, Dilip K. 1986 "Military models of policing: comparative impressions." *Canadian Police College Journal* 10:267–285.

Demers, Donald J. 1984 "Criminal justice spending in Canada: recent trends." *Impact* 2:4–11.

Dempsey, Hugh (ed.). 1977 *Men in Scarlet.* Toronto: McClelland and Stewart

Deszca, Gene 1988 "The communication of ideology in police forces." *Canadian Police College Journal* 12:240–268.

de Verteuil, Jacques 1987 "Metropolitan Toronto community policing survey working paper number 2: measurement of victimization." Ottawa: Statistics Division, Solicitor General of Canada.

Di Manno, Rosie 1996 "Why Toronto needs a black crime unit." *Toronto Star* (February 7): A7.

Dion, Robert 1982 *Crimes of the Secret Police.* Montreal: Black Rose Books.

Dolling, D. and T. Feltes (eds.) 1993 *Community Policing: Comparative Aspects of Community-Oriented Police Work.* Holzkirchen, Germany.

Dowling, John B., and Victor M. MacDonald (With Miles A. Protter) 1983 *The Social Realities of Policing: Essays in Legitimation Theory.* Ottawa: The Canadian Police College.

Downie, Brian M., and Richard L. Jackson 1980 *Conflict and Cooperation in Police Labour Relations*. Ottawa: Canadian Police College.

Dubienski, Ian 1981 "The police and the judiciary." Pp. 85–103 in W.T. McGrath and M.P. Mitchell, *The Police Function in Canada*. Toronto: Meuthuen.

Dumas, Evelyn 1975 *The Bitter Thirties in Quebec*. Montreal: Black Rose Books.

Dutton, Donald 1979 "A longitudinal study of police attitudes and values and their relationship to on-the-job behaviour." Ottawa: Solicitor General of Canada (unpublished).

Dutton, Donald, and Bruce Levens 1976 "The social service role of the police: domestic crisis intervention." Vancouver: United Way of the Lower Mainland.

Eck, John E. 1986 "The role and management of criminal investigations in the community." Pp. 107–121 in Donald Loree and Chris Murphy (eds.), *Community Policy in the 1980's*. Ottawa: Solicitor General of Canada.

Eck, John, and Nancy LaVigne 1994 *Using Research: A Primer for Law Enforcement Managers*. Washington: PERF.

Eck, John and David Weisburd (eds.) 1995 *Crime and Place*. Washington: PERF.

Engsted, Peter, and Michelle Lioy (eds.) 1978 *Workshop on Police Productivity and Performance: Report of the Proceedings*. Ottawa: Solicitor General of Canada.

Ericson, Richard 1981a "Rules for police deviance." Pp. 83–110 in Clifford D. Shearing (ed.) *Organizational Police Deviance*. Toronto: Butterworths Canada Ltd.

Ericson, Richard 1981b *Making Crime: A Study of Detective Work*. Toronto: Butterworths Canada Ltd.

Ericson, Richard 1982 *Reproducing Order: A Study of Police Patrol Work*. Toronto: University of Toronto Press.

Ericson, Richard 1983 *The Constitution of Legal Inequality*. Ottawa: Carleton University.

Ericson, Richard 1989 "Patrolling the facts: secrecy and publicity in police work." *The British Journal of Sociology* 40: 205–226.

Ericson, Richard, K. Haggerty, and K. Carrierre 1993 "Community policing as communications policing" in D. Dolling and T. Feltes *Community-Oriented Police Work*. Holzkirchen, Germany: Felix-Verlag: 37–70.

Ericson, Richard 1994 "The division of expert knowledge in policing and security." *British Journal of Sociology* 45: 149–175.

Ericson, Richard and Kevin Haggerty 1997 *Policing the Risk Society*. Toronto: University of Toronto Press.

Evans, Peter 1974 *The Police Revolution*. London: George Allen & Unwin.

Farmer, David 1978 "Research and police productivity: the United States experience." Pp. 120–133 in Peter Engsted and Michelle Lioy (eds.), *Workshop on Police Productivity*. Ottawa: Solicitor General of Canada.

Fidler, Richard 1978 *RCMP: The Real Subversives*. Toronto: Vanguard Publications.

Fisher, E.G., and Henry Starek 1978 "Police bargaining in Canada: private sector bargaining, compulsory arbitration and mediation-arbitration in Vancouver." *Canadian Police College Journal* 2:133–161.

Fletcher, Joseph 1989 "Results of the survey of racial prejudice." Toronto: Department of Political Science, University of Toronto.

Fleury, Barbara, and Ann Suzon 1988 "The historical development of police unionism: three case studies from British Columbia." Vancouver: M.A. thesis, Simon Fraser University.

Forcese, Dennis, P. Begin, and D. Gould 1979 "Policing in a multicultural society: Ottawa Police Force relations with immigrant and public housing residents." Ottawa: Departmental working paper, Sociology and Anthropology, Carleton University.

Forcese, Dennis 1980 "Police unionism: employee–management relations in Canadian police forces." *Canadian Police College Journal* 4(2): 79–129.

Forcese, Dennis, and Joseph Cooper 1985 "Police retirement: career succession or obsolescence?" *Canadian Police College Journal* 9:413–424.

Forcese, Dennis 1993 "Community policing and collective agreements." Toronto: Police Association of Ontario Conference Proceedings.

Forcese, Dennis 1994 "Seizing the reform agenda." Toronto: Police Association of Ontario Conference Proceedings.

Forster, Steve 1997 "Road slugs and warriors." *Ottawa Citizen* (November 7): C1;C4.

Friedmann, Robert R. 1992 *Community Policing.* New York: Harvester Wheatsheaf.

French, Richard, and André Beliveau 1979 *The RCMP and the Management of National Security.* Montreal: Institute for Research on Public Policy.

Galloway, Robert, and Laurie Fitzgerald 1992 "Service quality in policing." *FBI Law Enforcement Bulletin* (November): 1–7.

Gammage, A., and S. Sachs 1972 *Police Unions.* Springfield, IL: C.C. Thomas.

Gandy, John 1979 *Liaison Group on Law Enforcement and Race Relations.* Toronto: Social Planning Council.

Gandz, Jeffry 1990 "The employee empowerment era." *Business Quarterly* (Autumn):74–79.

Gentel, William D., and Martha L. Handman 1979 *Police Strikes: Causes and Prevention.* Washington: International Association of Chiefs of Police.

Genz, John, and David Lester 1976 "Authoritarianism in policemen as a function of experience." *Journal of Police Science and Administration* 4:9–13.

Germann, A.C. 1971 "Changing the police—the impossible dream?" *The Journal of Criminal Law, Criminology and Police Science* 67 (3):416–421.

Gervais, C.H. 1992 *The Border Police.* Waterloo: Penumbra Press.

Gillmor, Don 1988 "The shooting of J.J. Harper." *Saturday Night* 103 (December):43–52.

Goff, Colin H., and Randall J. Kimm 1987 "Seriousness of crimes: a comparison of Canadian and American chiefs of police and detachment commanders." *Canadian Police College Journal* 11:1–12.

Goffman, Erving 1961 *Asylums: Essays on the Social Situation of Mental Patients and Other Inmates.* Garden City: Anchor Books, Doubleday & Co.

Goldsmith, Andrew 1985 "Collective bargaining by municipal police officers: management under threat?" Toronto: Unpublished dissertation, University of Toronto.

Goldstein, Herman 1990 *Problem-Oriented Policing*. Philadelphia, PA: Temple University Press.

Gould, Larry 1995 "Can an old dog be taught new tricks: teaching cultural diversity to police officers." Montreal: Unpublished paper, Annual Meeting of the Canadian Sociology and Anthropology Association.

Grant, Alan 1980 *The Police—A Police Paper*. Ottawa: Law Reform Commission of Canada.

Gray, Charlotte 1990 "Mountie Makeover." *Saturday Night* (April): 11–13.

Great Britain 1962 *Royal Commission on the Police*. London: Her Majesty's Stationary Office.

Great Britain 1975 *Race Relations Research: A Report to the Home Secretary by the Advisory Committee on Race Relations Research*. London; Her Majesty's Stationary Office.

Greene, J.R., and S.D. Mastrofski 1988 *Community Policing: Rhetoric or Reality*. New York: Praeger.

Greene, J.R., and R.B. Taylor 1988 "Community-based policing and foot patrol: issues of theory and evaluation." in J.R. Greene and S.D. Mastrofski (eds.), *Community Policing: Rhetoric or Reality*. New York, Praeger: 195–224.

Greenwood, P., J. Chaiken, and J. Petersilia 1975 *The Investigative Process*. Lexington: Lexington Books.

Greenwood, P., and J. Petersilia 1977 *The Criminal Investigation Process*. Santa Monica: Rand.

Grimshaw, Roger, and Tony Jefferson 1987 *Interpreting Policework: Policy and Practice in Forms of Beat Policing*. London: Allen & Unwin.

Grosman, Brian A. 1975 *Police Command*. Toronto: Macmillan Co. of Canada Ltd.

Grosman, Brian A. 1978 "Police leadership in a changing society." *Canadian Police College Journal* 2:351–355.

Grosso, Sonny, and Philip Rosenberg 1978 *Point Blank*. New York: Grosset and Dunlap.

Groves, T., T. Moore, and K.E. Renner 1980 "An approach to problems in police-community relations." *Journal of Community Psychology* 8:357–363.

Halpern, Stephen 1974 *Police Associations and Department Leaders*. Lexington, MA: D.C. Heath.

Hann, Robert G., James McGinnis, Phillip Stenning and A. Stuart Farson 1985 "Municipal police governance and accountability in Canada: an empirical study." *Canadian Police College Journal* 9:1–85.

Hanna, Donald G. 1988 "Community perception of police." *The Police Chief* (November): 60–61.

Harring, Sidney 1981 "Policing a class society: The expansion of the urban police in the late nineteenth and early twentieth century." Pp. 292–313 in D.F. Greenberg (ed.), *Crime and Capitalism*. California: Mayfield Publishing Co.

Harris, Richard N. 1973 *The Police Academy: An Inside View*. New York: John Wiley & Sons.

Hart, P., A. Wearing, and B. Heady 1995 "Police stress and well-being: integrating personality, coping and daily work experiences." *Journal of Occupational and Organizational Psychology* 68: 1–16.

Henshel, Richard L. 1981 "Why police abuses will keep on growing." *The Toronto Star* (August 30):F1.

Henshel, Richard L. 1983 "Police misconduct in metropolitan Toronto: a study of formal complaints." Toronto: York University Lamarsh Research Program.

Higley, Dahn D. 1984 *O.P.P.: The History of the Ontario Provincial Police Force*. Toronto: The Queen's Printer.

Hochstedler, E., R. Regoli and E. Poole 1984 "Changing the guard in American cities: a current empirical assessment of integration in twenty municipal police departments." *Criminal Justice Review* 9:8–14.

Horn, Jo 1991 "The future of crime prevention: Inter-agency issues." In Donald Loree and Robert Walker (eds.), *Community Crime Prevention: Shaping the Future*. Ottawa, Minister of Supply and Services Canada: 115–136.

Horne, David, Dennis Forcese, and Lester Thompson 1989 "Gloucester Police Force Public Needs Survey: Preliminary Findings." Ottawa: Carleton University.

Horne, David, and Dennis Forcese 1990 "Nepean Police Force Public Needs Survey." Ottawa: Carleton University.

Horne, David 1993 "Public opinion surveys: implications for police organizations." *Canadian Police College Journal* 16: 263–281.

Horne, Martie (ed.) 1984 "History of the Ottawa Police Force 1827–1983." Ottawa: Unpublished paper, The History Collaborative, Department of History, Carleton University.

Hornick, J., B. Leighton, and B. Burrows 1993 "Evaluating community policing: the Edmonton project." In J. Hudson and J. Roberts, *Evaluating Justice*. Toronto: Thompson Educational Publishing: 62–92.

Horrall, S.W. 1980 "The Royal North-West Mounted Police and labour unrest in Western Canada, 1919." *Canadian Historical Review* LXI:169–190.

Howard, Ross 1996 "Police killings linked to death wish." *Globe and Mail* (November 4): A3.

Huey, John 1991 "Nothing's impossible." *Fortune* (September 23):134–140.

Hunt, R.A. 1986 "The planning and management of change in a police department: the London experience." Pp. 51–71 in Donald Loree and Chris Murphy, *Community Policing in the 1980's*. Ottawa: Solicitor General of Canada.

Hylton, John H. 1980 "Public attitudes towards crime and the police in a prairie city." *Canadian Police College Journal* 4:243–276.

Institute for the Study of Labour and Economic Crisis 1982 *The Iron Fist and the Velvet Glove: An Analysis of the U.S. Police* (3rd ed.). San Francisco: Crime and Social Justice Associates.

International Association of Chiefs of Police 1977 *Critical Issues in Police Labour Relations*. Washington: International Association of Chiefs of Police.

Isbester, Fraser 1974 "Asbestos 1949." Pp. 163–196 in Irving Abella (ed.) *On Strike: Six Key Labour Struggles in Canada 1919–1949*. Toronto: James Lorimer & Co.

Jackson, R.L. 1980 "Police labour relations in Canada: a current perspective." Pp. 35–62 in Bryan M. Downier and Richard L. Jackson (eds.), *Conflict and Cooperation in Police Labour Relations*. Ottawa: The Canadian Police College.

Jackson, R.L. 1983 "Police management under fiscal restraint: the labour relations aspect." *Canadian Police College Journal* 7:230–242.

Jackson, R.L. 1986 "Canadian police labour relations in the 80's: new environmental concerns." *Canadian Police College Journal* 10:86–138.

Jacobs, David, and David Britt 1978 "Inequality and police use of deadly force: an empirical assessment of a conflict hypothesis." *Social Problems* 26:403–412.

Jacobs, David 1979 "Inequality and police strength: conflict theory and coercive control in metropolitan areas." *American Sociological Review* 44:913–925.

Jaffe, Peter, and Judy Thompson 1979 "Family consultant service with the London Police Force— a description." *Canadian Police College Journal* 3:115–125.

Jain, Harish C. 1988 "The recruitment and selection of visible minorities in Canadian police organizations: 1985–1987." Hamilton: Working paper No. 315, Faculty of Business, McMaster University.

Jain, Harish 1992 *Issues in Recruitment of Visible Minority Police Officers in Canada.* Ottawa: Solicitor General Canada.

Jamieson, Stuart 1973 *Industrial Relations in Canada* (2nd ed.). Toronto: Macmillan of Canada.

Jayewardene, C.H.S. 1973 *Police and the Changing Society.* Ottawa: Department of Criminology, University of Ottawa.

Jayewardene, C.H.S., and C.K. Talbot 1990 *Police Recruitment of Ethnic Minorities.* Ottawa: Canadian Police College.

Jennings, John 1977 "The Plains Indians and the law." Pp. 50–65 in Hugh Dempsey (ed.), *Men in Scarlet.* Toronto: McClelland and Stewart.

Johnson, Bruce C. 1976 "Taking care of labor: the police in American Politics." *Theory and Society* 3:89–117.

Johnson, Kenneth 1978 "The missing link in police education: retirement counselling." *FBI Law Enforcement Bulletin* 47:29–30.

Johnson, T.A., G.E. Misner, and L.P. Brown 1981 *The Police and Society.* Englewood Cliffs: Prentice-Hall.

Juliani, T.J., C.K. Talbot, and C.H.S. Jayewardene 1984 "Municipal policing in Canada: a developmental perspective." *Canadian Police College Journal* 8:315–385.

Juris, Hervey A., and Peter Feuille 1973 *Police Unionism.* Lexington, MA: D.C. Heath.

Kaminer, Wendy 1994 "Crime and community." *The Atlantic Monthly* (May):111–120.

Kankewitt, Bill 1986 *The Shattered Badge: The Story of Ed Donovan, Stress Cop.* Toronto: Methuen.

Kaplan, Fred 1997 "New York fixes its broken windows." *Globe and Mail* (February 1): D4.

Katz, Donald R. 1977 "The 'misdemeanor murder' of Joe Campo Torres." *Rolling Stone* (December 29, 1977):53–61.

Kelling, George 1986 "The changing function of urban police: the historical and political context of community policing." Pp. 11–22 in Donald Loree and Chris Murphy (eds.), *Community Policing in the 1980's.* Ottawa: Solicitor General of Canada.

Kelling, G.L., T. Pate, D. Dieckman, and C.E. Brown 1974 *The Kansas City Preventive Patrol Experiment.* Washington: National Institute of Justice.

Kelly, Nora, and William Kelly 1973 *The Royal Canadian Mounted Police: A Century of History.* Edmonton: Hurtig Publishers.

Kelly, William, and Nora Kelly 1976 *Policing in Canada.* Toronto: Macmillan of Canada.

Kennedy, Leslie W. 1991 "The evaluation of community-based policing in Canada." *Canadian Police College Journal* 15: 275–289.

Kinsey, Richard, John Lea, and Jock Young 1986 *Losing the Fight against Crime.* Oxford: Basil Blackwell

Kirkham, George 1974 "A professor's 'street lessons.'" *FBI Law Enforcement Bulletin*: 1–9.

Kirkham, George 1976 *Signal Zero.* New York: J.P. Lippincott.

Kirkham, George L., and Laurin A. Wollan Jr. 1980 *Introduction to Law Enforcement.* New York: Harper & Row.

Klein, J.J., Jim Webb, and J.E. DiSanto 1978 "Experience with the police and attitude towards the police." *Canadian Journal of Sociology* 3:441–456.

Klockars, Carl B. 1985 *The Idea of Police.* Newbury Park: Sage Publications.

Koenig, Daniel J. 1975a "Police perceptions of public respect and extra-legal use of force: a reconsideration of folk wisdom and pluralistic ignorance." *Canadian Journal of Sociology* 1(3): 313–324.

Koenig, Daniel J. 1975b *RCMP Views of Themselves, Their Jobs and the Public.* Victoria: Office of the Attorney General, Province of British Columbia.

Koenig, Daniel J. 1980 "The effects of criminal victimization: judicial or police contacts on public attitudes toward local police." *Journal of Criminal Justice* 8:243–249.

Koenig, Daniel 1991 *Do Police Cause Crime?* Ottawa: Canadian Police College.

Koller, Katherine. 1990 *Working the Beat.* Edmonton Police Service.

Kraska, Peter, and Lovis Cubellis 1997 "Militarizing Mayberry and Beyond" *Justice Quarterly* 14 (December): 607–630.

Kroes, William 1978 *Society's Victim—The Policeman: An Analysis of Job Stress in Policing.* Springfield, IL: Chas. C. Thomas.

Lambert, John R. 1970 *Crime, Police and Race Relations: A Study in Birmingham.* London: Oxford University Press.

Larson, Richard C. 1972 *Urban Police and Patrol Analysis.* Cambridge, MA: MIT Press.

Lee, John Alan 1981 "Some structural aspects of police deviance in relations with minority groups." Pp. 49–82 in Clifford D. Shearing (ed.), *Organizational Police Deviance.* Toronto: Butterworths.

Lefkowitz, Joel 1975 "Psychological attributes of policemen." *Journal of Social Issues* 31:3–26.

Leinen, Stephen 1984 *Black Police, White Society.* New York: New York University Press.

Levens, Bruce R. 1978a "Domestic crisis intervention—a literature review of domestic dispute intervention training programs (part 1)." *Canadian Police College Journal* 2:215–247.

Levens, Bruce R. 1978b "Domestic crisis intervention—a literature review of domestic dispute intervention training programs (part 2)." *Canadian Police College Journal* 2:299–328.

Levens, Bruce R. 1978c "Domestic crisis intervention—domestic disputes, police response and social agency referral." *Canadian Police College Journal* 2:356–381.

Levi, Margaret 1977 *Bureaucratic Insurgency*. Lexington, MA: D.C. Heath.

Lewis, Clare 1981 "The police and the Crown." Pp. 104–113 in W.T. McGrath and M.P. Mitchell (eds.), *The Police Function in Canada*. Toronto: Methuen.

Lewis, Clare 1990 "Report of the Race Relations and Policing Task Force." *Canadian Police College Journal* 14:202–214.

Lewis-Horne, Nancy, and Dennis Forcese 1993 *Differential Police Response and the RCMP*. Ottawa: RCMP Community Policing series.

Linden, Rick, and Candice Minch 1980 *Women in Policing: A Review*. Ottawa: Report to the Ministry of the Solicitor General.

Linden, Rick, and Candice Minch 1982 "Women in policing: a review." Winnipeg: University of Manitoba Institute for Social and Economic Research.

Linden, Rick 1983 "Women in policing: a study of lower mainland RCMP detachments." *Canadian Police College Journal* 7:217–229.

Linden, Rick 1984 "Women in policing: a study of the Vancouver Police Department." Ottawa: Ministry of the Solicitor General.

Linden, Rick 1985 "Attrition among male and female members of the RCMP." *Canadian Police College Journal* 9:86–97.

Linden, Rick, and Cathy Fillmore 1993 "An evaluation study of women in policing." Pp. 93–116 in J. Hudson and J. Roberts, *Evaluating Justice*. Toronto: Thompson Educational Publishing.

Lipset, Seymour Martin 1969 "Why cops hate liberals—and vice versa." *The Atlantic* (March):76–83.

Liversedge, R. 1973 *Recollections of the On-to-Ottawa Trek*. Toronto: McClelland & Stewart.

Loree, Donald 1985 "Police in a plural society." *Canadian Police College Journal* 9:391–412.

Loree, Donald, and Chris Murphy (eds.) 1986 *Community Policing in the 1980's: Recent Advances in Police Programs*. Ottawa: Solicitor General of Canada.

Loree, Donald 1988 "Innovation and change in a regional police force." *Canadian Police College Journal* 12:205–239.

Loree, Donald (ed.) 1989 *Future Issues in policing: Symposium Proceedings*. Ottawa: Canadian Police College.

Loree, Donald (ed.) 1989 *Research Leaders in Policing: Symposium Proceedings*. Ottawa: Canadian Police College.

Lundman, Richard J. (ed.) 1980a *Police Behavior: A Sociological Perspective*. New York: Oxford University Press.

Lundman, Richard J. 1980b *Police and Policing: An Introduction*. New York: Holt, Rinehart and Winston.

Lunney, Robert 1989 "The role of the police leader in the 21st century." Pp. 197–213 in Donald Loree (ed.), *Future Issues in Policing: Symposium Proceedings*. Ottawa: Canadian Police College.

Maas, Peter 1973 *Serpico*. New York: Viking.

McAlary, Mike 1987 *Buddy Boys: When Good Cops Turn Bad*. New York: G.P. Putnam's Sons.

McCabe, S., and F. Sutcliffe 1978 *Defining Crime: A Study of Police Decisions*. Oxford: Basil Blackwell.

MacDonald, Jake 1983 "Pete and Jack." *Quest Magazine* (March):49–60.

MacDonald, Victor, and M.A. Martin 1986 "Specialists and the personnel structure of Canadian police forces." *Canadian Police College Journal* 10:189–226.

McDonald, W.F. (ed.) 1997 *Crime and Law Enforcement in the Global Village*. Cincinnati: Anderson Publishing.

McDougall, Allan K. 1988a "The police mandate: the modern era." *Canadian Police College Journal* 12:141–174.

McDougall, Allan K. 1988b *Policing: The Evolution of a Mandate*. Ottawa: Canadian Police College.

McElroy, James, C. Cosgrove, and S. Sadd 1993 *Community Policing: The CPOP in New York*. Beverly Hills, Sage.

McGahan, Peter 1984 *Police Images of a City*. New York: Verlag Peter Lang.

McGinnis, James 1985a: "Career development in a municipal policing: part 1." *Canadian Police College Journal* 9:154–206.

McGinnis, James 1985b "Career development in municipal policing: part 2." *Canadian Police College Journal* 9:254–293.

McGrath, W.T., and M.P. Mitchell (eds.) 1981 *The Police Function in Canada*. Toronto: Methuen.

Macleod, R.C., and D. Schneiderman (eds.) 1994 *Police Powers in Canada*. Toronto: University of Toronto Press.

McMahon, Maeve W., and Richard V. Ericson 1984 *Policing Reform: A Study of the Reform Process and Police Institution in Toronto*. Toronto: Centre of Criminology.

McQuaig, Linda 1981 "Prosecuting the enforcers." *Maclean's* Magazine (January 19):53–54.

Maddox, Charles W. 1975 *Collective Bargaining in Law Enforcement*. Springfield, IL: Charles C. Thomas.

Mann, Edward, and John A. Lee 1979 *The RCMP versus the People*. Don Mills: General Publishing.

Manning, Peter K. 1977 *Police Work: The Social Organization of Policing*. Cambridge, MA: MIT Press.

Manning, Peter K. 1980 *The Narcs' Game: Organizational and Informational Limits on Drug Law Enforcement*. Cambridge, MA: MIT Press.

Manning, Peter 1996 "Policing and reflections." *Police Forum* 6: 1–5

Manwaring-White, Sarah 1983 *The Policing Revolution*. Brighton: The Harvester Press.

Marin, Rene J. 1980 "The handling of complaints against policemen." *Canadian Police College Journal* 4:130–147.

Mark, Robert 1977 *Policing a Perplexed Society*. London: Allen and Unwin.

Mark, Robert 1978 *In the Office of Chief Constable*. London: Collins.

Marquis, M. Greg 1987 "Working men in uniform: the early twentieth century Toronto Police." *Society History* XX (40):259–277.

Marquis, M. Greg 1989 "Police unionism in early twentieth century Toronto." *Ontario History* LXXXI (2): 109–128.

Martin, M.A. 1978 "Police personnel administration survey." *Canadian Police College Journal* 2:177–189.

Martin, M.A. 1979 "Issues in higher education for police." *Canadian Police College Journal* 3:214–236.

Martin, Susan E. 1982 Equal versus equitable treatment: policewomen and patrol work." Pp. 101–121 in Phyllis L. Stewart and Muriel G. Cantor (eds.), *Varieties of Work*. Beverly Hills: Sage.

Marx, Gary T. 1978 Alternative measures of police performance." Pp. 15–32 in Richard C. Larson (ed.) *Police Accountability: Performance Measures and Unionism*. Lexington, MA: Lexington Books.

Maslach, Christina, and Susan E. Jackson 1979 "Burned-out cops and their families." *Psychology Today* (May): 59–62.

Massingham, Carolyn 1977 "When police strike: the Victoria police strike of 1923." Pp. 287–294 in Kerry L. Milte and Thomas A. Weber (eds.), *Police in Australia: Developments, Functions, Procedures*. Sydney: Butterworths.

Mayhall, Pamela A. 1984 *Police–Community Relations and the Administration of Justice* (3rd ed.). New York: John Wiley & Sons.

Meredith, Nikki 1984 "Attacking the roots of police violence." *Psychology Today* (May):20–26.

Mery, Kesley 1971 "Between police and public: a widening gap." Pp. 242–255 in Walt McDayter (ed.) *A Media Mosaic*. Toronto: Holt, Rinehart and Winston.

Miller, Wilbur 1977 *Cops and Bobbies*. Chicago: University of Chicago Press.

Milton, Catherine 1972 *Women in Policing*. Washington, DC: Police Foundation.

Miyazawa, Setsuo 1992 *Policing in Japan*. Albany: State University of New York Press.

Moffatt, R.E. 1981 "Crime prevention through environmental design." Winnipeg: Canadian Congress for the Prevention of Crime.

Monteiro, Lynette 1982 "Crying the blues: our cops—good, bad, or just indifferent." *Ottawa Magazine* (December):22–39.

Moore, Mark Harrison 1992 "Problem-solving and community policing." In Michael Tonry, *Modern Policing*. Chicago, University of Chicago Press: 99–158.

Moran, Theodore K. 1976 "Judicial-administrative control of police discretion." *Journal of Police Science and Administration* 4:412–418.

Mosse, George L. (ed.) 1975 *Police Forces in History*. Beverly Hills: Sage Publications.

Muir, R. Graham 1987 "Fear of crime: a community policing perspective." *Canadian Police College Journal* 11:170–196.

Munn, J.R., and K.E. Renner 1978 "Perceptions of police work by the police and by the public." *Criminal Justice and Behavior* 5:165–180.

Murphy, Chris, and Graham Muir 1985 *Community-Based Policing: A Review of the Critical Issues*. Ottawa: Solicitor General of Canada.

Murphy, Chris, and J. de Verteuil 1986 "Metropolitan Toronto community survey." Ottawa: Research and Statistics Group, Solicitor General of Canada (Working Paper).

Murphy, Chris, and Savvas Lithopoulis 1988 "Social determinant of attitudes towards police: findings from the Toronto community policing survey." Ottawa: Research Division, Police and Security Branch of the Solicitor General of Canada (Working Paper).

Murphy, Chris 1992 *Problem-Oriented Policing*. Ottawa: RCMP Community Policing.

Nadelmann, E.A. 1993 *Cops across Borders*. University Park: Penn State University Press.

Neiderhoffer, Arthur 1967 *Behind the Shield: The Police in Urban Society*. New York: Doubleday and Co.

Neiderhoffer, Arthur, and Abraham S. Blumberg (eds.) 1976 *The Ambivalent Force: Perspectives on the Police* (2nd ed.). Hinsdale, IL: The Dryden Press.

Normandeau, André 1990 "The Police and Ethnic Minorities." *Canadian Police College Journal* 14:215–229.

Normandeau, A. 1993 "Community policing in Canada: a review of some recent studies." *American Journal of Police* XXII: 57–74.

Norris, Donald F. 1973 *Police–Community Relations: A Program that Failed*. Lexington, MA: Lexington Books.

Northrup, David 1996 "Public perceptions of police treatment of minority groups and the disadvantaged." *ISR Newsletter* (Winter): 4–5.

Ontario 1962 Royal Commission on Police

Ontario 1962 *Task Force on Policing in Ontario* (The Hale Report). Toronto: Ministry of the Solicitor General.

Ontario 1973 *Task Force on Policing in Ontario* (The Hale Report). Toronto: Ministry of the Solicitor General.

Ontario 1976 *Report of the Commission on Ottawa-Carleton* (The Mayo Report). Ottawa: Commission on Ottawa-Carleton.

Ontario 1977 *Report of the Royal Commission of Metro* (The Robarts Report). Toronto: Royal Commission of Metro Toronto.

Ontario 1979 *Report of the Commission of Waterloo* (The Palmer Report). Waterloo: The Commission on Waterloo.

Ontario 1991 *Community Policing Series: Shaping the Future*. Toronto: Ministry of the Solicitor General: Queen's Printer for Ontario.

Ontario 1992 *A Police Learning System for Ontario*. Toronto: Ministry of the Solicitor General.

Ontario 1993 *Police Services Act*.

Parks, Evelyn 1970 "From constabulary to police society." *Catalyst* 5:76–97.

Paul, Raymond 1982 *The Thomas Street Horror*. New York: Ballantine Books.

Peak, Ken, Robert Bradshaw, and Ronald Glensor 1992 "Improving citizen perceptions of the police: 'back to basics' with a community policing strategy." *Journal of Criminal Justice* 20: 25–40.

Peak, Kenneth, and Ronald Glensor 1996 *Community Policing and Problem Solving*. Englewood Cliffs, NJ: Prentice-Hall.

Penner, Norman 1979 "How the RCMP got where it is." Pp. 107–121 in Edward Mann and John Alan Lee, *RCMP versus the People: Inside Canada's Security Service*. Don Mills: General Publishing.

Pennsylvania 1974 *The Pennsylvania Crime Commission Report on Police Corruption and Quality of Law Enforcement in Philadelphia*. The Commonwealth of Pennsylvania.

Perrier, David C. 1978 "Police professionalism." *Canadian Police College Journal* 2:209–214.

Perrier, David C., and Reginald Tower 1984 "Police stress: the hidden foe." *Canadian Police College Journal*: 5–26.

Perrott, Stephen, and Donald Taylor 1995 "Crime fighting, law enforcement and service provider role orientations in community-based policing." *American Journal of Police* XIV: 173–195.

Piliavin, Irving, and S. Briar 1965 "Police encounters with juveniles." *American Journal of Sociology* 70:206–214.

Piliavin, Irving 1973 "Police–community alienation: its structural roots and a proposed remedy." Andover, MA: Warner Modular Publications.

Pitman, Walter 1977 *Now is Not too Late*. Toronto: Task Force for the Council of Metro Toronto.

Post, G.M. 1992 "Police recruits: training tomorrow's workforce." *FBI Law Enforcement Bulletin*. 61: 19–24.

President's Commission on Law Enforcement and Administration of Justice 1967 *The Challenge of Crime in a Free Society*. Washington, DC: U.S. Government Printing Office.

Punch, Maurice (ed.) 1983 *Control in the Police Organization*. Cambridge, MA: MIT Press.

Reiner, Robert 1978a *The Bluecoated Worker*. Cambridge: Cambridge University Press.

Reiner, Robert 1978b "The police in the class structure." *British Journal of Law and Society* 5:166–184.

Reiner, Robert 1978c "The police, class and politics." *Marxism Today* (March):69–80.

Reiner, Robert 1980 "Fuzzy thoughts: the police and law-and-order politics." *Sociological Review* 28:377–413.

Reiner, Robert 1985 *The Politics of the Police*. New York: St. Martin's Press.

Reiner, Robert 1992 *The Politics of the Police* (2nd ed.). Toronto: University of Toronto Press.

Reiss, Albert J. 1971 *The Police and the Public*. New Haven: Yale University Press.

Richardson, James F. 1970 *The New York Police: Colonial Times to 1901*. New York: Oxford University Press.

Roach, Lawrence T. 1986 "Implementing community based policing in the London Metropolitan Police." Pp. 75–95 in Donald Loree and Chris Murphy, *Community Policing in the 1980's*. Ottawa: Solicitor General of Canada.

Roberg, Roy, and Jack Kuykendall 1997 *Police Management* (2nd ed.). Los Angeles: Roxbury Publishing.

Robinson, Cyril D. 1975 "The mayor and the police—the political role of the police in society." Pp. 227–316 in George L. Mosse (ed.), *Police Forces in History*. Beverly Hills: Sage Publications.

Robinson, C., R. Seaglion, and J.Olivero 1994 *Police in Contradiction.* Westport: Greenwood Press.

Royal Canadian Mounted Police 1967 *An Historical Outline of the Force.* Ottawa: Information Canada.

Royal Canadian Mounted Police 1983 "Police services community project." Ottawa: Crime Prevention Centre, RCMP "HQ."

Rubenstein, Jonathan 1973 *City Police.* New York: Ballantine Books.

Ruchelman, Leonard 1974 *Police Politics: A Comparative Study of Three Cities.* Cambridge, MA: Ballinger Publishing Co.

Russell, Francis 1975 *A City in Terror: 1919 The Boston Police Strike.* New York: The Viking Press.

Sallot, Jeff 1979 *Nobody Said No.* Toronto: James Lorimer.

Sanders, William B. 1977 *Detective Work: A Study of Criminal Investigation.* New York: The Free Press.

Saunders, Charles Jr. 1970 *Upgrading the American Police: Education and Training for Better Law Enforcement.* Washington: The Brookings Institute.

Savage, Louise, and Trish Ault 1985 *Police Officers and Public Safety—Use of Lethal Force by and against Police.* Ottawa: Solicitor General Canada.

Sawatsky, John 1976 "Guilt by association: how the Mounties got their men." *The Canadian Review* (December):23–29.

Sawatsky, John 1980 *Men in the Shadows: the RCMP Security Service.* Toronto: Doubleday Canada Ltd.

Scanlon, Joseph 1981 "Coping with the media: police–media problems and tactics in hostage-takings and terrorist incidents." *Canadian Police College Journal* 5:129–148.

Schaer, Joan 1994 "Employee assistance programs." Toronto: Proceedings, Ontario Police Association Annual Conference.

Shackleton, Doris F. 1975 *Tommy Douglas: A Biography.* Toronto: McClelland and Stewart.

Shackleton, Doris F. 1977 *Power Town: Democracy Discarded.* Toronto: McClelland and Stewart.

Scheingold, Stuart 1984 *The Politics of Law and Order.* New York: Longman.

Schemo, Diana 1994 "A common bond." *New York Times* (October 24): 10.

Schmidt, Wayne W. 1976 "Recent developments in police civil liberties." *Journal of Police Science and Administration* 4:197–202.

Schnelle, John, R.E. Kirchner, M.P. McNees and J.M. Lawlor 1975 "Social evaluation research: the evaluation of two police patrolling strategies." *Journal of Applied Behaviour Analysis* 8:353–365.

Schreiber, E.M. 1974 "The public's feelings toward policemen in the USA and Canada." Arlington, VA: U.S. Army Research Institute (unpublished paper).

Scott, Peter 1986 "The current climate of Canadian policing: prospects for change." Pp. 41–50 in Donald Loree and Chris Murphy (eds.), *Community Policing in the 1980's.* Ottawa: Solicitor General of Canada.

Seagrave, Jayne 1992 "Community policing and the need for police research skills training." *Canadian Police College Journal* 16:204–211.

Seagrave, Jayne 1997 *An Introduction to Policing in Canada*. Scarborough: Prentice-Hall.

Sewell, John 1985 *Police: Urban Policing in Canada*. Toronto: James Lorimer.

Shearing, C., M. Farnell, and P. Stenning 1980 *Policing for Profit*. Toronto: University of Toronto Press.

Shearing, Clifford D. (ed.) 1981 *Organizational Police Deviance*. Toronto: Butterworths.

Shearing, Clifford D., and Phillip C. Stenning 1981 "Modern private security: its growth and implications." *Crime and Justice: An Annual Review of Research* 3:93–245.

Sherman, Lawrence (ed.) 1974 *Police Corruption: A Sociological Perspective*. New York: Anchor Books.

Sherman, Lawrence 1978 *The Quality of Police Education*. San Francisco: Jossey-Bass Publishers.

Sherman, Lawrence 1986 "Effective community policing: research contribution and considerations." Pp. 125–140 in Donald Loree and Chris Murphy (eds.), *Community Policing in the 1980's*. Ottawa: Solicitor General of Canada.

Siegel, Micki 1980 *Cops and Women*. New York: Tower Books.

Silbert, Mimi 1992 "Job stress and burnout of New York police officers." Pp. 657–663 in K. McCormick and L. Viana, *Understanding Police*. Toronto: Academic Press.

Silver, Allan 1966 "The demand for order in civil society: a review of some themes in the history of urban crime, police and riot." Pp. 1–24 in David Bordua (ed.), *The Police: Six Sociological Essays*. New York: John Wiley & Sons.

Skolnick, Jerome 1969 *The Politics of Protest*. New York: Ballantine.

Skolnick, Jerome 1975 *Justice Without Trial* (2nd ed.). New York: John Wiley & Sons.

Skolnick, Jerome and Harvey Fyfe 1993 *Above the Law*. New York: The Free Press.

Skoog, D., and E.D. Boldt 1980 "Native attitudes toward the police." *Canadian Journal of Criminology* 22:354–359.

Southgate, Peter 1984 *Racism Awareness Training for the Police: Report of a Pilot Study for the Home Office*. London: Home Office.

Sparrow, Malcolm 1988 "Implementing community policing." *Perspectives on Policing*. Washington: U.S. Department of Justice (November):1–7.

Sparrow, Malcolm K., Mark H. Moore, and David M. Kennedy 1990 *Beyond 911: A New Era for Policing*. New York: Basic Books.

Spitzer, Steven 1981 "The political economy of policing." Pp. 315–340 in D.F. Greenberg (ed.) *Crime and Capitalism*. California: Mayfield Publishing Co.

Spitzer, Steven, and Andrew T. Scull 1977 "Privatization and capitalist development: the case of the private police." *Social Problems* 25:18–29.

Spring, W.R. 1984 "A critical examination of productivity in policing." Ottawa: RCMP "HQ" Division.

Standfest, Steven 1996 "Focus on stress: the police supervisor and stress." Beverly Hills, MI: Unpublished paper, Department of Public Safety.

Stanley, Paul R.A. 1976 *Crime Prevention through Environmental Design.* Ottawa: Solicitor General of Canada.

Stansfield, Ronald T. 1996 *Issues in Policing: A Canadian Perspective.* Toronto: Thompson Educational Publishing.

Stark, Rodney 1972 *Police Riots.* Belmont, CA: Wadsworth Publishing Co.

Stebbins, R., and C. Flynn 1975 "Police definition of the situation." *Canadian Journal of Criminology and Corrections* 17:334–353.

Stenning, Phillip C. 1980 "The role of police boards and commissions as institutions of municipal police governance." Montreal: Annual Meeting of the Canadian Political Science Association.

Stenning, Philip C. 1981a *Legal Status of the Police.* Ottawa: Law Reform Commission of Canada.

Stenning, Philip C. 1981b "The role of police boards and commission." Pp. 161–208 in Clifford D. Shearing (ed.), *Organizational Police Deviance.* Toronto: Butterworths.

Stenning, Philip C. 1981c *Police Commissions and Boards in Canada.* Toronto: Centre of Criminology.

Stenning, Philip C. 1989 "Private police and public police: Toward a redefinition of the police role." Pp. 169–192 in Donald Loree (ed.), *Future Issues in Policing: Symposium Proceedings.* Ottawa: Canadian Police College.

Stenning, Philip 1994 *Police Use of Force and Violence Against Members of Visible Minority Groups in Canada.* Ottawa: Canadian Centre for Police–Race Relations.

Stinson, Arthur 1985 "Evaluation: police-community intercultural education program." Unpublished.

Stoddard, Ellwyn R. 1974 "A group approach to blue-coat crime." Pp. 272–304 in Lawrence Sherman (ed.), *Police Corruption.* New York: Anchor Books.

Stroud, Carsten 1983 *The Blue Wall: Street Cops in Canada.* Toronto: McClelland and Stewart.

Stroud, Carsten 1987 *Close Pursuit: A Week in the Life of an NYPD Homicide Cop.* New York: Viking.

Sykes, Richard E., and John P. Clark 1975 "A theory of deference exchange in police-civilian encounters." *American Journal of Sociology* 81:584–600.

Sykes, Richard E., and Edward E. Bent 1983 *Policing: A Social Behaviorist Perspective.* New Brunswick, NJ: Rutgers University Press.

Talbot, C.K., C.H.S. Jayewardene, and T.J. Juliani 1984 "Policing in Canada: a developmental perspective." *Canadian Police College Journal* 8:218–288.

Taylor, Ian, Paul Walton, and Jock Young 1973 *The New Criminology: For a Social Theory of Deviance.* London: Routledge and Kegan Paul.

Taylor, Ian 1980 "The law and order issue in the British general election and the Canadian general election of 1979: crime, populism and the state." *Canadian Journal of Sociology* 5:285–311.

Teed, E.L. 1981 "Canadian police and defence counsel. Pp. 114–125 in W.T. McGrath and M.P. Mitchell (eds.), *The Police Function in Canada.* Toronto: Methuen.

Tenzel, James H., and Victor Cizankas 1973 "The uniform experiment." *Journal of Police Science and Administration* 1:421–424.

Tenzel, James, H., Lowell Storms, and Hervey Sweetwood 1976 "Symbols and behavior: an experiment in altering the police role." *Journal of Police Science and Administration* 4:21–27.

Thomas, Charles W., and Jeffrey Hyman 1977 "Perceptions of crime, fear of victimization, and public perceptions of police performance." *Journal of Police Science and Administration* 5:305–317.

Tomovich, V.A., and D.J. Loree 1989 "In search of new directions: policing in Niagara Region." *Canadian Police College Journal* 13:29–54.

Toronto 1986 *Proposed Guideline for Recruitment and Selection of Visible Minority Police Offices in Canada.* Greater Toronto Region Working Group on Policing Multicultural, Multiracial Urban Communities: Metro Toronto Police Force Personnel Services.

Tremblay, Pierre, and Claude Rochon 1991 "D'une police efficace a une police informee: Lignes directrices d'un programme global de traitement de l'information." *Canadian Journal of Criminology* 33: 407–420.

Trojanowicz, Robert 1986 "Neighbourhood foot patrol: the Flint, Michigan experience." Pp. 95–106 in Donald Loree and Chris Murphy (eds.), *Community Policing in the 1980's*. Ottawa: Solicitor General of Canada.

Trojanowicz, Robert, and Bonnie Bucqueroux 1994 *Community Policing: How to Get it Started.* Cincinnati: Anderson Publishing Co.

Turner, C. Frank 1973 *Across the Medicine Line*. Toronto: McClelland and Stewart.

Ungeleider, Charles 1985 "Police intercultural education: promoting understanding and empathy between police and ethnic communities." *Canadian Ethnic Studies* XVII:51–66.

United States 1967 *The Challenge of Crime in a Free Society*. Washington, D.C.

United States 1996 *Statistics Bulletin*. U.S. Bureau of Justice.

Van Kirk, Marvin 1977 *Response Time Analysis: Executive Summary*. Kansas City, MO: Kansas City Police Department.

van Maanen, James 1975 "Police socialization: a longitudinal examination of job activities in an urban police department." *Administrative Science Quarterly* 20:207–228.

Van Maanen, John and Ralph Katz 1979 "Police perceptions of their work environment." *Sociology of Work and Occupations* 6: 31–58.

Victor, Michael I. 1977 "Regulations between known crime and police spending in large United States' cities." *Sociological Focus* 10:199–206.

Vincent, Claude L. 1979 *Policeman*. Toronto: Gage Publishing.

Vincent, Claude L. 1990 *Police Officer* (new edition of [1979] *Policeman*). Ottawa: Carleton University Press.

Violanti, John 1995 "The mystery within: understanding police suicides." *FBI Law Enforcement Bulletin* 64: 19.

von Stein, J. 1996 *Race Relations Training in the Police Curriculum in Canada: A Content Analysis.* Ottawa: Canadian Centre for Police–Race Relations.

Walker, Christopher R. 1987 "The community police station: developing a model." *Canadian Police College Journal* 11:273–318.

Walker, Christopher, and S. Gail Walker 1989 *The Victoria Community Police Stations: An Exercise in Innovation.* Ottawa: Canadian Police College.

Walker, Sandra, Christopher Walker, and James McDavid 1992 *The Victoria Community Police Stations: A Three-Year Evaluation.* Ottawa: Canadian Police College.

Wambaugh, Joseph 1975 *The Choirboys.* New York: Delacorte Press.

Warner, Barbara 1997 "Community characteristics and the recording of Crime." *Justice Quarterly* 14: 631–650.

Wasson, David K. 1975 *Community-Based Preventive Policing: A Review.* Ottawa: Solicitor General of Canada.

Webb, Stephen D. 1975 "Causes, manifestations and the resolution of stress among police officers." Victoria: University of Victoria Department of Sociology.

Weiner, Norman 1974 "The effect of education on police attitudes." *Journal of Criminal Justice* 2:317–328.

Weiner, Norman 1976 *The Role of Police in Urban Society: Conflicts and Consequences.* Indianapolis: Bobbs-Merrill Co.

Weiner, Norman 1977 "The educated policeman." *Journal of Police Science and Administration* 4:450–457.

Westley, William 1956 "Secrecy and the Police." *Social Forces* 34:254–257.

Westley, William 1970 *Violence and the Police.* Cambridge: MIT Press.

Whitaker, Reg, and Gary Marcuse 1994 *Cold War Canada.* Toronto: University of Toronto Press.

White, Julie 1980 *Women and Unions.* Ottawa: Canadian Advisory Council on the Status of Women.

Wiley, Mary Glenn, and Terry L. Hudik 1980 "Police–citizen encounters: a field test of exchange theory" Pp. 78–90 in Richard Lundman (ed.), *Police Behavior.* New York: Oxford University Press.

Willet, Terrence, and Philip Chitty 1982 "Auxiliary policing in Canada—an overview." *Canadian Police College Journal* 6:188–192.

Wilson, James Q. 1969 "What makes a better policeman?" *The Atlantic* (March): 129–135.

Wilson, James Q. 1978 (1969) *Varieties of Police Behavior.* Cambridge, MA: Harvard University Press.

Wilson, James Q., and George Kelling 1982 "Broken Windows." *The Atlantic Monthly* (March):28–38.

Wilt, G. Marie, and James Bannon 1976 "Cynicism or realism: a critique of Niederhoffer's research into police attitudes." *Journal of Police Science and Administration* 4:38–45.

Winterton, Don 1985 *Recruitment, Training and Police Multicultural Liaison in Canada.* Ottawa: Secretary of State for Multiculturalism and the Canadian Association of Chiefs of Police.

Woods, Gerald 1984 "Costs of municipal police services." *Impact* 2:13–22.

Zwelling, Marc 1972 *The Strikebreakers: The Report of the Strikebreakers Committee of the Ontario Federation of Labour and the Labour Council of Metropolitan Toronto.* Toronto: New Press.

Index